CW00732340

Currency Overlay

Currency Overlay
A Practical Guide

Published by Risk Books, a division of Incisive RWG Ltd

Haymarket House
28–29 Haymarket
London SW1Y 4RX
Tel: +44 (0)20 7484 9700
Fax: +44 (0)20 7484 9758
E-mail: books@riskwaters.com
Sites: www.riskbooks.com
　　　www.riskwaters.com

Every effort has been made to secure the permission of individual copyright
holders for inclusion.

© Incisive RWG Ltd 2003

ISBN 1904339 174

British Library Cataloguing in Publication Data
A catalogue record for this book is available from the British Library

Managing Editor: Sarah Jenkins
Copyeditor: Romilly Hambling
Assistant Editor: Tamsin Kennedy

Typeset by Mizpah Publishing Services, Chennai, India

Printed and bound in Spain by Espacegrafic, Pamplona Navarra

Foreword

There is evidence all around us that the world is becoming a smaller place. Never before have goods, services, people and capital flowed around the globe as freely and in as great a volume as they do today. Each time one of these flows crosses a currency border, an inherent foreign exchange event takes place.

There is a growing appreciation by the originators and recipients of these cross-border flows that currency movements can greatly affect the value and risk associated with them. This recognition of foreign exchange risk – particularly by the institutional investment community – has become one of the primary drivers of growth in the global foreign exchange market, which with an average daily turnover in excess of US$1.2 trillion is the largest single capital market in the world.

When an asset moves from one underlying currency to another, an opportunity presents itself. At the heart of that opportunity is the decision whether or not to hedge the currency risk, which in itself can have a great impact on the return profile for the asset owner. As asset market returns revert to pre-1990s levels, and as risk control and disclosure requirements gain ever more attention, the issue of currency risk increasingly moves from the periphery of the overall investment decision to the core. Whether this risk is handled in-house or by a specialist currency overlay manager, the discipline of currency overlay is becoming an important tool for all global financial asset managers looking to maximise their performance.

This book by Dr Hai Xin offers a surprisingly rare overview of currency overlay. It is jargon-free, objective and detailed, and as such is accessible to financial asset administrators, investment advisers and consultants as well as academics. Fund managers, in particular, will here find help in making an informed decision on how best to deal with currency risk in their investment portfolios. Those who don't have a currency management programme will find the information they need to set one up or choose one from the market; those who do have such a programme will find an objective yardstick for detailed policy review.

Currency Overlay: A Practical Guide provides comprehensive coverage of such subjects as defining and decomposing currency returns, choosing currency management styles and managing currency overlay. Optimisation and hedge ratios, benchmark design and performance measurement, options pricing theory and dynamic hedging, foreign exchange research and emerging market currencies all come in for consideration. The very topical area of online forex dealing and e-commerce is also addressed. Dr Xin draws on years of direct experience in advising institutional investors to offer the reader an enlightened, in-depth and relevant overview of the entire discipline.

We trust that this important text will bring about a greater appreciation of currency risk management and that it will become a point of reference for the financial market on the increasingly vital topic of currency overlay.

Robert Garwood
Managing Director, Fixed Income, Rates and Currencies
UBS Investment Bank
September 2003

Contents

About the Author

Hai Xin has been a financial engineer with the investment bank division of UBS (previously SwissBank Corporation, SBC Warburg, SBC Warburg Dillon Read, Warburg Dillon Read, and UBS Warburg – a succession of names that betokens a small anecdote in the consolidation of the banking sector) since 1996. The team of which he is a member, FX Financial Engineering, is a specialist group within FX Distributions at UBS that provides bespoke solutions for UBS's corporate and institutional clients. Between 2000 and 2002 Hai Xin was permanently inside the "Chinese wall" of UBS's investment banking division, advising on currency risks embedded in merger and acquisition (M&A) transactions. Prior to joining UBS he worked as a researcher at AstraZeneca Treasury.

Hai obtained his PhD in quantitative finance from Imperial College, London, and MSc in economics from the London School of Economics, both part of the University of London. His bachelor's degree is in electronics and information science. Dr Xin is also a director and major shareholder of a start-up ethnic health food manufacturing company based in the UK.

Acknowledgements

The idea of this book started, out of frustration, in late 2000. Working as a risk management advisor at UBS, I had been asked in the previous few years to field questions on the whys and hows of currency overlay posed by our clients. Equipped with little more than a few marketing presentations from overlay managers and a handful of academic papers photocopied at the LSE library, I took on the challenge with zest. It was difficult to find any materials that were from a reasonably neutral source and/or with a reasonable degree of practical relevance at the time. My colleagues and I had to improvise as we went along, doing our own data analysis. My first impression of currency hedging was that it seemed nothing special, that all that was needed was a healthy dose of common sense, careful handling and interpretation of data, and a pragmatic approach. Several years on the impression has not really changed that much, except, perhaps, for the fact that the more I learn, the less I realise I know – just like everything else in life I suppose. This book is a review of what I have learnt so far. Neutrality, pragmatism and common sense were the goals I set for myself when I worked on it.

I should clarify a little further what I mean by claiming that the book is "neutral". While I have tried to remain as objective as possible, I am, nevertheless, implicated by the fact that I work for a bank that provides currency products and services. I have quoted UBS's research materials in several places and have used its online foreign exchange services as an example in Chapter 9. Naturally, many banks, including UBS, would probably claim that their research and their services were among the best – if not the best – available, and it is up to the reader to judge the validity, or otherwise, of such claims. In my opinion the services provided by the top-tier foreign exchange banks are fairly similar and they are only differentiated at the margins and in specialist niche areas. The decision to include UBS materials was more a matter of convenience than anything else; it would have been awkward for me to obtain material produced by other banks or, when I was privy to such material, to obtain copyright permissions for obvious reasons. When used, UBS materials are clearly identified and the decision on whether to include them was made solely on the basis of whether, in my opinion, they contributed to the purposes of the book. Most of the data analysis examples used here – especially in the areas of risk quantification, trading models, benchmark construction and option volatility studies – are available (or will soon be available) as customisable online tools in the Currency Overlay section of UBS's website.

My gratitude, first and foremost, goes to UBS. UBS is my first employer to have been a bank and, despite all the dim views and misgivings about banks I have heard and held over the years, it has been a surprisingly progressive and pleasant bank to work for. I wish to thank the following former and present colleagues: Mike Sutherland and Rob Garwood, for moral and practical support – they paid my bills (as Rob did when I was lying in bed in 2002, in response to which my parents, both former officials in a communist regime for considerable periods of time during the last century, became given to commenting that capitalism was not so bad after all); Simon Jagot and Martin Wiedmann, ex- and current bosses of Mike and Rob, for giving the go-ahead for this extracurricular, and in more than one way, extravagant project; Bob Jackson, for inspirational common sense and straight talking – he will, however, be disappointed that "Roger's Profanisaurus", which he gave me as a present, is not quoted in this book; Dr John Gavin, for explaining convoluted statistics in simple dots and lines, and, together with my friend and ex-colleague Alexandra Fruechtl, for saving my life, just narrowly, in Cuba; and Jason Perl, for calm and sensible advice. Other previous and current UBS colleagues helped at various stages, some before the idea of the book was conceived: Toby Angel, Stephanie Aufan, Rupert Brindley, Gary Brinson, Hagen Britz, Charlie Brown, Matthew Burden, Tom Clarke, Sarah Docx, Carol Gary-Tatti, Leslie Grant, Reine Gunnarsson, Graham Harris, Andreas Homberger, Hans Hsu, Ed Hulina, Shahab Jalinoos, Katy Walton Jones, Elke Kroll, Joachim Kruse, David Landi, Benjamin Lenhardt Jr, Linda Leaney, Brian Lewis, Andrew Lloyd, Ian Martin, Doug Millowitz, Mansoor Mohi-uddin, Dr Stefano Nappo,

Jo Prince, Dr Jonathan Roberts, Kristina Ross, Fabian Shey, Grant Wade, Dr Jamie Walton, Julian Wantling, Simon Williams, Tim Wolton, David Wright, Stephen Wright and Yue Wu.

I thank Sarah Jenkins, managing editor of Risk Books, for her kindness, patience and good humour. My gratitude also goes to Sarah's colleagues at Risk, Stephen Fairman and Tamsin Kennedy, for their professionalism. I also extend my thanks to Romilly Hambling who copy-edited this work with great care and diligence. I would also like to thank the following people for their help: Keith Darlington, Astra Zeneca; Dave Murphy, Record Currency Management; Michael Huttman, Millennium Global Investments Limited; Daniel Stark of Daniel B. Stark & Co.; Dr Wai-Ping Liu, Key Asset Management (UK) Ltd; Dr Helga Meier, McKinsey & Co.; Gerry Salkin, Imperial College, University of London; Mannus Stolk, Master Foods (Mars B.V.); Nancy Shanahan, Parker Global; Hélie d'Hautefort, Overlay Asset Management; Richard Qiu, InterSec Research Corp.; Neil Wardley, Lehman Brothers; and Adrian Franken, MSCI, Inc.

Last and certainly not least, I thank my parents for things they consider not to matter (they do), and they will probably not remember (I do). For babysitting me, once again, in my thirties, in 2002. My mother, out of retirement, has started taking English lessons in a bid – despite my blatant discouragement – to read the book. Bless her. I am also grateful for Hui Wang, one of my childhood friends, who helped me generously.

The opinions expressed in this book are mine alone. They do not necessarily reflect the opinions of my employer, UBS. And it is safe to add that they do not reflect those of my own food company either. Any errors and omissions are entirely my own responsibility.

Hai Xin
hai@xinhai.co.uk
London, June 2003

1

Introduction

The real trouble with this world of ours is not that it is an unreasonable world, nor that it is a reasonable one. The commonest kind of trouble is that it is nearly reasonable, but not quite. Life is not an illogicality; yet it is a trap for logicians. It looks just a little more mathematical and regular than it is; its exactitude is obvious, but its inexactitude is hidden; its wildness lies in wait.

G. K. Chesterton, Orthodoxy

In this chapter we give some background information on currencies, the currency market and currency risk management. The chapter starts with a brief summary of the history of modern currencies, from Bretton Woods to the dotcom bubble. We then look at some facts about currency markets: the players, liquidity, types of transaction and so on. Section 1.3 presents a list of questions related to the so-called currency-hedging debate. Each is reviewed and its relevance to the debate is evaluated. In later chapters we will return to many of these questions. The concept of currency overlay is introduced in Section 1.4, which reviews evidence of the globalisation of the investment universe and studies of the usefulness of currency hedging from the academic literature. A more detailed discussion of currency overlay, its many definitions and practical aspects is postponed until Chapter 3. Readers will find a summary outline of the book's contents in Section 1.5.

1.1 A BRIEF HISTORY OF MODERN CURRENCIES

The Bretton Woods Conference in 1944, held just as the Second World War was coming to an end, is one of the most important landmarks in the history of modern currencies. Emerging from the ashes of the old system of free-floating gold- or silver-anchored currencies, the new international monetary system was designed to provide stability for war-ravaged economies. Its key ingredients were the convertibility of the US dollar into gold at a fixed rate and the establishment of the International Monetary Fund (IMF) to monitor the new system. Other countries were obliged to peg their respective currencies to the US dollar. The "par levels" were periodically "re-fixed" (devaluation and revaluation by another name) to reflect the misalignment of values, but the whole arrangement essentially created an otherwise fixed exchange system in which central banks intervened on both sides of the currency market to maintain the peg. The Bretton Woods system is sometimes called "US dollar-based gold-exchange standard". Trading activities, on a minuscule scale compared with today's, were usually concentrated around the time when these "re-fixes" occurred.

In 1967 the Bank of England defended the peg between the British pound and the US dollar against speculators. Although a few other central banks entered the foray to assist the Bank of England, for the first time since the Bretton Woods Conference the speculators won the battle. Unfortunately (or fortunately, as many a free-market thinking economist would argue) this was not the last time. A new era had dawned, and it was not long before the battered US dollar–gold convertibility was suspended – in 1971, by President Nixon, after several more attacks on the fixed-rate system by the speculators.

The new floating-rate system commenced two years later, in 1973, by which time the advance of electronic communication technology, coupled with the large increases in both international trade flows and capital flows, had set the stage for the new global foreign exchange market. On that stage there was an ever expanding cast of importers/exporters, speculators, banks, exchanges and institutional investors alongside the central banks. Towards the end of the 1970s currency trading was dominated by large banks and brokers. The end of that decade also saw the emergence of the European Monetary System (EMS), in which the new currency unit, the ECU, was introduced to represent a basket of participating European currencies and the member currencies were managed around ECU parity within a prespecified band. The system was repeatedly attacked and was effectively abandoned in 1992–93 when the British pound and Italian lira made their infamous exits.

The first half of the 1980s was characterised by the steady appreciation of the US dollar against a host of other currencies, but this trend was reversed in the second half of the decade. Interventions in the currency markets were seen as necessary by many, and they were regularly carried out by major central banks to induce currencies to move in a particular direction. This type of activity was much less common in the 1990s, when the general view was that central banks should not intervene except perhaps to dampen volatility in the short-term, and that such intervention should be sparing and effective and have little impact on the long-term equilibrium value of a currency.

In 1992 European countries signed the Maastricht treaty, which drew up the blueprint for the new single currency as well as the unified monetary policies for the member states. In the ensuing few years leading to the debut of the euro in 1999, member countries struggled to fulfil the criteria for joining the single currency. The euro has so far had a tumultuous gestation, a reasonably smooth birth, and a loveless infancy.[1] The 1990s also witnessed the phenomenal growth in foreign exchange derivatives, the complete dominance of electronic trading/broking at the expense of other dealing methods, and the whole-scale consolidation of banks active in foreign exchange trading.

Foreign exchange is a mature industry now, with a commoditised product range and razor-thin bid–offer spreads. The volume in the foreign exchange market, in terms of both cash and derivatives, began to fall in the last few years of the old millennium, induced probably by the appearance of the euro and a gradual withdrawal of speculative capital (which flew to stock-markets around the world). There were fewer banks and, in every one of them, fewer employees. The talk of a single world currency, toyed with almost a hundred years ago when gold acted like one, resurfaced, but this time people were talking about the ubiquitous "e-currency", where a countryless and borderless electronic point system would assume most, if not all, roles traditionally fulfilled by currencies, like the chips in a casino – this particular casino being the world wide web. That proved to be a tulip-shaped bubble (much to my and my colleagues' relief). Money from investors and speculators is back in the foreign exchange market in 2002 and 2003, with other investment arenas offering lean pickings.

1.2 SOME FACTS ABOUT THE FOREIGN EXCHANGE MARKET
1.2.1 Who uses it and why
Major participants in the foreign exchange market include:

❑ commercial banks;
❑ investment banks;
❑ central banks and supernational banks;
❑ corporations;
❑ fund managers (including those of mutual funds, pension funds, insurance funds, etc.);
❑ hedge funds; and
❑ private individuals.

Although one of the original purposes of foreign exchange was to facilitate international trade, only a small percentage of the global foreign exchange volume (probably less than 1%) is directly linked to trade and service flows. Investors, speculators, arbitrageurs and hedgers of varying sizes are active in the currency markets. Some view foreign exchange as a distinctive asset class and seek excess return by buying and selling currencies. Others may not treat foreign exchange as asset class; rather, their need to buy and sell currencies arises from investment decisions to buy and sell securities denominated in foreign currencies and/or to hedge the currency risks. Many use currency instruments to manage their funding and short-term liquidity. In addition, there are central banks and similar institutions that may trade currencies towards a particular target level to dampen market volatility or to manage a country's foreign exchange reserves.

1.2.2 Types of trade, transparency and transaction cost
Foreign exchange transactions can be classified into three main types according to their counterparties:

❑ trades between customers and banks;

❏ trades directly between banks (interbank); and
❏ brokered trades between banks.

Given the size of the market, the volume in each category is difficult to measure and it varies with time and different currency pairs. Around a third of the total trades are customer-related and the remaining two-thirds are interbank trades. Traditionally there are more direct interbank trades than brokered ones, but the trend over the recent few years has been to a growing proportion of brokered trades, particularly electronically brokered trades.

Most foreign exchange transactions are conducted over the counter (OTC) between counterparties, with one, or, more likely, both of them being market-makers.[2] This market microstructure results in a paradoxical characteristic of the foreign exchange market: although the trading volume is massive, transparency is low. Information on a given transaction is usually not known beyond the two parties involved. Foreign exchange prices distributed by information vendors, such as Reuters or Bloomberg, are not necessarily transaction prices.

Bid–offer spreads in the foreign exchange market are very small, usually a couple of basis points. Market-makers (mostly banks) generally make money by taking positions rather than capturing the bid–offer spread. Academic as well as anecdotal evidence suggests that profit is usually made when the market is thin (eg, emerging market currencies) and/or volatility is high (eg, Japanese yen in 1997–98, euro in 2002) and/or an important announcement is made or about to be made (eg, unexpected change of interest rate).

1.2.3 Market size, major currencies and concentration

Foreign exchange is the biggest capital market, with an average daily turnover at US$1.2 trillion according to the latest Triennial Central Bank Survey of Foreign Exchange and Derivatives Market Activities 2001, published by the Bank for International Settlements (BIS) in 2002. The already gigantic figure of US$1.2 trillion represents a 19% decline compared with US$1.49 trillion in 1998. This was also the first time that the turnover showed a decrease since the survey started in 1989 (see Figure 1.1). If we look at the trades by their counterparties, the percentage of interbank trades in the total turnover fell from 64% to 59% (still representing the majority of

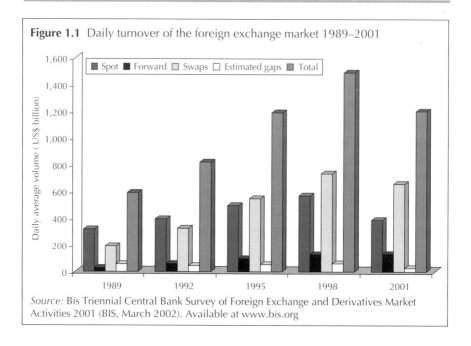

Figure 1.1 Daily turnover of the foreign exchange market 1989–2001

Legend: ■ Spot ■ Forward □ Swaps □ Estimated gaps ■ Total

Y-axis: Daily average volume (US$ billion)

X-axis: 1989, 1992, 1995, 1998, 2001

Source: Bis Triennial Central Bank Survey of Foreign Exchange and Derivatives Market Activities 2001 (BIS, March 2002). Available at www.bis.org

currency trades), mainly due to the expansion of electronic brokers. Those between banks and non-financial counterparties also dropped, from 17% to 13%. However, trades between banks and financial counterparties increased in share from 20% to 28%, reflecting the growing activity of asset managers in the currency market.

The US dollar appears in 90% of the trades as one of the legs, whereas the euro, Japanese yen and sterling account for 38%, 23% and 13%, respectively. The euro/US dollar is the most frequently traded currency pair, capturing 30% of turnover. It is followed by US dollar/yen (20%), sterling/US. dollar (11%) and US dollar/Swiss franc (5%).

Another important feature of the foreign exchange market is its market concentration. There are two general trends: the number of banks in the foreign exchange business has been declining, and the big banks are getting even bigger. This is corroborated by the BIS survey as well: the number of banks participating in the last three surveys were 2,417 in 1995, 2,205 in 1998 and 1,945 in 2001. Also, the number of banks accounting for 75% of the turnover were, in the US, 20 (1995), 20 (1998) and 13 (2001); and in the UK, 20 (1995), 24 (1998) and 17 (2001).

Table 1.1 Turnover of OTC and ETD derivatives (US$ billion)

	1995	1998	2001
Foreign exchange	688	959	853
Forward/swap	643	862	786
FX options	41	87	60
Interest rate	151	265	489
Total OTC derivatives	800	1,263	1,387
Total ETD, of which:	1,222	1,373	2,179
Foreign exchange	17	12	10
Interest rate	1,205	1,361	2,169

Source: BIS Triennial Central Bank Survey of Foreign Exchange and Derivatives Market Activities 2001 (BIS, March 2002). Available at www.bis.org. ETD data from FOW TRADE data, Futures Industry Association, and various futures and options exchanges. Reported monthly data were converted into daily averages on the assumption of 18.5 trading days in 1995, 20.5 days in 1998 and 19.5 days in 2001.

1.2.4 Recent trends in OTC and exchange-traded currency derivatives

The volume in the OTC foreign exchange derivatives market also declined in 2001, making a sharp contrast to the rapid growth in the interest rate derivatives market. If the trend continues, OTC interest rate derivatives may overtake currency derivatives in the next survey. Table 1.1 summarises the OTC turnover data for both currency and interest rate derivatives. We include exchange-traded derivatives (ETD) for comparison. It is easy to see that the volume of exchange-traded currency contracts is minimal compared with that of interest rate contracts.

In the OTC foreign exchange derivatives business, intra-bank trades declined by 18% (at US$503 billion out of a total of US$853 billion, still a dominant portion) and trades between banks and non-financial customers declined by 31%. Trades between banks and financial customers increased by 32%, again reflecting the increasing activities of institutional fund managers.

1.3 WHAT IS SPECIAL ABOUT CURRENCIES?

There are various reasons why currencies may be considered special in the context of international investment. These reasons are often linked to something known as the "currency-hedging debate", which revolves around the question whether an investor who invests in foreign currency-denominated assets should hedge the embedded currency risk.[3] The question is as old as global investment itself. While the latter has gained general acceptance – if with the occasional dissenting voices – 15 years of debate on the question of hedging the associated currency risk has not produced a consensus. Far from it. Sometimes the hedging debate is formulated in a rather more specific way: "Should an investor (passively) hedge 0%, 100%, 50% or 77% of the currency exposure associated with international investment?"[4] Another related, but slightly different, question is whether active currency management can add value. Investigation in this field has followed two routes, one looking at the predictability of currency movements (a topic which we review in Chapter 4), and the other examining the historical performance of active currency managers (the evidence on this will be considered in Chapter 3).

In the following sections we take a brief look at some of the statements that usually feature in (and, more often than not, spoil) the currency-hedging debate. Our emphasis here is not on demonstrating that a particular statement is right or wrong: many of the questions are, in our view, open-ended and are likely to remain so. A definitive answer to any of these questions may require a number of assumptions and restrictions, resulting at times in a quagmire of arguments and counterarguments. We instead emphasise the point that, irrespective of one's answer, currency risk in a portfolio is real and needs to be managed.

1.3.1 Currency trading is a zero-sum game

The argument that currency trading is a zero-sum game comes in two related forms:

1. One market participant's currency gain is another one's loss and therefore currency trading is a zero-sum game. Taking transaction costs into consideration, it is probably a negative-sum game.
2. In the long run, currency impact washes out: you gain one day and you lose another.

The first point is probably correct if we define gain and loss in pure cash terms over a very short time. For a given buyer X, there will be a seller Y on the other side, and one's gain is clearly the other's loss. In practice, many factors come into play when gains and losses are defined. This can be done in a variety of ways – for example, relative to certain benchmarks, short-term or long-term, in percentage terms, or with or without adjustment for risk. The sum of these gains and losses is probably not zero.[5]

The second point is probably correct too if we are looking at a horizon as long as, say, 8–10 years and if we include cases where investors' base currencies are different. For shorter horizons, however, currency fluctuation is significant, and for certain base currencies the historical returns may have been consistently positive or negative.

If we assume that both assertions are correct, can we conclude that currency risk should not be managed? We do not think so.

Not everyone in the currency market is profit-driven. For example, central banks and corporations are active in the market to dampen volatility and to hedge their exposures, respectively. Hence, they seek non-monetary "gains" from trading in the currency market. In fact, only a very small proportion of the gigantic currency transaction volume is there purely for profit motives. It is therefore possible to trade currencies for excess returns, ie, the returns in excess of risk-free interest rates.

One major motivation for managing currency risk is to make people accountable for the risks they take. Even if currency movements average out in the long-term, there are still plenty of short-term fluctuations. Although some still maintain that these can be disregarded if we accept the long-term zero-return argument, they increasingly impact real performances through peer group ranking and other performance measurement practices.

1.3.2 Currency movements represent random walks and are unpredictable

A wealth of literature documents the difficulties of predicting exchange rates using structural or time-series models. Frankel and Rose in their well-regarded 1995 survey on the subject concluded that traditional macroeconomic models of foreign exchange determination have relatively little explanatory power. They also expressed doubt about the value of further time-series modelling of exchange rates at high or medium frequencies using fundamental models. However, the research effort in the area has shown no sign of slowing down since their study. On balance, the body of evidence seems to support the claim that currency moves can be predicted, if only partially. Many of the later models focus on quantitative methods, especially those taking non-linear features of exchange rate movements into account. The line between technical analysis and quantitative analysis has become much finer thanks to the availability of data and computing power. The quest for the "Holy Grail" continues, and we discuss foreign exchange prediction models in Chapter 4.

Again, the predictability question is not the same as the currency risk management question: an investment manager who believes that currency moves are intrinsically unpredictable – and there is plenty of evidence to back up this view too – still faces currency risks. The latter are quantifiable (and possibly predictable too, see Chapter 8), and we firmly believe they should be measured and taken into account.

1.3.3 Is foreign exchange a separate asset class?

There is no consensus on whether foreign exchange is a separate asset class. We think that it is probably not in the traditional sense. Without being too technical, a type of asset can be considered a separate asset class if:

❏ the returns on the asset are not highly correlated to returns on existing asset classes or their combinations;
❏ the returns on the asset are correlated to known systematic risk factors, for example, market access return, inflation, changes in industrial productions, etc.;[6]
❏ there is a risk premium for assuming these systematic risks; and
❏ capital is needed to invest in such asset.

Currency returns are not highly correlated to the returns of other asset classes. However, the explanatory power of the commonly used risk factors is limited when applied to currency movements; there is no evidence that a stable currency risk premium exists; and capital is not necessary to establish currency positions. Hence my view that currency is not a separate asset class in the traditional sense.

Currency is viewed by many investment managers as a *tactical* asset class (equities and bonds are strategic asset classes)

Table 1.2 Comparison of strategic and tactical assets

Item	Strategic assets	Tactical assets
Risk premium	Stable	No stable premium
Expected return	Positive	None from passive investment
Capital	Employed	Net capital not required
Source of return	Passive investment	Active management
Confidence of return	High confidence of decade-long return	Uncertainty

Source: Ronald G. Layard-Liesching, Pareto Partners, London

for the following reasons:[7]

❑ the correlation between managed currency returns and those from strategic assets is low (we have not seen a comprehensive analysis on this point, but many recent studies of hedge fund performance provide anecdotal evidence);

❑ projected returns are positive (some evidence has been presented in recent years, though not without qualification; this is reviewed in Chapter 3, Section 3.8); and

❑ capital requirements are low (generally true).

If all these are true, a mean–variance model will allocate into such tactical assets.

Ronald Layard-Liesching of Pareto Partners, London, a foreign exchange overlay specialist, proposes the distinction between a strategic asset and a tactical asset set out in Table 1.2.

Also, the answer to the question whether currency should be treated as a separate asset class does *not* need to be the same as one's view on whether currency risk should be managed. Currency risk is an avoidable consequence of global investment, irrespective of whether or not currency is viewed as a separate asset class or whether excess return can be generated from it.[8] Since it is a risk factor, it should be managed under the proposed risk measurement and risk accountability framework.

Many asset managers adopt a pragmatic approach to the question of whether currency constitutes a separate risk class. For example, UBS Global Asset Management uses the classification of

Table 1.3 UBS Global Asset Management's investment categories

Core portfolio	Alpha-intensive	Opportunistic
Global equities	Hedge funds	TIPS
Developed & emerging markets	Global natural resources	Sector funds
Global fixed-income		Mortgages
Developed & emerging markets		Corporate debt
US high-yield bonds		REITs
Private equities		Foreign real estate
Real estate equity		Currencies
		Dynamic trading strategies

Source: UBS Global Asset Management, 2001. TIPS, Treasury inflation-protected securities; REIT, Real estate investment trusts.

its investment categories given in Table 1.3. Currencies are listed in the opportunistic investment category. Some asset managers may consider currencies as alpha-intensive (ie, not quite an asset class in the traditional sense but with a high likelihood of consistently yielding excess returns) or even include currencies in their core portfolios.

1.3.4 Currency is part of global diversification, but hedging reduces diversification benefit

It is typically claimed that unhedged international equities give better diversification than hedged equities because the correlation between domestic equities and hedged foreign equities is generally higher than if the foreign equities are unhedged. However, this argument is flawed as the reduction in correlation is expected if currency returns are not correlated with the equity returns.[9]

Generally speaking, if one adds a random variable (in this case, currency returns) to one of the correlated variables (domestic and foreign equity returns), the correlation between the latter will be reduced. The higher the currency volatility, the more the correlation is reduced. If currency volatility is very large relative to equity volatility, the correlation between unhedged foreign equity returns and domestic equity returns can approach zero as the true correlation becomes drowned by the noise produced by currency movements. And this is more or less the case for international bond portfolios. Currency volatility generally dwarfs bond volatility, so returns from unhedged foreign bonds typically exhibit low correlation with those from domestic bonds.

The impact of currency hedging should be measured by comparing the hedged portfolio risk with the unhedged portfolio risk. On this measure empirical evidence, including that surveyed in Section 1.4.4, suggests that hedging can reduce portfolio risk. But again, this is not without controversy as the conclusion depends on how one measures portfolio risk and what assumptions are used for correlations, etc.

1.3.5 Unlike equity or bonds, currency does not attract a risk premium

Both equities and bonds attract a risk premium, which is the return in excess of risk-free interest rates. For currencies, the risk premium is not clearly defined. Historical analysis conducted along these lines has produced inconclusive results – after all, we have meaningful foreign exchange data for less than two decades, and this is deemed insufficient to conduct a useful significance test.[10] Using what is available and some fancy statistical tools, some conclude that emerging market currencies attract a risk premium (before they experience a landslide devaluation, that is![11]). As for the currencies of developed economies, there seems to be no evidence to suggest that taking systematically long or short positions will be rewarded by a risk premium.

But then there are a host of phenomena (termed "puzzles" in the financial literature) that seem to contradict the zero-premium assumption, and these phenomena are usually linked to the unexplained profits/losses from holding currency positions in a particular manner – one of them being forward bias (discussed in the next section). The current consensus seems to be that there probably *is* a currency risk premium but that it is highly unstable and can be either positive or negative. Capital asset pricing model (CAPM) theory incorporating currencies links currency risk premium to factors such as the aggregate risk-aversion of investors based in different countries and the net asset positions of countries, amongst others. This point will be discussed again in Chapter 5,

Section 5.2, where the topic of currency and CAPM is reviewed. However, the practical relevance for a currency overlay manager is probably limited.

Some argue that since forward contracts are in zero net supply and gains by some counterparties are offset by losses for the others, currency offers no risk premium. But this argument is flawed. One can think of stock index futures that are also in zero net supply where, nevertheless, it is generally accepted that equity investment attracts a risk premium.

1.3.6 Forward bias (uncovered interest rate parity)

Currencies trade in both spot and forward markets. The difference between spot and forward prices, the "forward point", is determined by the interest rate differential between the currencies. The forward price is derived from an arbitrage relationship rather than from some consensus expectation in the market (as an example of the latter, forward interest rates *are* based on a market consensus expectation of where interest rates will be in the future). This is an interesting and very important distinction, and we will expand on it in Chapter 2, Appendix 2C. Nevertheless, to avoid arbitrage, currency spot prices should converge to the corresponding forward prices. But in general they do not. This is so-called "forward bias" and is frequently quoted as evidence of inefficiency in the currency market and as one of the major puzzles of international finance.

Forward bias is widely used as the basis for currency trading strategies, which are sometimes referred to as "value-trading". Various explanations for the effectiveness of such strategies have been offered, for example:

❏ *Time-varying risk premia* As the forward price rate may incorporate a risk premium, the spot price will not converge to the forward price even if the market is efficient.
❏ *Misspecification of the expectation* In this view, the spot is still expected to converge to the forward price, but the way we define the expectation is wrong. For example, there might be a potentially disastrous scenario that is priced in the forward but has not yet happened (the "peso problem" again). Therefore a test result relying on the historical data cannot capture this

latent move – although if we had a sufficiently large data set the problem would disappear.

Forward bias is a very important topic and has been thoroughly investigated in both the theoretical and the practical literature. In our view, it still represents a valid model for active trading, even in its naive form. However, this is not a reason to ignore currency risk. If anything, profit made through forward bias-based strategies should also be evaluated against the risk involved. The topic of forward bias will be revisited in more detail in Chapter 4, Section 4.5.1.

1.3.7 Autocorrelation (trends and countertrends)

Empirical evidence suggests, though not conclusively, that currency returns show positive autocorrelation over longer horizons (namely, an up move is more likely to be followed by another up move) and negative autocorrelation at a tick-by-tick level (an up tick is more likely to be followed by a down tick). The former is widely exploited by market participants, and there are countless articles and books on the subject. A short overview is provided in Chapter 4, Section 4.5.2. The latter has only been investigated empirically in recent years with the availability of data and the computer power to handle large databases, and this will be the topic of Section 4.5.2 in Chapter 4.

Is the existing evidence enough to provide a basis for taking trading decisions? Probably. One indirect proof is simply that the majority of active players in the currency trading arena can be classified as trend players of sorts. While the trend-following models are growing in sophistication, there is, however, growing evidence to indicate that the returns they give have been dwindling over recent years.

The positive autocorrelation over longer horizons has been attributed to the herding behaviour of market participants and the self-fulfilling property of trend following among other things (see next section). The tick-level negative autocorrelation is said to be linked to microstructural features:

❏ Market-makers' order books are skewed in different directions and they will skew their prices accordingly. Actual prices may touch different sides of the bid–offer spread from different banks in succession (ie, a buying transaction from one bank is more likely to be followed by a selling transaction from another bank).

❏ Heterogeneous traders react to a piece of news differently.

1.3.8 The currency market is efficient

Here the argument against currency hedging says that, because the currency market is very efficient, there is no point in trying to beat the market price, which summarises all available information. Such attempts are deemed fruitless.

The foreign exchange market is always commented on for its huge volume and liquidity. However, there is no consensus on the efficiency of this market. Chapter 4 reviews several models used by participants that are said to exploit inefficiencies in the foreign exchange market.

The debate on whether the efficient market hypothesis is applicable to the foreign exchange market is not confined to empirical matters. Many commentators question the assumptions that have to be made to ensure the validity of the efficient market hypothesis. It assumes that investors (a) are rational and (b) that they aim to maximise profit. However, numerous studies, both theoretical and empirical, demonstrate that investors may not be rational. In fact, it is common to observe herding behaviour among investors (when they are often known as "noise traders"). Many researchers attribute excessive short-term fluctuations in exchange rates to such herding behaviour.[12] The noise traders may overreact to news and generate exchange rate movements that have little relation to fundamentals. In this case exchange rates may be reacting to noise rather than news and movements could simply induce further movements through a feedback mechanism.

Also, the assumption about the profit-maximising objective of market participants may not apply to all – for example, to central banks, whose mandates generally require them to dampen fluctuation rather than seek profit. It is possible that this type of trading activity can generate patterns in exchange rates and present arbitrage opportunities.

The efficiency of the foreign exchange market is a wide-ranging question that relates to many of the points discussed earlier in this section. Any answer to the question will probably have to be balanced with a myriad of qualifications and, in our opinion, may not offer much guidance on what to do about currency risk. We shall therefore maintain a pragmatic approach and focus on risk measurement and accountability.

1.3.9 Purchasing power parity (PPP) prevails in the long run

The concept of PPP goes back to an early work of Cassel (1916) and simply measures the similarity of consumption opportunities in different countries. Following the law of one price, similar consumption baskets in different countries should have the same price tag. If not, exchange rates should adjust until they are. In international finance there are two versions of PPP:

❑ *Absolute PPP* The exchange rate between the currencies of two countries should be equal to the ratio of the average price levels in the two countries.
❑ *Relative PPP* This focuses on the relationship between the inflation rates in two countries and the change of the exchange rate between the countries' currencies over a certain period. If relative PPP holds, exchange rate shifts perfectly mirror inflation differentials and have no influence on the valuation of asset returns in real terms.

Consumption baskets and prices are reasonably easy to measure (though not so easy with all the twists and turns dreamt up by economists and statisticians), but observed currency prices have been shown to deviate consistently from their "parity values" suggested by PPP. Important and intuitive as it is, in practice PPP has only limited value as a foreign exchange determination model. It can be damaging to use it as a reason to reject the practice of measuring and managing currency risks. We will review PPP models in detail in Chapter 4, Section 2.

1.3.10 Summary

Through this brief exposition of what is special about currencies, we hope to have established that a clear-cut answer (or lack of) to any one of the questions we considered may not be directly linked to the question whether currency risk should be recognised and managed. Many of the questions are linked to, if not derived from, foreign exchange research and they will be the main subject of Chapter 4.

There are two more topics to cover in considering what is special about currencies, and these are:

❏ *Excess volatility* Macroeconomic models consistently fail to account for the level of exchange rate volatility.
❏ *Volatility memory (clustering)* This refers to the high autocorrelation of short- and long-term volatility.[13]

The first will be discussed in Chapter 4, Section 4.2. The second, volatility clustering, offers opportunities for excess returns. In fact, the whole subject of currency volatility is so important that it will be reviewed in Chapter 7.

1.4 FOREIGN EXCHANGE RISK MANAGEMENT AND CURRENCY OVERLAY

1.4.1 Renewed interest in foreign exchange risk management

The question of foreign exchange risk management in the context of global portfolio management has been around for as long as global portfolio management itself. Extensions have been made to the CAPM to incorporate foreign exchange (see Chapter 5, Section 5.2). There are also numerous empirical studies on the different aspects of foreign exchange risk management. However, there is no agreement on how foreign exchange risk should be managed in an international portfolio. In fact, as we have seen, there is no consensus on whether there *is* foreign exchange risk in such a portfolio.

The recent renewed interest in foreign exchange risk management from the fund management industry can be attributed to the following factors:

❏ Demographic changes have resulted in an explosive growth of the global asset management industry.
❏ Increasingly large proportions of assets under management are invested globally in pursuit of higher returns and/or diversification.
❏ International capital flows have a substantial, and sometimes sustained, impact on exchange rate movements as compared to traditional factors such as current account balances. Increased capital flows are one of the factors contributing to the heightened volatility of currencies.

❏ Investors are paying closer attention to returns and risks on their investments by looking at league tables and other performance indicators. Currency movements can produce highly undesirable swings in performance.

❏ A highly liquid and efficient foreign exchange spot and options market to price, transfer and manage risk has emerged. The depth of this market and its capacity for innovation continue to break new ground.

❏ Cheapening computing power and availability of data make risk separation, optimisation and performance attribution much easier.

❏ New risk measurement methodologies, such as value-at-risk, have been developed and are gaining wide acceptance.

The regulatory environment in most parts of the world is moving towards a tighter, fairer, more transparent approach. Requirements such as mark-to-market accounting and minimum funding levels compel fund managers to be more alert to currency risks. The poor performance of stockmarkets around the world after the burst of the dotcom bubble has also propelled investment managers into focusing on investment policy, including currency policies. In its quarterly survey the *Defined Contribution Universe Summary*, published in 2003, Mercer Investment Consulting, a pension fund consultancy, stated that nearly 70% of defined-contribution plans in the US now put out an investment policy statement compared with 57% two years ago. Many funds, in the process of clarifying the role of asset allocation and risk responsibility, have started to reconsider the question of currency in international investment and the management of currency risks. In a 2002 survey by JP Morgan Fleming Asset Management (2003) on alternative investment strategies, 9% of correspondents said they used currency overlay, 25% were considering whether to do so, and the remaining two-thirds did not use it.

1.4.2 The growing global market and its consequences for investors

This are plenty of books and databases on the scope and depth of the global capital market and investment, the rapid expansion of which provides the backdrop for the topic of currency management.

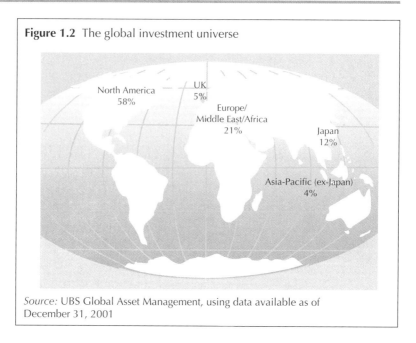

Figure 1.2 The global investment universe

North America
58%

UK
5%

Europe/
Middle East/Africa
21%

Japan
12%

Asia-Pacific (ex-Japan)
4%

Source: UBS Global Asset Management, using data available as of December 31, 2001

We present some charts here that are more relevant to the purpose of this book.

According to an estimate by UBS Global Asset Management (2002) using end-of-2001 data, the total investable capital market around the world stood at around US$60.5 trillion, of which more than half was accounted for by North American markets. The exact breakdown is shown in Figure 1.2.

Not only has the investment universe been expanding, the companies in traditional markets are also becoming more global. In a research report published in 2001, the US investment bank Morgan Stanley estimated that nearly a quarter of the revenue from US companies listed in the S&P100 Index can be attributed to non-US sources. The picture is similar for other major economies, with the exception of Japan, which derived an even larger portion of its corporate revenue from overseas sources. This phenomenon adds a new dimension to currency management: currency risk may be indirect, and investment in domestic stocks does not necessarily provide insulation for investors.[14]

Direct holding of international assets has been increasing for investors based in all major economies. Figure 1.3 shows the

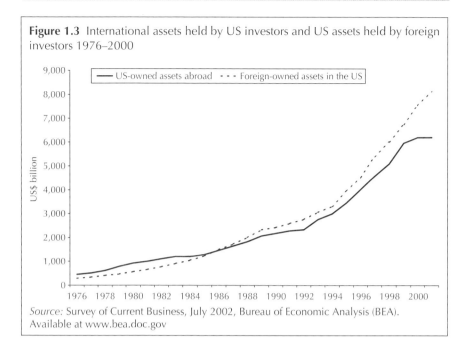

Figure 1.3 International assets held by US investors and US assets held by foreign investors 1976–2000

Source: Survey of Current Business, July 2002, Bureau of Economic Analysis (BEA). Available at www.bea.doc.gov

holdings of international assets by US investors along with those of US assets by foreign investors over the last 25 years.

The proportion of pension fund assets allocated to international bonds and equities varies in the developed countries. Figure 1.4 shows the estimated allocations for Australia, Canada, France, Germany, Japan, the Netherlands, Switzerland, the United Kingdom and the United States. Foreign equities and bonds are shown in shaded diagonal blocks, and the total amount of pension fund assets for each country is included at the top. One can see that there is considerable variation in international allocation between different countries (one principal reason for which is regulatory restrictions). With the size of pension fund assets in each country growing, both the percentage and the total amount invested in international assets are expected to increase. When we compare the 1995 figures for asset allocation with those for 2000, the last year when InterSec Research Corp. compiled the data, we see that allocations in foreign bonds and equities have gone up in all countries except Canada, and significantly so for France, Germany, the Netherlands and Switzerland, whose allocations have nearly doubled.

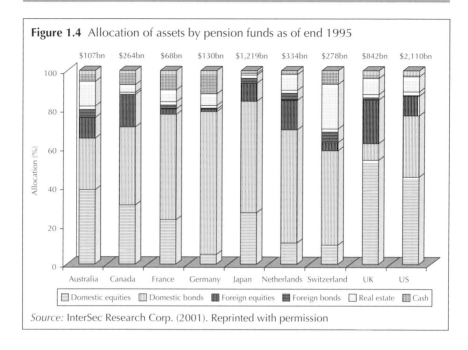

Figure 1.4 Allocation of assets by pension funds as of end 1995

Source: InterSec Research Corp. (2001). Reprinted with permission

And, finally, Figure 1.5 shows the holdings of foreign equities as a percentage of total portfolio assets for UK insurance companies, pension funds and trusts for the period 1964–2000.

Overall, the trend is clear: the investment universe is increasingly global and investors' exposure to foreign assets continues to grow. Against this background, considerations of currency risk become increasingly relevant.

1.4.3 Should currency risk be hedged? Some questions and answers

Whether currency risk should be hedged is a question that lies at the centre of the so-called "currency-hedging debate", and the answer is clearly worth considerably more than sixty-four thousand dollars. In many ways the whole book is about this question. However, we do not think one should seek simple yes or no answers that are applicable under different sets of objectives and constraints. In my opinion, currency risk is real and can be substantial, especially given the expansion of the global investment universe. Currency risk should be measured separately from the

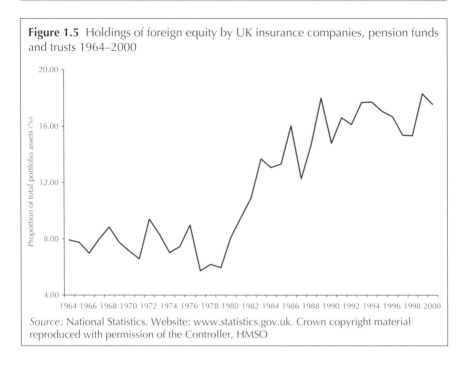

Figure 1.5 Holdings of foreign equity by UK insurance companies, pension funds and trusts 1964–2000

Source: National Statistics. Website: www.statistics.gov.uk. Crown copyright material reproduced with permission of the Controller, HMSO

underlying risks. Moreover, currency risk should be entrusted to managers with comparative advantage. Nor do we necessarily propose that a currency be hedged, either passively (using a predefined hedge ratio) or actively; a fund can choose to leave currency risk unhedged as a strategic and informed decision. However, if such a decision *is* made it is my belief that a fund should centralise the currency risk at the fund level and measure the performance of the underlying managers as if they were investing on a fully hedged basis. Later in the book we will provide a balanced overview on the whys and some practical techniques for the hows. Below we divide the question whether currency should be managed into several sub-questions and provide brief answers. Detailed answers are given in the relevant chapters.

Q1: Does passive hedging add value – ie, add value defined in terms of relative return?
Most existing studies of the subject fall into this category. There is, unfortunately, no conclusive answer. The results are usually

heavily dependent on the sample period and the base currency of choice. The question is similar to whether going consistently long or short a currency will yield systematic returns.

Q2: Does passive hedging add value in terms of risk reduction (and therefore in terms of risk-adjusted return)?
The answer to this question is not necessarily data-dependent and a commonsensical answer seems to be yes. Indeed, many studies have shown that hedging is effective in reducing portfolio volatility – more so for bond and balanced portfolios than for equity portfolios. In practice, currency hedging is like shooting at a moving target, rendering the surgical removal of currency risk all but impossible. There are a handful of articles that highlight the limitations of currency hedging, in particular Froot (1993), which disputes the long-term (more than three years for equities and more than five years for bonds) effectiveness of hedging.

Q3: Does passive hedging impair the diversification benefit of currency?
A host of articles published around 1990 asserted that hedging increased the correlation between asset classes. But such claims have since been discredited. If currency movements represent white noise, uncorrelated to underlying assets, passive hedging may indeed increase the correlation between foreign and domestic asset classes. Removing such white noise will clearly have no effect on diversification. There is no definitive answer to the question whether currency moves are random noise. In practice, many people assume that they are not correlated with underlying asset returns.

Q4: (a) Does active currency management add value? (b) Are currency movements predictable?
The answer to whether actively managing currency risk can add value is not conclusive. Evidence that it does comes mostly from overlay managers and investment banks. Two recent studies on the performance of overlay managers, both by pension fund consultants (Watson Wyatt and Frank Russell Company), show impressive historical returns, but they should be viewed with caution.[15] There is a huge body of material on the predictability of currency movements, and this is reviewed in Chapter 4.

Q5: Is the answer to the currency-hedging question different for bonds and equities?
Probably yes. Currency volatility is usually much greater than bond volatility and currency exposures are often hedged as a matter of course. The risk reduction benefit for equities is much smaller.

Q6: Can currency hedging add value by other means?
We believe this to be one of the most important and overlooked issues in the currency-hedging debate, and we think that the disciplined approach associated with currency overlay is capable of bringing real benefit to an organisation. The manager of one of the largest pension funds in the world said, on the basis of their experience with currency overlay, that the greatest benefit of currency hedging is the clarification of responsibility for risk. To undertake currency hedging properly the first thing one needs to do is to know, and continuously monitor, one's investment positions and resulting currency exposures. This exercise of clarifying risk responsibility may well bring many benefits to the fund. In our experience, those funds which run currency overlay programmes typically have clearly defined roles and responsibilities and their internal communication appears to be more efficient. It would be interesting to see whether this is reflected in the overall performance of such funds.

1.4.4 How does the evidence in favour of currency hedging stack up?

In this section we survey the empirical evidence on the question whether currency risk should be hedged. We focus on the most frequently quoted articles and, where possible, we have chosen studies by authors who are not involved in the overlay industry. The results are presented in Table 1.4. It is impossible to give detailed consideration to every article as many adopt a unique approach in dealing with the subject. Some of these, for example, hedge ratio, Sharpe ratio-based optimisation and parameter uncertainty, will be discussed later in the relevant sections of the book.

Our aim in including this rather long survey is to allow readers to make up their own minds on the currency-hedging debate. The evidence available so far, as reviewed in Table 1.4, is summarised in the points below:

❏ currency hedging is generally beneficial in terms of risk reduction, more so for bonds and balanced portfolios than for pure equity portfolios;
❏ the impact of currency hedging on returns or risk-adjusted returns (eg, Sharpe ratio) is unclear;
❏ hedge ratios obtained from CAPM-style optimisation using Sharpe ratios are generally not very practical, and the optimisation method is very sensitive to the expected returns used in the optimisation process;
❏ in *ex ante* studies a unitary hedge ratio (100%) works better than optimised hedge ratios;
❏ the impact of hedging is different for different base currencies;
❏ forward bias-based hedging strategies generally work, as do some other quantitative strategies;
❏ the hedge ratio may also depend on other factors, such as investors' risk appetite and the cost of hedging.

1.4.5 Currency overlay: what it is and what it is not

The concept of currency overlay means different things to different people and currency overlay managers, in our view, have done very little to demystify it. In many sales pitches and published articles by currency overlay managers which we have seen currency overlay is presented as a means to earn extra returns for next to nothing and/or to reduce portfolio volatility, again, for next to nothing. Otherwise there is very little information on how they obtain their upward-sloping cumulative return curves (also known as "equity curves") or downward-sloping (at least to a point) risk curves. Unstated assumptions may have been made to get these numbers, which means that the conclusions must certainly be viewed with caution.

In this book, currency overlay is defined as a process whereby currency risk is managed separately from the underlying investment. It is, therefore, a form of currency hedging. The underlying investment can be bonds, equities, real estate and so forth. These are typically, but not necessarily, denominated in a currency other than the investor's home currency.

Table 1.4 Should currency risk be hedged? A review of the empirical evidence

Study/Underlying/ Period/Base currency	Main conclusions	Other features
Eun and Resnick (1988) *Exchange rate uncertainty, forward contracts and international portfolio selection* Equities 1979–85, weekly USD	Full currency hedging can increase the gains from international equity diversification	❑ Covers CAD, FRF, DEM, JPY, CHF and GBP ❑ Both *ex ante* and *ex post* ❑ Shows exchange rate risk to be non-diversifiable due to high cross-correlations ❑ Hedging results in significant performance improvement by reducing parameter uncertainty
Perold and Schulman (1988) *The free lunch in currency hedging: implications for investment policy and performance standards* Bonds, equities and balanced portfolios 1977–87, quarterly USD	Hedging significantly reduces currency risk without sacrificing the expected return	❑ Uses quarterly real USD return[16] ❑ Not based on optimisation ❑ Full currency hedge reduces equity volatility by 20–30%, bond volatility by 35–60% ❑ Authors estimate that transaction cost for a six-month rolling programme is 0.12% per annum
Thomas III (1989) *The performance of currency-hedged foreign bonds* Bonds 1975–88 USD	Hedging significantly improves the performance of foreign currency-denominated government portfolios	❑ *Ex post* study covering DEM, JPY, GBP, FRF, CAD and NLG ❑ Not based on optimisation ❑ Currency risk decreases from average 15% per annum to 8% with hedging; at portfolio level, from 12% to 5%

AUD, Australian dollar; CAD, Canadian dollar; CHF, Swiss franc; DEM, Deutschmark; EUR, euro; FRF, French franc; GBP, sterling; JPY, Japanese yen; NLG, Dutch guilder; USD, US dollar.

Table 1.4 (continued)

Study/Underlying/ Period/Base currency	Main conclusions	Other features
		❏ Risk reduction is consistent but returns are not consistent in sub-periods
Burik and Ennis (1990) *Foreign bonds in diversified portfolios: a limited advantage* Bonds 1978–87 USD	US-based investors benefit only marginally from investing in currency-hedged foreign bonds, and when hedging cost is considered, investing in foreign bonds is not worthwhile	❏ Uses *ex post* optimisation over Sharpe ratio with different asset classes ❏ In unconstrained optimisation, optimiser chooses hedged foreign currency bonds; however, the efficiency loss is very small when hedged foreign currency bonds are excluded ❏ Sharpe ratios for US, unhedged and hedged foreign bonds are, respectively, 0.22, 0.13 and 0.25 in this study
Eaker and Grant (1990) *Currency hedging strategies for internationally diversified equity portfolios* Equities 1975–88 USD	Hedging is beneficial, and a forward bias-based hedging strategy provides superior performance to a fully hedged strategy	❏ Covers CAD, DEM, USD, JPY, CHF and GBP ❏ *Ex post* results
Hauser and Levy (1991) *Optimal forward coverage of international fixed income portfolios* Bonds 1983–88 USD	Hedging is more beneficial for shorter-maturity foreign bonds	❏ *Ex post* study ❏ Covers USD, JPY and DEM bonds ❏ Currency risk decreases from 95% to 75% as maturity of foreign bonds increases from 0.5 to 5 years ❏ Forward bias-based hedge shows the best performance improvement

Study	Details	Findings
Nesbitt (1991) *Currency hedging rules for plan sponsors* Equities 1973–89 USD	Hedging is beneficial but hedge ratio decreases with cost of hedging. Hedge ratio also depends on portion of assets allocated internationally as well as investor's risk appetite	□ A pragmatic approach linking cost of hedging and hedge ratio □ Based on the idea that investor is willing to give up 0.28 basis points for a 1% reduction in portfolio volatility
Froot (1993) *Currency hedging over long horizons* Equities and bonds 1802–1990 GBP	For shorter horizons hedging reduces volatility. For horizons longer than five to eight years, foreign stocks/bonds display greater return volatility when hedged than not	□ USD investments □ Real returns instead of nominal returns □ Minimum variance hedge ratio reduces from almost 100% at short horizons to an average of 35% at a 5–10 year horizon
Glen and Jorion (1993) *Currency hedging for international portfolios* World bond portfolio, world equity portfolio, balanced portfolio 1974–90, monthly USD	Hedging is beneficial, though more so for world bond and balanced portfolios than for world equity portfolios	□ Both ex ante and ex post □ Includes significance tests and out-of-sample performance □ Optimised hedge ratio does not significantly outperform unitary or universal hedge ratio[17] □ Black's universal hedge ratio does not provide statistically significant performance □ Forward bias-based strategy provides significant improvement over a fully hedged strategy
Halpern (1993) *Investing abroad: a review of capital market integration and manager performance* Bonds and equities 1988–90 USD	The timing of country allocation shows that underlying managers do not have skills to forecast currency movements. A small amount of exploitable inefficiency present in foreign exchange forward market	□ Actual allocation and performance data for 18 managers makes this the only study we are aware of to use such data. □ Forward inefficiency is the only alternative tested in the study

AUD, Australian dollar; CAD, Canadian dollar; CHF, Swiss franc; DEM, Deutschmark; EUR, euro; FRF, French franc; GBP, sterling; JPY, Japanese yen; NLG, Dutch guilder; USD, US dollar.

Table 1.4 (continued)

Study/Underlying/ Period/Base currency	Main conclusions	Other features
Levich and Thomas (1993b) *The merits of active currency risk management: evidence from international bond portfolios* Bonds 1976–90 USD	Rule-based active management significantly improves portfolio performance as measured by Sharpe ratio	☐ Covers DEM, GBP, CHF, JPY and CAD ☐ Incorporates transaction costs, carry ☐ Bootstrap-based significance test ☐ Sharpe ratios: unhedged, 0.29; fully hedged, 0.38; active, 0.75 ☐ Filter rule and moving average rule
Eun and Resnick (1994) *International diversification of investment portfolios: US and Japanese perspectives* Equities, bonds, balanced Portfolios 1978–89, monthly USD, JPY	For US-based investors hedging is beneficial both *ex ante* and *ex post*; for Japan-based investors, only *ex post*	☐ Covers CAD, FRF, DEM, JPY, CHF, GBP and USD ☐ Both *ex ante* and *ex post* ☐ Hedging gain is more significant for bond and balanced portfolios but less so for equity portfolios ☐ The gain with international diversification is greater for US-based investors than for Japan-based investors[18]
Jorion (1994) *A mean–variance analysis of currency overlays* Bonds and equities 1978–91, monthly USD	Currency hedging is generally beneficial. However, overlay-style separate optimisation is not as efficient as full optimisation[19]	☐ Forward bias-based strategy adds value ☐ Uses *ex post* optimisation over Sharpe ratio with different asset classes ☐ Author acknowledges that the *ex post* result is of little relevance to actual portfolio management ☐ Optimisation results in hugely implausible hedge ratios, eg, as high as 1450%; no position in German underlying assets but taking 52% short position in DEM, etc.

Annaert (1995)
Estimation risk and international bond portfolio selection
Bonds
1985–91, weekly
USD, DEM, JPY

Hedging reduces both portfolio risk and estimation risk considerably, more so for USD and JPY-based investors. However, for USD, DEM and JPY-based investors, hedging has been expensive due to forward bias

❑ *Ex ante* optimisation based on Sharpe ratio, closely following Eun and Resnick (1988) but with bonds as underlying
❑ Covers 15 different currencies, of which eight later joined EUR and four track EUR closely (hence smaller benefit of hedging for DEM-based investors)
❑ Alternative estimators which are designed to deal with estimation risk do not work as well when short-sale constraints are imposed

Braccia (1995)
An analysis of currency overlays for US pension plans
Equities and bonds
1980–93
USD

Optimal hedge ratio is as high as 0.80 if cost of hedging is zero. However, hedge ratio is much lower, averaging 0.30, when a 55 basis points cost is included

❑ Covers DEM and JPY
❑ Portfolio consists of US and international equities, US and international bonds
❑ Some curious correlation figures: for example, correlation between JPY (DEM) and international bonds is 0.84 (0.64)
❑ Author explains: "correlations among asset classes and the currencies are low enough to provide adequate diversification without incurring the added cost associated with currency hedging"

Clarke and Kritzman (1996)
Currency management: concepts and practices
Equities and bonds
1980–93
USD, GBP, DEM, FRF, JPY, AUD, CAD

No consistent pattern found to indicate that hedging either enhances or reduces returns; currency hedging, however, consistently reduces asset risks

❑ Currency hedging reduces risks in equity/bond investment by average 8% and 24%, respectively
❑ Both return and risk figures seem high in this study. For example, unhedged bond risk typically over 20% and hedged bonds about 13–19%

AUD, Australian dollar; CAD, Canadian dollar; CHF, Swiss franc; DEM, Deutschmark; EUR, euro; FRF, French franc; GBP, sterling; JPY, Japanese yen; NLG, Dutch guilder; USD, US dollar.

Table 1.4 (continued)

Study/Underlying/ Period/Base currency	Main conclusions	Other features
Eun and Resnick (1997) *International equity investment with selective hedging strategies* Equities 1978–94 USD	Currency hedging marginally benefits international equity investments. Active strategies such as forward bias-based hedging and writing options provide enhanced results	❒ Covers CAD, FRF, DEM, JPY, CHF, GBP and USD ❒ Out-of-sample tests and ex ante strategies; simulation ❒ Deals with parameter uncertainties ❒ Overall, option-writing strategies performed the best
Larsen and Resnick (2000) *The optimal construction of international diversified equity portfolios hedged against exchange rate uncertainty* Equities 1983–88, monthly USD, FRF, DEM, NLG, CHF	A full currency hedging strategy combined with minimum-variance optimisation on local currency excess returns outperforms other hedging/ optimisation combinations	❒ *Ex ante* study covering equity indices from 14 countries ❒ Definition of local currency excess return similar to that of Karnosky and Singer (1994) – see Chapter 6, Section 6.6 ❒ Results consistent for investors based in different currencies
Reiner (2000) *Practical active currency management for global equity portfolios* Equities 1972–99, monthly USD	Passive hedging reduces portfolio performance. However, a moving average rule outperforms both hedged and unhedged portfolios	❒ *Ex post* study covering FRF, DEM, JPY, GBP and USD ❒ Sharpe ratio is reduced from 0.26 to 0.18 when currency is fully hedged for a portfolio with a 40% foreign asset allocation ❒ Local currency indices are used as the "hedge indices" (see Chapter 6, Section 6.4)

VanderLinden, Jiang and Hu (2002)
Conditional hedging and portfolio performance
Bonds and equities
1976–97
FRF, DEM, JPY, GBP, USD

For US-based investors, full hedging does not improve Sharpe ratio for equities but it does for bonds. Results are different for different base currencies

❏ *Ex post* optimisation
❏ A forward bias-based strategy, using both real and nominal interest rates, performs better in all cases
❏ In bond portfolios, Sharpe ratio improves uniformly with higher hedge ratio. In equity and balanced portfolios it peaks before declining at higher hedge ratios

de Roon, Nijman and Werker (2003)
Currency hedging for international stock portfolios: the usefulness of mean–variance analysis
Equities
1975–98, monthly
USD

Hedging is utility-dependent. Passive hedging is only beneficial for investors with very high risk-aversion. It is not beneficial for investors with mean–variance utility. Forward bias-based hedging leads to significant performance improvement

❏ *Ex post* optimisation using regression, covering G5 currencies
❏ Hedge ratio from optimisation highly variable, sometimes running into thousands of percentage points, whether to hedge or to speculate

AUD, Australian dollar; CAD, Canadian dollar; CHF, Swiss franc; DEM, Deutschmark; EUR, euro; FRF, French franc; GBP, sterling; JPY, Japanese yen; NLG, Dutch guilder; USD, US dollar.

Table 1.5 Currency overlay: what it is and what it is not

It is ...	It is or does not ...
One method of managing currency risk	A "magic product" that will bring
A useful framework for quantifying currency risks in a portfolio and accommodating a variety of styles for managing them	certain excess returns or reduce portfolio risks
	Necessarily view currency as a separate asset class
A tool for measuring performance depending on a fund manager's core competency	Necessarily trade currency actively
An exercise that clarifies risk responsibility and improves internal communication	Necessarily involve financial wizardry

While we defer a detailed discussion on the subject to Chapter 3, a list of what currency overlay is and is not is presented in Table 1.5.

1.5 ABOUT THIS BOOK

This book provides a guide to currency overlay management for investment portfolios from a practitioner's viewpoint. Our aim is that it should be a reference work for investment managers whose investment decisions and results are affected by currency fluctuations and who currently use, or plan to use, an overlay method to manage their currency risks.

As far as we know, the book is the first comprehensive and objective attempt to treat the subject from a practitioner's viewpoint. Most of the topics it covers were raised by UBS's wholesale clients, including mutual funds, hedge funds, pension funds, insurance funds and sovereigns. The author felt the need to undertake such a project after an extensive search failed to locate a single book that dealt with the various aspects of currency overlay for practitioners in a relevant manner and/or at an appropriate technical level.

Currency Overlay is intended as an accessible reference guide for anyone working in the investment management industry. For a fund manager who does not have a currency management programme (and there are many), the book will provide all the materials he or she needs to set one up or to choose one from the market. For those fund managers who have a currency management policy in place, it will provide an objective yardstick for performance review.

The field is not new. Currency risk is an unavoidable consequence of the rising volume of global investment which has been one of the main themes in investment management for the last 20 years or so. The concept and practice of currency overlay first appeared in the late 1980s and have gained acceptance in recent years as more and more investment managers invest abroad and their performance comes under ever closer scrutiny.

There are many books and numerous research articles on several important subjects in the field: notably, on option pricing theory, on technical analysis, on the efficiency of the currency market, and on currency determination from a macroeconomic perspective. These topics are generally more relevant to currency traders and researchers interested in currency trading. Other materials in the field consist mainly of articles by various leading practitioners preaching on the merit of currency overlay and offering a glimpse of their proprietary management methodology, and one cannot help treating such statements with a sense of scepticism. There has been comparatively little effort to provide guidance on how one should establish a framework to manage currency risk in practice and how various research results on currency trading fit into this framework.

As the present book is a practical guide, we assume minimum technical background on the part of readers apart from a basic knowledge of investment management. However, we provide references wherever appropriate for more technical readers.

1.5.1 Structure of the book

To establish whether currency hedging should be used for a particular portfolio and to develop an appropriate currency overlay programme requires consideration of a number of topics. These are listed below along with the chapter in which each is discussed:

❏ the impact of currency on the portfolio's risk and return (Chapter 2);
❏ the special features of currency vs other asset classes (this chapter and also Chapter 4);
❏ whether to adopt a passive hedging policy – possibly a passive hedge ratio (Chapter 5);
❏ the suitability of active management (Chapter 2 and Chapter 4);

❏ benchmarks and performance measurement (Chapter 6);
❏ the suitability of currency derivatives (Chapter 7);
❏ emerging market currencies (Chapter 8); and
❏ relevant online technology and e-commerce (Chapter 9).

Chapter 3 is devoted to an overview of currency overlay – what it is, how it is done, who are the main players and so on. Some important questions about overlay management will be discussed in later chapters. For example, in Chapter 4 we review various foreign exchange models and modelling techniques and the choice of overlay style. In Chapter 5 we include a theoretical digression on currency's role in modern portfolio theory as well as in the CAPM. We list common approaches to determining an optimal hedge ratio for currencies and discuss their suitability in real life. Chapter 6 deals with selecting a currency benchmark and measuring currency management performance. Chapter 7 focuses on the relevance of option pricing theory, in particular to dynamic overlay style, with a general overview of the use of derivative instruments in currency risk management. The question of whether to have a separate policy for emerging market currencies is discussed in Chapter 8. Chapter 9 includes a short excursion on currency liquidity and how it varies with changes in the foreign exchange marketplace, in particular the rapid emergence and spread of online dealing platforms. We include two examples to show what kind of services an institutional asset manager can expect from a bank and a multi-bank platform. The book concludes with a summary of the key arguments followed by a step-by-step check list for someone who is intending to set up a currency overlay.

1.5.2 Related publications

Four publications, all from the Association for Investment Management and Research (AIMR), cover aspects of the topic similar to those dealt with in this book. *Managing Currency Risk* (AIMR, 1997) and *Currency Risk in Investment Portfolios* (AIMR, 1999) are conference proceedings offering a potpourri of contradicting opinions by an assortment of academics and practitioners, usually overlay managers. Ramaswami's (1993) monograph *Active Currency Management*, which looks at the non-linear dependencies in current returns and profitable trading strategies, is far too empirical and data-dependent for the purpose of investigating currency risk management in the context of global investment. The closest in objectives and layout to our book is Clarke and Kritzman (1996), *Currency Management: Concepts and Practices*. A tutorial with reviews on currency management concepts and principles, it presents an algebraic representation of currency hedging in a mean–variance setting (assuming stable multivariate normal distributions) and tables of risks and returns of historical hedged vs unhedged performance. But many important topics are not covered and the restrictive assumptions employed may limit its practical relevance.

Four other books on currency risk management cover a similar range of topics to this book. Eun and Resnick's (2001) *International Financial Management* provides a comprehensive, if academic, exposition but only a very short section on currency risk in international investment. *The Currency Hedging Debate*, edited by Thomas III (1990), contains a collection of 18 articles, some previously published (in 1986 and 1989), by both academics and practitioners. Some of these have been reviewed in Section 1.4.4. Both Bennett (1997), *Managing Foreign Exchange Risk: How to Identify and Manage Foreign Currency Exposure*, and Smithson and Smith (1998), *Managing Financial Risk: A Guide to Derivative Products, Financial Engineering, and Value Maximization*, are geared more towards corporate users.

1 And, we must add, a resilient entry to its childhood by the time this book went to press. The single currency has regained almost all of its lost value since its launch against the US dollar, sterling and the Japanese yen.
2 For more information on foreign exchange market structure and its implications, see Lyons (2002). Also refer to Chapter 4, Section 4.3 for market structure and exchange rate forecast.
3 We define currency hedging as using financial means to neutralise the impact of currency fluctuations on returns, denominated in a base currency, from investment denominated in, or impacted by, foreign currencies. Currency overlay is a method of implementing hedging. We will defer the definition of currency overlay until Chapter 3, Section 3.3.
4 77% is Black's universal hedge ratio; see Chapter 5, Section 5.5.
5 See footnote 5 of Chapter 5 on Siegel's paradox for an illustration of percentage gains. Appendix A of Chapter 4 contains an example where both central bankers and speculators make money out of intervention but over different horizons.
6 Commonly used factors in the academic literature include excess market returns, market capitalisation relative to GDP, balance of trade relative to GDP, inflation, changes in industrial production and credit spread. In a global setting, the factors can be excess return on world market index, world dividend yield, world inflation, changes in world industrial production, slope of the US interest rate curve, oil price, US corporate bond–treasury spread, etc.

7　Sometimes it is called a "managed alpha asset", or just "alpha asset". The traditional assets are beta assets due to CAPM pricing relationships. Hedge funds can be seen as a type of alpha asset.

8　Some commentators therefore label currency as an exposure rather than an asset.

9　See Chapter 2, Section 2.3.3, for a further note about the correlation between currencies and equities.

10　See Chapter 5, Section 5.2.2.3 for a discussion of currency risk premium and references.

11　See the "peso effect" in Chapter 4, Section 4.5.1.

12　See, for example, Banerjee (1992) and Shleifer and Summers (1990).

13　For references see Baillie (1996), Andersen *et al.* (2000), Ederington and Lee (1993) and Granger and Ding (1996).

14　Refer to Chapter 2, Section 2.3.3 for more detailed discussion.

15　Hersey and Minnick (2000) and Baldridge, Meath and Myers (2000).

16　Perold and Schulman (1988) contend that quarterly data are better suited for this kind of analysis as risk measures calculated over shorter time windows (eg, monthly or weekly) tend to underestimate the risk as they fail to account for the changes in mean.

17　In Glen and Jorion's setting a passive foreign exchange hedge ratio is chosen and implemented. Then additional currency positions are taken on the basis of the result of CAPM optimisation. They show that the second optimisation does not provide additional value in the out-of-sample tests. The result corroborates practical observations that most currency managers do not use CAPM-type optimisation to determine currency weights.

18　During the sample period, the US dollar appreciated against the Canadian dollar, French franc and sterling and depreciated against the Deutschmark, Japanese yen and Swiss franc. The yen appreciated against all other currencies. It is puzzling why under the circumstances hedging did not improve the portfolio performance. Closer inspection of the data shows that the yen-denominated domestic bond portfolio had the highest Sharpe ratio, which proved difficult to beat.

19　See Chapter 5, Section 5.4 on optimisation styles.

2

A Primer on Currency Risk

2.1 INTRODUCTION

This chapter starts with a review of the basic definitions of return in the currency management context. Some simple examples are used to show that different calculation methods can give different results, where the differences can easily be comparable in magnitude to the expected returns from an active currency overlay programme. We therefore draw up some guidelines on the most suitable definitions of return for use in currency management. We include a summary of risk measures in Appendix 2D.

We then proceed to a descriptive tour of currency risks and returns in global portfolios, illustrated by reference to two well-known return indices. We limit our attention to results that are not too sensitive to different sample periods or calculation methods – namely, the risk reduction that is achievable through currency hedging – but do not consider historical hedged versus unhedged returns. There are plenty of published materials in the area, and some analytical software and tools allow this type of analysis to be conducted on the fly.

The chapter continues with a general overview of the pros and cons of different approaches to currency risk management and to currency trading.

We conclude with a section on the key theme of the book: the need for risk awareness and a disciplined approach to currency risk management. In our opinion, the most vital question in the currency risk management debate in a portfolio management setting is not whether one should hedge risks, but rather *whether currency risk is clearly defined and quantified*. The answer to the question whether to hedge or not will be the by-product of a clear definition of currency risk and the existing risk/return policy of the portfolio.

2.2 DEFINING AND DECOMPOSING CURRENCY RETURNS

Many attempts to investigate the currency risk in international investments are either flawed or unnecessarily complicated due to the lack of a consistent approach. Concepts of return are often confused – for example, *ex ante* vs *ex post* returns, spot vs forward returns, domestic vs foreign interest rates, bond/equity returns expressed in one currency vs *hedged* into the currency, the total return on a benchmark bond portfolio vs the short-term interest rate in the same currency, etc. In this section we present a brief overview of the relevant concepts of return. Short summaries of risk and correlation measures are included in Appendices D and E at the end of the chapter.

Return can be either absolute return or relative return. The latter is the return computed relative to a specific benchmark. Return can also be *ex ante* or *ex post* (see Section 2.2.5). Returns for currencies can be more difficult to define than returns on, say, bonds and equities. So we will first look at a stylised example to help us approach the problem of definition gradually.

Example 2.1 A US dollar-based investor invests US$1.0 million in a Japanese monetary fund. The market prices are:

❏ spot exchange rate is 100 Japanese yen per US dollar (denoted USD/JPY in subsequent sections);[1]
❏ three-month forward exchange rate is 98.46 USD/JPY;
❏ three-month Treasury bill yield is 6.50% (in US dollars); and
❏ three-month Japanese government bond (JGB) yield is 0.25% (in Japanese yen).[2]

To obtain the yen funds needed to purchase units in the Japanese monetary fund, the investor can conduct a spot currency transaction to convert the US$1.0 million into yen at the current spot rate. He receives ¥100.0 million and the proceeds are invested.

Three months later the spot exchange rate moves from 100 to 110 USD/JPY and the ¥100 million investment has turned into ¥100.0625 million.[3] What is the return on currency? What is the relevance of Treasury bill and JGB yields? And would the result be different if the money were invested in an equity or bond fund? Would the return calculation be different if the currency were fully or partially hedged? We will consider these questions in the next sub-sections.

2.2.1 Absolute return when underlying investment return is certain

Here are a few commonly used methods, or return measures, for calculating the absolute return on currency.

Method I The first is a straightforward calculation of how much the Japanese yen has depreciated during the three-month period on a spot-on-spot basis. This method is often used by journalists and other financial commentators to calculate currency moves, and the results are sometimes referred to as "headline" currency returns.

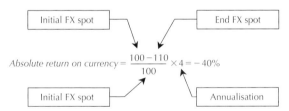

$$\textit{Absolute return on currency} = \frac{100-110}{100} \times 4 = -40\%$$

Method II Some people may argue that the first method is more relevant for US dollar appreciation than yen depreciation. To calculate the latter, one needs to redenominate the exchange rate as US dollars per Japanese yen rather than the conventional Japanese yen per US dollar as in Method I. Again, during the three-month period, on a spot-on-spot basis:

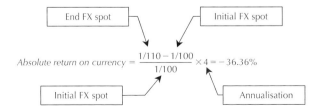

$$\textit{Absolute return on currency} = \frac{1/110-1/100}{1/100} \times 4 = -36.36\%$$

The difference between Methods I and II can be attributed to the way percentage returns are calculated. To take an extreme example, an increase from 1 to 10 is 900%, but a corresponding decrease from 1 to 110 is only 90%. In practice, the difference is usually not this large because the change in a given period is small if not negligible. The difference disappears if one uses log-returns.

Method III Similar to Method I, but instead of spot-on-spot one uses spot-on-forward and the exchange rates are expressed in Japanese yen per US dollar:

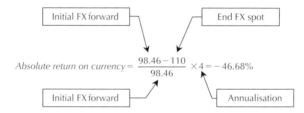

We observe that the return in this case, -46.48%, is lower than the return obtained with Method I. This is because the Japanese yen is trading at a premium to the US dollar. In other words, the yen is "expected" to be stronger in the future. Therefore, its depreciation against the US dollar is even more pronounced when set against this "expectation". However, the forward price is not an "expectation" of the future spot price in a strict sense – unlike forward interest rates calculated from the yield curve, which is the market forecast of future interest rates. The foreign exchange spot–forward relationship is based on a no-arbitrage relationship. This is an important distinction but not totally relevant to what we are trying to concentrate on here. For further details see Appendix 2C.

Method IV Similar to Method II, but with the three-month forward rate replacing the initial spot rate.

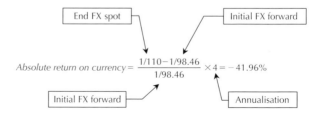

Method V From a cashflow viewpoint, the investor has US$1.0 million to start with. If he liquidates his investment in Japanese yen at the end of month 3 and converts the proceeds into US dollars at spot, a return can be calculated from the net return as follows:

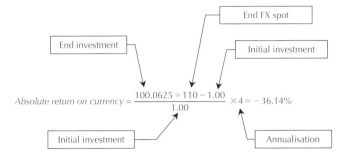

Method VI Similar to Method V but with a small adjustment as, strictly speaking, the return in Method V is not a return on currency as it includes the return on the Japanese yen monetary fund, which yields 0.25% per annum. In fact, the same adjustment can be made to the other methods as well.

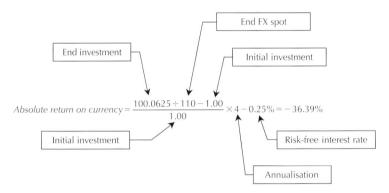

It is worrying that the return figures in such a simple example can differ by so much, and none of them seems particularly wrong! The discrepancies are particularly alarming in view of the fact that historical or expected average returns from active currency management amount only to tens of basis points per annum. If used by unsuspecting portfolio optimisers, different calculation methods could radically alter asset allocation decisions. This is one of the reasons why some empirical studies produce conflicting evidence with the same data set.

2.2.2 Selecting a suitable return measure

With a confusing array of alternative measures to choose from, it is important to be clear about which one should be used. Although we do not think there ought to be a universal measure suitable for different types of investors, here are a few general guidelines:

❏ it should be consistent with the return measures used for other asset classes and should be readily usable in optimisation together with other asset classes if needed;

❏ it should be capable of reflecting the economic impact of currencies on investments;

❏ it should be investable (hedgeable); a portfolio manager can reproduce the return almost exactly (after taking transaction costs into account) if he chooses to by following some predefined rules irrespective of actual market moves;

❏ it should not give a portfolio manager incentive or disincentive to hedge or not to hedge currency risk beyond what is prescribed by a currency benchmark;

❏ it should be able to take the use, and hence of cost, of capital into account;[4]

❏ it should be relatively easy to apply to both benchmark and actual portfolios for return/risk calculations; and

❏ it should reduce the dead-weight return – the portion of return where neither currency manager nor underlying manager is responsible (see Chapter 6, Section 6.3)

Whereas the discrepancy caused by different base currencies is easy to deal with (for example, by using log-returns rather than simple returns), the choice between spot-on-spot and spot-on-forward is less obvious. Many people argue that it is dependent on whether an investor hedges his currency exposure. Sometimes another question is dragged into the discussion: does the forward rate give a better forecast of the future spot rate than the current spot rate? We will revisit both questions later, in Chapter 6, Section 6.4 and Chapter 4, Section 4.5.1, respectively. In this book, unless specified otherwise, we use log-returns on a spot-to-forward basis.

Cashflow-based methods (Methods V and VI) are widely used for performance evaluation purposes. As portfolios are marked-to-market during each period, the returns can then be computed from the difference in valuation. The change in valuation results from change in the underlying investment and change in currency prices. To separate these effects, one can hold other factors constant and allow only one to vary. But, to do that in practice, there are quite a few choices to make and each will affect the end result. We will take a look at this in Section 2.2.3. There is another advantage of using cashflow-based methods: that the computed returns are intrinsically investable. However, one has to be careful as a return might be investable at a portfolio level but not so when split into its components.

2.2.3 Absolute return when underlying investment return is uncertain

Since the return calculation is central to many of the topics in this book, we will explore it a little further. In Section 2.2.1, the return on the underlying investment was fixed and known at the beginning of the investment period. The picture can be further complicated by the fact that the return on the underlying is not known at the beginning. To illustrate this we will rework Example 2.1 using equities.

Example 2.2 A US dollar-based investor invests US$1.0 million in Japanese stocks. The market prices are:

❏ spot exchange rate is ¥100 per US dollar;
❏ three-month forward exchange rate is 98.46 USD/JPY;
❏ three-month Treasury bill yield is 6.50% (in US dollars);
❏ three-month JGB yield is 0.25% (in Japanese yen).

The Nikkei Index stands at 10,000 at the beginning of the investment and goes up to 11,000 (adjusted for dividends) after three months.

As in Example 2.1, the investor can conduct a spot currency transaction to convert the US$1.0 million into Japanese yen at the current spot rate. He receives ¥100.0 million and invests the proceeds in local stocks. Let us assume that the investor's return follows the Nikkei exactly. The spot exchange rate again moves from 100 to 110 USD/JPY and the ¥100 million investment turns into ¥110 million. What is the return on currency?

The calculation for Methods I through IV remains the same since the return on the underlying investment does not feature in the calculation. We can repeat Method V here.

Method V(b) In cashflow terms, the investor has US$1.0 million to start with. If he liquidates his investment in Japanese yen at the end of month 3, he is left with ¥110 million. If he then converts the proceeds into US dollars at the spot rate, a return can be calculated from the net return as follows:

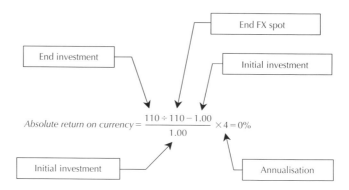

This is clearly wrong as the Japanese yen has depreciated against the US dollar over the period and the currency return should not be zero. It is not difficult to observe that the underlying investment produces a return of 40%, which subsidises the negative currency return. How should we deal with this?

We want a return calculation method which produces a return that is investable. From a foreign exchange hedging viewpoint, the above return is not investable as one does not know at the outset what the final Japanese yen asset will be. So, two practical questions need to be asked:

1. How much is exposed?
2. Is the hedge static or it is adjusted during the three-month calculation period?

The choice for the first question is usually one of the following:

❑ current valuation, denominated in Japanese yen; in our example this is ¥100 million;
❑ current valuation, denominated in US dollars, ie, US$1 million;
❑ future valuation at the forecast growth rate, denominated in Japanese yen. If we assume that the investor expects the Nikkei to grow by 5% over the three months, then the exposed amount is ¥105 million;

❏ future valuation at the forecast growth rate, denominated in US dollars; this is US$1.0664 million (=105 million 98.46);
❏ future valuation at the Japanese yen risk-free growth rate, denominated in Japanese yen; this is ¥100.0625 million;
❏ future valuation at the US dollar risk-free growth rate, denominated in US dollars; this is US$1.01625 million.

Obviously, each will yield slightly different returns if we recalculate the returns using Method V(b).

The second question – whether the exposure (and the hedge) is adjusted during the calculation period – is also relevant. For example, if half way through the three-month period the Nikkei has gone up from 10,000 to 10,500, the initial exposure amount has clearly changed. Will the investor elect to adjust the exposure or leave the hedge static? If he adjusts the exposure, the new calculation of the return will have to reflect the fact that half way through the period the USD/JPY exchange rate will also have changed. Clearly, the adjustment too will affect the final return calculation and so needs to be defined beforehand.

2.2.4 Relative return

Relative returns are more commonly used in the fund management industry, and here calculation of the return on a currency is even more plagued by ambiguity. One commonly used term is "excess return". For other types of asset, excess return is defined as the absolute return from investment less the return on a risk-free asset. What, then, is the excess return on a currency? As demonstrated earlier, the definition of the absolute return can vary, and so can the definition of the return on a risk-free asset. These are the usually quoted alternatives:

❏ since the expected currency return is zero, one can use one of the absolute returns obtained in the previous section as the excess return;[5]
❏ a foreign currency can trade at a premium (more expensively) or discount (cheaply) relative to the spot exchange rate in the forward market, and some use the forward point (difference between spot and forward) as the expected return on a currency.[6]

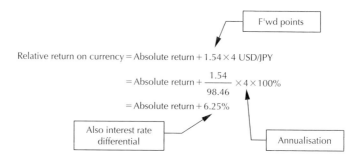

Some people follow the general rule of using risk-free rate in the calculation of excess return, but in our example which currency should we consider, the US dollar or the yen?

This is a very important question in currency risk management and its significance goes well beyond obtaining a more "accurate" return measure. We will defer detailed discussion on this point until Chapter 6, where we look into the question of index calculation and performance measurement.

2.2.5 Ex ante vs ex post

Ex ante (meaning viewed "from before") return is the forecast or expected return, which can be used in asset allocation, optimisation and portfolio construction. *Ex post* ("from after") return is the realised return, and it can be used in performance attribution and risk management.

As we have seen in Chapter 1, Section 1.4.4, many earlier studies of currency risk management are *ex post*. Optimisation techniques are applied to *ex post* returns and variance–covariance matrices to examine the impact of currency hedging. The practical relevance of this type of result is very limited as, when a portfolio manager makes a trading decision, he only has historical price data up to the point at which he makes that decision. So he will have to decide whether to use the available historical data or, instead, to use some form of forecast. If the historical analysis is conducted incorporating this constraint, the results can be drastically different from those obtained using a complete *ex post* data set. More recent studies take this vital practical constraint into consideration and their results – for instance, on currency optimisation and the use of a unitary hedge ratio – are considerably more relevant to real-life currency management.

There is no consensus on how to derive *ex ante* returns on currencies. For most fund managers, the *ex ante* return on a stock consists of:

❏ the risk-free interest rate;
❏ the equity premium (estimates of which range from 4% to 8%), modulated by
❏ the forecast β of the stock.[7]

Unfortunately, for currencies these three terms are not easy to define. A discussion of this point and of currency in a CAPM framework in general is included in Chapter 5.

The commonly seen approaches to deriving *ex ante* currency returns are:

❏ direct forecast (rather than through a forecast of β);
❏ assume that currency movements are essentially random walk and use zero return for currencies;
❏ use the *ex post* returns from the last period or the historical average as the forecast (*ex ante*) return;
❏ use interest rate differentials (forward points);
❏ use the risk-free interest rate (domestic/foreign).

There is an interesting issue here regarding the *forward* return on a currency (last two points) as opposed to the *forecast* return of a currency (first three points). Forward returns are derived through a no-arbitrage relationship, whereas forecast returns can be formed in a variety of ways (see Chapter 4). Forward returns are "achievable", but they are not necessarily the best forecast of the foreign exchange rate in the same way that forward interest rates are the best forecast of interest rates. As forward returns are achievable, we generally recommend their use as the baseline for return calculation. Other forecast-based returns can be defined relative to forward returns. We include a short discussion on the interesting and important distinction between forecast and forward in Appendix 2C.

2.2.6 Nominal return vs real return

For many investment managers, the nominal – or monetary – return is sufficient. However, pension funds and some insurance funds use real returns in assessing their asset/liability position as their liabilities are usually longer-term in nature and are linked to the rate of future inflation. Some people argue that the return on foreign currencies tends to be positively correlated with domestic inflation (when domestic inflation is high a domestic currency is more likely to weaken against foreign currencies). Therefore, the argument goes, investors should retain more foreign currency exposure than is suggested by nominal risk/return measures. As stated above, the relationship between domestic inflation and foreign currency return says, in essence, that purchasing power parity (PPP) holds. (Chapter 4, Section 4.2 surveys both theoretical and practical aspects of PPP.) The consensus is that PPP does hold in the long run (longer than about 8–10 years) but that the exchange rate can deviate significantly from its equilibrium value, and the process of reverting to where it "should" be can take a long time. In practice, decision-makers face a trade-off between accepting the short-term fluctuations caused by currencies in order to pursue long-term benefit, or managing the fluctuations at the potential cost of long-term benefit. In our opinion the balance is tilted towards the latter because:

❏ the benefit of managing fluctuation is easily measurable but the benefit of long-term diversification is not;
❏ in the current environment of stable and low inflation the benefit of diversification is perhaps not as appealing as before; and
❏ transparency requirements and league tables accentuate, rightly or wrongly, the importance of managing short-term fluctuations.

There are a handful of empirical studies on the subject, but their conclusions are generally dependent on the assumptions and data set used.[8] A theoretical debate is well beyond the scope of this book, where instead we choose to focus on issues of more practical interest: nominal return and risk measures.

2.3 A SIMPLE DESCRIPTIVE TOUR OF CURRENCY RISKS

Foreign exchange fluctuations can have a considerable impact on the risks and returns of global investment. Over any given short period (up to three years), it is not atypical to observe that 40% to 80% of the total risk on a foreign bond investment is attributable to movements in exchange rates. For equity investments, foreign exchange moves often account for 5–30% of the total risk. It is, however, difficult to make a definitive statement on the long-term impact of foreign exchange return on the total return as it is heavily dependent on the sample period and the base currency of choice. Some commentators refer to periods during which the US dollar appreciated or depreciated and conclude that one should have hedged or stayed unhedged. This kind of remark will not provide guidance for a fund manager making decisions in real life as no one has the luxury of peering into the future with a rear-view mirror. The question of the long-term impact of currency on returns, defined in nominal terms, is the same as asking whether the impact of currency washes out in the long term. There is a considerable volume of evidence to show that it probably does, albeit over a very long horizon (the impact having a half-life of about three to five years).

In this section we take a look at the implications of currency risk for international investment from several different angles:

❏ short-term vs long-term contribution;
❏ correlations between foreign exchange and the underlying; and
❏ bonds vs equities.

2.3.1 Short-term vs long-term contribution

The two panels in Figure 2.1 show the MSCI EAFE Index in both local currency terms and in terms of the US dollar and Japanese yen, hedged and unhedged.[9] Note that the local currency index is only a weighted average of country index returns and is not investable. We see that, over a long period, hedged and unhedged indices follow a similar pattern, indicating that the main driver is the underlying equity returns. On the question whether hedging is beneficial in terms of total return, one can at best answer that it depends on the period and the base currency you choose to consider. Also, it is evident from Figure 2.1 that there may be long periods of time during which the unhedged index underperforms its hedged counterpart and vice versa.

In Figure 2.2 we show the two-year rolling volatility series computed from the returns series displayed in Figure 2.1. The volatility of the hedged indices closely tracks that of the local index as currency fluctuations are removed from both series. In contrast to total returns, where we cannot make a general observation on whether

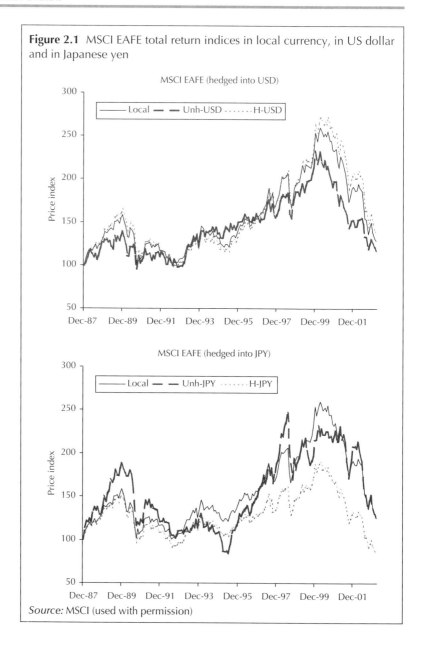

Figure 2.1 MSCI EAFE total return indices in local currency, in US dollar and in Japanese yen

Source: MSCI (used with permission)

hedging is beneficial, we can see clearly that currency hedging generally reduces portfolio volatility. The average volatilities for local currency returns and hedged returns are 15.25%, 15.36% (hedged into US dollars) and 15.26% (hedged into yen), respectively, over the whole period. The average unhedged volatility is 16.26% (unhedged US dollars) and 19.34% (unhedged yen). The risk reduction from currency hedging is therefore 7.6% for a US-based investor and 21.1% for a Japan-based investor if we use volatility as the risk measure. If we use variance as the risk measure, risk reduction is 14.6% and 37.7%, respectively. However, we also notice that the risk reduction is not constant over time and that there are some periods when the risk of hedged portfolios is as great as or even greater than that of unhedged portfolios. However, these figures are comparable to those quoted in many academic and practical studies of currency risk as a proportion of overall portfolio risk. For example, Eun and Resnick (1994) separate the decomposed portfolio variance into four parts:

1. variance of the underlying investment in local currencies;
2. variance of the exchange rate moves;
3. covariance of the above; and
4. cross-product terms (negligible).

For a US-based investor investing into the French, German, Japanese, Swiss and UK equities markets, the averages of the four terms above, expressed as the relative contribution to total portfolio variance, are (ranges in parentheses):

1. variance of the underlying investment in local currencies: 63.04% (47.24%, 72.02%);
2. variance of the exchange rate moves: 34.06% (21.32%, 50.68%);
3. covariance of the above: 1.17% (-10.8%, 14.06%);
4. cross-product terms (negligible): 1.81% (0.38%, 2.56%).

Eun and Resnick calculated these figures using data from 1978 to 1994, but they are similar to later calculations by, for example, Larsen and Resnick (2000) and Clarke and Kritzman (1996). The latter presented a similar calculation for a range of base currencies.

The two panels in Figure 2.3 show the Lehman Brothers' US Aggregate Index, both in US dollar terms and in sterling and Japanese yen, hedged and unhedged. In this case, the hedged sterling index consistently outperforms its unhedged counterpart but it is not conclusive for Japan-based investor. The hedged sterling (Japanese yen) index consistently performs better (worse) than the US dollar index, probably reflecting the impact of forward

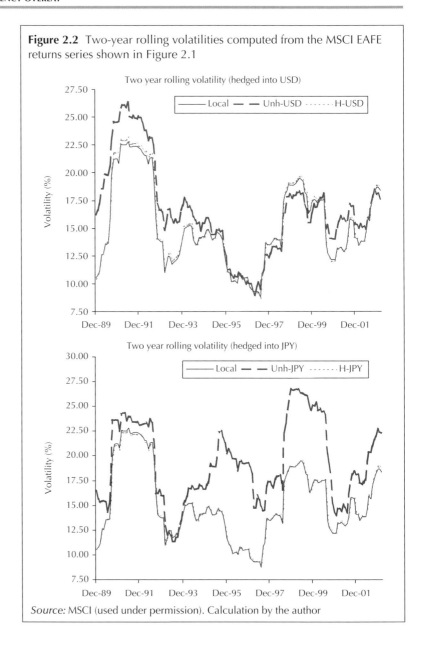

Figure 2.2 Two-year rolling volatilities computed from the MSCI EAFE returns series shown in Figure 2.1

Source: MSCI (used under permission). Calculation by the author

bias: hedging into sterling is beneficial due to interest rate differentials, but this is not so for the Japanese yen.

In Figure 2.4 we show the computed two-year rolling volatility series for the returns series in Figure 2.3. As in Figure 2.2, the

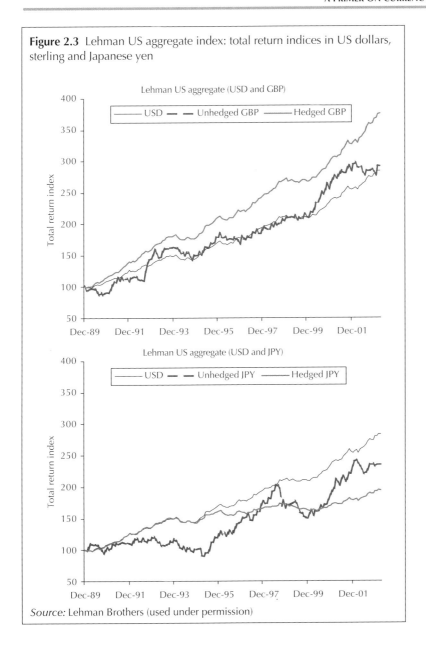

Figure 2.3 Lehman US aggregate index: total return indices in US dollars, sterling and Japanese yen

Source: Lehman Brothers (used under permission)

volatility of the hedged indices closely tracks that of the local index as currency fluctuations are removed from both series. However, the risk reduction is much more significant than for equity port-folios. The average volatilities for US dollar returns and hedged

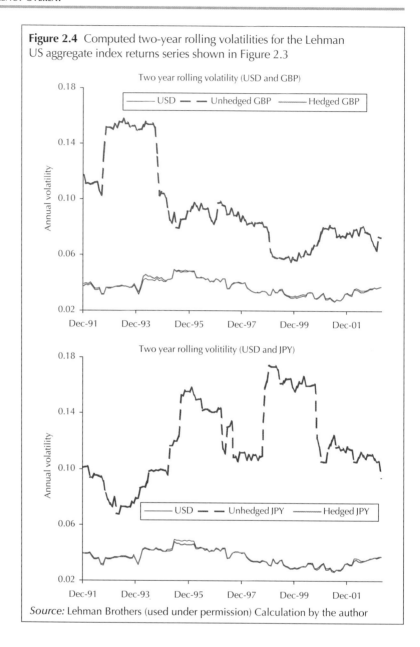

Figure 2.4 Computed two-year rolling volatilities for the Lehman US aggregate index returns series shown in Figure 2.3

Two year rolling volatility (USD and GBP)

Two year rolling volitility (USD and JPY)

Source: Lehman Brothers (used under permission) Calculation by the author

returns are 3.70%, 3.70% (hedged into sterling) and 3.66%, respectively, over the whole period. The average unhedged volatility is 9.42% (unhedged US dollar) and 3.66% (unhedged Japanese yen). The risk reduction from currency hedging is therefore 60.7% for a sterling-based investor and 69.3% for a Japan-based investor if we use volatility as the risk measure. If we use variance as the risk measure, the risk reduction is 84.5% and 90.6%, respectively. The risk reduction is fairly consistent over the period. Again, as Eun and Resnick (1994) calculated, for a US-based investor investing into French, German, Japanese, Swiss and UK equities markets, the averages of the four decomposed variance terms listed earlier, expressed as the relative contribution to total portfolio variance, are (ranges in parentheses):

1. variance of the underlying investment in local currencies: 15.78% (5.39%, 32.09%);
2. variance of the exchange rate moves: 66.20% (44.78%, 83.36%);
3. covariance of the above: 16.84% (3.64%, 24.66%):
4. cross-product terms (negligible): 1.20% (0.19%, 1.94%).

More up-to-date calculations (with similar results) can be found in Annaert (1995) and Clarke and Kritzman (1996), both of which contain data for different base currencies.

The nominal-return-based approach, however, is not without criticism. Throughout the book, we use the nominal returns to compute the risk measures. It can be argued, however, that the investor's risk is really to the real return rather than to the nominal return. Using this argument and a long-term data series (going back 200 years!), Froot (1993) looked at the impact of hedging in the long term. He used the real returns on US dollar-denominated assets in the domestic currency (in this case, sterling), the real return being the US dollar return adjusted for spot foreign exchange movements and inflation in the UK. He argued that the real exchange rate is mean-reverting over the long term, and this observation is borne out by his long data series. When the real exchange rate is mean-reverting, currency hedging is not effective in the long term. Hedging introduces interest rate differentials to the long-term performance, which may even increase the portfolio variance. Froot concluded that although hedging is effective in the short term, its effectiveness ceases beyond five years for equities and eight years for bonds. He also noted that the minimum-variance hedge ratio declines from close to 100%, as argued by Perold and Shulman (1988), to an average of about 35% over a horizon of five to ten years. He argued that if short-term currency fluctuation is not a major concern for investors, they should not hedge currency simply to avoid transaction costs. Froot's (1993) data series covers several currency regimes, including the old gold and silver (bimetallic) standard, the gold standard and the current floating-rate regime, so one may question the particular relevance of his results for the current foreign exchange environment. Also, the method overlooks the risk-reducing and return-enhancing benefits that a sound currency-hedging programme can bring.[10]

2.3.2 Correlation

The correlations between currencies and the underlying asset returns have been investigated both theoretically and empirically. As far as we know, there is no consensus on how such correlation should be properly defined. Quite a few studies we have seen calculate the correlation between currency returns and foreign asset returns denominated in the *domestic* currency. It is difficult to interpret the correlation coefficients obtained in this manner as the latter already contains the exchange rate element. Our own recommendation is that one calculate correlation using exchange rate returns, spot-on-forward and hedged underlying returns. This may be a more cumbersome calculation, but it is more suited to the task of currency risk management. The calculation can be simplified by correlating exchange rate returns, spot-on-spot and underlying returns denominated in local currencies. As long as interest rate differentials are not large and/or are reasonably constant, the calculated results will be similar.

Many people comment that the correlation between bonds and currencies is high whereas that between equities and currencies is low. If one calculates correlation coefficients using domestic returns and currency returns, the above conclusion is the natural result. This is because currency volatility is usually higher than bond volatility, so returns on foreign bonds denominated in the domestic currency will be predominantly currency fluctuations. For equities, the effect is much less dramatic simply because equity volatility is typically higher than currency volatility. So correlation calculated in this way does not offer any insight into whether there are intrinsic links between currencies and the underlying, nor on whether currency fluctuations should be removed. We will comment further on the correlation between currencies and bonds or equities in the next two sections.

It is a well-recognised feature in currency risk management that correlations between currencies and underlying assets are not constant. In a recent paper Goetzmann, Li and Rouwenhorst (2001) show that the diversification benefits of global investing are not constant, and that these benefits are currently low compared to other periods in the history of capital markets. The authors decompose diversification benefits into two parts, a component that arises from variation in the average correlation across different national markets, and a component due to variation in the investor opportunity set. There are periods, like the last two decades, in which the opportunity set expands dramatically and the benefits of diversification are driven primarily by the existence of marginal markets. In other periods, such as World War I and the two following decades, risk reduction is due to low correlations among the major national markets. They infer that periods of globalisation have both benefits and drawbacks for the international investor. Globalisation expands the opportunity set, but diversification relies increasingly on investment in emerging markets. They conclude that the global correlation structure is not constant between various periods.

The instability in the correlation between currencies and the underlying assets undermines the validity of many analyses in currency management. For example, when one uses CAPM optimisation to determine optimal currency weights or to find the optimal hedge ratio, one has to be extra careful as the results may vary significantly when different sets of correlations between currencies and the underlyings are used. This is a topic we will return to in more detail in Chapter 5.

2.3.3 Stock prices and currency fluctuations

It has generally been assumed that the correlation between stock or equity prices and currency moves is zero or close to zero. The assumption enabled one to equate country exposure to currency exposure and simplified the task of quantifying currency risk because, historically, global equity management has been structured around country allocation. Country allocations were first chosen and the stock picking was then conducted within countries. The currency risk associated with a particular shareholding was fully allocated to the corporation's headquarters or trade listing location.

However, over the last 10 to 20 years, the environment in which corporations operate has undergone considerable change and the corporations have reacted accordingly, primarily by going global themselves. These days, many corporations have to be viewed and valued as a portfolio of activities across different currencies. However, matters are not as straightforward here as they might appear, and a simple breakdown of a corporation's revenue into different currencies will not necessarily reveal the true extent of its currency exposure. A range of factors come into play:

❏ many corporations actively manage their exposure to currencies through various financial instruments and through the currency mix of their debt;
❏ many corporations maintain excess capacity in different countries as an operational hedge – they can shift production from one location to another in response to persistent currency moves;
❏ some corporations have pricing power which enables them to pass on exchange fluctuation to consumers;
❏ in some situations corporations can be indirectly exposed to exchange movement if their competitors are exposed;
❏ some corporations have changed their functional currencies.[11]

It could be argued that every corporation merits a separate model that delves into these factors, but in a portfolio management context this is clearly undesirable. We think that the market-based approach proposed by Solnik (1993) offers a valid and practical alternative to investigate the issue. He assumed that equities are priced globally with currency risk taken into account. Therefore, if we regress the historical returns of a particular stock on the domestic index return, foreign index returns and the movement of foreign currencies against the domestic currency, we can obtain the sensitivity of the stock's returns to all the factors – especially to currency moves. These sensitivity estimates are called "loadings", which in option pricing terminology are equivalent to deltas.[12] A holding in a particular stock can then be decomposed into different currency-sensitive parts which can be aggregated across a portfolio. The problem with this approach is that a corporation's exposure to currencies can change dramatically following a particular corporation action.

Jorion (1990) suggested that an alternative measure of foreign currency exposure can be obtained by regressing individual firm stock returns against the market return and exchange rate movements. This measure of the sensitivity of stock returns to exchange rates provides a net-of-hedging measure of foreign currency exposure, since market returns should already take into account any hedging activities undertaken by the firm. This approach has been applied to various data sets by Amihud (1994), Bartov and Bodnar (1994), Donnelly and Sheehy (1996) and Kedia and Mozumdar (1999), extended to multiple exchange rates by Miller and Reuer (1998), and applied to different return horizons by Chow, Lee and Solt (1997). Of these studies, only the UK study by Donnelly and Sheehy found statistically significant results for the sensitivity of stock returns to exchange rate changes, which they attributed to the relative openness of the UK economy. Although the Jorion measure is a theoretically appealing measure of foreign currency exposure, the existing empirical evidence indicates that the exposure coefficients are highly volatile and not generally related to foreign operations (see Kedia and Mozumdar, 1999).

A practical assumption on the correlation between hedged equities and currency returns is that it is zero. If one calculates the correlation coefficients over a reasonably long period, they are usually small and not significantly different from zero.

2.3.4 Bond prices and currency fluctuations

Several academic studies look into the risk factors that determine bond returns, but very few have examined the relationship between currencies and international bond returns.[13] Driessen, Melenberg and Nijman (2000) used weekly bond index data from 1990 to 1999 for Germany, the US and Japan and principal component analysis to detect the factors that impact bond returns. They used both currency-hedged and unhedged indices, and their results shed light on the question of bond prices and currency fluctuation. They found that currency fluctuations do seem to explain a portion of the variability of unhedged bond returns (about 25%); however, they concluded that there is no reward in bearing currency risk.

Annaert (1995) found that exchange rate fluctuations imply higher correlations between returns, and thus higher estimation risk. He also computed the correlations between local bond returns and exchange rate returns for investors based in the US, Germany and Japan investing in a range of bond portfolios in 15 countries.

They are usually very low and not significant. Of 42 such correlation coefficients which he reported, only seven were significant at the 1% level, most of them falling between −10% and +10%.

Again, a practical assumption on the correlation between hedged bonds and currency returns is that it is zero, but this may be more controversial. If one calculates the correlation coefficients over a reasonably long period, as for hedged equities they are small and not significantly different from zero. However, hedging decisions on bond portfolios are usually made on strategic grounds simply because of the relative magnitude of currency volatilities, which renders this sort of agonising assumption unnecessary.

2.3.5 A word of caution for unsuspecting readers of statistics

We have avoided being overzealous in the above sections in terms of presenting table after table of volatilities, correlations and so on. Plenty of these can be found in the references listed in Chapter 1, Section 1.4.4, and in the marketing materials provided by overlay managers and other involved parties. One reason for their frequent use is that this type of analysis is increasingly easy to conduct with the availability of data and computing capabilities. An important reason for our caution here is that summary statistics, such as volatilities and correlation coefficients, may gloss over vital information and lead to erroneous conclusions. For example, both are informative measures for normal or near-normal distributions. However, the informativeness can break down when we move away from normal distributions – especially that of correlation coefficients, which can be heavily influenced by a handful of outliers. Statistical remedies abound, but they can quickly move into realms beyond a busy practitioner's will or ability to reach. One remedy we invariably find useful and reliable is a chart. Before making a decision based on computed correlation coefficients, it is always helpful to take a quick look at a scatter plot of the correlated variables to see if there are data points that are way out of line with the rest. This is only common sense, but more often than not we find it in preciously short supply.

2.4 CHOICE OF CURRENCY MANAGEMENT STYLES

Many of the debates listed in Chapter 1, Section 1.3 are linked to one main question: should one hedge or not? Once a decision is taken, there are more questions to answer. Should one be passive or active? Should one be fundamental or technical? Should one be discretionary or quantitative? These questions can, to a certain extent, be answered scientifically, and that is our main subject for the whole of Chapter 4. However, there are many areas where the evidence is not conclusive and a learned judgement is often called for in practice. Also, there are many practical constraints that are not reflected by looking only at different performance measures. In this section we summarise the pros and cons of the different management approaches we have seen in practice.

2.4.1 A do-nothing approach

This is still one of most commonly adopted approaches by investment managers and the rationales cited include the zero-sum game, random walk and long-term wash characteristics of currency movements. A fine yet fundamental distinction has to be made here:

❏ Some investment managers have decided to leave their currency exposures unmanaged after detailed reviews of the fund's investment risk exposures, objectives and constraints in addition to empirical and theoretical evidence on the pros and cons of currency management. We think this is a valid approach since, as mentioned earlier, evidence on the benefit of active currency management is mixed and it is a judgement call for a fund to adopt a particular style. However, the important thing is that currency risk is recognised (and hopefully communicated to investors).

❏ Other investment managers simply decide to leave their currency risk exposure unmanaged. We believe that this is a head-in-the-sand approach and, although in the long-term currency impact may indeed cancel out, this approach leaves an important source of risk unaccounted for. The approach can also be manipulated by some investment managers to hide the consequences of poor investment decisions and incompetence. We have seen many investment managers switch from this type of do-nothing (which we label "passive" do-nothing) approach to the first type ("active" do-nothing) over recent years and the trend continues.

2.4.2 Active vs passive vs dynamic

With a passive management style one typically refers to a foreign exchange benchmark with a *fixed* hedge ratio; the foreign exchange manager will automatically execute hedging orders to that fixed hedge ratio and he has no flexibility in terms of deviating from the benchmark.

An active management style is generally employed *in addition* to a passive management style – only in a currency fund is active management used on its own. In this style the foreign exchange manager can deviate from the benchmark hedge ratio by under-hedging or overhedging and/or take positions in currency pairs where the fund does not have an underlying position.

There are various foreign exchange management styles that fall between these two. For example, in static option replication the manager calculates a delta using an option pricing model and adjusts the hedging automatically.[14] This is known as a "dynamic" style. It is passive in the sense that the foreign exchange manager does not deviate from the benchmark. But it is also active because the benchmark hedge ratio changes with change in the spot rate.

In the next three sections we briefly summarise the advantages and disadvantages of these management styles.

2.4.2.1 A passive approach
Pros:

❏ A passive style is easier to implement and monitor.
❏ If the fund is not very big, there is no need to have foreign exchange experts as bond portfolio managers can manage the currency risks.
❏ It is more intuitive to communicate to investors/sponsors/fiduciaries (people are more likely to accept the zero-sum game argument that foreign exchange returns average out over time than go through technical details on why foreign exchange is special and how it can add return).
❏ It has a relatively low direct cost.

Cons:

❏ A passive style is not able to capture additional returns.

❑ The manager cannot react to short-term opportunities which are characteristic of the currency market (for example, the long-run correlation between currencies and equities is typically close to zero, but in the short run it may be positive or negative for a considerable time; a passive management style will not be able to respond to this and may actually increase the overall risk of the fund).

❑ It may lead to cashflow problems as losses on the hedging contracts need to be settled in cash and a passive management style cannot adjust to adverse cashflow situations.

2.4.2.2 An active approach

Pros:

❑ Active management gives scope for yield enhancement. Various short-term opportunities such as trends, forward premiums and technical predictions can be exploited.

❑ In-house specialists' performance can be benchmarked to publicly available currency benchmarks.

❑ Part of the risk exposure can be outsourced.

❑ Risk reduction (without giving up expected returns) can be pursued as a separate objective.

❑ Cashflow can be a decisional variable.

❑ Last but not least, a fund employing an active approach can easily adapt to the risk budgeting process. Namely, it allocates its assets according to the active level of risk it runs in different risk classes.

Cons:

❑ An active style is slightly more difficult to implement and monitor as there will be additional "active positions".

❑ One needs currency specialists.

❑ Investors/sponsors/fiduciaries have to be convinced that active management does not equate to taking wild bets on currencies.

❑ There is also a need for relatively sophisticated risk-measurement and control systems (though this may be an advantage given the increasingly strict reporting requirements for pension funds around the world).

2.4.2.3 A dynamic approach

The dynamic approach is linked to option pricing theory. An option can be viewed as a hedge plus an insurance contract in case the exchange rate goes against the hedge, all for an upfront premium. The dynamic approach attempts to replicate the payoff profile of any option but actively adjusts the hedge ratio according to some specific rules that will be discussed in Chapter 8. The aim is to own an option without paying the option premium – at least, not all of it. A similar approach exists for equity portfolios, and it is sometimes called portfolio insurance.

In a nutshell, a dynamic approach tries to beat the market – in this case not the currency spot market but the currency options market. We will review the relevant empirical evidence for its effectiveness, again in Chapter 8.

Pros:

❑ As one hedges with an insurance contract, there is no worry about whether a currency goes up or down.
❑ The cashflow problem associated with currency hedging can be mitigated (relative to a passive hedge, one will have a smaller hedge contract to settle when the exchange rate moves unfavourably).
❑ There is no need to pay a large upfront option premium.
❑ Sometimes a currency options market does not exist or is not liquid enough to facilitate an option-based hedging transaction, in which case the "DIY" hedging provides a viable alternative.
❑ There is no need to hire a full team of researchers/analysts/ decision-makers as the dynamic approach is still relatively straightforward.

Cons:

❑ Beating the currency options market may not be easy (and there is no conclusive evidence that it can be beaten).
❑ Now that options markets are becoming increasingly commoditised, success in the past is no guarantee of success in the future.
❑ A dynamic approach is not as easy to communicate to investors.
❑ How frequently one undertakes dynamic hedging is largely an empirical optimisation problem and is based on the premise that history will repeat itself.

2.4.3 Trading styles

Fund managers make their trading decisions on the basis of a range of market signals, and the way they do this is referred to as a "trading style". Broadly speaking, depending on which types of signal a fund manager pays more attention to, trading styles can be divided into "fundamental" and "technical". And depending on how closely the signal is followed, trading styles can be divided into "discretionary" and "systemic".

In the following sections we present a brief overview of the different trading styles, with a full discussion deferred until Chapter 4. A classification of the major players in the currency management market can be found in Chapter 3, Section 3.10.

2.4.3.1 Fundamentalists: the failure of macroeconomics

Exchange rates are often viewed as the barometer of a country's (relative) economic health, and their close link to macroeconomic variables is obvious. However, like many other relationships in the world of economics and finance, the exact relationship between exchange rate movements and economic fundamentals has proven to be elusive. There are many so-called structural models that try to use the state of, and the changes in, economies to explain such movements. These models have become an integral part of the curriculum of economic education. Many in the investment management industry will have some memories of these models from their student days, and it is not surprising to see that many currency managers base their trading decisions on the forecasts provided by macroeconomic indicators. The bad news is that these structural models have left a string of unresolved puzzles, and so far they have not been able to consistently outperform a simple random-walk model either in the short-term or over the medium to long-term.

Now it is generally accepted that the way macroeconomic variables work their way through into exchange rates is probably more complicated than a simple linear regression can reveal. Also, there may well be factors other than macroeconomics at play in determining exchange rates, and with the rapidly changing conditions in global capital markets, old factors may drop out and be replaced with new ones.

The message here may be a sombre one, but we nevertheless think that one of the most basic and intuitive assumptions – that strong economies lead to strong currencies – still holds true, as long as one is willing to augment the basics and the intuition with a good dollop of scepticism and pragmatism.

2.4.3.2 Chartists: entering the mainstream?

Many people, especially those with a formal economic education, baulk at the very thought of basing currency-trading decisions on chart patterns with fancy names like "head and shoulder", "morning star" and "three river bottoms". Very little attention has been paid by the academic world to this ancient art. There are many practical books covering all manner of charting techniques, and readers will find references in Chapter 4, Section 4.4. Chartist methods (also called technical analysis) have a considerable following in the currency-trading community, especially spot traders and short-term speculators. But the number of spot traders and short-term speculators in the currency world has steadily declined in recent years. Some fund managers acknowledge that they use technical analysis as part of their decision-making input, especially for "timing" transactions.

In the past we have felt rather ambivalent about this particular trading style used on its own. However, the advent of large data sets and cheap computing power has perhaps begun to swing the pendulum in the chartists' favour. Many research papers have been published in the field and some interesting results are emerging. We shall wait and see.

2.4.3.3 Judgementalists: on the wane?

There are managers who may utilise a variety of input variables but who make trading decisions mainly on the basis of their own judgement. This is referred to as a "judgementalist" or "discretionary" trading style (although one should note here that all trading styles have an element of judgement in them). Many who have worked long enough in the currencies market can tell a few stories of legendary position-taking in the "good old days": of sheikhs and magnates and cowboys (and ordinary folks managing other people's money), of dealing from yachts and skiing slopes and taxis, of buying and selling "yards" of this and that and then reversing the deal moments later realising a mistake had been made, of breathtaking amounts of money made and lost over a very short period of time.[15] With the increasing emphasis on transparency, style specialisation and risk management, there are probably fewer and fewer purely discretionary players in the market these days, although those remaining can point to some quite consistent and impressive results.[16]

2.4.3.4 Quants: gaining in importance

Quants – quantitative analysts, or people using quantitative methods – base their trading decisions on the numerical output of certain models. They are also called "system traders" or "black-box traders". This is an area that has enjoyed tremendous growth over recent years, driven by an increasing emphasis on quantitative measurement of all aspects of the investment management process and the availability of computing power. Willingly or otherwise, fund managers are turning to quantitative research and risk management to cope with today's complex and increasingly global trading strategies.

Due to its growing importance, we devote large portions of Chapters 4 and 7 to review and discussion of quantitative methods in currency trading and risk management.

2.5 RISK SEPARATION AND RISK RESPONSIBILITY

Throughout this book our aim is to present a full picture of the many issues involved in the currency management discussion while, as far as possible, remaining impartial by presenting both sides of the argument on a particular question. As mentioned in Chapter 1, some sales pitches (including many originating in the currency overlay industry) leave the reader with the impression that hedging currency risk is definitely return-enhancing or risk-reducing or both. Such conclusions should be viewed with scepticism. As we saw, many of the issues implicit in such assertions remain unresolved, and if by discussing these we can help investment managers (and, ultimately, investors) to make an informed judgement we have achieved our main objective.

However, there is one issue we would like to take a stance on: we believe that currency does represent a risk in a global investment portfolio and that the risk needs to be managed. If the book has a mission statement, this is it. On the basis of existing evidence it cannot be concluded that managing currency risk produces excess returns and/or reduces portfolio risk. Nevertheless, we consider that, overall, currency management is value-adding due to the disciplined approach it brings to a fund and the risk awareness and responsibility it helps to establish.

Before an investor or a fund manager plunges into detailed debate on whether or not to hedge, a risk measurement framework should be established and risks quantified. During the process all relevant parties, such as plan sponsors, plan managers and investment consultants, should be involved and risk awareness should be promoted.

Throughout this book we maintain that currency risk should be separated out from other risks – a simple test of which is: at any given time, does a fund know how much foreign exchange risk it is running?

To be able to answer that question, a fund would need to have a separate foreign exchange benchmark in addition to its usual bond/equity and/or general benchmarks.

However, a fund may decide not to manage foreign exchange risk even if it is separated out! Conversely, a fund may decide to "manage" foreign exchange risk even though the foreign exchange risk has not been distinguished. This can be a dangerous practice.

After currency risk has been separated, equity managers and bond managers can still take currency positions (for example, as part of investments in foreign equities/bonds), but now they will be rewarded/penalised if the positions fail to produce the required returns. This will avoid those situations where managers make bundled decisions on both underlying and currency and then blame underperformance on the currency but attribute the benefits of favourable currency movements to their own foresight.

Compared with equity or bond investment, currency overlay management is special because it is intrinsically linked to the underlying investments. One prerequisite for running a currency overlay efficiently is to have a clear picture of these. In many an investment organisation we have come across, especially those produced by sector consolidation, obtaining such a picture is no small feat. The process of investigating, establishing and periodically reviewing currency overlay management (not necessarily active overlay management itself) can, in our view, bring significant benefit to an institution and, ultimately, to its investors. It would be interesting to see a comparison of the performance of funds that ignore currency risk with that of funds with a clearly defined currency policy and a centralised currency risk pool, but we have not come across such studies to date.

A key concept we promote in the currency-hedging debate is that of "core competency": investment managers should be allowed to do what they are good at and their performance ought to be measured on the same basis.[17] The concept is important when formulating a consistent yet flexible currency management framework at both macro and micro levels.

For example, a fixed-income manager whose core competency lies in country outperformance may wish to retain a high degree of control over currency allocations if returns are an important factor in his investment decisions. In this case, currency risk ought to stay with the manager. However, his performance should still be measured with respect to two risk factors: one being the relative outperformance of the fixed-income investment with currency risk completely hedged, the other being currency movements. On the other hand, in the case of a fixed-income manager whose core competency is to predict the future shape of the yield curve or the relative movements between several yield curves in different currencies (excluding currency effects), the currency risk should be transferred and his performance should then be measured on a fully hedged basis.

Likewise, for an equity manager who specialises in stock picking, currency forecasting is unlikely to be his core competency, so this ought to be transferred and his performance measured on a fully hedged basis. Some equity managers specialise in country allocation, and some may even declare core competency in currency forecasting, in which case they should retain control over currency allocations as well. Again, in this situation their performance should be measured with respect to two risk factors – one, the relative outperformance of the equity investment with currency risk completely hedged, and the other the currency movements.

APPENDIX 2A: UNCOVERED INTEREST RATE ARBITRAGE

Uncovered interest rate arbitrage describes the relationship between the expected returns on monies denominated in different currencies. Basically, when the expected returns are measured in the same currency they should be equal.

For example, if interest rates for the Japanese yen and US dollar are 0% and 2% per annum, respectively, and the current spot exchange rate is 100.00 Japanese yen per US dollar, then in one year's time the yen is expected to appreciate against the US dollar by 2%. This way, the return on US dollars, 2%, is the same as the expected return on the yen expressed in US dollars (0% interest rate plus 2% of appreciation).

What, then, would be the *covered* interest rate arbitrage? In the above example, the return on the yen is expected, not guaranteed, since we do not know what the actual USD/JPY spot exchange rate will be in one year's time. One can, however, effect a hedging transaction, selling ¥100 million forward at a fixed price in order to remove that uncertainty. This transaction is called the covered interest rate arbitrage. This arbitrage relationship, not the expectations of market participants, determines the forward prices for foreign exchange. This point is discussed further in Appendix 2C.

The Japanese yen, with a lower interest rate than the US dollar, will be traded more expensively against the US dollar in the forward market. The yen is also said to trade at a premium, whereas the dollar is said to trade at a discount.

Violation of the uncovered interest rate arbitrage is called forward bias. This is an important concept in foreign exchange trading and is discussed in Chapter 4, Section 4.5.1.

APPENDIX 2B: THE CORRELATION TRIANGLE

There is a simple geometric relationship between the volatilities and correlations of three currency pairs formed from three currencies.

Let us define some notation:

❑ σ_{AB} is the volatility of the currency pair A/B; it is expressed as the annualised standard deviation of returns on currency B measured in currency A.

❑ $_A\rho_{BC}$ is the correlation between currencies B and C with respect to currency A; specifically, it is the correlation between returns on B measured in A and returns on C measured in A.

We can now draw a volatility and correlation triangle using the US dollar, sterling and Japanese yen as an example (Figure 2B.1). In this figure, volatility is a length and correlation is (the cosine of) an

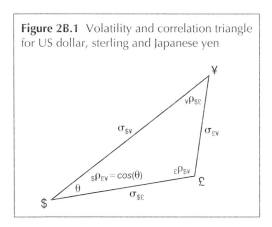

Figure 2B.1 Volatility and correlation triangle for US dollar, sterling and Japanese yen

angle. Given any three products it is always possible to draw this triangle. By definition, the volatility and correlation values bear exactly the relationships shown. In particular, given any three of the values depicted, the remaining three can be determined by trigonometry. The following relationship holds:

$$\sigma^2_{\$¥} = \sigma^2_{£¥} + \sigma^2_{£\$} - 2\sigma_{£¥} \times \sigma_{£\$} \times {}_{£}\rho_{\$¥}$$

Two kinds of volatility are normally observed in the foreign exchange market: the actual volatility and the implied volatility. In our example we could use the historical data for the past three months to calculate the actual volatilities between the pairs GBP/USD, USD/JPY and GBP/JPY. If we then re-plotted the tri-angle and made the three sides proportional to the calculated actual volatilities, we could read off the correlation between any two currency pairs directly from the triangle (though when you do this for yourself be sure to get the sign of the correlation right). The results of this exercise are the same as the correlations estimated directly from the daily changes in the exchange rate.

Similarly, you can use the three-month implied volatilities for the three currency pairs and plot the triangle once more. This time, the correlation you read off the chart is the implied correlation. Loosely interpreted, the implied correlation is where the market thinks the correlation is going to be for the next three months. If we assume that the market is efficient, then that would be the best fore-cast for the future correlation.

If the actual and implied correlations are wildly out of line with each other, some people would make certain trades to exploit this situation.

APPENDIX 2C: FORECAST, FORWARD AND NO-ARBITRAGE PRICE

Some people claim that the forward foreign exchange rate, derived from the covered interest rate arbitrage relationship discussed in Appendix 2A, represents the market consensus forecast of where the exchange rate will be in the future. The analogy would be that the forward interest rate, derived from, for example, interest rate futures or forward rate agreements (FRAs), represents the market consensus forecast of where the interest rate will be in the future. Whereas the latter statement is true, the same cannot be said of the forward foreign exchange prices as it comes via a different route: the arbitrage relationship. We will spend a little more time in Chapter 7 considering why the arbitrage relationship is so funda-mental to modern financial theory. For the time being, it suffices to say that whenever an arbitrage price exists it dominates the fore-cast price. In other words, the prevailing market price will be the arbitrage price rather than the forecast price. Anyone quoting the forecast prices will face almost certain financial ruin. How so? Because arbitrageurs can enter into an agreement with him on one side and use the arbitrage relationship to fix the price on the other. The arbitrageurs can therefore lock in risk-free profit – well, market risk-free at least because he can go bankrupt and the arbitrageurs face credit risk. Here is an example:

Example 2.C.1

❏ Spot USD/JPY rate = 100.00.
❏ One-year interest rates for US dollar and Japanese yen are 2% and 0%, respectively.
❏ Dealer X is quoting one-year forward USD/JPY at 98.10.

Note that the no-arbitrage forward price is $100 \times (1 + 0\%)/(1 + 2\%) = 98.04$.[18]

An arbitrageur can contract with X to sell US$1 million and buy ¥98.10 million at 98.10 in one year's time. The arbitrageur can then borrow ¥98.04 million and sell them on the spot market at 100.00, receiving US$0.9804 million. Let us suppose that he deposits the proceeds at the 2% US dollar interest rate.

In one year's time the US dollar deposit matures to US$1 million. The arbitrageur delivers the US$1 million to X and receives ¥98.10 million. He then uses this to repay the Japanese yen loan of ¥98.04 million, making a net profit of ¥0.06 million. Note that this is irrespective of what the spot USD/JPY rate might be in one-year's time, so it is free from market risk. And the arbitrageur could do any amount to multiply the profit.

What might happen to X? If he decides to hedge his spot currency risk, he will do exactly the opposite of what the arbitrageur has done and end up losing ¥0.06 million for certain. If he leaves his position open, he would be exposed to any changes in the USD/JPY spot exchange rate as he will have to sell yen and buy dollars in the spot market to settle his contract with the arbitrageur. If we assume that, almost surely, he does not get his prediction right all the time, he will almost certainly face financial ruin.[19]

APPENDIX 2D: RISK MEASURES

Roughly speaking, risk measures can be divided into two categories: symmetrical and asymmetrical. With symmetrical measures, risk is defined in terms of a probability-weighted dispersion of results around some reference point, for example, the mean or an expected value. Both negative and positive values can affect this type of risk measure. Risk measures in this category include standard deviation, tracking error, mean-Gini and some lesser-known ones such as entropy.

Asymmetrical risk measures concentrate only on the values and probabilities below the reference point. Measures in this category include expected value of loss, safety-first, semivariance and value-at-risk. In the context of currency risk management there is not a lot to add to the general discussion on risk measurement, and in the rest of this Appendix we will limit our discussion to a few relevant concepts.

2D.1 Standard deviation

This is still the most commonly used risk measure. Typically, historical foreign exchange data for a certain period and with a certain frequency are used to compute the standard deviation of the log-returns. When the standard deviation is annualised, the result is also called the "actual volatility". In practice there are some choices to make here:

❏ How long a period (also known as the "sample period") should one choose? If it is too short, extending only over the recent past, the computed standard deviation will be heavily influenced by the latest events (or lack of them) and so may vary somewhat in value. If it is too long, it may contain information from the distant past, since when the currencies might have undergone structural change. In practice, a three- to five-year sample period is often used. Generally speaking, trading institutions use shorter sample periods than investment management institutions.

❏ What frequency (also called "window") should be used? The common choices are daily and monthly. When monthly data is used, care should be taken that the data points are non-overlapping. In other words, the time windows should not share data points apart from beginning and end points.

❏ Which mean return should be used? There are three main alternatives when calculating standard deviations: sample mean, zero or interest rate differentials. The sample mean is the default in commonly used software packages such as MS Excel. For longer windows, using the interest rate differential is more "correct" from a non-arbitrage point of view, but most people tend to ignore this due to the cumbersome data requirements. For financial institutions with a short investment horizon, the choice of mean return does not present a major problem. However, for investment managers with longer horizons the choice of mean return can have serious implications for the risk measure and asset allocation decision.

❏ Whether to weight the data and which weighting method to use. It is generally assumed that all data points, recent and not so recent, have the same significance and so weighting is not applied. However, in some situations it may make sense to treat the more recent data points as carrying more relevant information. One frequently used method is to weight the data points by a decay factor – generally an exponential function.

❑ Whether to use simple returns or log returns. Simple returns can be used in place of log returns, usually with marginal impact on the estimated standard deviation.

There is a very long and extensive line of investigation on the normal distribution assumption in relation to its implications for the calculation of standard deviation. The currency market has offered a most fruitful field for research on the normal distribution assumption because of its continuous and liquid trading. In fact, the standard deviation of future currency movements is itself traded through the currency options market – as option implied volatility. There are also very liquid markets for the so-called "wings" and "skews" in the currency market.[20]

2D.2 Implied volatility

As mentioned above, the standard deviation of future currency movements is actively traded in the currency options market and, if we ignore some minor technicalities, it represents the market consensus forecast of future foreign exchange volatility. Various studies generally support the idea that implied volatility does contain incremental information about future volatility than, say, historical volatility, and it offers a realistic, forward-looking alternative to historical volatility as a risk measure. Also, additional information such as wings and skews can be utilised to better describe the underlying risks.[21] Implied volatility is particularly useful for emerging market currencies, where events tend to cluster. If one uses historical volatility, depending on the window used for calculation, risks may not be properly taken into account. In an extreme example, the historical standard deviation for a pegged currency may be zero, which can grossly underestimate the risk. In such cases implied volatility is a much better indicator of the risks involved in a currency.

2D.3 Value-at-risk (VAR)

VAR has gained a foothold in the area of risk management in recent years and different versions of it are now the default risk measure for almost all investment banks. It is also used in areas such as trading desk risk limits, trading portfolio risk management, capital allocation and performance measurement. Its application to investment management has been hampered by a few problems, notably the choice of mean return (discussed earlier in this Appendix), the longer holding horizon and the lack of theoretical foundation. These problems are being tackled on both theoretical and practical fronts and we are optimistic that VAR will soon become a standard component in an investment manager's toolbox.

2D.4 Extreme value theory (EVT) and aggregate VAR

The traditional risk measure of standard deviation works well only if return distributions are normal. Financial prices and returns, however, are typically not very well approximated by normal distributions. Value-at-risk methodology makes two major extensions to standard deviation: it works well with portfolios; and the underlying distribution does not have to be normal. In essence, value-at-risk is a cut-off level of maximum losses: a 99% confidence level VAR is simply the 99th percentile highest loss from a portfolio over a specific period. In other words, 1% of losses may turn out to be higher. The problem is that VAR does not concern itself with the properties of this 1% tail – which in a sense is where the real risk is.

In the world of finance these tails are typically fat – ie, they contain more extreme values than is predicted by a normal distribution. EVT explicitly models the distribution of extreme returns. For example, if we take the worst return over a certain period and if we look at many periods, we will have a series of worst returns. If we plot these returns, we get an extreme return distribution – that is, only those events that fall in the tail of a normal distribution. EVT simply tries to find a distribution that best describes this extreme distribution. It may not fit the "typical" returns that fall under the main part of a normal distribution, but it should fit extreme returns much better than the normal distribution. Armed with the new distributions, you can make more accurate predictions about extreme returns. In the world of the normal distribution, events beyond more than about four to five standard deviations simply won't happen because the predicted probability of such events is so close to zero. In the world of EVT, they do happen, and they happen with a much more realistically predicted probability than a normal distribution can provide. In other words, EVT is a much more powerful measure for the quantification of tail risks.

EVT has some disadvantages:

❑ It requires advanced statistical/data-mining techniques;
❑ It is data-intensive;
❑ Greater flexibility in modelling may lead to erroneous results if the parameters are not carefully investigated;
❑ Distributions may not be stationary.

Along the same line of investigation, aggregate VAR (also known as conditional VAR, mean shortfall or expected loss) can be seen as an average VAR (AVAR). Traditional VAR represents a cut-off point above which the outcome is assured with a given confidence level. AVAR goes beyond that point and tries to work out the (probability-weighted) average of losses if they do occur. Various studies have shown that AVAR is superior to the traditional VAR and most other traditional risk measures used by the fund management industry.[22]

APPENDIX 2E: CO-DEPENDENCE

Co-dependence refers to the tendency for two or more variables to move together. Correlation is a measure of co-dependence between variables, but it is not the only measure. There are a host of problems associated with the correlation measure despite its ubiquitous use, and in this Appendix we take a brief look at some of them.

Co-dependence between currencies and the underlying investment, be it bonds or equities, is often cited as a reason both for and against foreign exchange risk management. There are several issues here:

❑ The relationship, if exists, is unlikely to be linear, so a simple calculation of correlation can be misleading. We therefore use co-dependence instead to highlight the difference.
❑ Some point out that, for a global equity portfolio, currency-hedged returns from different equity markets are more highly correlated than the unhedged returns. They argue from this that currency hedging reduces the benefit of diversification and so should not be undertaken.[23]
❑ The long-term average of the correlation of foreign exchange movements with the underlying equity exposure is close to zero. Some commentators suggest that foreign exchange risk, resembling white noise, should be hedged.

❏ The correlation between foreign exchange and bonds may be significantly different from that between foreign exchange and equities, and it deserves separate treatment.

❏ There is a growing body of evidence that, as with equities, correlations between foreign exchange rates increase significantly during periods of market turbulence.

❏ There is no satisfactory structural model of the correlation between foreign exchange and underlying investments. One main reason is that the linkage between foreign exchange and real or nominal factors is very hard to establish.

Correlation is the most commonly used measure for co-dependence, but its practical application is fraught with errors and difficulties. Simple but frequently made mistakes include:

❏ Calculating correlation on foreign exchange levels rather than on returns.

❏ Using overlapping data with no correction (we have seen this done in a research report on currency overlay by the global head of risk management in a well-known investment bank).

❏ Making such statements as: "if the price of A goes up, the likelihood of the price of B going up is 70%" based on a correlation between A and B of 70%.

Ordinary correlation assumes that the risk factors are multivariate normal. If we plot a scatter graph of a pair of price changes, the data points should form a roughly elliptical area. However, most real data sets do not exhibit linear relationships like this (a line parallel with the long axis of the ellipse), and scatter plots of bivariate data are rarely elliptical. There are various "robust" correlation measures, but they have not been widely used in foreign exchange risk management. Blyth (1996) summarised several non-linear correlation measures that may be applicable to financial data; these involve, for example, transforming the underlying data series or calculating local correlations.[24] The key non-linear measure he proposed involves modelling the dependence between two variables using a particular functional form (which can be estimated parametrically if one assumes a particular form of function or it can be estimated non-parametrically). We hope to see some further research in this area.

Like implied volatility, implied correlation is also a traded "commodity". Correlations can be "implied" from implied volatilities via a correlation triangle (see the detailed example in Appendix 2B). Correlations are also traded directly through some exotic instruments (such as the "correlation swap"). Unlike implied volatility, we have not seen a report on the comparative usefulness of implied correlation for forecasting future correlation. For emerging market currencies, where actual correlation suffers from problems with the data, implied correlation provides a useful alternative. Clearly, future research on the use of implied correlation for asset allocation will be useful.

Along with EVT, copula techniques have received considerable attention from academics and practitioners in recent years. When one moves away from the centre of a distribution to the tail(s), correlation is no longer very well defined as tail distributions are highly unlikely to be normal. Copulas offer a more general way of describing the co-dependence between risk factors in that:

❏ They do not presume a normal distribution. In fact, it does not assume any distribution.
❏ They attempt to find a way to describe the probability of observing return factors below certain given levels.

As an example of the second point, we might want to know what is the probability of both the EUR/USD rate and Nasdaq "tanking" (falling) more than 5%. Of both tanking more than 10%? Of the EUR/USD rate tanking more than 10% but Nasdaq more than 5%? And so on. Copula methodology tries to find ways to describe how these probabilities are linked to one another.

A direct application of copulas is multivariable EVT. If you have extreme value distributions for different risk factors, how do you put them together to get an extreme value distribution for the portfolio? Copula techniques (and there are many different candidates for copulas) can be used to define the co-dependence of the various risks.

The disadvantages of copula techniques are as for EVT: they call for advanced statistical/data-mining techniques and are data-intensive; the greater flexibility in modelling can lead to erroneous results if; and distributions may not be stationary.

1 A clear expression of a foreign exchange unit is currency A per currency B, where the former is the numerator currency (aka counter currency or foreign currency) and the latter is the denominator (aka base currency or domestic currency). A commonly used short form is currency B/currency A, and this convention is followed throughout the book.

2 See Appendix 2A for an illustration of how to calculate the forward exchange rate from the spot rate and domestic/foreign interest rates. Also, in our examples we use simple compounding for simplicity.

3 Here we assume that there is no uncertainty regarding the outcome of the investment. Obviously, in practice both the yield and the capital may well be different after three months. This is dealt with in the second example.

4 Capital usage for currency trading is usually not as easily defined as, say, that for cash investments in bonds and equities. Some argue that currency trading requires zero capital as it is conducted entirely on credit (they might not be of the same opinion if they actually tried to obtain credit lines from, say, a bank to trade currencies). Clearly, using the notional amount of currency trades as capital usage may not be appropriate either as relatively few currency trades are actually funded this way. The answer lies somewhere between these two polar cases. Many funds employ a VAR-based approach similar to those used by banks to compute their capital requirements. This is a general problem for any fund using any form of derivative instrument and therefore is not dealt with in this book.

5 See Chapter 1, Section 1.3 for a discussion of zero return.

6 See Appendix 2A.

7 The β of an instrument is its standardised covariance with its class of instruments as a whole. Thus the β of a stock is the extent to which it follows movements in the overall market (after Chase/Risk Publications, 1996).

8 See, for example, Prajogi, Muralidhar and van der Wouden (2000) and Muralidhar and van der Wouden (2000).

9 MSCI EAFE Index: an international equity performance index prepared by Morgan Stanley Capital International Inc. EAFE stands for Europe, Australia and Far East.

10 Risk may include other aspects of the return distribution which the variance measure adopted by Froot (1993) may not be sufficient to capture. For example, the risk can be defined as extreme losses.

11 A functional currency is the currency in which a corporation chooses to report its results. A corporation may have several functional currencies, and the functional currency can be different from that of the country where its shares are listed.

12 The delta of an option describes its premium's sensitivity to changes in the price of the underlying (Chase/Risk Publications, 1996).

13 See, for example, Knez, Litterman and Scheinkman (1994) and Litterman and Scheinkman (1991).

14 Static replication is a method of hedging an options position with a position in standard options whose composition does not change through time (Chase/Risk publications, 1996).

15 A yard is a billion of something.

16 A postscript: these remarks were made in early 2001. At the time of publication (2003), discretionary styles and proprietary trading in currencies had staged a comeback of sorts. Opportunities in other assets have been limited since our original remarks were made.

17 Another topic that has been referred to occasionally in the currency-hedging discussion is the fund manager's career horizon. It starts with the assumption that in the long-term the impact of foreign exchange volatility averages out and, if fund managers hold their job for the long-term, they can afford not to be concerned about currency fluctuation – which, indeed, was the situation five or seven years ago. Nowadays, a fund manager's tenure is much shorter (estimated to be around three years), and it is therefore much more important for him to manage the short-term fluctuation induced by currencies.

18 We use a straightforward interest rate calculation here for simplicity.

19 In fact, market forces will, in all probability, make sure that he does not survive all that long.

20 See Chapter 7, Sections 7.6 and 7.8.2 for more details.

21 See Juzczenko and Maillet (2001) for an example of how to incorporate these kinds of "higher-order" risk measures in a CAPM framework.

22 For references see Embrechts, Klüppelberg and Mikosh (1997), Artzner *et al* (1999), Basak and Shapiro (1998), Kroll and Kaplanski (2000a and 2000b).

23 This argument is not as plausible as it sounds. With two correlated variables, if we add random noise to one of the variables the correlation between the two variables will decrease. In the extreme where the random noise is several magnitudes greater than the variation of interest, the correlation will approach zero as it is drowned in the random moves.

24 See also Bjerve and Doksum (1993).

3

Currency Overlay Management

3.1 INTRODUCTION

This chapter examines the concept and practice of currency overlay. After brief historical summary, we look at some of the rather divergent definitions of currency overlay before defining our own concept in a very broad context. We then present generic illustrations to show how a currency overlay programme may function in practice. Section 3.6 is largely devoted to two commentaries from the financial press that illustrate recent trends, in particular the increasing readiness of funds to outsource their overlay requirements from external specialist firms. The next section describes the services provided by an overlay manager, illustrated by panels that follow a fund's currency manager and the bank currency salesperson she deals with through a typical hectic day. In Section 3.8 we turn to a detailed consideration of historical performance in the form of two studies of overlay management and two publicly available monthly indices of overlay performance. Section 3.9 reviews practical aspects of outsourcing currency management: mandates, costs and how to evaluate the services on offer. After a consideration of trading styles and how to avoid the risk associated with a single style, the chapter closes by describing another significant external service: foreign exchange prime brokerage by a hub bank.

Some important related topics are deferred until later chapters. For example, in Chapter 4 we review various foreign exchange models and modelling techniques and the choice of overlay style. In Chapter 5 we make a digression into currency's role in the CAPM and optimisation, and we list common approaches to identifying an optimal hedge ratio for currencies. Chapter 6 deals with selecting a currency benchmark and measuring currency management performance. Chapter 7 focuses on the relevance of option pricing theory – in particular to the dynamic overlay style – with a general overview on the use of derivative instruments in currency risk management. Chapter 8 looks at the question whether emerging market currencies should be treated differently.

3.2 ORIGINS AND DEVELOPMENT OF CURRENCY OVERLAY

The concept of currency overlay first surfaced in the late 1980s when specialists began to provide disciplined currency management services to fund managers with international investment portfolios. The specialist currency overlay industry has grown in size and depth since its early days. However, in recent years a more notable area of growth has been (and is expected to continue to be) from traditional investment managers who start running overlay programmes internally and offer such services to their (captive) customers. We believe that future growth in the currency overlay business will be mainly from this type of "organically" grown service within firms.

Auxiliary business areas have been catching up too. For example, consultants such as the Mercer Group, Watson Wyatt and Frank Russell Company have collected performance data on currency managers that can be used by clients in their search for suitable managers. There are also publicly available performance indices, for example, those provided by Parker Global Strategies and Daniel B. Stark & Co. Some service providers now combine currency overlay with an "FX prime brokerage" service. We will return to these topics later in the chapter, and in Chapter 9 we will discuss currency overlay and e-commerce in foreign exchange.

3.3 DEFINITIONS OF CURRENCY OVERLAY

There are many different interpretations of the currency overlay concept. At one end of the spectrum, currency overlay means that currency risk is hedged. At the other end it means that currency is viewed as a separate asset class and positions in currencies are taken for speculative gain. And in between flourish various hybrids.

Some view a passive currency-hedging programme with a fixed hedge ratio as the most basic form of currency overlay. In this type of programme existing hedges are periodically adjusted according to changes in the underlying and rolled forward. These hedges will (partially) neutralise the fluctuation in the value of the foreign currency investment caused by exchange rate movements. Generally, the hedge ratio is set beforehand, possibly through an optimisation process, and it is fixed irrespective of overall trends in the currency market. Risk control is the main objective of a passive hedging programme.

In many sales pitches by overlay managers, currency overlay is described as a way of actively adjusting hedge ratios in anticipation of exchange rate moves: keeping currencies fully hedged when the exchange rate is expected to move unfavourably and fully unhedged otherwise. The rationale behind this is that currency moves are governed by a different set of variables than traditional asset classes. Specialists can use their skills, based on an intimate knowledge of how the currency market functions or on superior trading models, to predict currency moves. Extra return is the main objective of an active hedging programme.

More recently, the concept of currency overlay has increasingly come to be linked to the active management of currency risks. Today's overlay manager tries to achieve a balance of yield enhancement *and* risk control. The motivations for overlay managers vary:

❏ Most state, implicitly or explicitly, that the currency market is inefficient and hence provides arbitrage opportunities. The inefficiencies manifest in many different ways: mean-reversion, trending, range-boundedness, responsiveness to various signals, etc.
❏ Some claim that, by actively managing currency risks, they can reduce the impact of a negative cashflow related to a passive hedging programme.
❏ Some say that by concentrating on the major currency exposures in a portfolio they can reduce transaction costs and exploit the diversification effect between currencies.
❏ Others believe that they can reduce the risk of a currency-induced valuation disaster by adopting a dynamic approach.

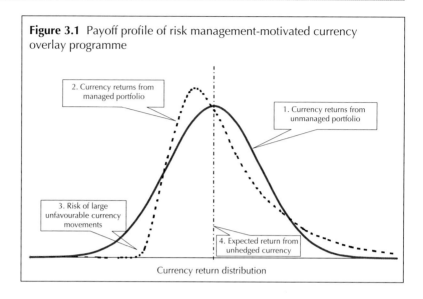

Figure 3.1 Payoff profile of risk management-motivated currency overlay programme

The approach is illustrated in Figure 3.1, where the dashed curve shows the shift in the distribution of currency returns that is the aim of an overlay programme. The symmetrical, solid line follows a normal distribution, representing the random walk view of currency returns. The dashed curve is skewed to the right, indicating that the likelihood of large losses is reduced, whereas the likelihood of large profits is increased. There may also be an increase in the likelihood of small losses.

3.3.1 A working definition

Overlay (noun): a covering; anything laid over to alter the appearance.
We now set out our own definition of currency overlay:

> Generally speaking, if the decision on currencies is taken separately from the other investment decisions, and if this currency decision is executed by specialist managers with pre defined risk/return objectives and other operational parameters, then this process is called currency overlay and the specialist managers are known as overlay managers.

Some refer to the currency decision as the "investment decision", while others prefer to call it the "hedging decision", and in practice the specialist managers are sometimes fixed-income portfolio managers. Overlay is not confined to currencies; for example, a fund might run a derivatives overlay on top of its normal asset allocation process. The derivatives overlay manager can use, say, a bond–equity total return swap to alter the bond–equity split of his investment portfolio.

The key ingredient in the above definition is that the decision process for currencies is formalised in the same fashion as other types of strategic and/or tactical investment decisions taken by the fund. In particular, the currency decision is *functionally separated* from the other decisions. In Chapter 5, Section 5.4 we will see that taking a separate decision does not equate to taking the decision separately. Currency decisions can be made at the same time as the decisions on other asset classes. Or they can be made after those decisions and when implicit currency exposures are known. The overlay programme will have a predefined risk/return objective, risk control parameters and performance measurement procedure.

The asset allocation decision is the central decision for a fund. The overlay can run "alongside" or "on top of" the asset allocation process. In the derivatives overlay example given above it is *on top of* the asset allocation process because it alters the asset allocation. Most overlay programmes – in particular currency overlay – run *alongside* the asset allocation process.[1]

3.3.2 Risk separation is key

In our view, then, the key theme in a currency overlay process is risk separation. In this book, when we talk about "foreign exchange overlay", we assume or imply that there is a framework present to separate out the foreign exchange risk element during the investment process. The framework comes into play from the point before the investment action is taken, when dealing with issues such as investment policy, risk/return objectives and constraints, and optimisation. Then it covers the execution of investment decisions and risk control. It finishes with performance measurement and attribution.

In our definition, currency overlay has more to do with risk measurement and risk responsibility than with whether one should or should not hedge currency risks or whether currency is a separate asset class. It has to be stressed that running an overlay programme does not necessarily mean treating foreign exchange as a separate asset class – a point on which much of the debate on the merit of currency risk management has centred. Some funds run a currency overlay merely to execute passive hedging as required and execute any additional currency transactions needed to neutralise the currency positions from the active underlying positions. This type of overlay can centralise currency dealings and reduce transaction costs. Moreover, currency risk is monitored (though not actively managed) centrally. Funds running this type of overlay, which we would call passive currency overlay, probably do not view currency as a separate asset class. Other funds allow the overlay managers to take active positions in addition to execution and monitoring roles as in a passive currency overlay. The implicit assumption is that trading currencies can either bring extra return or further reduce risk or both. Clearly, currency *is* treated as a separate asset class, either strategic or tactical. In our view, the distinction in risk-adjusted performance terms between a pure currency fund and an active overlay fund is small.[2]

3.4 WHAT AN OVERLAY PROCESS LOOKS LIKE IN PRACTICE

Now we will look at the structure of a real-world currency overlay process. In fact, this tends to differ considerably from one programme to another, so in this section we present three flow charts to illustrate typical aspects.

Figure 3.2 shows the relationships between a plan sponsor, consultants and the investment manager and how currency decisions can be taken at different stages of the investment process. The consultant(s) advises the plan sponsor on the extent of the currency risk in his or her portfolio and whether overlay is suitable for managing currency risk. He also advises on the choice of overlay manager(s) if external overlay specialists are deemed appropriate (point 3 in Figure 3.2). The plan sponsor awards mandates with or without specific instructions on currencies (a mandate is an agreement on how certain assets should be managed; see Section 3.9.1) Points 4–6 in Figure 3.2 are included in the mandate. Sometimes a plan sponsor will strip the currency part from the underlying and award a separate currency mandate to a currency specialist.

The investment manager allocates assets under the guidelines that have been established in the mandate and attempts to outperform the designated benchmark. At the asset allocation level, the investment manager may or may not make an explicit decision on

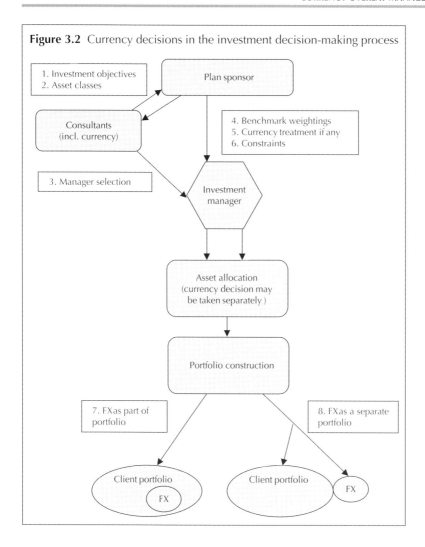

Figure 3.2 Currency decisions in the investment decision-making process

currency weightings (many do). If the currency decision is not made at that stage, it can be made later, once the exposures from the underlying positions have been aggregated. The asset allocation and currency decisions are then passed on to the portfolio construction team and eventually are reflected in mandate-compliant portfolios. Depending on how currency risk is specified in the mandate, some of these portfolios may have currency allocation as an integral part. Others may have a separate currency overlay

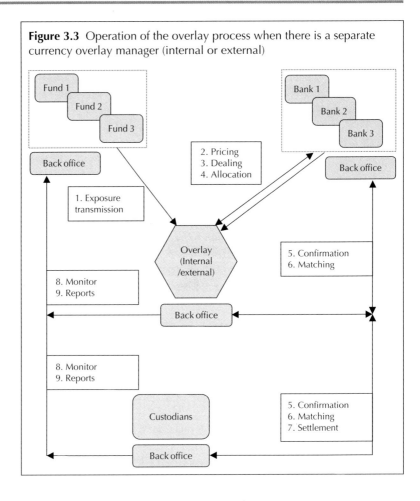

Figure 3.3 Operation of the overlay process when there is a separate currency overlay manager (internal or external)

portfolio that is constructed under the guidelines of either the plan sponsor or the investment manager.

Figure 3.3 shows how a currency overlay manager operates. Note that here as well as in Figures 3.2 and 3.4 the overlay manager can be either internal or external. The exact compositions of the underlying portfolios are communicated to the overlay manager. The overlay manager decides whether to hedge passively according to his mandate or to take active positions. He has a variety of decision variables: timing, amount, to hedge directly or through crosses, spot or forward or options, etc. Different mandates may require different implementations of the same strategy. All the

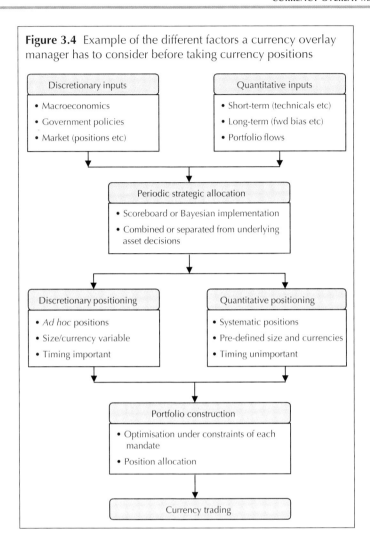

Figure 3.4 Example of the different factors a currency overlay manager has to consider before taking currency positions

Discretionary inputs

• Macroeconomics
• Government policies
• Market (positions etc)

Quantitative inputs

• Short-term (technicals etc)
• Long-term (fwd bias etc)
• Portfolio flows

Periodic strategic allocation

• Scoreboard or Bayesian implementation
• Combined or separated from underlying asset decisions

Discretionary positioning

• *Ad hoc* positions
• Size/currency variable
• Timing important

Quantitative positioning

• Systematic positions
• Pre-defined size and currencies
• Timing unimportant

Portfolio construction

• Optimisation under constraints of each mandate
• Position allocation

Currency trading

required transactions are netted to arrive at the dealing amounts, which are hedged with external counterparties.

Figure 3.4 shows the range of factors – quantitative, discretionary, fundamental, technical and so on – a currency overlay manager may have to consider in deciding on his currency positions.

3.5 ADVANTAGES OF EMPLOYING CURRENCY OVERLAY
The key benefit of a currency overlay approach lies in the discipline it brings with it. An overlay process simply cannot function properly

without a clear picture of what is being overlaid on to. It is not unusual to come across funds where the overall picture of the risk incurred is woefully inadequate – in some cases with disastrous consequences that have made newspaper headlines. An overlay programme should be part of a fund-wide risk management framework in which responsibilities are clearly defined, exposures aggregated in a timely manner, risk properly monitored and performance measured.

Additionally, a properly designed and executed overlay can ensure that:

❑ exposure to currency risks in a portfolio is controlled in an efficient, timely and low-cost manner;
❑ investment decisions are made and implemented on the basis of each asset class's own risk/return characteristics rather than in a bundled manner;
❑ currency overlay specialists, either internal or external or both, can be used to manage risk and/or to seek returns;
❑ certain functions, such as transaction netting and cash management, within a fund can be centralised at a higher level to improve efficiency; and
❑ more choices are available to the investors, trustees and plan sponsors.

The smooth implementation of an overlay programme requires participation from almost all sectors of a firm and the expertise gained will therefore be beneficial to the efficient running of the firm as a whole. The story of Calpers, the US$160 billion Californian public employees' pension fund, is perhaps quite telling. In October 1999 Calpers announced that it planned to take the management of large tranches of non-US assets in house, citing the expertise developed through a currency overlay process that allowed it to manage risks associated with international investment more efficiently. The plan was approved in November 2000 and a "shadow" trading programme was initiated at the same time. In August 2001 staff recommended to the investment committee that trading should start with real money. The benefits of using overlay, they stated, included risk reduction, cost savings, a greater diversity of investments and expertise in foreign exchange management that could lead to the creation of an active currency programme.

The disadvantages associated with an overlay programme may include:

❏ there is no *a priori* theoretical justification for managing currencies (though active management of other asset classes could be rejected on similar grounds);
❏ the requirement for timely valuation and aggregation of currency exposures across the overlaid assets;
❏ the cost of hiring external overlay specialists or managers or of buying equipment for internal overlay specialists; and
❏ organisational resistance to separating out a specific risk factor from others; this may arise because some investment managers like to attribute gains produced by favourable currency moves to their expertise and poor performance to unfavourable currency moves.

3.6 TRENDS AND OPPORTUNITIES IN CURRENCY OVERLAY

Currency overlay management has been gaining acceptance in the global investment community in recent years, and the main trends we have observed can be summarised as follows:

❏ the growing application of a risk management-motivated approach to currency risk;
❏ continuing expansion of the established market in overlay specialist services and, more importantly, the increasing adoption of internal currency overlay management programmes;
❏ more efficient delivery of external overlay services through online technology and lower costs;
❏ more players are moving towards a quantitative, model-driven approach;
❏ the increasing (if with reluctance) level of transparency on performance in the overlay market;
❏ more players are using options as instruments or volatility as a trading signal in overlay programmes.

Previously a niche topic confined to a handful of specialists, currency overlay has gradually assumed a role on the main stage of investment management. This is reflected in the increasing press coverage of the topic. According to a Reuters report in late 2001, "Fund managers, faced with growing exposure to overseas markets and a dismal track record on currency management, are increasingly turning to experts for advice."[3] The article claimed that the number of specialist currency overlay managers will grow fast as governments ease pension restrictions and fund managers try to insulate their returns from currency swings. It suggested that the new UK financial reporting standard, FRS 17, would put pressure on UK-based pension funds to pay closer attention to short-term risks such as currency risk, and it attributed the low adoption of currency overlay in the UK to "peer pressure" whereby pension funds will not deviate from the unhedged benchmark which is the industry standard. Two stories from *Financial News*, reproduced here to give a flavour of what is going on, paint a similar picture. Mercer, a pension fund consultant, has compiled a database of currency overlay managers and it offers a performance comparison service to its pension fund clients.

PANEL 1 CURRENCY OVERLAY ON THE AGENDA
William Hutchings, *eFinancial News*, July 9, 2001

(Reproduced by the kind permission of Financial News. For further information visit www.efinancialnews.com. © Copyright 2000 eFinancialNews.com Ltd)

Currency overlay has finally started to appear on the agendas of large UK pension schemes, according to investment consultant William M. Mercer. Mercer has been working hard to persuade its UK clients to invest more in overseas markets, but does not want them to take currency risk too. Bill Muysken, head of global research at the firm, says: "Investing more overseas makes sense. It does not make sense to have more currency exposure."

Accordingly, Muysken and his colleagues have been raising the issue with pension plan sponsors. As an issue, currency overlay has been around for at least 12 years. But for most of that time no more than a handful of reliable managers have offered it as a separate service. Muysken says: "The number has been growing recently. Our global database has grown to 36, of whom about two-thirds have a UK office. We are now confident that, when we raise the issue with trustees, we can offer to bring them as many managers as they would want to look at."

Trustees are being encouraged to challenge their assumptions by the minimum funding requirement and FRS 17, the new accounting standard. Both of these focus attention on short-term risk. Simultaneously, currency managers now have track records that include periods of US dollar strength and weakness and of global macroeconomic crisis.

James Binny, a senior investment manager at Gartmore, says: "Currency management always tends to perplex people and the industry has not helped by overcomplicating it. I now spend half my time on what I call education, hoping I'll be remembered when the time comes to give mandates." Binny has come across a number of typical answers to his question: "Why don't you manage your currency risk?" The first is that the scheme invested overseas to diversify. He says: "The first bit of currency exposure does diversify your risk, but then it is just extra risk. You should hedge 90% of your currency." Then, many trustees believe exchange rate fluctuations tend to even out over time. Binny believes they may well do so: "But you may have to wait an awfully long time." Conversely, many UK trustees are labouring under the impression that sterling always tends to fall in value. "In fact, over the last 10 years sterling has been flat, and over the last five it has been strong."

Paul Duncombe, a deputy managing director at State Street Global Advisors specialising in currency management, adds to Binny's comments: "When you hedge against currencies, you also pick up the interest rate differential." As an example, he compares the returns from European assets between 1979 and December 2000. If they were denominated in deutschmarks (subsequently, euros), the UK investor enjoyed a return of 1% per annum, with a volatility of 9%. If the foreign currency was hedged back into sterling, the UK investor enjoyed a return of 3.8% per annum, with virtually no volatility.

PANEL 2 UK PENSION FUNDS WARM TO CURRENCY OVERLAY MANDATES
N. Mehra, eFinancial News, March 14, 2000

Consultants are warming to the idea of encouraging pension funds to hedge their bets on currency overlay mandates, according to State Street Global Advisors (SSgA). State Street, which has recently won a $250m currency overlay mandate from a leading UK pension fund, insists that pension fund trustees and their advisers are becoming braver about hedging their bets. With the increased popularity of specialist investment managers, and the use of both passive and active management, consultants are becoming less ambivalent to the currency process of investment

A currency manager receives reports from a custodian of the fund's net currency exposure and it can then take positions to manage that exposure in line with its views in an attempt to add value. It aims to outperform a benchmark exposure relative to tracking error – or produce a high information ratio relative to a sensible tracking error.

Typically investors have regarded currency as being managed together with the country and stock selection process, but this tends to leave the exposure unhedged. The bad press surrounding hedging tools and funds has also left many pension schemes and consultants fearing volatility. UK managers generally favour balanced management, even where this has not produced strong returns, and currency selection has not been an area where manager expertise has been demonstrated. Most UK funds invest more than 25% of assets in a foreign currency – a large currency exposure to leave to chance.

SSgA has added 2.9% per annum over five years ending 1999, at an active risk level of 2.3%, giving an information ratio of 1.3%. Many active equity managers would be delighted if they produced a ratio of 0.5% or 0.75%, says Kanesh Lakhani, marketing director at SSgA. Increasingly consultants are advising their pension funds clients to have some sort of benchmark for currency mandates.

The growth of specialist management in Europe is enabling managers to more easily assess which portfolios are generating the largest returns and this has increased the popularity of [the] currency overlay process. While there will be an additional investment manager to monitor, the mechanics of the process are simple, says Lakhani.

The US has a history of specialist arrangements and the main US players – JP Morgan, Pareto Partners, Bridgewater Associates, SSgA and Goldman Sachs Asset Management – account for around 80% of most active currency overlay mandates in the US, UK and Australia combined.

3.7 CURRENCY OVERLAY MANAGERS – WHAT DO THEY DO?

The specialist currency overlay market is dominated by a handful of large players – a table listing key players and summaries of the investment philosophies of the four largest can be found in Appendix 3B.

A specialist overlay manager traditionally provides services that encompass the whole overlay process, including:

❑ risk quantification;
❑ passive hedging;
❑ active trading using its proprietary methods;
❑ trade confirmation and settlement; and
❑ performance measurement.

The specialist receives a fee plus a performance-related fee for the series of services. Because many of these services are essentially identical for different clients, clearly there is significant benefit due to economies of scale for the specialist to grow large. Recent years have seen some changes in this area:

❑ Some players, including banks, custodians and many online start-ups, are offering automated services that cover risk quantification and performance measurement.
❑ Banks, custodians and online portals also offer online transaction tools that allow their clients to carry out transactions (include passive hedging) with greatly improved efficiency and low cost. These tools usually conduct trade confirmation and settlement automatically – see Chapter 9 for more details.
❑ Many traditional investment funds choose to set up internal overlay programmes (sometimes by buying specialist currency overlay outfits) instead of using external specialists, taking advantage of the new services mentioned in the previous points.
❑ Increasingly frequently a currency overlay service is offered as part of a range of products provided by a fund for its clients to pick and mix.

The core competency of a currency overlay manager can now be more narrowly defined as a skill in active trading using its proprietary methods. The methods, or "trading styles", can be different, and these are discussed further in Section 3.10. The decision-making process is illustrated in Figure 3.4. One important factor in distinguishing between overlay managers, aside from management style, is track record. This is the subject of the next section.

Internal overlay managers operate in a similar fashion: since nearly all the non-core services provided by the specialist (external) overlay manager are shared with other asset managers within the fund, the internal overlay managers naturally focus on active trading. They often have the added responsibility of quantifying and monitoring the risk-reduction benefit of the passive hedging programme – a function that often is not adequately carried out for many funds which employ external overlay managers.

Panel 3 illustrates some of the points in this section by describing a day in the life of Cheryl, a currency overlay manager. For comparison, Panel 4 takes us through the same day for Graham, a currency salesperson working in a bank who advises on and executes the larger foreign exchange transactions required by the bank's clients, including the fund Cheryl works for. Both characters are, of course, fictitious.

PANEL 3 DAY IN THE LIFE OF CHERYL, A CURRENCY MANAGER AT FUND Z

		Comments
7:30	Reads market commentaries from various sources: what's happened in North American and Asian time zones, major flows, today's key currency-influencing events, technical analysis.	There are many different currency trading styles and different types of information may be required.
8:00	Internal meeting to decide on monthly currency positions. Views from the currency team are combined using a scoreboard mechanism: USD/JPY is strongly bearish. Also, equity managers say they are halfway through implementing yesterday's asset allocation decision: overweight JPY equity and underweight USD equity. The balance will be done today when the US opens. Net additional FX flow is around $250 million.	Effective internal communication ...

... and timely information on the |
| 8:30 | Cheryl checks the daily asset revaluation reports provided by custodians summarising currency positions and FX hedge adjustment needed *vis-à-vis* benchmark. Liaises with portfolio construction team to implement USD/JPY decision across appropriate mandates, taking constraints into consideration. Total amount | underlying positions are vital for optimal currency management. |

		Comment
	needed to implement USD/JPY view is estimated at around $500 million.	
9:00	Takes call from Graham, an FX salesperson at Bank A, confirming that the additional credit line required for a new fund is in place.	Good salesperson can provide value-added information and ideas. Typically, a buy-side currency manager has two to five main sales contacts with different banks.
9:05	Continues chatting with Graham about today's market. Graham mentions that UBS has changed its mid-term EUR forecast from bearish to bullish. There is also a large exotic USD/JPY option position with barrier at 120.00. Cheryl says Fund Z may need to sell some USD/JPY today. Graham suggests that acting earlier today is better than later as the option barrier is likely to cap any upside moves. However, the US GDP figures (1330 GMT) may contain surprises. Market is neutral on average but Bank A is negative.	Existing market positions, especially barrier options, can significantly affect the price movement. Market sentiment matters too.
10:30	Launches Bank A's FXTrader to request some small spot/forward and swap prices. Two-way prices come back. Hits deal button. The deals will be automatically confirmed and settled. Details of deal automatically load into his own system.	More and more market players are using FX on-line dealing platforms, especially for smaller routine transactions.
11:00	Final USD/JPY adjustment known from portfolio construction team. Need to sell $750 million. Cheryl decides to wait for a little.	

		Comments
11:30	Graham calls. There are rumours that US GDP figures will be disappointing. Cheryl leaves a limit order to sell $600 million at 119.80, with stop-loss at 119.35, OCO (one cancels the other), partial fill okay, GTC (good till cancelled). Market price is 119.65.	This is some FX-specific lingo, but it's soon picked up.
12:45	Graham again. US dollar sold off, market price is now around 119.05. Sold $450 million at 119.80 during a brief rally and the balance $150 million at 119.35. Average price 119.6875. Graham thinks risk is further to the downside.	
12:47	Asks Graham the price in $250 million. He quotes: "figure -10". Deal at 119.00 to sell a further $250 million. All-in-average 119.4853. She asks him to roll the deal to one-month date.	The FX market is very liquid and clients can specify any settlement date subject to credit or collateralisation agreements.
13:30	US figures even worse than expected. Spot 118.55. Confirms to Graham how the deal will be split between different funds.	
14:00	Works on currency overlay part of a presentation to be given to a pension fund client jointly with equity managers.	More and more clients are looking at systematic trading models for return enhancement.
15:30	Meets Bank B's quantitative analyst and internal analyst to discuss the back-testing result from a systematic trading model. Suggests testing the results using stop-loss orders.	A clearly defined and monitored performance measurement system is essential for good currency risk management.

	Comments
16:30	Internal meeting to review performance figures from last month.
18:30	Beer with Graham.

PANEL 4 DAY IN THE LIFE OF GRAHAM, A CURRENCY SALESPERSON AT BANK A

7:00	Reads market commentaries, political and economic news, technical analysis. Speaks to colleagues in Far East on major overnight flows and client orders. Speaks to traders about big positions. Discusses today's key currency-influencing events with strategists.
7:30	Starts calling important clients for morning updates. ❑ Update on Hungarian florint for Fund Tango as they have a large investment in the country. ❑ Goes through a multi-legged accumulating hedging strategy with Fund Lima, who use derivatives extensively for currency management. Lima asks about the impact of volatility skew on the structure; Graham promises to get back to him. ❑ Chats to spot USD/JPY traders about market liquidity and positioning. Today is the rebalancing day for Fund Z. Fund Z may have a large USD/JPY transaction after Graham chats to colleagues in Equity Division covering Fund Z.
8:30	Conference call with Lima and quantitative analyst on skew and other "high moments". In a rare quiet moment, Graham listens. Lima wants to change the fixing arrangement of the structure. This is not a standard request and cannot be handled by existing modules. Graham promises to call back in an hour. Quantitative analyst is on the case. He liaises with Exotic Traders and Risk Controls.
8:45	Calls credit officer about the limits for one of Fund Z's new sub-funds.
9:00	Calls Cheryl at Fund Z to inform her of new credit line.

9:05   Chats with Cheryl about today's market and gives additional information from spot traders. She says Fund Z may need to sell USD/JPY.

9:30   Calls Lima with price for new structure.

10:00   Lima calls back and deals. Graham confirms details and price over the phone. He inputs the deal into the internal risk management system and the risk is split into spot, forward and volatility and hedged by relevant traders. Informs Back Office to confirm this tailored deal manually (most deals are confirmed automatically).

10:30   Sees online notifications: Fund Z is dealing some spot and forward using the online dealing tools. Green light on notification panel indicates that things are in order. Confirmation and settlement are automatic.

11:00   Conference call with Fund Delta and his own e-marketer on implementing straight-through processing (STP) with Delta. It cuts processing costs for Delta and reduces trading errors dramatically. Delta mentions that their newly acquired US subsidiary has a separate currency unit.

11:30   Calls Cheryl at Fund Z to update after strategist shouts across on latest rumour about US GDP figures. Obtains a limit order from Fund Z. Inputs orders into the system and speaks to USD/JPY spot trader about the order.

12:00   Chats online with his counterpart in the US, passing on the information about subsidiary from Delta. Monitors movements in USD/JPY, liaises with spot trader.

12:45   Sudden large moves in USD/JPY. Calls Cheryl to inform her that Fund Z's order is partially filled at the level but stop-loss is triggered on remainder. Confirms verbally to Fund Z.

12:47   Fund Z asks for a spot USD/JPY price in $250 million notional in competition with another bank. Fund Z does not deal initially as not happy with spread from either bank. Graham queries the spot trader on liquidity and the large exotic option positions. Speaks to Cheryl on improvement. Fund Z deals.

14:00	Called by colleague in Equities. One of his clients, Fund Papa, is reviewing currency policy for their equity portfolios. Agrees to join Steve for a meeting with client along with a quantitative analyst.
15:30	Goes to quantitative analyst's desk and explains Fund Papa's request. Also enquires about progress on portfolio currency analysis and trading tool quantitative analyst team is working on. Quantitative analyst mentions a new systematic hedging idea in Hungarian florint prepared for another client.
16:00	Calls Fund Tango to book meeting. Confirms with Cheryl where to meet for a beer after work.

3.8 HISTORICAL PERFORMANCE

Measuring the historical performance of currency overlay pro-grammes, managers or providers is difficult as quality data are not usually publicly available. When they are available, they are nor-mally reported by the overlay managers themselves and thus are liable to survival bias – the bad performance of certain programmes may not be included. Measuring the contributions of overlay man-agers has some unique difficulties: for example, many overlay man-dates have restrictions that may affect a manager's performance; the impact of forward points should be properly accounted for; and the performance should be net of interest.

In this section we first review two studies of the historical per-formance of currency overlay managers and then take a detailed look at two publicly available foreign exchange performance indices that can be used for performance evaluation.

3.8.1 Two studies of manager performance

There are two recent studies on the performance of overlay man-agers, both by pension fund consultants, one from UK-based Watson Wyatt and the other by the US-based Frank Russell Company. Both reports show impressive historical returns, but they should be viewed with caution for the reasons discussed above.

Hersey and Minnick (2000) of Watson Wyatt Investment Consulting looked at returns and risks in more than 200 accounts from 20 currency overlay managers. They found that "across all accounts, the value-added number since inception stands at 1.55% as of year-end 1998, while dollar and non-dollar accounts generated 1.52% and 0.93% in excess return respectively." In a later update (Hersey and Ogunc, 2000), the value added for all accounts was 1.34% at the end of 1999, while the added values were 1.37% and 0.67% for dollar and non-dollar based accounts, respectively.

In the second study, by Baldridge, Meath and Myers (2000) of Frank Russell, 18 firms with US$85 billion in currency overlay assets provided return series for 241 accounts managed during various periods from December 31, 1988, to June 30, 1999. The authors found that "a majority of institutional clients who have hired active currency specialists to overlay their multi-regional equity portfolios have experienced positive returns. The performance has been shown to be universal against any benchmark and against any base currency." They comment that "the combination of positive success ratios, consistent excess returns, and low tracking errors present an intriguing case for considering active currency overlay strategies to enhance an investor's global portfolio. Certainly, the managers we have studied have added value for their investors." The authors found that the average currency overlay manager had achieved an average of 1.48% excess return per year relative to the client-selected currency benchmarks in the 10 years through to 1999 with an average tracking error of 2.63%. Of the 241 accounts they examined, 180 or 75% had added value since inception and 81% over the preceding five years. The tracking error fell between US fixed income and US equity and significantly below that of a non-US equity portfolio.

They reported some other interesting findings as well. For example, the performance of an overlay programme can be affected by the benchmark itself and by whether the mandate is symmetrical or asymmetrical (referring to whether or not the overlay manager can take positions on both sides of the benchmark).

3.8.2 Published indexes of overlay performance
The only two publicly available data sources we are aware of are those from Parker Global Strategies (PGS) and Daniel B. Stark & Co.[4] The Parker FX Index is a performance-based benchmark which measures both the reported and the risk-adjusted returns of

currency managers. The managers run either pure currency funds or currency overlay funds.

The actual performances of programmes included in the index are collected regularly by PGS and an average is taken across all of them with equal weighting so that large managers do not dominate the results. The average returns are used to construct the index, which is published monthly. In fact there are three indexes as the programmes are further divided into "Systematic" (rule-based trading (34)) and "Discretionary" (technical, fundamental, and quantitative based trading (13)). The main Parker FX Index is based on 47 programmes managed by 36 firms located in the US, Canada, the UK, Ireland and Switzerland and covering more than US$6 billion in overlaid assets. To qualify, a programme has to oversee at least US$10 million in equity capital, with approximately US$30 million in currency exposures managed on behalf of outside clients.

PGS does not reveal which funds are included in the index, but we can gather from its monthly public announcements that names such as FX Concepts, Bridgewater Associates, Gaia Corp., Goldman Sachs Asset Management, Millennium Global Partners, FX Quadrant, Coral Rock Investment, Lawrence Financial Ltd., and UBS Currency Funds are included. The Parker FX Index was launched in December 1996, but the historical index levels go back to 1986. PGS's president, Ms Virginia R. Parker, who developed the index, is well known for the Ferrell FX Index which was launched in late 1991. Table 3.1 gives recent performance data for all three Parker indexes (the data used in the table are also available on PGS's website at www.parkerglobal.com).

The Parker FX Index is based on a proprietary model developed by PGS to measure the unleveraged (risk-adjusted) performance of managers who invest in currencies as an asset class, and the company claims that it is the first to calculate pure currency alpha, or manager skill. The gist of the risk-adjustment process is to normalise the standard deviation of the returns of included programmes to 5% per annum. PGS applies its model to the performance of a representative currency portfolio or composite, net of fees and excluding interest (based on short-term US Treasury bill returns), for each currency manager.

Because of the deleveraging procedure, one can easily calculate Sharpe ratios from the data given in Table 3.1. Because returns in

Table 3.1 Historical performance of Parker Global Strategies FX indexes (%), January 1986 to February 2003

	Reported*			Risk-adjusted†		
	Parker FX Index	Parker Systematic Index	Parker Discretionary Index	Parker FX Index	Parker Systematic Index	Parker Discretionary Index
February 2003	0.16	0.05	0.44	0.03	−0.02	0.52
Year-to-date	2.61	3.40	0.45	1.28	1.34	0.38
Last 3 months	6.59	8.40	1.75	3.31	3.35	2.20
Last 6 months	5.18	6.07	3.18	2.40	2.27	3.85
Last 12 months	12.56	14.10	8.29	5.76	5.20	10.31
Last 24 months	15.82	17.06	12.23	6.41	5.72	13.44
Last 36 months	22.59	24.11	17.71	6.95	6.32	11.85

*Net of fees, including interest.
†Net of fees, excluding interest and scaled to a 5% volatility.
Source: Parker Global Strategies (reproduced with permission)

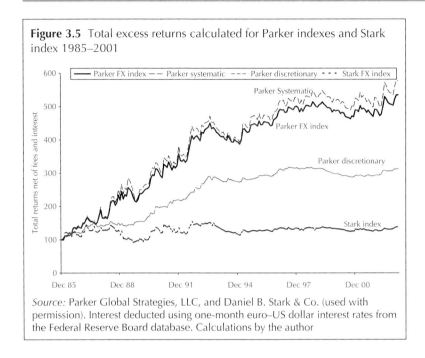

Figure 3.5 Total excess returns calculated for Parker indexes and Stark index 1985–2001

Source: Parker Global Strategies, LLC, and Daniel B. Stark & Co. (used with permission). Interest deducted using one-month euro–US dollar interest rates from the Federal Reserve Board database. Calculations by the author

the right-hand (risk-adjusted) panel attract a risk of 5% per annum, the Sharpe ratio is simply the annualised returns divided by 5%. The Sharpe ratios obtained are generally around 0.50–1.0, which is typical for currency overlay.

The Stark index has a similar composition with around 50 accounts covering US$5 billion in assets. The company does not keep a record of participating accounts but the number has been stable over the last few years. The index was launched in 1995 but historical levels go back to 1982. When an included account exits, the historical returns are not adjusted. The index is net of fees but, unlike the PGS indexes, is not adjusted for interest. Stark does not provide a risk-adjusted index or style sub-indices.

Figure 3.5 shows the historical performance of the three Parker indexes and the Stark index. The returns are net of fees and exclude US dollar interest rates, but they are not deleveraged using PGS's methodology.[5] The exclusion of interest has a significant impact on the long-term performance of the indices. Compared to the Parker indexes, the historical performance of the Stark index has been much lower, with an average monthly excess return of 0.26%.

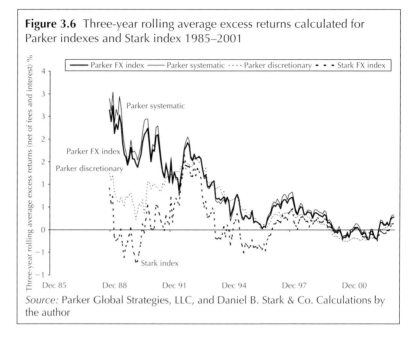

Figure 3.6 Three-year rolling average excess returns calculated for Parker indexes and Stark index 1985–2001

Legend: Parker FX index ——— Parker systematic ···· Parker discretionary – – Stark FX index

Source: Parker Global Strategies, LLC, and Daniel B. Stark & Co. Calculations by the author

Average monthly excess returns for the Parker indexes are between 0.60% and 1.00%. The discrepancy is probably due to the fact that the Parker indexes are equally weighted among the participating accounts whereas the Stark index is weighted by assets or capital. (It is worth noting that, if real, the discrepancy implies that large mandates or managers have not performed as well as smaller ones.)

We have also computed the three-year average excess returns for all four indexes, and the results are shown in Figure 3.6.[6] We can observe that, broadly, excess currency returns have been diminishing over the last 17 years. However, before we can draw any meaningful conclusions from this, we need to take a look at the corresponding risk levels embedded in such returns. Figure 3.7 shows the annualised three-year rolling standard deviations of excess returns, and it is easy to see that there has been a corresponding decrease in the return volatilities – probably the result of increasingly rigorous risk management practices employed by currency managers and, to a lesser extent, of a general decline in currency volatility over the period. One can also see that the risk levels are generally lower for discretionary styles.

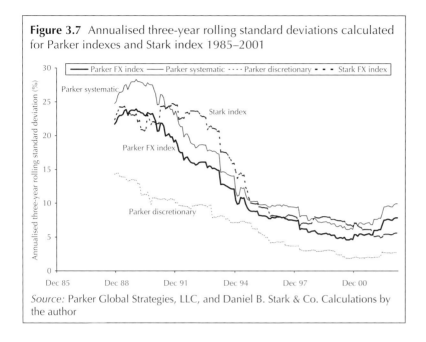

Figure 3.7 Annualised three-year rolling standard deviations calculated for Parker indexes and Stark index 1985–2001

Source: Parker Global Strategies, LLC, and Daniel B. Stark & Co. Calculations by the author

Combining the data in Figures 3.6 and 3.7, we can obtain rolling Sharpe ratios for the indices, and these are shown in Figure 3.8. In general, the curves are more likely to lie above zero than below, indicating the value enhancement provided by active currency management. There may have been a broad decline over time, but it is not as pronounced as in Figure 3.6. The risk-adjusted performance was poor between 1999 and 2002, largely coinciding with the period of the weak euro. It has staged a recovery since mid-2002, reverting to its historical average level of around 0.50 for the Parker indexes and 0.10 for the Stark index.

Finally, we calculated the correlations between these foreign exchange indices and indices on the underlying assets using monthly returns for the period 1993 to 2003. For equities we used MSCI EAFE equity indices in local currency, hedged and unhedged into US dollar and Japanese yen, and for bonds we used the Lehman Brothers' US Aggregate Index in US dollars, hedged and unhedged into Japanese yen. The results are presented in Table 3.2. We can see, in the shaded area, that the active currency returns generally have low correlation with the underlying asset returns, suggesting the benefit of diversification.

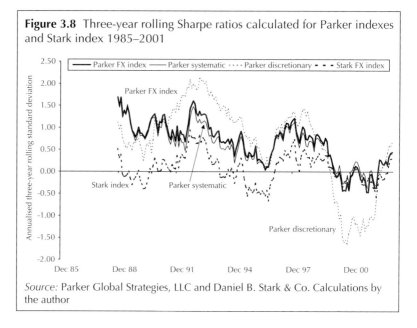

Figure 3.8 Three-year rolling Sharpe ratios calculated for Parker indexes and Stark index 1985–2001

Source: Parker Global Strategies, LLC and Daniel B. Stark & Co. Calculations by the author

Overall, the historical performance lends a degree of support to the deployment of active currency management. However, the Parker and Stark indexes cover a fairly small universe of the overlay management industry and many questions remain unanswered:

❑ What are the potential biases associated with small samples in particular and with such performance indexes in general?[7]
❑ What is the impact of mandate-specific constraints?
❑ What is a more appropriate deleveraging method?
❑ Should the interest be deducted before or after deleveraging?
❑ Are the risks and risk-adjusted returns different for different currency trading styles?

We can certainly expect better disclosure, better databases and more independent research in this area, in the same way that independent research on the performance of hedge funds thrived after better-quality performance data became available in recent years.

3.9 OUTSOURCING CURRENCY MANAGEMENT

There are no general rules on whether currency management should be outsourced or not as many factors come into play,

Table 3.2 Correlations (%) between foreign exchange index returns and underlying asset returns 1993–2003

	Parker FX	Parker Systematic	Parker Discretionary	Stark	MSCI EAFE LocCcy	EAFE Unhgd USD	EAFE Unhgd JPY	EAFE Hedged USD	EAFE Hedged JPY	Lehman Unhgd USD	Lehman Unhgd JPY	Lehman Hedged JPY
Parker FX	100	99	63	80	−3	0	−4	−4	−3	9	1	9
Parker Systematic		100	53	78	−3	−2	−3	−4	−3	7	3	8
Parker Discretionary			100	58	−1	7	−7	−2	−1	15	−7	17
Stark				100	−3	−1	−5	−4	−4	16	2	15
MSCI EAFE LocCcy					100	89	79	100	100	−7	3	−7
EAFE Unhgd USD						100	49	89	89	−5	−31	−4
EAFE Unhgd JPY							100	79	79	−5	60	−7
EAFE Hedged USD								100	100	−7	3	−8
EAFE Hedged JPY									100	−7	3	−8
Lehman Unhgd USD										100	29	99
Lehman Unhgd JPY											100	27
Lehman Hedged JPY												100

LocCcy, local currency; Unhgd, unhedged.

Source: Parker Global Strategies, LLC, and Daniel B. Stark & Co., MSCI, and Lehman Brothers (used with permission). Calculations by the author

113

including the size of the fund, its managers' core competencies, system capacity, restrictions imposed by existing mandates and so on. Many medium to large investment management firms outsource a portion of their exposure to external managers while keeping the rest managed by internal specialists as a basis for performance comparison. Financial theory suggests that internal managers may take on more total risk and/or relative risk than external managers because they are less likely to be replaced and that they are less likely to underperform a benchmark than external managers. These predictions have been substantiated by performance data for mutual fund managers but not yet for overlay managers (Elton, Gruber and Blake, 2001).

3.9.1 The overlay mandate

A currency overlay mandate, like other investment mandates, is a service-level agreement signed between the overlay manager and the investor. It specifies the scope of the currency management service provided to the investor by the overlay manager during a specific period of time. It is awarded by the investor to an overlay manager(s), often after a beauty parade. Pension fund trustees usually use the advice provided by consultants. Mandates are legally binding and renewable on expiry at the investor's discretion.

Apart from various legal inclusions and exclusions, an overlay mandate usually contains the following parts to specify how it is to be carried out:

❑ description of the service provided;
❑ description of both parties' obligations and limits on liabilities;
❑ description of the investment philosophy;
❑ description of how the overlay process takes place;[8]
❑ description of how third parties (such as counterparties to foreign exchange transactions and custodians) are involved;
❑ description of position restrictions;
❑ description of benchmarks and performance calculation methods;
❑ fees (typically a management fee plus a performance-related fee); and
❑ warning of risks.

A fictitious overlay mandate is shown in Appendix 3A as an example. Unfortunately the interesting parts – for example, details of trading models and historical performance – are contained in various annexes that are usually not made public.

3.9.2 Cost of currency overlay
Generally speaking, four main types of cost are associated with hedging currency exposure:

❏ management fees;
❏ transaction costs;
❏ opportunity costs; and
❏ the effect of the discount/premium of the forward contract.

3.9.2.1 Management fees
Management fees for overlay are around 15 basis points, with a range of 5–25 bp, depending on the size of the programme and the nature of the assignment. Trading and custody costs associated with currency hedging can total approximately 25 bp annually, some of which would be incurred irrespective of whether a currency overlay programme was in place. With the increased levels of commoditisation and competition in the currency markets, both management fees and trading costs have come down considerably during the last decade, although more recently there has been some stabilisation. Some overlay managers charge performance-related fees. On the other hand, some funds offer a "free" currency overlay service if clients choose the same fund for their underlying mandates. Here the management fee for the overlay service is, in effect, bundled together with that for the underlying portfolios.

3.9.2.2 Transaction costs
If a fund is thinking of running a currency overlay internally, it needs to estimate the transaction costs that may be involved. The question of transaction cost is not unique to foreign exchange trading and it has been investigated both theoretically and empirically. Historically, estimated transaction costs for an overlay programme typically ranged from 12 to 25 bp for execution, another 5–20 bp for settlement and around 10 bp for custody. But these figures have come down significantly in recent years, thanks to automation and competition. Current estimates are 3–15 bp for execution, 1–5 bp for settlement and 2–5 bp for custody.

Table 3.3 Bid–offer spreads (basis points) in spot rate, swaps and options

	Currency pair					
	EUR/ USD	USD/ JPY	GBP/ USD	EUR/ JPY	USD/ ZAR	USD/ MXN
Spot	1.7	1.7	1.8	2.1	30.6	4.8
One-month swap	0.1	0.1	0.1	0.1	1.8	2.6
One-month ATMF vanilla option						
Including spot/swap spread	3.3	3.3	3.3	3.3	74.0	11.5
Excluding spot/swap spread	2.3	2.3	2.3	2.3	57.3	8.0

ZAR, South African rand; MXN, Mexican peso; ATMF, at-the-money forward.

One main determinant of the transaction costs for a particular programme is its estimated trading volume, which obviously varies from fund to fund depending on its trading style. It is worth bearing in mind that certain foreign exchange trading costs may be incurred whether an overlay programme is used or not. Hence, only the extra trading volume associated with overlay should be included in a cost/benefit analysis for such a programme.

Table 3.3 shows the typical bid–offer spread for some commonly used foreign exchange instruments assuming normal market conditions and normal market size (up to US$30 million equivalent in euro/US dollar, US dollar/Japanese yen, sterling/US dollar and euro/Japanese yen and up to US$10 million equivalent in US dollar/ South African rand and US dollar/Mexican peso).

3.9.2.3 Opportunity cost

Some people use the term opportunity cost to refer to the fact that the investor might not always have sufficient cash reserves to settle currency forward contracts, in which case it might be necessary to liquidate other assets with higher expected returns. Of course, there will also be occasions when the investor experiences gains from settling forward contracts that can be applied to assets with higher expected returns. The problem is discussed in Chapter 9; in practice this cost is usually ignored.

Opportunity cost is also referred to in situations where, because a large trade can distort the market and give rise to liquidity cost, one executes a trade slowly to minimise the liquidity cost and as a result may miss an investment opportunity. This may be more relevant in equities markets than in foreign exchange as most trades can be comfortably accommodated.

3.9.2.4 Forward premium/discount
There is substantial empirical evidence to show that since 1973 the forward rate has systematically and significantly overestimated subsequent changes in the spot rate. On balance, hedgers have suffered losses when they sold currency forward contracts at a discount or purchased them at a premium. The topic is covered in Chapter 4, Section 4.5.1. Since the evidence is inconclusive, however, we think it should not be part of the cost consideration. Such systematic discrepancies may form the basis for strategic decisions by a fund if they are considered to present arbitrage opportunities. A forward bias-motivated programme of this type should be assessed separately in terms of its own returns and risks.

3.9.3 Evaluating the service
The evaluation of currency overlay managers follows the general rules used in evaluating other types of investment manager. We list a few specific points in this section. These are the key performance areas one needs to consider when selecting or evaluating an external overlay manager.

3.9.3.1 Track record
❏ Are there long-term, multi-currency track records?
❏ Are risk measures such as tracking error, overall risk reduction and worst performance provided?
❏ Are the performance results simulated?
❏ Are the performance results AIMR-PPS/GIPS or FRAG audited?[9]
❏ Can client references be provided? In particular, are there clients who have terminated overlay programmes?
❏ Can results be provided for several accounts with different base currencies, different passive hedge ratios, different benchmarks and different risk levels?

3.9.3.2 The organisation

❏ How long has the staff been there? Are the results, or have the results been, dependent on one person?

❏ Are the key members of staff experienced? What is the turnover of key members of staff?

❏ Does the team communicate effectively?

❏ Who owns the overlay management company and what profit-sharing schemes are in place?

3.9.3.3 Research

❏ Is there a clear mission statement on where and how potential market inefficiencies can be identified and explored to add value?

❏ What are the unique features of the approach?

❏ Is the approach supported by both academic and practical evidence?

❏ Is the data management sufficient? Robust? Is there enough capacity?

❏ Is the research conducted to reflect actual trading conditions? For example, transaction costs, *ex ante*, liquidity and so on.

❏ Are there established procedures to document and review research results?

3.9.3.4 Processes

❏ Is there an efficient process to implement strategies on each client portfolio in compliance with portfolio-specific mandate constraints?

❏ Is performance measured and attributed in a way that is unbiased and consistent?

❏ Are there processes and people to deal with client enquiries and other aspects of client services?

❏ Are there documented procedures and processes for risk management, in particular, of operational risks?

❏ Are client and transaction data properly backed up?

❏ Is there emergency back-up of, for example, people, systems, locations, etc.?

❏ Are there procedures to deal with potential conflicts of interest? For example, those arising from proprietary trading, trade

aggregation and allocation, commissions from trading counter-parties, etc. Is there a suitably qualified compliance officer?
❏ Is there effective separation between trading and administration?

3.10 TRADING STYLES

Overlay can be either active or passive. Active management styles can be classified further according to the trading style employed. Depending on what forms the *basis* of a currency decision, the trading style can be either technical or fundamental. And depending on *how* the decision is made, the trading style can be either discretionary or quantitative. The latter is also known as a black-box, systematic, or model-driven style. In practice, many overlay managers use a mix of all styles but with a certain emphasis. For example, a discretionary fundamental overlay manager may rely on macro-economic indicators for long-term positioning but use technical indicators for the timing of establishing the positions.

This choice of one style rather than another, along with the basis for the choice, is a central feature of currency overlay programmes and allows us to classify different overlay service providers according to their trading style. This is done in Figure 3.9, where we have plotted some of the largest using their stated currency investment objectives (these are summarised in Appendix 3B). The coordinates are those used in the classification of active management styles described in the previous paragraph: technical vs fundamental and discretionary vs quantitative.

One could also classify the commonly used trading indicators using the same figure. For example, technical models such as head-and-shoulder and relative strength index (RSI) belong to the top left-hand quadrant, whereas econometric models based on purchasing power parity (PPP) and its variants can be placed in the bottom right-hand quadrant.[10]

3.10.1 Avoiding style risk

Studies have shown that for most global portfolios based in US dollars, euros, sterling or yen, the main exposures are to the three other currencies in the group. In other words, the currency risk is highly concentrated, so it can be risky to leave all the currency exposures to a single-style overlay manager. If his style is out of

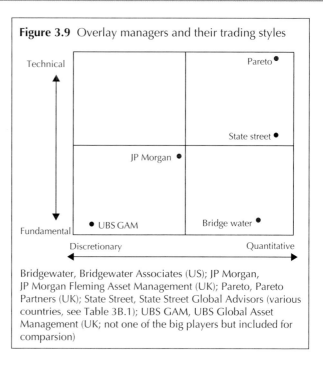

Figure 3.9 Overlay managers and their trading styles

Bridgewater, Bridgewater Associates (US); JP Morgan, JP Morgan Fleming Asset Management (UK); Pareto, Pareto Partners (UK); State Street, State Street Global Advisors (various countries, see Table 3B.1); UBS GAM, UBS Global Asset Management (UK; not one of the big players but included for comparsion)

synch with market movements, even temporarily, currency hedging may lead to heavy losses.

Many overlay managers use several styles at the same time to benefit from the potential diversification. This approach is similar to the "multi-style/manager" approach that has been gaining popularity in the equity/fixed-income investment community – leading the field here are Frank Russell Company and Northern Trust Global Investors. The logic of the approach lies in the assumption that the performance of a specific style is difficult to predict and that the length and depth of a style cycle are also unpredictable.[11] This may leave the portfolio overly exposed to a particular style.

In practice, several styles are combined to reduce style risk and improve consistency of performance. For instance, a black-box overlay manager may employ several styles, a couple of them based on momentum trading but differing in speed of response, another based on counter-trend signals and yet another based on volatility forecasting. By the same token, an investor may wish to divide his currency portfolio into two or three parts and hire more than one overlay manager to do the job. The disadvantage of this approach used to be cost, but with more players entering the currency overlay market and the widespread use of on-line dealing and straight-through processing the cost is expected to fall further.

3.11 OVERLAY AND PRIME BROKERAGE

Prime brokerage is a service that is typically provided by large investment banks. It allows the customers to deal with a host of third-party banks ("spoke" banks) in the name of the service-providing bank (the "hub" bank) using the latter's credit lines. In the US prime brokerage has been widely used by institutional managers, especially hedge funds and commodity trading advisors (CTAs), for several years, but it is quickly catching on in Europe and the Far East.

The advantages for a client of using a prime brokerage arrangement are obvious: much more efficient confirmation and settlement processes; centralised, and therefore more efficient, collateral management; and the need to negotiate and maintain only one set of legal documentation instead of many with a range of counterparties. Its disadvantages include the increased visibility of client positions – which have to be reported to both hub and spoke banks – though this can usually be dealt with by a confidentiality agreement between the relevant parties, and the concentration of credit risk. Fees charged by hub banks are relatively low – typically US$10–20 per US$1 million face value.

Figure 3.10 illustrates the structure of a foreign exchange prime brokerage service. Although not shown in the diagram, the hub bank can be one of the spoke banks too. The hub bank receives a fee income for the use of its balance sheet and trade management facility. And the spoke banks can do business with counterparties where otherwise they might not be willing to take on the credit exposure.

The combination of prime brokerage and currency overlay is only starting to gain acceptance.[12] Looking at the overlay process depicted in Figure 3.3, it is clear that an overlay manager may have to manage relationships with multiple funds (the clients) as well as multiple banks. In some cases, a currency overlay mandate may include clauses specifying which banks are to be used for the

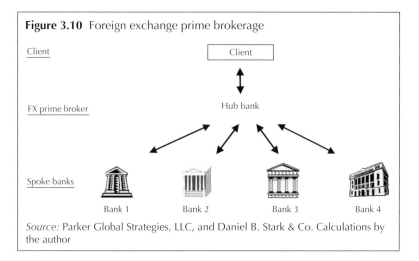

Figure 3.10 Foreign exchange prime brokerage

Client

Client

FX prime broker

Hub bank

Spoke banks

Bank 1   Bank 2   Bank 3   Bank 4

Source: Parker Global Strategies, LLC, and Daniel B. Stark & Co. Calculations by the author

foreign exchange transactions. As the number of mandates increases, the manager has to navigate an increasingly complex web of banking relationships, each costly and time-consuming to establish and maintain. Furthermore, a currency overlay operation can be exposed to a large settlement risk as running overlay typically involves opening and closing many forward positions. Worse, the opening and closing of a particular position is often done with different banks to make it more difficult for others to "read" one's moves. Such actions result in large cashflow movements between the custodian bank and the relationship banks during settlement and therefore create settlement risk.

These practical difficulties in running currency overlay can be solved or alleviated by having a foreign exchange prime broker in whose name the client conducts all currency trades. In this scenario, the client has only one foreign exchange relationship bank, the hub bank, whose credit risk the client bears. At the same time, the client continues to enjoy the liquidity and competition provided by the spoke banks. Settlement risk on the client side is largely eliminated as it (or its custodian bank) has to settle net only with the hub bank. Implementing and running a currency overlay is therefore greatly simplified. As shown in the lower part of Figure 3.11, the negotiation can be standardised between different clients (and their custodian banks), the same overlay manager and

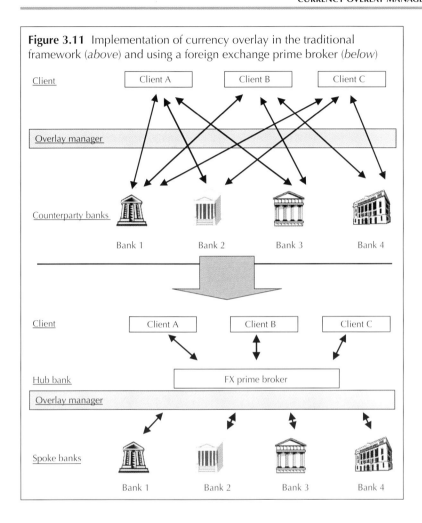

Figure 3.11 Implementation of currency overlay in the traditional framework (*above*) and using a foreign exchange prime broker (*below*)

the same prime brokerage bank. In the traditional framework, the negotiation would be between different clients, the overlay manager and a host of different foreign exchange counterparty banks, as in the upper part of Figure 3.11.

APPENDIX 3A: A TYPICAL OVERLAY MANDATE

THIRD-PARTY MANAGED ACCOUNT AGREEMENT

between

MILLENNIUM ASSET MANAGEMENT LIMITED
(Manager)

and

MILLENNIUM GLOBAL INVESTMENTS LIMITED
(Investment Manager)

and

CLIENT

Millennium Asset Management Limited	Millennium Global Investments Limited
P O Box 100	5th Floor
Sydney Vane House	64 St James's Street
Admiral Park	London SW1A 1LY
St Peter Port	Tel: 44 207 663 8900
Guernsey GY1 3EL	
Tel: 44 1481 739 930	

This THIRD-PARTY **MANAGED ACCOUNT AGREEMENT** dated XXX, (the "Agreement") is made by and between **MILLENNIUM GLOBAL INVESTMENTS LIMITED** of 64 St James's Street, London, SW1 1NF (the "Investment Manager"), **MILLENNIUM ASSET MANAGEMENT LIMITED** of P O Box 100, Sydney Vane House, Admiral Park, St Peter Port, Guernsey, GY1 3EL (the "Manager") hereafter collectively referred to as "Millennium" and **CLIENT,** of XXX (the "Client").

WHEREAS, the Client appoints the Manager and Investment Manager to carry out contingent liability transactions, the risks of which are outlined in Appendix A the currency overlay programme shall be referred to hereafter as "Investment Account". The initial size of the investment account is outlined in Appendix A.

WHEREAS, the Client desires to retain Millennium as the Client's Investment Advisor for the trading activities set forth herein pursuant to the terms and conditions set forth in this Agreement, Millennium desires to service the Client pursuant to such terms and conditions and such terms and conditions being therefore applicable both, singly as well as jointly, to Millennium Global Investments Limited and Millennium Asset Management Limited unless otherwise specified in this Agreement.

NOW, THEREFORE, in consideration of the premises set forth above, the parties hereto hereby agree as follows:

1) **AUTHORISATION TO MILLENNIUM TO ENTER ORDERS FOR THE ACCOUNT**. The Client appoints Millennium as its sole attorney-in-fact with respect to the Account to buy, sell or otherwise trade in currencies and in currency options thereon in such amounts, at such prices and at such time as Millennium may determine, subject to the Initial and Subsequent Account Size. The Client hereby gives and grants to Millennium full power and authority to act for the Client and on the Client's behalf to do every act and thing whatsoever requisite, necessary or appropriate to be done in connection with this power of attorney as fully and in the same manner and with the same force and effect as the Client might do or could do if personally present, and the Client hereby ratifies all that Millennium may lawfully do or cause to be done by virtue of this power of attorney so long as leverage limits in Section 3 hereof are complied with.

Millennium shall have discretionary authority to make all trading decisions for the Account, without prior consultation with the Client and without prior notice to the Client with respect to such trading decisions.

Millennium acknowledges and agrees that Millennium is not authorised to transfer or cause to be paid or delivered to third parties or to itself/herself/himself any securities or other property held in the Account, except within Millennium's authority to complete a transaction as described in this agreement.

Any and all transactions effected by Millennium for the Account shall be subject to the constitution, by-laws, rules, regulations, orders, and customs and usage's of the exchange or market where executed (and of its clearinghouse, if any), and to the applicable provisions of federal, state, and provincial law and to the rules, regulations, and orders promulgated from time to time thereunder. Millennium shall not be liable to the Client as a result of any action taken by Millennium which is necessary to comply with any such constitution, by-law, rule, regulation, order, custom, usage, act, or statute.

Under the United Kingdom Financial Services and Markets Act 2000 the Investment Manager is a member of the Financial Services Authority ("FSA") and, as such, is regulated by the FSA. The Manager acknowledges and agrees that the Manager has a full understanding of the nature and suitability of the investment in which the Investment Manager is likely to invest on behalf of the Client and the potential risks, if any, involved with these investments. The Manager agrees that the Investment Manager, its representatives or employees may call upon the Manager by telephone, or otherwise communicate orally with the Manager, without express invitation and that the Manager will forfeit any right conferred by section 56 of the Financial Services and Markets Act 2000 to treat as unenforceable any investment agreement entered into in the course of, or in consequence of, such a call.

The Investment Manager, Manager may not hold any Client investments or Client monies. In the event that any investments are received by the Investment Manager or Manager and any monies received by the Investment Manager or Manager as a result of the realisation of any Investments shall be transferred to the clearing broker (or such other person or entity, from time to time providing clearing services to the Manager and/or to the Client on behalf of the Manager) appointed by the Client. The monies and assets of the Account will be held by the clearing broker and/or its nominees and will be registered in the name of the Client, or in the name of the nominees of the clearing broker for the account of the clearing broker on behalf of the Client.

With respect to the trades in currencies and currency options made on behalf of the Account the sum of the long positions in all currencies and delta equivalent for options on currencies shall not exceed the Account Size.

2) **REPRESENTATION OF CLIENT**. The Client represents and warrants that (i) the Client has full power and authority to execute and deliver this Agreement and to purchase, sell, trade and

own currencies as contemplated by this Agreement and the individuals executing and delivering this Agreement for and on behalf of the Client have full power and authority to do so on behalf of the Client and (ii) this Agreement has been duly and validly authorised, executed and delivered on behalf of the Client and is a valid and binding agreement of the Client enforceable in accordance with its terms.

3) **REPRESENTATION OF MILLENNIUM**. Millennium represents and warrants that (i) Millennium has full power and authority to enter into this Agreement and to perform its obligations and provide the services required of it under this Agreement and (ii) this Agreement has been duly and validly authorised, executed and delivered on behalf of the Millennium and is a valid and binding agreement of Millennium enforceable in accordance with its terms.

4) **FEES**. The Client agrees that fees will be paid as follows:
   a) *Management Fee.* In consideration of and in compensation for the management services to be rendered by Millennium to the Account under this Agreement, the Management Fee, which is calculated monthly, shall be taken as a percentage of the Account's programme size payable monthly in arrears. For the purposes of this agreement the Management Fee is equal to XXX basis points of the programme size per annum.

Incentive Fee. In consideration of and in compensation for the management services to be rendered by Millennium to the Account under this Agreement, XXX basis points of any net profit achieved on currency trades in a calendar quarter (the first commencing XXX); high water mark and loss carry forward will apply whereby any net loss in an accounting period has to be made good in the subsequent period or periods before performance fee can be earned; payable quarterly.

   b) If this Agreement shall be terminated on a date other than at the end of a quarter, Management and Incentive Fees shall be calculated as if such termination date were the end of the quarter. The Client shall be billed for Management Fees and Incentive Fees accrued to the date of such termination and the Client's obligation to pay future fees shall terminate.

The Client shall not be entitled to a refund of any Management Fees and Incentive Fees paid or accrued to the date of the termination of this Agreement.

c) Following the end of each quarter, Millennium shall send to the Client a statement for Management Fees and/or Incentive Fees that are due and owing to Millennium. A statement shall be deemed sent to the Client upon Millennium sending an e-mail to the Client and depositing such statement in the mail in a first-class, postage pre-paid envelope addressed to the Client and shall be deemed delivered to the Client personally whether actually received or not. A statement shall be deemed correct and shall be conclusive and binding on the Client unless a written or verbal objection from the Client has been received by Millennium within ten business days after the statement has been mailed by Millennium.

d) Millennium acknowledges and agrees that all fees will be calculated in the Client's base currency, XXX. Should Millennium request payment of fees in a currency other than XXX, the Client's month-end rate will be used for conversion and subsequent payment. Therefore for the purposes of the agreement, Millennium will be issued fee payments in XXX.

5) **TERMS AND CONDITIONS FOR TERMINATION**. This Agreement shall terminate upon 90 days written notice to the other party. Notice shall be deemed given on the close of business on the day such notice is actually received by Millennium or the Client. Termination shall be effective on the date such written notice is given pursuant to Section 13 of this Agreement. If either party terminates this Agreement, Incentive Fees shall be calculated (and, if due, paid) as if the termination date of the Account were the end of the calendar quarter. Upon delivery of a termination notice, open positions in the Client's Account will be liquidated as expeditiously as reasonably possible. When this Agreement is terminated by the Client pursuant to this Section 5, the Client shall be liable for all costs, expenses and losses incurred in liquidating open positions upon termination.

6) MANAGEMENT OF OTHER ACCOUNTS BY MILLENNIUM; TRADING BY MILLENNIUM FOR ITS OWN ACCOUNT(S).

a) The services rendered hereunder are not exclusive and the Client acknowledges that Millennium presently advises and manages other client accounts and intends to do so in the future. Millennium reserves the right to charge different fees from those described above for other accounts for which it directs trading. Millennium and its principal(s) may also trade for their own account(s) as allowed under all applicable laws and agree that the Client can have reasonable transparency, which may include trade details specific to Millennium's own accounts.

b) The Investment Manager will place orders for the execution of transactions on behalf of the Client on a net best execution basis. Net best execution is a combination of commission rates and prompt, reliable execution. Brokers may be paid an above average commission for superior or difficult execution. Consistent with the policy of seeking the net best execution, the Investment Manager may, in allocating brokerage, take account of the research capabilities of the various brokerage firms with whom the Manager or the Client has established appropriate accounts and credit alliance. Research services (which are not soft commissions) furnished by brokers through whom the Investment Manager affects transactions may be used by the Investment Manager in servicing other accounts, and not all such services may be used by the Investment Manager for the benefit of the Manager or the Client which pays the brokerage commission which results in the receipt of such research services. The Manager, on behalf of the Client, authorises the Investment Manager to bunch or aggregate orders for the account of the Client with orders of other managers and to allocate the aggregate amount of the investment between the Client and other customers in the manner in which the Investment Manager shall deem appropriate, providing that the allocation is in accordance with fair allocation rules set up by the FSA and that any obligations on the part of the Client arising from the transaction, or limited to the Client's *pro rata* share of the transaction.

c) The Investment Manager may place a large order to purchase or sell a particular investment for the account of the Client and the accounts of several other managers. Because of the prevailing trading activity, it is frequently not possible to receive the same price, rate or execution on the entire volume of investments purchased or sold. When this occurs, the various prices may be averaged and the Client will be charged or credited with the average price or rate and the effect of the aggregation may operate, on some occasions, to the disadvantage of the Client. Although, in such an instance, the Client will be charged the average price or rate, the Investment Manager will make the underlying records reflecting the actual transaction available to the Client and the Manager upon request of the Client or the Manager. The Investment Manager, however, is not required to bunch or aggregate orders.

d) The Investment Manager is not permitted to act as a principal to any transaction with or on behalf of the Manager or the Client.

e) The Investment Manager may not enter into soft dollar arrangements with brokers prior to receiving consent from the Client and the Manager

7) **GOVERNING LAW.** This Agreement shall be governed by, and construed in accordance with the law under which the Adviser's business is organised as set forth in the first paragraph of this Agreement, that is Guernsey. The Client acknowledges and agrees however that to the extent the Adviser delegate's power and authority hereunder to a Sub-adviser, the laws and regulations applicable to such a Sub-adviser's activities that is England will apply to the Sub-adviser's activities for the Investment Account.

8) **ASSIGNMENT.** This Agreement shall not be assignable by any party without the written consent of the other party.

9) **DURATION AND TERMINATION.** After the first anniversary, this Agreement may be terminated at any time by either party upon 90 days written notice. The Client will pay the fees of the Adviser prorated to the date of termination and provided that the Client shall honour any trades entered but not settled before the date of any such termination.

Upon termination, except as the Client may otherwise direct, the Investment Account will be liquidated in an orderly manner and the assets therein after settlement of all amounts outstanding from such account shall be transferred to the Client.

10) **SECTION HEADINGS.** The section headings in the Agreement are for convenience of reference only and shall not be deemed to interpret or modify the provisions of this Agreement.

11) **ENTIRE AGREEMENT.** This Agreement contains the entire understandings between Millennium and the Client with respect to the Millennium matters described herein; is intended to be a complete and exclusive expression of this Agreement; and supersedes any other agreements or understandings of the parties with respect to such Millennium matters.

12) **AMENDMENTS/SEVERABILITY.** This Agreement may not be altered, amended or modified without the signed written consent of each party.

No provision of this Agreement may be amended or waived unless such amendment or waiver is in writing and signed by the parties. No amendment or waiver of any provision of this Agreement may be implied from any course of dealing between the parties or from the failure of either party to assert his or its rights under this Agreement on any occasion or series of occasions.

If any provision of this Agreement is, or at any time shall become, inconsistent with any present or future law, rule, regulation, or ruling of any jurisdiction, court, or regulatory body, exchange, or board having jurisdiction, such provision shall be deemed rescinded or modified to conform to such law, rule, regulation, or ruling and the remaining provisions of this Agreement shall not be affected thereby and shall remain in full force and effect.

13) **NOTICES.** Any notices required to be given shall be in writing and sent by (i) e-mail to mgibson-stark@millenniumglobal.com and dgirard@fundmanagement.net and (ii) certified or regis-tered mail, return receipt requested, overnight courier or facsimile (provided receipt is confirmed by telephone) to Millennium at 64 St James's Street, London SW1A 1NF, England, Attention: Maria Gibson-Stark and to the Client by (i) e-mail: xxx and (ii) certified or registered mail, return receipt requested overnight courier at Client xxx, (provided receipt is

confirmed by telephone). Either party may change its address by giving notice in writing to the other party stating the new address. Commencing on the tenth (10th) day after the giving of such notice, such newly designated address shall be the party's address for the purpose of all notices or communications required or permitted to be given pursuant to this Agreement.

14) **CONFIDENTIALITY.** The Client understands that the trading method employed by Millennium is proprietary and that the advice provided hereunder by Millennium is for the exclusive use of the Client. The Client agrees not to disclose any of Millennium's trading recommendations, advice or analysis to any third party without Millennium's prior written consent. The Client agrees to treat all such communication related to the Account as confidential. Millennium may become privy to confidential and proprietary information of Client, including its affiliates and clients, while rendering its services to the Client, Millennium agrees to treat all such information as confidential. This clause shall survive the term of this agreement.

15) Millennium's obligation hereunder is to act in good faith and due care and not responsible for any act or omission hereunder in the absence of willful misconduct or negligence.

IN WITNESS WHEREOF, the parties hereto have caused this Managed Account Agreement to be duly executed by their respective authorised representatives as of the date above written.

CLIENT

By:
Title:

By:
Title:

MILLENNIUM ASSET MANAGEMENT LIMITED

By:
Title:

MILLENNIUM GLOBAL INVESTMENTS LIMITED

By:
Title:

Appendix A: Investment guidelines and additional powers and disclosures

Investment Objective

The investment objective of the overlay programme is twofold:

a) **Primary objective**

Millennium will seek to strategically hedge Client's portfolio of US Dollar based Hedge Funds into Swiss Francs. The primary objective being to negate the risk associated with the implicit US $ underlying exposure. It is anticipated that this will be achieved by use of a forward and options hedging programme that will incur certain costs.

b) **Secondary objective**

Millennium will also pursue a moderate active currency risk exposure management in order to seek positive returns and cover costs of the strategic hedge, and opportunistically add value.

c) **Aggressiveness factor**

It is understood that the degree of aggressiveness of the secondary objective will be moderate. As such, this proposal and its related constraints (see hereunder) have been designed not to add material volatility to the underlying investments into the US dollar hedge fund of funds, which is expected to be the main source of active returns.

There can be no assurance that the above investment objectives will be achieved. Furthermore, the value of the Investment Account may fall as well as rise. The types of transactions, which it is anticipated the Adviser will effect for the Client, may result in losses.

Investment guidelines and benchmark

Performance will be reported on a monthly basis in the following way:

❏ Benchmark Performance: 100% hedge into Swiss Francs
❏ Maximum Deviation from   40%
   Benchmark:
❏ Excess Performance: Millennium's Activity minus Benchmark

❏ Benchmark Calculation: Benchmark is one month short $,
                             long Swiss francs is monitored by
                             a separate Benchmark account
                             where we fully hedge the
                             underlying account size from the
                             customer using a 100% hedged
                             sell US dollars against Swiss
                             francs rolled over on a monthly
                             basis.

The Adviser is hereby granted and shall have full power and discretionary authority to enter into transactions for and to invest and
re-invest the assets constituting the Investment Account in such a
manner as it may deem appropriate given the objectives of the
Client including, but not limited to, the authority to trade, buy, sell
or otherwise acquire, hold or dispose of the following instruments:

Permitted currencies
The Investment Account can invest in any of the currencies held by
the "Client" account and cross/proxy hedge in any of the following currencies:

Europe:	Swiss Franc
	Euro
	Sterling
	Danish Krone
	Norwegian Krone
	Swedish Krona
Dollar Block:	US Dollar
	Canadian Dollar
	Australian Dollar
Other Currencies:	Japanese Yen

Maximum exposure constraints
Following discussions in reference to acceptable risk/return objectives with client, we are suggesting constraining the maximum net
deviation from benchmark in the following way:

1. 50% Euro
2. 40% Canadian Dollar
          Sterling
3. 30% Japanese Yen

4. 25% Danish Krone
         Norwegian Krone
         Swedish Krona
5. 15% Australian Dollar

Symmetric mandate
Authorised maximum: 140% Swiss Franc

Instruments
1. Spot and forward currency contracts   Authorised
2. Currency option contracts   Authorised
3. Futures   Not authorised
4. Emerging Currencies   Not authorised

Programme size
❏ Currency Overlay Programme: up to US dollar XXX million
❏ The currency of the Investment Account for reporting purposes
  shall be Swiss Francs.
❏ The net aggregate size of open currency forward contracts and
  currency option positions measured on a net delta cash equivalent basis must not exceed the programme size, at the point of
  trade inception, safe for opportunistic hedging into Swiss Francs
  which is authorised up to 140% of mandate size.
❏ The Client may adjust the programme size from time to time on
  prior written notice to the Adviser.

Reconciliation's and valuations
Provided on a monthly basis, and agreed with the Prime Broker.

APPENDIX 3B: CURRENCY OVERLAY SERVICES – THE BIG PLAYERS

Due to its technical requirements and economies of scale, the specialist currency overlay market is dominated by a handful of big
players. Table 3B.1 lists the main firms based on the information we
have collected in mid-2003. Russell Mellon Analytical Services and
a few pension funds consultancy firms maintain databases on the
performance and other details of overlay managers/accounts, the
access to which requires a fee. The rapid expansion of on-line foreign exchange dealing, the spread of foreign exchange modelling

Table 3B.1 Main players in the external currency overlay services market

Company	Currency only	Remarks
A.G. Bisset & Co.	Y	Return seeking and highly systematic. Models based on price history.
Barclays Global Investors	N	Mainly return seeking. Mainly systematic.
BNY Overlay Associates	Y	Mainly risk control. Highly systematic.
Bridgewater Associates, Inc	N	Return seeking and highly systematic. Models based on price history. Fundamental based models.
Credit Suisse Asset Management	N	Mainly return seeking. Mainly discretionary.
First Quadrant Limited	N	Return seeking. Mainly fundamental.
FX Concepts	Y	Mainly risk control but account dependant. Both systematic and discretionary.
Gartmore Investment Management plc	N	Mainly return seeking. Systemic. Models based on fundamentals.
GK Investment Management	Y	Mainly risk control. Systematic. Models based on price history.
Goldman Sachs Asset Management International	N	Mainly return seeking. Discretionary with model-based output. Both fundamental and technical.
JP Morgan Fleming Asset Management	N	Mainly return seeking. Both fundamental and technical. Both systematic and discretionary.
Lee Overlay Partners Limited	Y	Return seeking. Mainly fundamental. Both systematic and discretionary.
Mellon Capital Management	N	Mainly return seeking. Mainly systematic, based interest rate differentials.
Millennium Asset Management Limited	Y	Mainly return seeking. Mainly fundamental. Mainly discretionary.

Table 3B.1 (continued)

Company	Currency only	Remarks
Overlay Asset Management	Y	Mainly return seeking. Highly systematic. Models based on historical prices and implied volatility.
Pareto Partners	N	Mainly risk control. Highly systematic.
Principal Global Investors	N	Mainly return seeking. Both systematic and discretionary. Both fundamental and technical.
Putnam Investments	N	Mainly return seeking. Mainly fundamental.
Record Currency Management Limited	Y	Mainly risk control. Highly systematic. A form of option replication.
Windham Capital Management	Y	Main return seeking but also offer risk control programme. Highly systematic. Models based on interest rate differentials and momentum.
State Street Global Advisors UK Limited	N	Mainly return seeking. Both technical and fundamental. Systematic.

Source: Parker Global Strategies, Russell Mellon Analytical Services, company websites

capacity, the availability of both market and performance data and extra services provided by custodian banks and/or prime broker- age services (which are necessary for overlay programmes) may help to bring down the entry barrier in this market.

Below we take a brief look at the investment philosophies of the several large players in the specialist overlay market. Much of this material was taken directly from the companies' marketing litera- ture and websites. Their models and historical performances are, however, proprietary.

3B.1 Bridgewater associates

❏ 25 years' experience of running currency overlay. Currently man- age approximately US$31 billion in currency overlay portfolios,

US$14 billion as pure overlays and US$17 billion together with the underlying assets.

❑ The overlay process is fundamental and systematic.

❑ Indicators include relative inflation rates, relative real growth rates, relative external account balances, relative interest rates, and global capital flows.

❑ Manages currency overlay on a variety of benchmarks, including fully hedged, unhedged, partially hedged and options-hedged.

❑ Company website: www.bridgewaterassociates.com. Site has research articles on currency risk management, including on emerging market currencies.

3B.2 JP Morgan Fleming asset management

❑ Exploits market inefficiencies through fundamental and technical analysis.

❑ Combines quantitative model with qualitative input from research and portfolio management teams, partly discretionary, partly model-driven.

❑ Models to quantify the degree of over- or undervaluation for a particular currency pair by looking at the demand for goods and assets between two counties.

❑ Technical model gives short-term trend indicator.

❑ Qualitative indicators include central bank interventions, political events, mergers and acquisitions, and global investment impacts.

❑ Core strategies are tailored to each account based on the client's hedging benchmark, base currency, target return, risk profile and investment guidelines.

❑ US$18.7 billion in external active currency overlay assets as of end of 2002.

❑ Company website: jpmorganfleming.chase.com.

3B.3 Pareto partners

❑ Founded 1991, assets under management US$31.8 billion as of the end of 2002.

❑ Investment philosophy on currency management: value is added by controlling risk of loss.

❑ Believes that the global currency market is inefficient in risk/return terms due to the de-synchronisation of global economies and the different investment objectives of major market participants. Also believes that it is not possible to forecast currency returns, with any consistency, over the short term (less than two years).

❏ Focuses on estimating and managing the currency risk embedded in international investment portfolios rather than attempting to forecast future currency returns.

❏ Statistical model-based approach designed to capture the upside while controlling of risk of loss. An improved version of dynamic hedging.

❏ No subjective override is permitted within the modelling process.

❏ The trading team closely monitors counterparty risk and transactions are evenly distributed among counterparties for efficient execution and to minimise market impact.

3B.4 State street global advisors

❏ Believes that currencies as an asset class behave very differently than bonds and equities and that an active manager can capitalise on the inefficiencies inherent in these markets and add value to an international portfolio over time.

❏ Believes that an active approach works better than a dynamic hedging or option-based approach.

❏ Uses both technical and fundamental indicators. The first is based on historical price patterns through data mining. The second is based on the historic relationship between economic data and currency prices.

❏ Two types of model: one a trend model and the other a so-called "fair value" model.

❏ A rule-based system brings the model outputs together and sets portfolio positioning. Over- or underweight and the size of those positions are driven by the strength of signals.

❏ Positions are adjusted with currency volatility levels.

❏ Aims to add 150–200 basis points yearly to international portfolios.

❏ Company website: www.ssga.com. Contains research articles and periodic market summaries.

3.B.5 Millennium asset management limited

❏ Started offering active currency overlay service since 1994. Also offer a total return programme for investors seeking currency risk.

❏ Its currency overlay programme is designed to protect the value of foreign investments in periods of base currency appreciation, and tactically seek to add value through diversifying and/or cross hedging, within a client's defined constraints.

❏ Investment philosophy centres around the analysis of relative fundamental factors to help determine future market trends, combined with market dynamics analysis to focus entry and exit discipline.

❏ Quantitative techniques are used for portfolio construction. Stops are used with discipline to limit excessive losses.

❏ Company website is www.fundmanagement.net.

1   Some might ask what is the point of having such an overlay on top of the asset allocation process, which is supposed to be the core investment decision anyway. This type of derivative overlay approach was proposed a decade or so back when the use of derivatives was not as widespread and the asset allocation was achieved through cash instruments. A separate derivative overlay could then take advantage of various benefits the derivatives contracts had to offer while keeping the "derivatives risks" centralised. Nowadays derivatives risk is treated as part of the portfolio risks. The understanding, availability and usage of derivatives contracts have all improved significantly. There is little need to run a separate derivatives overlay.

2   A pure currency fund (many traditional fund managers as well as some hedge fund managers offer such funds) seeks excess return by investing in various currencies via different cash or derivatives instruments. Currency funds are sometimes distinguished by whether they invest exclusively in mature currencies (G7 or G10) or emerging market currencies. The fund will generally declare its risk control parameters but rarely restricts its investment to certain currencies or currency pairs beyond the aforementioned currency groups (mature or emerging currencies or both). It can usually leverage its positions as well.

These two aspects of pure currency funds are different from those of a currency overlay fund. The latter is normally restricted to dealing in predefined currencies in which underlying investments are made, and it is usually not allowed to take on leveraged positions either. (There are other differences too: for example, an overlay fund may be able to go short on a currency but not go long. This so-called "asymmetrical mandate" problem is discussed in Chapter 6, Section 6.9.4.) The impact of leverage can be dealt with if – admittedly a big "if" – performance from the currency funds is properly deleveraged (ie, using risk-adjusted returns). And the restrictions on currencies or currency pairs, as long as they are not too stringent, are unlikely to materially influence the performance of overlay funds either because the permitted currencies are usually G7 or G10 currencies anyway and trades in a restricted currency pair can usually be replicated by trades in permitted currency pairs. Therefore we are of the view that the performance of currency overlay funds should generally be comparable with the performance of pure currency funds. However, this is an area has not been thoroughly researched. In practice, we have come across some extremely restrictive currency overlay mandates, sometimes due to outdated statutory requirements, sometimes due to a lack of understanding of trustees. Clearly, the performance of overlay funds can be materially affected in such cases. We observe, however, that the general trend is to a gradual loosening or removal such restrictions (which are replaced by other risk control measures).

3 "Currency weary funds look to outsource FX headache" by Christina Fincher, Reuters, October 26, 2001.

4 Available at, respectively, www.parkerglobal.com and www.starkonline.com.

5 We have made adjustments to the Stark index to exclude interest using one-month euro–US interest rates.

6 The choice of the three-year horizon for evaluation is arbitrary. Over how long a period a currency manager's performance should be measured is an actively debated question. Three years is a fairly common choice, being the mean of the typical range of between one and five years. The fact that a fund manager's "career horizon" – how long on average he spends in the same job – is about the same length is probably more than coincidental.

7 We will discuss the general problems associated with performance-based indexes in Chapter 6, Section 6.10.

8 This part can be detailed and very technical. As illustrated in Figures 3.3 and 3.4, it may include specifications on how and when the exposure data are collected and by whom; how the data are transmitted to the overlay manager; how the decisions on currency positions are taken by the overlay managers; how the trading process works – in most cases, overlay managers deal with third-party banks *on behalf of* the investor rather than as a principal, and this needs to be clarified; how the settlement process takes place between overlay managers, custodian, third-party banks and the investor; how the trading positions are monitored and by whom; how the investor is kept updated on trading performance; how the periodic performance evaluation is carried out; how fees are calculated and collected; etc.

9 AIMR-PPS/GIPS refers to the Global Investment Performance Standards (GIPS), which are part of the AIMR's Performance Presentation Standards (PPS). PPS, of which GIPS is a part, are created and promoted by the AIMR and used by investment managers for creating performance presentations that ensure fair representation and full disclosure. The standards allow investors to directly compare the performance of different investment managers and help to build an environment of credibility and trust in the investment industry. Many countries have their locally adopted version of GIPS that is endorsed by AIMR. More information is available at www.aimr.com/standards/pps/pps.html. Likewise FRAG, the Financial Reporting and Auditing Group of the Institute of Chartered Accountants in England and Wales, puts out guidance and technical releases on professional standards. Further information is available at www.icaew.co.uk.

10 We thank Tom Clarke of UBS Global Asset Management for the suggestion. See Luca (2000) for definitions and examples of head-and-shoulder and RSI.

11 A style cycle is a period of time over which a specific style is useful, very useful, not useful and, sometimes, even terrible.

12 FX Concepts, a currency overlay specialist, was one of the earlier proponents of the combination of prime brokerage and currency overlay services. See Simotas (2002) and also www.fxconcepts.com for further information.

4

Foreign Exchange Research and the Choice of Currency Management Style

4.1 INTRODUCTION

What determines foreign exchange rates is an ancient question and, because of the changing conditions in global goods and capital markets, it is also a constantly evolving question. Possibly there never will be an answer – until we have a single world currency at any rate.

In the realm of modern investment management, where numbers and charts seem to carry much more weight than philosophies, theories or intuitions, investors typically rely on the results of quantitative analysis to choose a foreign exchange trading style: fundamental vs technical, or discretionary vs systematic. Some may also rely on the result of foreign exchange research to decide on a management approach: passive, active or dynamic. Paradoxically, the sheer multitude of academic research papers and practical studies in this area presents a barrier to many investors, and there are a number of reasons for this:

❏ most academic studies set out to prove or disprove certain macroeconomic or financial propositions (for example, the efficient market hypothesis), and their relevance to practical day-to-day decision-making in investment management is not obvious.
❏ many practical works in this field are too narrowly focused. Some, often those conducted by practitioners, have too much of

the sales pitch about them and lack objectivity. Others, aiming to uncover arbitrage opportunities, do not incorporate real-life constraints – for instance, that all decisions have to be taken *ex ante*, transaction costs need to be included, positions may have to be squared if risk limits are broken, or that one may not be able to transact at prices broadcast by information vendors, etc. One therefore has to treat these results with due scepticism.

❑ perhaps more importantly, despite the effort of generations of economists (from a variety of fields such as international economics, financial economics, behavioural economics and many more), statisticians, nuclear physicists, chartists, computer geeks, investment gurus, central bankers, minor speculators, astrologists and so on,[1] we are still debating some of the most basic questions, such as whether currency behaviour is predictable or whether currency is an asset class.

Our aim in this chapter is a modest one. We do not attempt to outsmart many of the authors referred to – which would be a tall order. Instead we adopt a practical approach that is firmly based on what has been reiterated many times in this book as our core tenet: *currency risk is real, it ought to be separated out from other risks, and someone should be made responsible for dealing with it.* So in this chapter we attempt to present a balanced account of some of the studies that have been done, including a consideration of the methodologies, and look at whether the findings can be incorporated into the decision-making process within an investment management framework. We provide a reasonably comprehensive survey for investment managers – particularly those who do not specialise in foreign exchange – of the research on foreign exchange rate determination and of various trading models that are used by many practitioners we have dealt with in the past.

We start with one of the oldest theories in foreign exchange determination – purchasing power parity (PPP) – which represents the "goods market view" of currencies. We then proceed to a simple survey of macroeconomic models where we adopt the now-standard "asset market view" of currencies. We merely skim the surface of technical analysis, which has been well researched and written on. Instead we draw the reader's attention to the quantitative models that have been gaining acceptance in the investment management industry over recent years. In fact, quantitative models now also incorporate ideas from both fundamental models and technical analysis, sometimes making it quite difficult to say which approach a model is based on.[2] (Another branch of quantitative models deals with option pricing, option market efficiency and option implied volatility. These are extremely important topics, even for investors who do not employ options in their trading, and they are therefore considered separately in Chapter 7.) The chapter finishes with a general discussion on the pitfalls of quantitative models and the scepticism one should apply when dealing with a career forecaster.[3]

4.2 PURCHASING POWER PARITY (PPP) BASED MODELS

PPP is one of the earliest concepts developed in the attempt to provide a theoretical basis for explaining what determines exchange rates. It represents the goods market view of currency and, as we saw in Chapter 1, Section 1.3.9, it is based on the idea that a given currency should have the same purchasing power for goods everywhere in the world. In this section we look at the two versions of PPP – absolute and relative. But first we consider the fundamental tenet of the theory, which is known as "the law of one price".

4.2.1 Law of one price

Put simply, the law of one price dictates that two identical goods should sell at an identical price. In the foreign exchange context, this means that two identical goods with prices denominated in different currencies should sell at an identical price when the prices are converted into a common currency. The enforcement of the law of one price comes from the powerful mechanism of arbitrage: if the prices are *not* the same, someone can make a risk-free profit by buying the goods in the relatively cheap currency and selling them in the relatively expensive currency, converting the proceeds through a currency transaction. In the process, either the prices of the goods will adjust or the exchange rate will adjust so that the arbitrage profit is eliminated and the law of one price is restored. The law of one price in fact expects the prices of the goods to adjust rather than the exchange rate itself.

Perhaps the most famous example of the application of this law is the Big Mac Index published periodically by *The Economist*, which explains the rationale behind the index as follows:[4]

> Burgernomics is based on the theory of purchasing-power parity, the notion that a dollar should buy the same amount in all countries. Thus in the long run, the exchange rate between two countries should move towards the rate that equalises the prices of an identical basket of goods and services in each country. Our "basket" is a McDonald's Big Mac, which is produced in about 120 countries. The Big Mac PPP is the exchange rate that would mean hamburgers cost the same in America as abroad. Comparing actual exchange rates with PPP indicates whether a currency is under- or overvalued.

4.2.2 Absolute PPP

To go from the law of one price to the theory of PPP, we need to introduce two further items. First, PPP invokes the law of one price in respect of two identical baskets of goods and services. Second, to achieve PPP, arbitrage will induce changes in the exchange rate rather than in the price levels themselves (remember that the law of one price originally requires the prices of the goods to adjust).

The PPP relationship becomes a theory of exchange rate determination if we introduce assumptions about the behaviour of arbitrageurs (eg, importers and exporters) in response to changes in the relative prices of national market baskets. If the law of one price leads to equalisation of the prices of one good between two markets, then it seems reasonable to conclude that PPP, describing the equality of market baskets across countries, should also hold. It follows from this that the exchange rate between two currencies should be the ratio of the prices of the two national baskets.

The PPP relationship is straightforward and intuitive and, indeed, perhaps the only one economists would agree is correct over time.

A frequently used term in talking about the PPP relationship is "half-life". Deviations of a nominal exchange rate from PPP take some time to rectify themselves, the average estimate of the half-life of this process being three to five years. This means, for example, that if the nominal US dollar/Japanese yen exchange rate appreciates from its PPP par level by 10%, it will, on average, take that amount of time for the deviation to mean-revert to 5% above the PPP par level. And even this does not necessarily offer guidance on the direction of the adjustment in the nominal exchange rate because parity can be restored not only through the exchange rate but by adjustment of the PPP par level itself brought about by relative price moments between the US and Japan.

4.2.2.1 Problems with absolute PPP theory

❑ Transportation costs and trade restrictions. For PPP to hold, one needs to assume that there are no transportation costs and no differential taxes or other types of restrictions applied between the two markets. However, these market imperfections do exist and they could drive the prices for identical goods apart. Generally, the greater the transportation costs, tax differentials and trade restrictions between two countries, the less likely it is that the exchange rate will reach the purchasing power parity level.

❑ *Costs of non-tradable inputs.* Identical goods may have non-tradable inputs. The difference between the burger prices listed above could well reflect non-tradable elements such as ground rent and labour costs.

❑ *Imperfect information.* For profit-maximising arbitrageurs to make rational decisions, they need perfect information. This condition is often violated in practice.

❑ *Relevance of other types of players.* PPP theory is based on current account transactions with its main focus on the goods market. It does not take the yield-seeking behaviour of investors into consideration. Some newer PPP models try to incorporate the impact of capital flows.

4.2.3 Relative PPP

Absolute PPP theory, as its name implies, concerns itself with absolute levels of prices and exchange rates. The alternative formulation links price changes – ie, inflation – to exchange rate movements. This version of the theory is known as relative PPP, and in essence it is the dynamic version of absolute PPP. It says, for example, that if inflation in the US is higher than in Japan, the dollar will depreciate against the yen by the differential between the inflation rates. This is very similar to the "covered interest arbitrage" statement in format but with the inflation differential replacing the interest rate differential.

4.2.3.1 Empirical testing

The common test for the validity of relative PPP compares changes in the exchange rate with the cumulative inflation differentials between two counties, typically over a very long period. The huge body of work in this area generally supports the notion that PPP *is* a factor in long-run exchange rate determination but that it offers very little guidance on short-term movements. Additionally, the following empirical results have been obtained by various researchers:[5]

❏ even over the medium-term, the consumer prices of tradable goods seem to suggest an absence of arbitrageurs as much as that of non-tradable goods;

❏ there is strong evidence to suggest that many monopoly producers charge different prices in home and foreign markets;

❏ the supposedly "broad" range of tradable goods which in theory tie down the exchange rate may not be that broad after all due to segmentation of the market and trading costs.

4.2.3.2 Examples of application

Some fund managers incorporate PPP-based forecasts into their asset allocation weightings. UBS periodically produces such a forecast using an improved, proprietary method to compute PPP exchange rates since 1995. The method augments the inflation differentials by the net foreign asset positions of two countries (which are calculated for each country on the basis of its accumulated current account balance). This is supposed to capture the effect of capital flows when investors balance their portfolios. UBS uses statistical methods to capture the dynamic behaviour of both the inflation differential and net foreign asset positions, and the forecast is also adjusted for potential interaction between these two factors.

Figures 4.1 and 4.2 show two examples of PPP exchange rates vs actual exchange rates for the euro/US dollar and euro/sterling. In each chart the central bold dashed line tracks the equilibrium PPP level for the respective currency pair, using the methods described above. The series is updated when the latest data on inflation and the current account balances become available. The actual spot exchange rates are shown as solid lines. They are much more volatile than the equilibrium PPP levels. The upper and lower

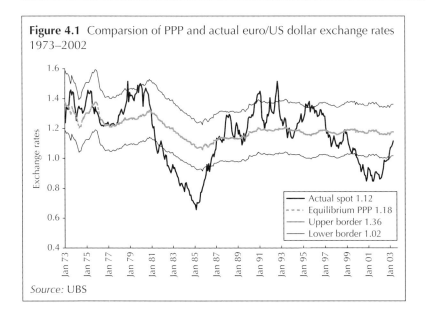

Figure 4.1 Comparsion of PPP and actual euro/US dollar exchange rates 1973–2002

Source: UBS

borders of the equilibrium PPP levels are computed using a proprietary method, similar to the Bollinger band method which we will describe later in this chapter (Section 4.5.2.5). The idea of the band is to provide an empirical range (with a moving centre) into which the actual spot exchange rate will fall with 95% likelihood. When the actual spot exchange rate goes outside the band, it indicates severe disparity between it and the PPP equilibrium rate. Accordingly, some investors take positions in the currency pair in anticipation of a mean-reversion.

Pairwise PPP forecasts may not be particularly useful as it can take a long time for the exchange rate to revert to its PPP level. One alternative is to look at the PPP deviations of a single currency against a range of currencies. If one sums up the absolute deviations, it may indicate the market opportunity available at that time. This practical approach tallies well with Kilian and Taylor (2001), which is reviewed in the next section.

4.3 BACK TO FUNDAMENTALS: MACROECONOMIC MODELS OF FOREIGN EXCHANGE DETERMINATION

A full survey of exchange rate modelling is clearly beyond our scope here – even a simple summary could extend this book unreasonably

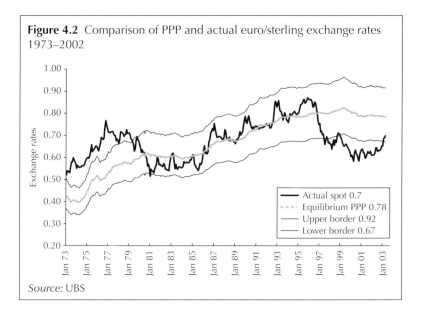

Figure 4.2 Comparison of PPP and actual euro/sterling exchange rates 1973–2002

Legend:
— Actual spot 0.7
---- Equilibrium PPP 0.78
— Upper border 0.92
— Lower border 0.67

Source: UBS

as such summaries can take up half of a standard international macroeconomics volume! Instead, in this section we will outline the main themes with the aim of illustrating the following ideas:

❏ this field of research is an ongoing one and the number of structural models is vast;
❏ many of the models are useful in certain respects, but none has proven particularly successful for forecasting;
❏ the complexity arises partly from the fact that many macroeconomic factors as well as microeconomic structures may influence exchange rates through a variety of channels, their (relative) influence may change over time and they may interact with each other.

4.3.1 A brief history of fundamental models

Broadly speaking, from a macroeconomic point of view an exchange rate can be expressed as a function of (1) current fundamentals and (2) the changes it is expected to undergo. This corresponds to taking the asset market view of the exchange rate (as opposed to the goods market view embedded in the theory of PPP) which has now been generally accepted both in theory and in practice and which states that the exchange rate is a just asset price determined so as to induce investors to hold the various assets available in a global economy.

The classical monetary models of exchange rate determination link exchange rates to money supplies and incomes: since an exchange rate is the relative price of foreign and domestic money, it should be determined by the demand/supply characteristics of these monies. In the simplest setting, price levels are assumed in general to be fully flexible so as to maintain national balances of payments, and PPP always holds. Lack of empirical support for the simple version of monetary models prompted researchers to seek alternative models, for example, models with "sticky" prices. The validity of PPP, even with various modifications, is not supported by empirical data and therefore the classical monetary model bears little resemblance to the reality. Nevertheless, it serves as a useful benchmark for later developments in the field.

The landmark work on exchange rate determination in the field of international economics was that by Mundell (1960) and Fleming (1962). Their model is characterised by rigid wages and prices, unemployment, and less-than-perfect capital mobility between countries. The emphasis here is on the balance of payment flows, whereas in the classical monetary model it is on the stock of money. The exchange rate is determined by the zero balance of payments condition on the combined current and capital account.

One research area on how expectations about an exchange rate can affect the rate itself relies on the so-called "rational expectation model" (also known as the canonical model of exchange rates). In this model all participants in the market maximise their utility rationally using all the information available to them at a given point in time. The seminal work here is Dornbusch's (1976) "overshooting" model, which introduced forward-looking expectation into the Mundell–Fleming framework. Some later models also incorporate announcements, news and rumours of current and future monetary policies, political factors and a variety of measurable or unobservable variables that may affect investors' demand for currencies. Speculative bubbles or "sunspots" can be included in an expectation framework to induce the observed fluctuations and trends in the currency market.

With the continued growth of world financial markets, the use of the balance of payments money account as an indicator of external balance was clearly inadequate, as international capital flows are orders of magnitude greater than balance of payment flows. One strain of models therefore incorporates other types of assets in a so-called "portfolio approach" where all economic agents choose to hold various types of domestic and foreign assets.[6] Because of its general set-up, it is better equipped to describe exchange rate adjustment in a world of mobile capital.

In an article in March 2000 entitled "Test-driving a new model – do currency-forecasting techniques need to be redesigned?" *The Economist* argued that the relative prices of financial assets in different countries matter more than the prices of goods. Investors will shift assets between countries (presumably much easier than shifting Big Macs) until expected returns are equal. Quoting a research note issued by Warburg Dillon Read (now part of UBS), the article noted that the US equity market is about four times as large as the stock of US Treasury bonds.[7] In 1990 it was only 50% bigger. Therefore, the article observes, the expected returns from equities in different currencies will matter for exchange rate forecasting. But this is not a foolproof route to accurate currency forecasts, noted the article, as forecasting the stockmarket returns will be just as difficult, if not more.

A new generation of exchange rate models emphasises non-monetary factors to replace the classical Keynesian framework of Mundell–Fleming and Dornbusch. These factors include fiscal variables such as government spending and productivity, wealth and household spending and price-setting mechanisms in an open economy. The new class of model is shown in stylised fashion in Figure 4.3. Some newer models also explore the impact of imperfect information, frictional trading in both goods and asset markets, heterogeneous agents and so forth (see Obstfeld and Rogoff, 1996, Chapters 4 and 10).

4.3.2 Empirical evidence on the validity of fundamental models

Fitting a model with so many variables is not an enviable task, and many such attempts have been rejected in empirical studies. With enough variables, of course, one can fit virtually any historical pattern, but what matters most is the out-of-sample

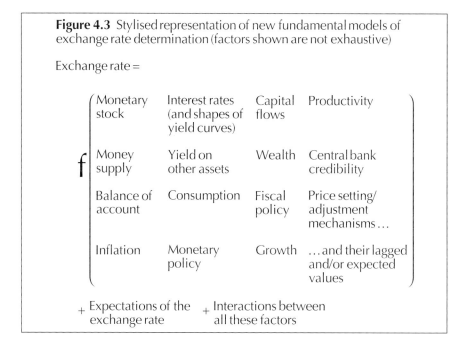

Figure 4.3 Stylised representation of new fundamental models of exchange rate determination (factors shown are not exhaustive)

performance. For nearly all macroeconomic models this has been empirically shown to be mediocre to say the least. Furthermore, over a medium-term horizon of one month to two years they fail to outperform naive random-walk models. This conclusion was demonstrated for various major currency exchange rates by Meese and Rogoff (1983a,b) and has also been confirmed by extensive empirical testing.

For a comprehensive and important survey of the literature on fundamental exchange rate models, see Frankel and Rose (1995).[8] They concluded that traditional macroeconomic models of foreign exchange determination have relatively little explanatory power, and they expressed their doubt as to the value of further time-series modelling of exchange rates at high or medium frequencies using fundamental models. They touched briefly on the subjects of technical analysis, microstructure and quantitative models. While acknowledging that the area of research is small, they noted that it is, nevertheless, potentially important.[9]

Economic fundamental models are usually constructed by employing multifactor regression or its variants. One can regress exchange rate movements on a range of economic indicators such as GDP growth, inflation, nominal short- and long-term interest rates, current account balances and trade deficits, consumer confidence, lagged changes, etc.[10] Although such models may prove to be useful for forecasting over the longer term, the publicly available models rarely give superior indicators for short- to medium-term trading to those produced by a random-walk model.

4.3.3 The use of fundamental models in practice and new angles of research

Empirical support for the various macroeconomic models is weak, but fundamental models continue to be used by many institutions – for example, central banks, treasuries or ministries of finance, government or private-sector think-tanks and academic institutions – for policy forecasts and academic purposes. Banks and their fund management clients typically use them on a discretionary basis. Some asset managers use the macroeconomic approach for currency management: for example, State Street Global Advisors, Millennium Partners and UBS Asset Management, among others. Their models are proprietary, but it is unlikely that any of these names would slavishly follow the trading signals given by a regression equation. In practice, macroeconomic indicators are often only part of the information set and it is common for a so-called "fundamental"-driven currency management style to include a fair proportion of discretionary elements in its trading decisions.

New statistical tools have been constantly applied in this field as well, many of them specifically selected to deal with the non-linear, multichannel and unstable way in which macroeconomic factors influence exchange rates. For example, models using neural network algorithms try to capture the fact that the same piece of economic data may go through different channels and potentially produce opposite effects. There are learning models (for example, Bayesian updating) that will update estimated coefficients as time progresses. There are regime-switching models that work under the assumption that exchange rates are determined by one of several relationships (regimes), and because one does not always know for sure which regime is in operation, that has to be estimated first. For example, a recent paper by Kilian and Taylor (2001) employs a variant of this type called the exponential smooth threshold autoregressive (ESTAR) model to link economic fundamentals (in this case, PPP) to exchange rate moves. Generally speaking, the more complicated models offer the flexibility to fit the data better – there are simply more knobs to turn. However, the ultimate test for a model lies in its ability to perform out of sample. This is where most models have failed to live up to expectations, so far.[11]

Kilian and Taylor (2001) also offer an interesting explanation for why it is difficult for (macroeconomics-based) forecast models to beat a simple random-walk alternative. They suggest that *on average* fundamental models do work, especially over the medium- to long-term horizon (1.5–3 years), but that they only work when the exchange rate deviates substantially from its fundamental equilibrium level. Such events are rare. Given that we normally work with exchange rate series less than 20 years long, we effectively only have around 10 non-overlapping data points to test the models. The chances are that we will not be able to obtain (enough) data points where fundamental forecast models would have soundly beaten the random walk. We may have to wait for a while, perhaps a long while, before that happens – assuming that governments and central banks will allow such large departures to happen in the first place.

This view offers a sombre outlook for forecasters. But new statistical techniques are being borrowed, invented and tested all the time and there is probably already a model around somewhere that can beat the random walk, if only marginally. Also, the risk management motive – which we consider at least as important as the return-enhancing motive, is less dependent on the existence of superior forecast models. We will discuss a few such statistical methods later in this chapter with relevant references.

4.4 TECHNICAL ANALYSIS

We will not dwell too much on the ins and outs of technical analysis (or chartist methods) in this section. This is not because of its conspicuous lack of logical underpinning in orthodox economic and financial theory, although this has been addressed in recent years. Technical analysis has a large following in the investment community and an industry of considerable size has evolved around it. There are a large number of works in the field. One excellent book, by Luca (2000), covers topics such as the fundamentals of technical analysis and how it applies to foreign exchange. There are thorough explanations and analysis of point and figure charting, candlestick charting, Gann methods and the Elliot wave principle. It also explains some quantitative methods of analysis – including all types of moving averages, oscillators and other indicators. The second edition includes a CD-ROM that lets readers test the methods presented, apply them to real trading and increase their proficiency in charting and chart analysis.

Another two books worth consulting are by a veteran in the area. Murphy (1999) is well regarded in the technical analysis community and is referred to as "the book" by many technical analysts. Murphy (1991) looks specifically into the linkage between different markets and is even more relevant today given the global integration of capital markets.

Despite its massive fan club around the world, in different markets and through the years, investors are increasingly sceptical about technical analysis.[12] The main reason is its highly subjective nature and lack of any logical foundation – some even place it in the same category as astrology. Recent efforts to address the criticism have followed two lines of approach.

The first line comes from within the profession, where there has been a consistent shift from an essentially *ad hoc* approach to a more disciplined approach. Gone are the days when research notes from investment banks were peppered with strange jargon and charts with outlandish names. These days, trading advisory notes will probably contain sections on historical performance or rule-based model forecasts, and the emphasis is more on consistency than on exotic patterns or terminology. As an example, Figure 4.4 is a screen shot of UBS's on-line technical analysis website. The inserts are the trading performance and forecast from their proprietary model, which uses neural network algorithms. Most large foreign exchange banks offer similar services.

The second line researches the effectiveness of technical analysis using quantitative methods. It thus represents an attempt to add some "science" to the "art" of technical analysis. To do this, rigid rules are created to replicate the styles in technical analysis.[13] The rules can then be rigorously checked by computers. Here the demarcation between model trading and technical trading becomes blurred.

Studies such as Sweeney (1986), Schulmeister (1988), Levich and Thomas (1993a), Taylor (1994), Kho (1996), Neely, Weller and

Figure 4.4 Screen shot of UBS's technical analysis site (available at www.ubs.com)

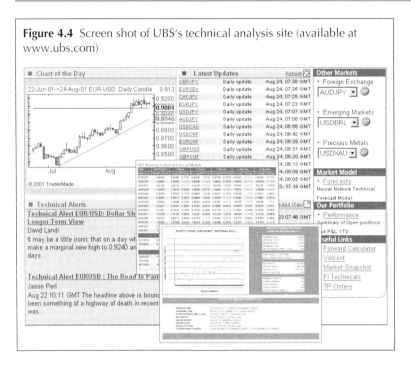

Dittmar (1997), LeBaron (1998, 1999) have lent support to the predictive power of pattern-based trading. Lo, Mamaysky and Wang (2001) use a systematic pattern recognition approach to evaluate some commonly used trading strategies on US stocks going back 31 years and find that some rules did produce economically significant returns. Osler and Chang (1995) tested the commonly used "head-and-shoulder" rule on daily exchange rate movements during the floating rate period and found that this rule too generated significant profit over the sample period. Levich and Thomas (1993a) obtained similar results using moving average and filter rules. Most of the results are essentially *ex post* – basically, they tell you that a certain rule fits past data well but offer very little guidance to an investor who has to decide *today* why head-and-shoulder is better than, say, morning star.[14]

To return briefly to the efforts to address the criticism of technical analysis. Two promising lines of enquiry look to make further advances along the second line: one applies technical trading rules to real-time tick data and the other employs a portfolio of trading rules. In addition, some recent studies from the field of behavioural finance have attempted to theorise the *raison d'être* of technical trading and why it is sometimes successful (Barberis, Shleifer and Vishny, 1998; Fama, 1998; and Hong and Stein, 1997). It is too early to predict what impact these may eventually have on the age-old art of chart reading.

4.5 QUANTITATIVE MODELS

This subject area overlaps with fundamental and/or technical models. However, according to *The Economist* of May 29, 1999, it has taken a quantum leap forwards largely for two reasons:

❑ a growing acceptance of quantitative techniques by mainstream investors, such as pension funds and even retail mutual funds; and
❑ with the falling cost and greater availability of computing power, managers increasingly use these methods to tweak their basis portfolio (though not as the sole basis for investment decisions).

The quantitative approach, in its different reincarnations, has been accepted into the mainstream of currency management philosophy and nearly all major currency overlay managers listed in Table 3B.1 employ some form of quantitative method.

Quantitative methods are sometimes referred to as number crunching or data mining in a context that primarily relates to the discovery of patterns and relationships in data. The focus is not necessarily on identifying logical or causal relationships, which is one of the main purposes of econometric modelling. However, in applications to foreign exchange, quantitative techniques have been adapted to certain special conditions relevant to the foreign exchange market. For example, some models might include complicated delays and other transformations of macroeconomic variables. These may not make sense from an economist's viewpoint but are nevertheless used in practice because they "work", whereas the economist's rational attempts to capture the behaviour of this market have all but failed.

Quantitative methods often have one or more of the following features:

❑ database management;
❑ machine learning and artificial intelligence;

❏ pattern recognition; and
❏ data visualisation.

People sometimes equate quantitative method with statistics, but this is not always the case. Historically, statistical analysis has focused mainly on hypothesis testing and fitting models to data. Statistical approaches usually rely on an explicit underlying probability model. It is implicit in any statistical model that human intervention is required for the generation of candidate hypotheses and models. In contrast, quantitative methods may include computer-automated exploratory data analysis, computer learning and artificial intelligence. Many of the methodologies used in quantitative methods originated in fields other than traditional statistics. For example, pattern recognition is arguably more part of computer science and engineering disciplines than of statistics. This also goes for genetic programming and neural network algorithms, which we will briefly discuss later.

Quantitative methods have been increasingly adopted by investment managers. The lure of potentially huge financial rewards is attracting many new entrants to the field. For example, in May 2001 *The Economist* reported on the effort by physicists and mathematicians from Oxford University to theorise the existence of patterns in financial prices that have not been arbitraged out. Using complicated techniques normally used to model complex natural systems, these researchers found that if many market participants think they see the same pattern, they may respond to the pattern in the same way. Thus, collectively, they may create a real pattern. Applied to US dollar/yen exchange rates between 1990 and 1999, their model detected enough selling and buying signals to yield a 380% profit. Reuters (September 12, 2001) also reported on the fledging research area of "ecophysics", where methods and techniques used in physics are applied to economics and finance to detect complex patterns. It noted the more convoluted approaches used in ecophysics than in traditional econometrics.

In this section we look at some examples of quantitative models, some of which are widely employed by currency managers, some are used by proprietary currency traders (one can only speculate on the exact details of such models), and some are freshly out of the academic ivory tower. We spend some time discussing how each model can be implemented by the practitioner himself and why the results should be treated with caution when used for real trading purposes. Our view is that well-constructed quantitative models may be able to offer some excess returns over time, but we doubt that there is some "Holy Grail" of currency trading models. Practitioners should research a particular trading model thoroughly before applying it, and the effectiveness of any model should be periodically reviewed. As the risk control aspect of currency overlay management is at least as important as return enhancement, we urge practitioners to look at the risk aspect of a currency overlay programme from a portfolio perspective.

4.5.1 Forward bias revisited

The earliest empirical work on forward bias was done a couple of decades ago (eg, Bilson, 1981, and Longworth, 1981) and the topic has received extensive scrutiny since. But unfortunately there is still little consensus on very much at all.

A common test for uncovered interest rate parity (or forward bias – see Chapter 1, Section 1.3.6) considers the following regression:

$$\text{Spot change} = \text{Intercept} + \beta \, (\text{Interest rate differential}) + \text{Disturbance}$$

If uncovered interest rate parity holds, the theoretical values of the coefficients are intercept $= 0$ and $\beta = 1$, ie, the return from holding spot is the same as the return on a forward, the latter being the interest rate differential. In practice, for a wide range of currencies and time periods, one finds estimated β significantly less than zero, with point estimates often below -1. In other words, when the interest rate differential "predicts" that the spot exchange rate will move in a certain direction and by a certain amount, the spot exchange rate actually goes in the opposite direction. So the expected return from holding open forward exchange positions is not zero (Froot and Frankel, 1989; Froot and Thaler, 1990). Investing in currencies with high nominal interest rates, for example, has provided better than expected results.

This is so-called forward bias. It defies economic intuition and possibly violates the principle of market efficiency. Various explanations have been offered, ranging from non-stationary risk premia through econometric mis-specification. Some researchers have accepted the puzzle as a fact of inefficient foreign exchange markets, a phenomenon that provides profitable trading opportunities. A profitable trading or hedging rule can be achieved by leaving all the exposures in the high-interest rate currencies open but hedging all exposures in lower interest rate currencies. In other words, a moneymaking strategy would be to bet against the forward rate.

A naive test of forward bias can be done quite easily: select a spot price for a particular day, using the interest rate differential to compute the forward price for a given maturity, then compare the actual spot price on the maturity date with the original forward price and calculate the gain and loss assuming one takes a long position in the higher-yielding currency. Repeat the exercise. Figures 4.5–4.8 illustrate this by showing cumulative profits/losses for investors based in different currencies. Note that the accumulation is done backwards in time so that any point on a line represents the cumulative profit/loss you may be able to accumulate up to now if trading started at that point in time. Accrued interest on the profit/loss and funding costs for the trade are ignored.

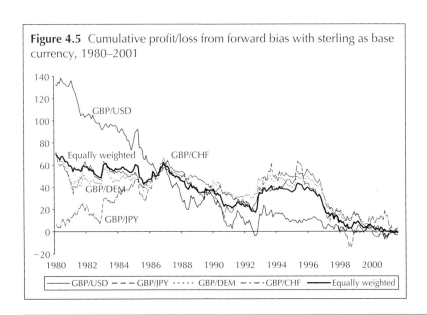

Figure 4.5 Cumulative profit/loss from forward bias with sterling as base currency, 1980–2001

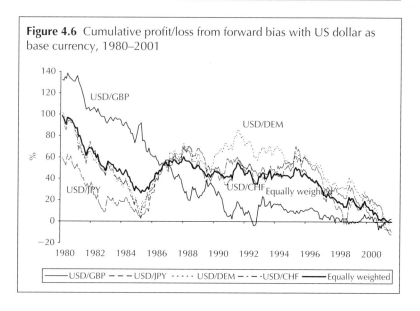

Figure 4.6 Cumulative profit/loss from forward bias with US dollar as base currency, 1980–2001

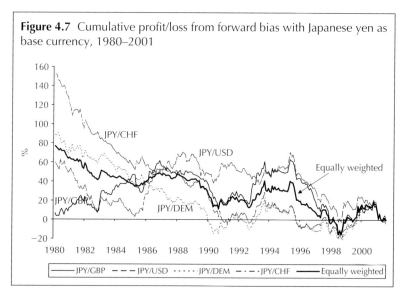

Figure 4.7 Cumulative profit/loss from forward bias with Japanese yen as base currency, 1980–2001

Figure 4.5 shows the cumulative profit/loss using sterling as the base currency. The strategy is to take long (short) positions in sterling if the sterling yield is higher (lower) than those of foreign currencies. It is the same as taking long (short) positions in sterling

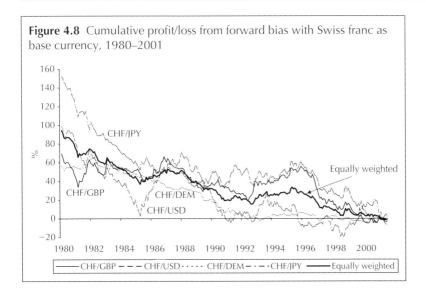

Figure 4.8 Cumulative profit/loss from forward bias with Swiss franc as base currency, 1980–2001

if sterling is trading at a discount (premium) in the forward market – ie, betting against the forward. One can easily see that there is a downward (ie, profitable) trend in three of the four currency pairs, and it is most persistent for sterling/US dollar. A 130% return over a 20-year period is impressive considering it is a zero investment strategy. However, the trend is not consistent across time and currency pairs. Depending on the currency pair and time period chosen for study, the conclusion can be different.

Eyeballing the four charts, one can see that the forward bias may provide some profit opportunity as most of the points lie above the zero-profit line, and this is true irrespective of the base currency in question. However, one has to bear in mind that the overall trend of a currency pair may play a dominant role here. Some currencies have consistently lower interest rates than others, so the cumulative profit/loss in such a currency largely reflects the overall trend in that currency pair. And even if it can be demonstrated that the phenomenon is statistically significant, is it sufficient to entice someone to trade? There are few issues one needs to consider.

❑ *Investment horizon.* It might take a long time for the assumed profit to materialise – can one wait that long?
❑ *Risk/return.* Does the return compensate for the risk?

❏ *Underlying.* Will someone enter currency positions solely to exploit the forward bias or will he consider such a move exclusively as a hedging issue?

❏ *Currency portfolio approach.* Should one consider each currency pair in isolation or should one optimise them as a portfolio of currencies?[15]

❏ *Transaction cost.* How will the transaction cost affect the performance?

❏ *Refining the naive approach.* Are there better ways to improve the performance?

Many of the questions listed above can be specific to a fund. Here we briefly discuss three examples relevant to the last point. It has been proposed that, instead of a naive approach where positions are entered as long as the interest rate differential is not zero, a position is entered only if the interest rate differential is above a certain level. The approach was tested by Kritzman (1993), who found that adding a trigger generally lowered performance.

Another improvement would be to base hedging decisions on estimated real interest rates. This was done in a study by Hazuka and Huberts (1994). Using an adaptive expectations model and assuming that a trailing six-month average of actual CPI inflation is a proxy for inflation expectations, they simulated buying currencies with high real interest rates and shorting currencies with low real rates. The strategy returned 3.7% annually over the 228-month test period. It beat an unhedged and a fully hedged benchmark portfolio by a considerable margin. They also found empirical support for a strategy based on purely nominal interest rate differentials, but not as strong as for a real rate differential-based strategy. In fact, the nominal and real interest rate differential-based strategies can be combined to yield even better results, and this exercise is done by VanderLinden, Jiang and Hu (2002). They find a uniform improvement of results when the two strategies are combined for US-based investors. Interestingly, this does not hold for investors based in non-US currencies.

Hodrick and Vassalou (2002) look at the dynamics of short-term returns and exchange rates in four economies: the US, UK, Germany and Japan. They argue that exchange rate drift can potentially be better modelled as a linear function of multiple country short rates as opposed to the usual practice of modelling it as a linear function of the interest rate differential of the two countries under consideration. Alternatively stated, the study explores whether the forward risk premium can be modelled better by incorporating multiple interest rates than by confining it to a single interest rate differential. In terms of empirical evidence, the authors show that, for various exchange rates under consideration, other country interest rate differentials matter. They conclude that, compared to the standard single- or two-country model, a multi-country model specification offers additional intuitive insight in understanding these realisations, but their primary focus is not on whether the improved model gives more trading profit.

So, if forward bias does exist, *why* does it exist? Here are a few explanations:[16]

❑ *Time-varying risk premia.* The forward rate may incorporate a risk premium, and it is possible that, on average, the risk premium tends to outweigh the trend change in exchange rates. Fama (1984) demonstrated that the negative β implies a negative covariance between the risk premium and the expected change in the exchange rates. He argued that this is problematic for the risk premium explanation as it implies that the risk premium is highest when the currency is expected to appreciate.[17]

❑ *Econometric mis-specification of the expectation.* In this view, the regression coefficient is a biased estimate of the population value, say, due to learning or peso effects (see Engel's 1996 survey). Another interpretation of forward bias involves so-called "peso problem" in the data – the current floating-rate period is still relatively young and markets are expecting a meltdown some time in the future but the event has not shown itself in the sample. Therefore a test result relying on historical data does not capture this latent move. If we had a sufficiently large data set, the problem would disappear.

❑ *Interest rate spread.* More recently, Phillips and Maynard (2001) have shown that estimates of beta are biased downwards due to the persistence of the interest rate spread.

❑ *Non-stationarity.* If both interest rate differentials and spot exchange rates are non-stationary, one cannot draw useful conclusions from a regression.

4.5.2 Variations on the theme of momentum

The majority of technical and quantitative trading methods are either based directly on the concept of momentum or have some element of momentum built into them.[18] Momentum is also known as "trending" or "autocorrelation", and investors who use such indicators are called momentum players or trend followers. However, there are also a small number of market participants who are counter-trend players. Some of these simply believe that taking counter-trend positions is profitable, but others may have a particular reason for doing so: one of the latter type are known as "gamma scalpers", and we will discuss their approach in Chapter 7, Section 7.8.1.

Techniques commonly used by trend watchers include filter rules and moving average rules, which are outlined below. Taylor and Allen (1992) among others have shown that the foreign exchange rate does exhibit some degree of autocorrelation that is not readily explained by the efficient market hypothesis. According to Fama (1965), the current exchange rate fully reflects all available information and therefore will only change when new information arrives. If we assume that the arrival of information flows is random, it follows that exchange rate moves should also be random.

4.5.2.1 Filter rules

Under a simple filter rule investors will buy when exchange rates increase by a certain percentage above their most recent trough and sell when they decrease by a certain percentage below their most recent peak.

There are endless permutations of the filter rule – see Murphy (1999) for more examples; many off-the-shelf graphing/active trading packages allow users to specify the filters (triggers) and the historical trading performance will be generated automatically.

4.5.2.2 Moving average rules

There are many variants of the moving average rule (some of which are called oscillators). A commonly used rule, also known as "the double crossing rule", stipulates:

❏ buy when a short-run moving average (say, five-day) cuts a long-run moving average (say, 150-day) from below;

❑ sell when a short-run moving average cuts a long-run moving average from above.

The idea is that the short-run moving average represents a quick market trend and the long-run moving average a slow one. When the quick one crosses the slow one from below, it indicates upward pressure on the exchange rate and hence the taking of a long position to exploit it. When the opposite occurs, it indicates downward pressure on the exchange rate and a short position would then be the obvious choice. There are no rules to determine suitable moving average windows for the short and long run. Generally some kind of optimisation procedure over the historical data is used to solve the issue empirically.

Again, the variation on this theme can be endless. The original moving average compares the current price with a moving average and the buy signal is generated if the current price is above the moving average and vice versa. It can be combined with a filter rule: a buy signal is generated only if the current price is x% higher than the moving average (so-called "hybrid rules"). Some people use three moving average curves rather than two, a clear-cut buy signal being generated only when the shortest trend line cross both longer trend lines and vice versa. A research paper by Dr J. Roberts (1999) of UBS modifies the moving average procedure: rather than a simple arithmetic average, he uses an exponentially weighted moving average to give more weight to more recent observations. Then a similar optimisation process is undertaken to find the "best" window lengths and the exponential decay parameter. The result shows an improvement over a simple arithmetic average.

4.5.2.3 Effectiveness

A substantial number of studies have shown that both types of trend-following rule have been profitable in foreign exchange markets even after adjusting for interest and transaction costs. Dooley and Shafer (1982) tested filter rules using US dollar/Deutschmark, US dollar/Japanese yen and US dollar/sterling over the period 1973–81 and found evidence of substantial profits for most of the filter parameters. Sweeney (1986), using daily US dollar/ Deutschmark rates over the period 1975–80, reported excess profits over buy-and-hold of 4% per annum for a 0.5% filter. LeBaron (1992) found persistent returns for various moving average rules compared with traditional time-series forecast methods using weekly exchange rates for sterling, Deutschmark and the yen against the US dollar between 1974 and 1992. Levich and Thomas (1993a) used three moving average rules for five currencies and found significant trading profit. Szakmary and Mathur (1997) found positive profit from moving average rules in both in- and out-of-sample tests in four out of five currencies investigated. They also reported that the trading rules are more profitable on Fridays and Mondays. Lee and Mathur (1996) looked at European currency spot rates between 1988 and 1993 and found that moving average rules are marginally profitable for Deutschmark/yen and Swiss franc/yen but not for sterling/yen, sterling/Deutschmark, Deutschmark/Swiss franc and sterling/Swiss franc. Kho (1996) also reported significant excess returns over the buy-and-hold strategy using selected moving average rules. Surajaras and Sweeney (1992) studied 950 moving average and filter rules in 15 currencies and concluded that moving average rules outperform filter-based rules in the foreign exchange market.

The reliability of this type of study has been questioned because:

❏ they generally rely on *ex post* data to discriminate one rule against another;
❏ they usually do not attempt to establish whether the excess return reported was specifically due to trends in foreign exchange rates or to some other statistical property or properties.

A commonly used method for resolving the second issue is "bootstrapping", whereby the original prices are permutated either randomly or according to a specific rule. Levich and Thomas (1993a) used a bootstrapping approach to examine the effectiveness of various filter and moving average rules over the period 1976–90. Their results indicate that if the data had been generated by a random walk, no trading profit would have been earned. This does not directly imply that exchange rates exhibit trends, but it eliminates the random-walk assumption.[19] The bootstrapping method has since become a very powerful tool for investigating non-linear price relationships (see Sullivan, Timmermann and White, 1998).

The *ex post* data may introduce bias as a rule that performs well against its peers on historical data but it is not necessarily a guarantee of superior performance when it is applied in the future. There is another potential source of bias. The rules and parameters tested in these studies are usually widely used ones and are probably chosen using some historical data set, leaving the possibility that there are better rules that do not get selected for testing. To alleviate the first problem, it is advisable to run the optimisation over a portion of the historical data and then apply the rule over the remaining portion to check validity. The second problem is not easy to deal with. In a recent study Okunev and White (2001) tested a wide range of moving average formulations and parameter values. They used moving averages to rank different currencies, trying to identify the most attractive and the least attractive. Their results indicate that the moving average trading rule specification impacts profitability minimally both during sub-periods and over the entire sample period, yielding a total return of 6% per annum across eight different base currencies.

4.5.2.4 Stop-loss and take-profit

Stop-loss and take-profit are widely used by investors either to limit future losses and/or to protect past gains. In general, if currency moves follow a random walk, the expected return on stop-loss and take-profit strategies will be less than from a buy-and-hold strategy. When the markets trend, stop-loss strategies will outperform buy-and-hold, whereas take-profit will underperform. Acar and Toffel (2000) tested the effectiveness of stop-loss and take-profit rules on the daily US dollar/yen exchange rate between 1984 and 2000 where positions were taken at random but a stop-loss or take profit order was executed if a prespecified level was breached. They found that a stop-loss strategy would have generated 1.95% per annum vs the interest differential of 0.62% per annum but that a take-profit strategy would have lost 1.70% per annum over the period. These are taken as indicative of the existence of a positive trend in the US dollar/yen market.

There are some more fancy formulations of stop-loss and take-profit strategies. For example, a stop-loss order can move with spot movements ("trailing stop-loss"). Some exotic options generate their own stop-loss/take-profit patterns. There has been very little research in the area apart from the literature on market micro-structure reviewed in Section 4.5.4. Given the wide application of these methods, more study is clearly needed.

4.5.2.5 Counter-trending and mean-reversion

There are two types of counter-trending model: one identifies the end of a particular trend and places a counter-trend trade to benefit from the trend reversal; the other executes a counter-trend trade irre-spective of what might happen next. The latter type is discussed in Chapter 7, Section 7.8.1. The first type of counter-trending is closely related to the following terms: divergence, over-bought/ sold signal, trend reversal, mean-reversion (also called the Ornstein–Uhlenbeck process), and again there are some examples in Murphy (1999).

One well-known example of a counter-trending model makes use of what is known as a Bollinger band. A Bollinger band is plot-ted as follows:

1. calculate, say, a 60-day moving average of the spot rate; this is variable 1.
2. calculate a 20-day standard deviation of spot moves using day-on-day percentage changes (variable 2).
3. calculate, say, two standard deviation levels both above and below the current moving average calculated in step 1 (variable 3).
4. plot variables 1, 2 and 3 against time. The two standard devi-ation data points will form a band that centres around the mov-ing average line and for much of the time envelopes the spot line. However, there may be points where the spot line goes out-side the band boundaries and later returns (which is meant to happen by design unless the spot rate follows a one-way train). By modifying variables 1–3 one can increase or reduce the number of crossing points.
5. since when the spot curve goes outside the band it is expected to return, the crossing point may provide a buy/sell signal.

We have not seen any literature on the effectiveness of this tech-nique for trading. The construction of a Bollinger band is mainly an empirical issue as the three variables are almost entirely arbitrary, and therefore an effectiveness test, both in sample and out-of-sample, would offer very little guidance to an investor.[20] That said, the phenomenon of herd behaviour might validate the heresy and a particular set of parameter values may turn out to be a consistent money-spinner.

4.5.2.6 *Why momentum might exist*

A few factors are thought to contribute to the existence of momentum in the currency market:

❑ herding behaviour of investors;
❑ the wide acceptance of systematic trading styles;
❑ market microstructure (Section 4.5.4);
❑ insider dealing (though this may not be an important factor in foreign exchange);
❑ certain risk management practices used by many investment institutions (eg, the use of stop-loss when price falls induce further declines).

4.5.3 Seasonality

Seasonality is one of the oldest topics in econometric modelling and quantitative trading and there used to be a considerable amount of research interest in the seasonality of foreign exchange prices; for example, Wasserfallen (1989) looked at the time of the day effect, Harvey and Huang (1991) at the day of the week effect in currency volatility, and So (1987) at the trading day effect.

In a relatively recent update, Cornett, Schwarz and Szakmary (1995) found (1) significant close-to-open and open-to-close effects, whereby most foreign currencies tend to weaken close-to-open (while the US market is closed) and strengthen when the US market is open, particularly during the first and last two hours of the US trading day; (2) significant day of the week effects: negative returns from Thursday close to Friday open (in equities or other asset markets there is often a weekend effect where the return is negative over the weekend); and (3) during the US trading day, significant positive returns between open and 8:30am on Wednesdays and significant negative returns on all currencies between 10:30 and 11:30 on Thursday.

However, the seasonality research in foreign exchange has now more or less dried up.[21] We can only speculate that the reasons may be:

❑ the underlying product is standardised, continuously traded and generally free of idiosyncratic features;

❏ participants in the foreign exchange market generally have much shorter investment horizons so that seasonality, if it exists, would be on a much shorter time scale, in which case it would be included in intra-day market microstructure research; and
❏ price transparency and liquidity have improved enormously.

Here we include a quickly assembled example to show how seasonality effects can be looked for in practice. A potentially fruitful line of investigation is to use tick-data to look for foreign exchange seasonality on a micro-scale, and this is reviewed in Section 4.5.4.

4.5.3.1 An example – the Wednesday effect

We use this example to illustrate how a quick-and-dirty test can be put together with very little programming effort. The Wednesday effect in the foreign exchange market has been studied before and it was thought to be caused by settlement issues: prior to 1981, all foreign currencies apart from the US dollar were settled in two business days but the dollar was settled in three. This led to relatively low demand for the dollar to avoid the five-day interest-free loan. However, a recent study by Thatcher and Blenman (2001) shows that the abnormal return pattern persisted after the settlement issue was dispensed with. The existence of the Wednesday effect may be attributable to the lower foreign exchange volatilities on Wednesdays in general.

Here we use the daily spot and forward data for sterling/US dollar, sterling/yen and euro/sterling from January 1990 to October 2001 to test this claim. The data source is DataStream. We assume that these rates are daily London close rates, which corresponds to 5–6pm, but this is unconfirmed. Obviously, an Asian opening price against the US close price on a Wednesday would be a better fit, but we have not tried to obtain those data.

Figure 4.9 shows the (reverse) equity curve for the following simple strategies: on a given Tuesday at 5pm one observes the rate of return from the day before (Monday 5pm if not a holiday) up to Tuesday 5pm. If the return is positive, a long position is taken and vice versa. The position can be in spot, one-month forward or three-month forward (shown as s, 1 and 3 following the currency symbols in Figure 4.9). The position is then closed at 5pm on Wednesday. We did not consider bid–offer spreads, nor the impact of forward

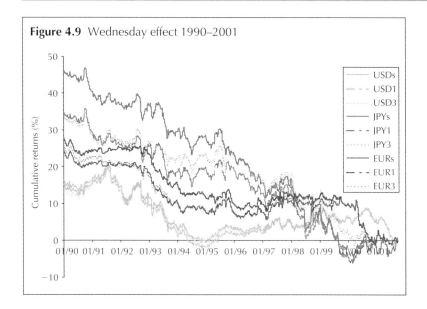

Figure 4.9 Wednesday effect 1990–2001

contract when rolled one day. The accumulative curve was calculated backwards in time so that at any given point along the curve it shows the cumulative profit one could have achieved if the strategy was initiated at that point.

The curves are generally downward sloping and above the x-axis, indicating their profitability (before taking transaction costs and one-day rolling cost into account). The return results are not spectacular, ranging from just over 1% per annum for the US dollar against sterling to around 3–4% for the yen against sterling. We use 2bp per transaction as a rough estimate for transaction cost and assume that the net rolling cost between long and short positions is zero. Dollar/sterling trades just break even (2bp × 50 weeks = 1% per annum), but yen/sterling trades make 2–3% per annum.

4.5.4 Market microstructure and high-frequency data

Market microstructure refers to detailed information on how a market functions: the relationship between counterparties, the sequence and manner in which they exchange information, who has what information at what time, how order flows affect traders behaviour, etc. It has become an actively researched area thanks to the availability of data over recent years.

Two characteristics of the foreign exchange market stand out in terms of market microstructure: low market transparency and quick inventory turnover. Most foreign exchange transactions are conducted over the counter with one or both counterparties being market-maker. This so-called dealership structure means that the transaction price and volume information is limited to the counterparties to the transactions only.[22] Some studies use the market-maker's own position – rather than price – data to construct forecast models.[23] In the foreign exchange market the information content of position data may be linked to inventory risk management, which is more important than in other dealership markets. The average inventory cycle of a foreign exchange trader may be as short as a few minutes, and inventory risk is therefore a crucial determinant of trader behaviour and foreign exchange price formation.[24]

Evans and Lyons (1999) present an interesting exchange rate prediction model that takes market microstructure into account. They propose that two factors influence changes in the short-term exchange rate, namely, order flows and overnight interest rates. Spot traders typically watch order flows and take positions accordingly. At the same time, their positions are affected by changes in overnight interest rates as they have to fund their positions. Evans and Lyons estimate their model for US dollar/Deutschmark and US dollar/yen rates using the following relationship:

$$\text{Daily spot change} = \beta1 \text{ (Change of overnight interest rate differential)} + \beta2 \text{ (Signed order flow)} + \text{Disturbance}$$

where $\beta1$ is the sensitivity of daily spot change to change of overnight interest rate differential (the differential being counter currency overnight interest rate – base currency overnight interest rate), $\beta2$ is the sensitivity of daily spot change to signed order flow ("signed" means that inflow is treated as positive and outflow as negative). As predicted, both β_1 and β_2 are positive and significant. The estimated R^2 improves substantially when signed order flow is included. Over 50% of daily changes in the US dollar/Deutschmark rate and 30% in the US dollar/Japanese yen rate are explained by the model – for comparison, fundamental models typically produce an R^2 below 10%. The model points to a new avenue of modelling where macroeconomic indicators can be combined with microstructure variables to improve predictive power. However, the order flows for foreign exchange are typically confidential for individual market-makers and they are often prohibited from entering trades using client order flows.

An interesting extension along this line over recent years has been to look at the expected currency flows from index trackers when the index they are tracking is scheduled for rebalancing. For example, the total amount of investment tracking the MSCI Index can be estimated, as can the "average" foreign exchange hedge ratio, albeit with less confidence. When MSCI announces a rebalancing action it is about to implement (for instance, due to free-floating adjustments), the resulting currency flows can be estimated. One can then model these to actual currency movements and assess their accuracy. This approach is slightly different from many commentaries produced by various investment banks and global custodians which look at aggregate cross-border bond/equity flows and foreign exchange movements. That relationship, if proven, is contemporary and therefore cannot be used directly for forecasting foreign exchange movements.

Another research direction takes advantage of the availability of high-frequency data, better algorithms and the computational power offered by ever faster computers. The leader is this area is Olsen Data AG, which was founded by Dr R. Olsen in 1985 and specialises in high-frequency data.[25] They have collected large amounts of data (for example, up to 10,000 non-equally spaced prices per day for the US dollar/Deutschmark spot rate) and developed trading systems based on analysis of the data set. They have published a host of papers on the subject.[26] For example, Dacorogna et al (1995) reported that by using five-minute price series over seven years for four currency pairs (US dollar/Deutschmark, US dollar/Swiss franc, US dollar/ French franc and Deutschmark/Japanese yen) and following a (proprietary) momentum-based model with realistic stop-loss orders, they manage to produce annualised excess profits ranging from 3.7% to 9.6% net of transaction costs. It is not clear whether interest rate differentials were properly accounted for in these results.

A counterpoint is provided by Neely and Weller (2001b), who used half-hourly data provided by Olsen. They concluded that, after reasonable transaction costs are taken into account, there is no evidence that excess profit can be made by trading on technical-based models. This is markedly different from their results using longer-horizon data, which are discussed in Section 4.5.5.1.

4.5.5 Other data-mining techniques

There are many other data-mining techniques, for which we offer the following rough categorisation.

❑ *Statistical methods and techniques:* neural networks, Bayesian updating, genetic programming, fractal space and chaos methods, co-integration and error correction, smooth transition autoregression (STAR), Markov switching, kernel regression and generalised method of moments (GMM). Some of these are explained in more detail later.

❑ *Different underlying:* instead of forecasting spot moves, implied volatilities and tail distributions are forecast. Here Garch family, vector autoregressive integrated moving average (VARIMA) and stochastic autoregressive volatility (SARV) models are used. Implied volatility can be traded via options and volatility swaps, and tail distributions can be traded through exotic-type instruments. Volatility forecasting will be reviewed in Chapter 7, Section 7.7.3.

❑ *New forecast outputs:* forecasts of spot ranges, support and resistance levels, trend-reversal points, or the time it takes for a spot to reach a certain level.[27]

❑ *New indicators:* equity flows, market participants forecast survey data, sentimental index, option skews and central bank intervention.

❑ *Risk management-focused approaches:* value-at-risk (VAR), VAR–CAPM, conditional VAR, extreme value theory (EVT), correlation structures, extreme correlation and copulas.

In the following sections we briefly review some of these approaches which we think merit consideration from a practitioner's viewpoint.

4.5.5.1 Genetic programming

Genetic algorithms are optimisation procedures inspired by the principles observed in natural evolution – hence this approach's alternative name of evolutionary programming. The technique was developed in the 1970s and has since found wide-ranging application. It has been particularly useful for problems where there are many possible solutions and/or it is difficult to rank these solutions into a logical order and/or there are multiple local optimal solutions that prevent the optimisation procedure from identifying the global optimal solution. The problem of searching for a profitable trading rule is of this kind.

The technique was first applied to the stockmarket in 1995. Neely and Weller (2001a,b) used a genetic programming approach to study technical trading in the foreign exchange market. The essence of their approach can be described as follows:

1. create an initial set of trading rules. These rules can be a random combination of arithmetic and logical operations on historical prices – eg, IF (average of last five days' prices is less than current price) THEN (go short by one unit). The initial set of rules is called the "first generation".
2. compute the trading profits generated by each rule and rank all the rules. Designate the rule which produces the highest profit as the "best rule".
3. randomly select two rules from the first generation, giving higher-ranked rules a better chance of being chosen. Use logical operators to combine the two rules to form a new rule, checking that the combination makes sense.
4. repeat Step 2 and obtain the best rule of the "second generation". If this is better than the best rule from Step 2, use it to replace that rule.
5. repeat Steps 2, 3, and 4 until some prespecified criteria are met.

Steps 1–5 constitute one "trial", and each trial generates one rule. If repeated, the whole process can generate another rule. Running 100 trials, Neely, Weller and Dittmar (1997) obtained an optimised set of 100 trading rules for a range of currencies using exchange rates from 1975 to 1980.[28] They then examined the performance of these rules over the period 1981–95. Their method stands out from many similar studies in two ways:

❑ rules were obtained using *ex ante* data and their performance was tested using *ex post* data. This resembles the situation faced by a currency manager who does not have the luxury of using future prices to optimise a trading rule. In fact, the rules were "manufactured" using six years' worth of price data and were applied to the next 15 years without modification, which is quite impressive.

❏ they tested a portfolio of 100 rules rather than a single rule. This again is very similar to the operation of a real-life currency management firm where multiple trading models/managers are functioning at the same time.

The authors reported positive excess returns on all six currency pairs under investigation, ranging from 102 basis points per annum for sterling/Swiss franc to 605bp per annum for US dollar/Deutschmark after taking transaction costs into account. The average was 287bp per annum. They found that the best-performing rules in different currencies differed significantly in terms of trading frequency. They used the bootstrap technique to test whether the excess returns could have been generated by some known statistical properties of the data and found that the models people normally use did not explain the profit their rules generated. The average trading frequency ranged from once every two weeks to once every three months.

The method is suitable for financial modelling not only because of its flexibility and robustness but also because of its objective of maximising trading profit. The set-up of their study is not dissimilar to that of some currency overlay managers in real life. Many of these use a portfolio of trading rules optimised over historical data, and these rules are the result of a continuous evolution. In fact, the result the authors reported, 2.87% profit before management fees, is similar in magnitude to the actual historical performance of some overlay managers (see Chapter 3, Section 3.8.1).

The downside of this approach is the fact that the rules are generated at random by a machine and are not necessarily transparent to human brains. The rules are generally nested, with several layers and many conditions on each layer. Most of them cannot be simplified. Therefore, for real trading purposes the portfolio of rules would have to be treated as a black box.

4.5.5.2 Bayesian updating

Bayesian updating is one type of learning model and is an approach that has been applied in many scientific and engineering disciplines (and beyond) for years – Thomas Bayes first introduced the principles of eponymous Bayesian updating more than 200 years ago. The idea behind it is reasonably straightforward: rather than treating the parameter in question (for example, a coefficient in a regression) as having a true, fixed value (a point) as in classic statistical models, one views the parameter as a random variable from a distribution with certain assumed properties (referred to as a "prior distribution"). The objective of estimation now becomes to recursively update the prior distribution with the latest data, which will tell us how well or badly the model performed in the last round. The updated distribution is called the "posterior distribution". In a way, it is not dissimilar to many other models that adjust the model parameters with the arrival of more information; the difference is that Bayesian updating stipulates a specific way on how the new information should be utilised. It has grown into a sprawling branch of applied statistics of its own, with books, journals, annual conventions and business enterprises devoted to its application. Its use in financial forecasting has been mainly in variance–covariance matrices (for asset allocation) because the technical specifications of Bayesian updating can lead directly to the estimation of these matrices. It is also widely used for comparing different types of forecast models. Direct application to return forecasting, however, has been patchy, partly due to the subjectivity involved in specifying the prior distribution. This is a general criticism of all Bayesian-type analysis.

We are aware of only two Bayesian foreign exchange return forecast models, one of which is produced by UBS.[29] This dynamically allocates weights using Bayesian updating procedures to three different sub-models (called "styles" in the model) for foreign exchange determination: a fundamental sub-model, a technical sub-model and a capital flow sub-model (using data from UBS's proprietary equity flow database). The set-up was motivated by the observation that all three models are valid for foreign exchange determination but that their relative importance changes over time.[30] The website provides some detailed reading material on how the model is estimated and what practical fudge factors are introduced (see Panel 1 for a brief introduction). It seems that the initial weights for the three styles were set at one-third each, but it is not clear how much of these arbitrary weights are propagated through to later forecasts. The simulated model has generated a return of some 40% between January 1999 and December 2001, although a large proportion (33%) was generated in 2000. The other Bayesian-type multiple factor model we know of is produced by Credit Swiss Asset Management, but details are insufficient to comment.

PANEL 1 FX KEY DRIVERS

(UBS Warburg promotion brochure, 2001, with collaboration from Bayesian Edge Technology and Solutions)

With countries following different policies, yet aiming at similar economic objectives, foreign exchange market participants cannot depend on the economics textbook to make sense of currency movements. In the old world of macroeconomic FX analysis, rules were simpler and stickier, and the FX trend was your friend. Trend reversals develop faster now, the long waves seem shorter, patterns are more complex, and – most importantly – the factors which move FX are in constant flux. Not only is there a lot more noise and a lot less signal, but multiple directional signals often don't point in the same direction ...

... We have sought out three aids to our visceral judgement of the state of the FX market. Our resultant product, UBS Warburg FX Key Drivers, has the following components, which are incorporated into the UBSW FX Strategy effort. The first is to take a total-portfolio approach and apply the latest developments in risk management to that portfolio. The second is to use dynamic Bayesian statistical approaches. Compared to simple regression analysis and other traditional statistical approaches, these represent a tremendous step forward in recognising which forces are dominating the market at any given time.

Finally, new sources of information must be mined for improved and more timely insights. Modern information technology makes possible the detailed analysis of this data, especially the tracking of capital flows on a daily and weekly basis from one major region of the world to another.

... New information comes regularly and randomly in the form of market movements, policy changes, newly announced economic data and so on. In a dynamic Bayesian statistical process, we start with the previous assessment of subjective probability, take the new information, and develop a new forecast and a new confidence assessment of that forecast. At the same time, this process generates a new appreciation of how potential errors may relate to other forecasts and positions in the portfolio.

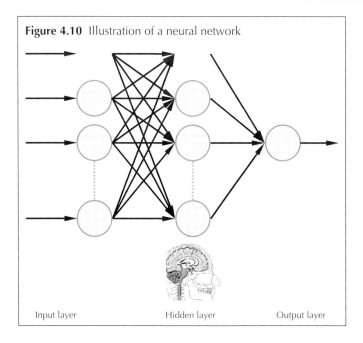

Figure 4.10 Illustration of a neural network

Input layer   Hidden layer   Output layer

4.5.5.3 Neural network algorithms

Neural networks are a class of systems modelled after the human brain that have been successfully applied in numerous pattern recognition and non-linear estimation problems. Just as the brain consists of millions of neurons that interconnect via synapses, neural networks are formed from a set of simulated neurons – each of which is a computational element – connected to each other in an analogous manner (Figure 4.10). Every neuron is capable of making optimal decisions in its micro-environs. As in the human brain, the strength of a neuron's connections may change (or be changed by the learning algorithm) in response to a presented stimulus or an obtained output, which enables the network to "learn". The output is a weighted average of the outputs of all neurons in the hidden layer.

Neural networks as models for forecasting exchange rates have been investigated in a number of studies, and the results generally support the claim that they outperform the random walk and some other linear forecasting models, although some studies have also reported mixed performance.[31] As neural network studies are usually designed to test out-of-sample performance, they closely resemble the practical situation where trading decisions have to be taken with no knowledge of future price moves.

Although neural network estimation is computationally intensive, the limited practical application of the technique can be attributed to certain arbitrary factors involved in model construction and estimation, for example:

❏ decisions about how many neurons and how many layers of neurons to include;
❏ the criteria used to evaluate performance;
❏ how to divide the sample into a training part (for optimisation) and a learning part (for updating);
❏ how to avoid overfitting the data – there can be many parameters to estimate and there is a tendency to use as many as possible to obtain the best in-sample performance.

If quantitative models are generally regarded as black boxes, some view neural networks as even blacker boxes. True, the estimation algorithms are more convoluted, but if proper software packages are used they are still relatively easy to implement.[32] These also allow estimation of ordinary least-square (OLS) regression-type outputs such as slope, t-tests and R^2 (although technically there may be some fiddle involved).

4.5.5.4 Markov-switching models

Markov-switching models are based on a premise that exchange rates can be described by a mixture of normal distributions – ie, it is assumed that there is more than one stable relationship between the variables concerned. For example, foreign exchange rates may be linearly associated with changes in relative bond yields. However, the *sensitivity* (ie, regression coefficient) of the relationship can take one of two values, which a forecaster cannot observe beforehand. A Markov transitional matrix characterises the likelihood of the sensitivity jumping from value to another. It is possible to estimate both values of the regression coefficient as well as the transitional matrix from the empirical data using optimisation procedures. Such models are better suited to capturing sharp and discrete changes in the economic mechanism that generates the data.

The motivation for using Markov-switching models is provided by the work of Engel and Hamilton (1990), Bekaert and Hodrick (1993), Engel (1994) and Engel and Hakkio (1997). All these authors document regime shifts in exchange rates and find that regime-switching models provide better in-sample fit and out-of-sample forecasts than random-walk specifications. Caporale and Spagnolo (2001) applied a Markov-switching model to East Asian currencies. They allowed the exchange rate to switch between two distributions according to a hidden Markov chain, one corresponding to a more stable and less volatile period and the other to a less stable, more volatile period. They compared the in-sample fitting and out-of-sample forecasting performance of random-walk, smooth transition autoregressive and Markov-switching processes when applied to nominal exchange rates and found the Markov-switching model to produce superior forecasts. They concluded from their results that such models would be able to handle the structural break that occurs when currencies are hit by a financial crisis.

Clarida *et al.* (2001) applied the Markov-switching method to the relationship between forward (of different maturities) and spot exchange rates. Their forecasting model significantly outperformed a random-walk benchmark as well as a variety of other models across a range of horizons and currencies in an out-of-sample test. For example, they reported that for the US dollar/Japanese yen pair their model improved the 52-week forecast efficiency by up to 90% over a random-walk alternative. The average improvement for a four-week forecast relative to random walk was about 25%, and for 52-week, 60%. These efficiency figures do not necessarily correspond to the magnitude of profit opportunities. They concluded that the forward premiums contain valuable information about future spot movements.

Practical implementation of Markov switching can be taxing for a user. One has to estimate several traditional stable linear relationships, *plus* the transitional probabilities of jumps from one state to another, *plus* the probability that a certain state is prevalent at any given time (as this is not observable). Equipped with all this information, one can then make one-step or several-steps ahead predictions. Application in the financial market is still relatively new and user-friendly packages should be available within a couple of years.

4.5.5.5 Nearest-neighbour methods

Most time-series forecasting methods treat price data as they happened over time, sequentially. An alternative is to look at the data "spatially" – you try to pick out those segments of historical data that look the most promising for the prediction of future spot moves irrespective of when they occurred. The nearest-neighbour approach explores this route. It searches through historical data series and locates a few sub-samples where these were the "nearest neighbours" in spirit (rather than in time) and makes predictions of the spot move over the next period based on what happened during those sub-sample periods. One can easily see the close similarity of this approach to that of a technical analyst. The latter looks at historical patterns, irrespective of how close they are to the current time, and fits the perceived historical pattern on to the latest data points to predict the next move in the market now.

A simple version of this is relatively easy to implement: you calculate the correlation of, say, last week's daily price changes with historical one-week price changes and select a few weeks for which the correlations are the highest. Then, because you have the actual outcomes, you look at what was the "correct" one-step-ahead forecast for those weeks. That information can now be used to forecast the one-step-ahead currency price change as of today.

Several academic studies have applied the nearest-neighbour approach to foreign exchange rate forecasting. For example, Lisi and Medio (1997) found that nearest-neighbour forecasting significantly outperformed a random-walk alternative. Fernández-Rodríguez, Sosvilla-Rivero and Andrada-Félix (1999) confirmed the superior performance of nearest-neighbour estimates vs random-walk or linear trend-following models. In a recent update, Fernández-Rodríguez, Sosvilla-Rivero and Andrada-Félix (2000) incorporated trading cost and carry. They found that, without transaction costs, annual returns given by a nearest neighbour-based trading rule were positive in eight out of nine currencies and that it significantly outperformed commonly used moving average rules.[33] When they included five basis points per transaction as the transaction cost and took carry into account, four out of nine currencies still showed positive returns, whereas trading based on different moving average rules resulted in losses in all cases when transaction costs were included. The study is limited in the sense that it only looks at EMS currencies and five basis points may be too high for the transaction cost. Moreover, the study does not consider the impact of one-off events such as the forced devaluation of sterling and the lira.

4.5.6 Some idiosyncratic currency modelling

In passing one should mention the numerous currency "models" (or relationships if model is too big a word) which are often mentioned by practitioners in the currency market but are probably too simple or too spurious to have received rigorous treatment in academic circles. For example:

❏ Canadian dollar exchange rates are said to be predicted by movements in the share price of Nortel;
❏ similarly, the Swedish krona is said to be influenced by share price changes in Ericsson;
❏ the South African rand tracks the price of gold (which makes up a sizeable portion of the country's exports);
❏ the target's currency will rise when a cash cross-border acquisition is announced;[34]
❏ the foreign exchange option skew (see Chapter 7, Section 7.6) is said to foretell movements in the yen spot rate.[35]

And the list goes on. Some may have a more rational foundation than others. But clearly, from what we have surveyed, foreign exchange determination is a complicated business and attributing it to a single factor may not be appropriate. Even over a short period of time there may be many factors, with complicated interactions, at work. Also, from a practical viewpoint, one needs to distinguish between a contemporary relationship and a sequential relationship. The former may well exist between, say, the Canadian dollar and Nortel's share price, but unless Nortel's share price is predictable, the relationship hardly offers much value for forecasting how the Canadian dollar will move.

4.6 SOME OTHER PRACTICALITIES[36]
4.6.1 Pitfalls of data-mining

Quantitative methods based on historical data are *ex post* and the problem of biased selection is all but unavoidable. Also, it need hardly be said that the results of many modelling exercises are not applied in real life with real capital outlay, or that they may never see the light of day if they do not perform well in statistical significance tests or promise mouth-watering returns. This very fact encourages researchers (and gold-diggers) to focus on particular data sets and/or testing methods that tend to turn in favourable results and disregard other data sets and testing methods, whether consciously or otherwise. Many publicly available trading models use the same data set for optimisation and subsequent testing of the optimised model. A good result here indicates no more than a good optimisation procedure and the model may not be as valuable for trading purposes as it seems.

When possible, a data mining-type model should be tested for its out-of-sample performance. The easiest way to achieve this is to split the sample into two sections, using one to estimate the model coefficients and the other to test its performance.

4.6.2 Objectives of forecasting in the financial market

Many empirical studies in the literature have examined the predictability of foreign exchange time series. A measure that is commonly used in these studies to compare the performance of various forecasting models is the mean-square forecasting error. However, the objective of forecasting in financial markets is to maximise the return from an investment over a given time horizon. Therefore, the sign of the forecast error can be much more important than its magnitude. For example, let us say the forward rate is 95 and there are two separate forecast rates of 90 and 120. When the time comes, the actual spot rate is 100. So, the forecast errors are 10% and 20%, respectively. But is the first forecast, with the smaller error, necessarily better? An investor who went by the forecast of 90 may have decided to hedge out his positions completely (or even go short on the currency) as the currency was expected to depreciate. However, the currency actually appreciates against forward. Therefore, the forecast with the bigger error, 120, would have been the profitable one.[37]

The majority of academic studies use various significance tests based on statistical theories, the most frequently used being Student's *t*-test. Again, a coefficient might be significant at the 95% or 99% significance level, but that does not necessarily equate to a moneymaking opportunity. The question the academic typically asks is, given an estimated value and the dispersion of such estimates, could the "true" value be so different from the estimate? He does not usually treat positive dispersions and negative dispersions differently. In contrast, the important question for the practitioner is, given the historical returns and the dispersion of such returns (and for him positive and negative dispersions obviously have a completely different significance), how can one replicate a particular return going forward, taking into account all the practical constraints such as bid–ask spread, other costs, position limits and mark-to-market limits, trading size and slippage, time zone, counterparty risks, margin/collateral requirements and cashflow management, etc. It is conceivable that a profitable trading rule may forecast poorly in the conventional sense but enable the trader to position correctly during large market moves.

4.6.3 Interpreting the results with care

LeBaron (1998) gave an example that is all too familiar in the real world of trying to make money with forecasting models. He found that the performance of dynamic strategies is greatly reduced when true out-of-sample, and therefore tradable, experiments are considered. He also found that the returns from dynamic strategies are far from normally distributed, with several large outliers. So the usual risk/return statistics, such as Sharpe ratio, can be misleading as they are based on a mean–variance world. An impressive excess return may have been the correct reward for bearing the kind of risk that is not reflected in the Sharpe ratio.

In practice, we find the single most useful tool (apart, of course, from common sense – lots of it) to protect oneself against glaring mistakes is a graph. Do not believe in average annualised historical excess return; check out the cumulative excess return curve and make sure it is reasonably smooth over time. Do not believe in standard deviation; use a histogram and make sure it is not patchy or lopsided to the left. Do not believe in correlation; look at a scattergraph instead, and treat any outliers with suspicion.

4.6.4 Be wary of career forecasters

Zitzewitz (2001) studied the optimal behaviour for career forecasters, especially with regard to the so-called exaggeration or anti-herding behaviour that is observed in practice. He assumes that (1) forecasters with high ability have opinions that, on average, depart more from the consensus and (2) clients are able to discern such departures from the consensus more quickly than they can exaggeration. He finds that forecasters are more likely to exaggerate when:

❏ they are underrated by their clients;
❏ the underlying variables are especially noisy; and/or
❏ the frequency of their forecasts is lower.

How have the foreign exchange forecasters fared? There have been few studies apart from some periodic league tables compiled by magazines and newspapers, whose rankings have been likened to a game of musical chairs.[38] In one more rigorous study, Elliott and Ito (1998) tested the three-month US dollar/Japanese yen forecasts from 42 companies over the period 1985 to 1996. They found that, on average, the survey data could be used to obtain a small positive profit but that the profit was highly variable.

4.7 SUMMARY: RELEVANCE OF FORECAST MODELS IN A PORTFOLIO MANAGEMENT CONTEXT

There are two key variables in any decision-making process: return and risk. Correspondingly, there are two types of forecast models: those forecasting spot and those forecasting volatility (including correlation).[39] For a portfolio manager, models forecasting spot can be used to enhance return directly and/or for portfolio insurance. Models forecasting volatility/correlation can be used to optimise diversification and/or enhance return. For those faced with the task of choosing one or more models from the vast array available for incorporation into a strategic implementation of a currency management style as well as in the practical day-to-day management of currency risk, we think the following points are worth emphasising:

❏ on balance, the existing evidence suggest that active currency trading models can produce economically significant profit;
❏ research effort put into identifying the model(s) suitable for a particular fund is more likely to pay off if models are tested out-of-sample incorporating real trading constraints;

❏ the availability of data, computing power and statistical packages does not necessarily make forecasting easier as the end aim
remains to beat the market rather than alternative models.

APPENDIX 4A: CENTRAL BANK INTERVENTION

Some people hypothesise that, in general, central banks around the
world trade in the currency markets to dampen volatility but not to
maximise profit. Clearly, the banks' motivation is different from that
of many other market participants, and therefore it may be possible
for speculators to profit from the difference. LeBaron (1999) showed
that most of the excess return generated with a (150-day) moving
average rate rule occurred the day *before* interventions by the US
Federal Reserve. Szakmary and Mathur (1997) documented a significant link between the monthly returns from trading rules and
changes in the foreign currency reserves of five central banks
(which serve as a proxy for intervention). However, both articles
investigated the return *before* intervention, which is useless for an
investor. Neely and Weller (2001a) applied a genetic programming
approach to the situation and let the programme optimise on, in
addition to historical price data, historical intervention data. They
obtained mixed results but concluded that their findings did support the view that intervention activity by central banks is a source
of profit for technical traders in the foreign exchange market.

In a recent study, Saake (2002) utilised daily exchange rate
intervention data from both the German Bundesbank and the US
Federal Reserve between 1979 and 1994. (The daily data are not generally available to the public.) He found evidence that central banks
earn profit from intervention and that technical trading rules (150-
day moving average) are unusually profitable on days on which
intervention takes place. He explained that the two conclusions are
not necessarily contradictory as the definitions of return on which
they are based are quite different: in the case of central bank intervention the profit is defined as long-term returns, whereas for technical trading rules it is made over a short period (days). He also
observed that central banks normally make big losses in the first
few days after an intervention (ie, the spot rate moves opposite to
what central bank wants to achieve) and that the gain is made in the
long-term as spot moves in the direction intended by the intervention. So we can infer that over the short term technical traders gain

at the expense of central banks. The question is: at whose expense do the central banks gain over the long-term if foreign exchange trading is zero-sum? It is unlikely that it is at the expense of technical traders as they go in and out of the market over short periods of time. We can only speculate that the losers are the many commercial foreign exchange users and those asset managers who do not explicitly manage foreign exchange risks.

Both the frequency and magnitude of central bank intervention have decreased over the recent years. If Saake's result is correct, this would result in a reduction of profit-making opportunities for technical traders, particularly the trend-followers. This may well explain the fact that returns on currency trading have been much smaller in recent years.

APPENDIX 4B: FOREIGN EXCHANGE AND CROSS-BORDER MERGER AND ACQUISITION ANNOUNCEMENTS

Common wisdom in the foreign exchange market is that if sterling-based company A buys US dollar-based company B, company A needs to buy dollars and therefore sterling depreciates against the dollar. A refined version of this says that the exchange rate goes down if it is a cash deal but not if it is a share deal. Many a flow watcher must be disappointed at the absence of the predicted flows.

Here we try to classify a few commonly seen deal structures and the foreign exchange flows through the market that one might expect as a result. There are, almost certainly, exceptions to every case presented below, but these are the ones we have worked on or know of. We start with the simplest scenario by making the following assumptions:

❏ *assumption 1* UK (only) listed Company A acquires US (only) listed Company B. Neither company has dominant shareholders.
❏ *assumption 2* Company B has no substantial operating or financial assets/liabilities denominated in other currencies.
❏ *assumption 3* There is no uncertainty (eg, timing, different due diligence outcome, deal going hostile, regulatory issues, etc.).

Example 1: All-share deal with a fixed exchange ratio

Company A issues new shares to the shareholders of Company B according to a *fixed ratio* (one old share in Company B for x new shares in Company A). There is no immediate foreign exchange impact for Company A, but shareholders of Company B are exposed to the sterling/US dollar exchange rate, even if they get American depositary receipts (ADRs).

Possible foreign exchange consequences

❏ Some of Company B's shareholders (not Company B itself) may sell sterling and buy US dollars to hedge their sterling-denominated assets (which they may dispose of). Or, perversely, Company B's shareholders may sell dollars in anticipation of ADRs they may receive and dispose of. Potentially, these shareholders could sell dollars and buy sterling. Activities of this kind have resulted in some substantial foreign exchange flows in recent years.

Example 2: All-share deal with a variable exchange ratio

Company A issues new shares to the shareholders of Company B according to a schedule (one old share in Company B for *x* new shares depending on the ratio of Company A and Company B's future share prices over a certain period).[40] Company A could be exposed to the sterling/US dollar exchange rate as, when the schedule is computed, its share price may need to be translated into dollars to calculate the ratio. This is not a cash exposure as Company A is only issuing shares. But Company A may nevertheless decide to hedge this "dilution exposure". The direction and size of the exposure will be dependent on the nature of the schedule, but Company A is likely to have a long sterling/dollar exposure. The exposure of Company B's shareholders is similar to Example 1 but the magnitude is different.

Possible foreign exchange consequences

❏ Company A may sell sterling and buy dollars to hedge.
❏ Some of Company B's shareholders (not Company B itself) may sell sterling and buy dollars to hedge their sterling-denominated assets.

Example 3: Cash deal with Company A issuing new equities

Company A pays US dollar-denominated cash to the shareholders of Company B and issues new equities. Company A is likely to be exposed to the sterling/dollar exchange rate. It is not a direct cash exposure as the main impact is the number of shares Company A has to issue. Once the sterling cash proceeds are obtained, Company A can:

❑ use spot/forward-type transactions to move funds into the dollar – this will create a foreign exchange flow and hedge the dilution exposure; or
❑ use a cross-currency swap[41] (exchanges of principles at both ends) with a short leg to obtain US dollar funds and the long leg serving as a currency hedge – this may largely eliminate foreign exchange flows (but not necessarily the dilution exposure).

Possible foreign exchange consequences
❑ Company A may hedge its dilution exposure by selling sterling and buying dollars.
❑ Company A may take delivery on such a hedge.
❑ If it does so, Company A may settle the hedge in cash. In such cases Company A or its agent may buy sterling and dollars to reverse the hedge.

Example 4: Cash deal with Company A using its own cash

Company A pays US dollar-denominated cash to the shareholders of Company B out of its current cash resources (typically smallish deals). Company A's cash could be denominated in any currency (XYZ or US dollars) and the direction of the foreign exchange flow, if any, may not be transparent to outsiders.

Possible foreign exchange consequences
❑ Company A may sell currency XYZ and buy US dollars.

Example 5: Cash deal with Company A issuing debt

Company A pays US dollar-denominated cash to the shareholders of Company B and funds this by borrowings (public or private). Company A could borrow in any currency it chose to.

❑ Usually, Company A will borrow in US dollars to fund a dollar-denominated acquisition. There will be no immediate foreign exchange flow.

❏ Or, it can borrow in any other currency and use a cross-currency swap with the short leg to obtain US dollar funds and the long leg serving as hedge. Again, there will be no immediate foreign exchange flow. When cross-currency swaps are used, Company A creates a synthetic liability in US dollars.

❏ Or, it can borrow in sterling (or currency XYZ) and use a spot/forward-type transaction to obtain US dollar funds. This will create an immediate foreign exchange flow. In this case, Company A's liability remains in sterling (or XYZ).

Possible foreign exchange consequences

❏ Company A may sell sterling (or XYZ) and buy US dollars if it pursues the third option. In fact, Company A could pursue a mixture of all three options to separate the borrowing decision from the liability currency decision.

4B.1 Complications

In reality, deals can much more complicated than in our stylised examples. To start with, the deal could be a mixed share/cash deal funded by a mixture of instruments. Many deals have escrows – put or call options embedded in them which can potentially delay part of the currency exposure/transactions for years. Some deals have a lock-in period barring share sales by certain parties, but foreign exchange exposure may be handled separately.

The violation of assumptions 1, 2 and 3 above may also change the nature of the exposure and ensuing foreign exchange flows.

Assumption 1

❏ Both Company A and Company B could be listed on more than one stock exchange. This will complicate the picture, especially if Company A issues shares.

❏ Company B may have one or more dominant shareholders and they may negotiate to receive in different currencies.

❏ Company B may be a subsidiary of Company C. Company A and Company C may agree the deal in US dollars but settle in another currency using some fixing arrangement. This can bring direct or indirect exposures to both Company A and Company C and they can use certain instruments to hedge this type of exposure.

Assumption 2

❑ Company B may have substantial assets/liabilities in other currencies and Company A's hedge can be different in terms of currency and/or magnitude.

Assumption 3

❑ There can be a host of uncertainty factors which may influence the timing and nature of a currency hedge. It is rare that a currency hedge, even if the direction and size is as expected, takes place at exactly the time the deal is announced or closed (the very time those foreign exchange flow watchers take notice of such deals). The hedge might have been put in place during the months leading up to the announcement. Or it might be effected any time between announcement and close, which in some cases can be years.

❑ Options are sometimes are used in such circumstances and the currency impact can be even more convoluted when an option is put on, unwound and/or rolled into forwards.

1   These are not necessarily listed in the order of who is more likely to get it right. The often-heard saying of someone in the business of forecasting currency movements runs along the lines of "he successfully predicted 13 out of the five US dollar bear periods in the last two decades". See Section 4.6.4 on career forecasters.

2   Recent surveys in this area can be found in Engel (1996) and Lewis (1995).

3   Readers interested in pursuing topics covered in this chapter further can consult the following books: Dunis and Zhou (eds) (1998), *Non-linear Modelling of High Frequency Financial Time Series*; Acar and Satchell (1997) *Advance Trading Rules*; Taylor (1986), *Modelling Financial Time Series*; and Pardo (1992), *Design, Testing, and Optimisation of Trading Systems*.

4   The Big Mac Index is available on *The Economist* website at www.economist.com/markets/Bigmac/index.cfm.

5   See Froot and Rogoff (1995), Rogoff (1996), Goldberg and Knetter (1997) and Taylor (2001) for discussions and reference.

6   It was originally introduced to augment the classical monetary model in order to explain the impact of "sterilised" foreign exchange intervention, where monetary supply is deliberately kept constant.

7   The figures were compiled shortly before the slump in the equity markets worldwide.

8   See also Isard (1995) and Taylor (1995).

9   These types of models have flourished in recent years. Frankel and Rose might make different observations on the depth and width of the research area now.

10 One potentially serious problem with macroeconomic data series is that most series have been revised since initial release. See Faust, Rogers and Wright (2001).

11 See, for example, Kilian (1999), Berkowitz and Giorgianni (2001) and Berben and van Dijk (1998).

12 Taylor and Allen's (1992) survey of trading strategies adopted by London foreign exchange dealers provides evidence of the popularity of technical analysis in foreign exchange markets. Dealers indicated that technical rather than fundamental analysis mainly determined their short-term, intra-day to one week, forecasting.

13 We thank an anonymous currency researcher/trader for pointing out that the rules can be based on fuzzy logic, like those he uses himself, and so do not need to be rigid.

14 See Sullivan, Timmermann and White (1998) for a discussion on statistical bias and Bessembinder and Chan (1998) for a discussion of the impact of transaction costs.

15 Baz *et al.* (2001) construct a simple mean–variance portfolio assuming that the expected change in the exchange rate is zero and the risk premium on currency investment equals the negative of the interest rate differential. They look at a portfolio of US dollars, Swiss francs, Japanese yen, Deutschmarks and sterling over the 1989–98 period in which, on average, short positions in yen and Swiss franc are taken vs long positions in sterling, Deutschmark and the dollar. They find that the Sharpe ratio of the portfolio, at 0.80, is higher than those of portfolios of US Treasury or global government bonds.

16 For further reference see Fama (1984), Hodrick (1987), Canova and Marrinan (1993) and Engel (1996).

17 See Clarida and Taylor (1997) for further details.

18 Billingsley and Chance (1996) report that of the commodity trading advisors (CTAs) trading only in specialised markets, 41.2% trade in bonds and interest rate futures, 30.9% trade currencies, 15.5% trade commodities and 12.4% trade stock index futures. Fung and Hsieh (2001) find evidence, using an option-based style attribution analysis on trend-following CTAs (most CTAs are trend followers) that currency markets are the most favourable for trend-following styles and stock indices the least favourable. Risk capital will probably deployed accordingly.

19 See Brock, Lakonishok and LeBaron (1992) for a detailed discussion of the bootstrapping technique.

20 There may be a theoretical link between the Bollinger band and so-called volatility clustering or Arch-type models. Interested readers may also wish to explore a modelling technique known as the threshold autoregressive process (see Enders and Granger (1998), Berben and van Dijk (1999) and Coakley and Fuertes (2001)).

21 Seasonality remains an actively researched topic in equities, commodities, weather derivatives, bonds and real estate.

22 Transaction prices for equities and many bonds have to be reported and are usually available to the public. Foreign exchange prices from vendors such as Reuters and Bloomberg are indicative and do not usually correspond to transaction prices. Recent work by Donielsson and Payne (2002) shows that indicative prices are more volatile than transaction prices and the bid–offer spread in indicative prices does not reflect market liquidity. Also, they show that indicative prices lag transaction prices by up to three minutes but that the lag disappears when the horizon is longer than five minutes. Their result has important implications for the testing of tick-level trading models on indicative prices.

23 This may not yield useful insight due to the asset substitution problem. Currency is one of the most commoditised assets and different instruments can provide near perfect substitution. For example, spot positions may be cross-hedged with forward positions, euro/US dollar positions may appear through euro/Japanese yen and US dollar/Japanese yen and vice versa.

24 See Bollerslev and Melvin (1994), Lyons (1995 and 2002), Evans and Lyons (1999).

25 Olsen offers asset management as well as forecasting services. More information on the company as well as high-frequency data research is available at www.olsen.ch/index.html.

26 For example, Dacorogna *et al.* (1993) and Pictet *et al.* (1992) in addition to the Dacorogna *et al.* (1995) study discussed here.

27 See Osler's (2000) article "Support for resistance: technical analysis and intraday exchange rates".

28 This is a very time-consuming exercise. The authors indicated that it would take a 120 MHz Pentium-based computer at least 81 days to repeat their computation.

29 For an equity return forecast model, see Cremers (2000). One reason why Bayesian updating is not widely used in foreign exchange forecasting is the general application of Arch/Garch-type models for that purpose. In approach they are very similar to Bayesian updating but without the restrictive priors.

30 The three sub-models are estimated simultaneously using a technique called seemingly unrelated regressions (SUR or SURE). SUR belongs to a class of statistical models known as vector autoregressions (or, somewhat confusingly, VAR). In layman's terms, VAR estimates several regressions at once to capture the interactions between them efficiently. VAR models have become increasingly popular in research work because (1) the estimation process is now standardised and included in many off-the-shelf packages and (2) many researchers focus on non-linearity in financial price data. And, finally, VAR is often combined with Bayesian analysis to improve accuracy and make efficient use of all available information.

31 See Weigend, Rumelhart and Huberman (1991), Kuan and Liu (1995), Hann and Steurer (1996), Zhang and Hu (1998), Hu *et al.* (1999), and Gabbi *et al.* (1999). For a comprehensive treatment see Azoff (1994).

32 There are many commercially available packages – for example, NeuroShell (www.wardsystems.com), Thinks (www.sigma-research.com/bookshelf/), BrainMaker (www.calsci.com), EXPO (www.lmt-expo.com) and Matlab (www.mathworks.com).

33 Short-dated moving average (one- and five-day) vs long-dated moving average (50-, 150- and 200-day).

34 See Appendix 4B for a detailed discussion.

35 A more obscure but no less entertaining version in the market attributes such clairvoyant powers to the average length of girls' skirts in Tokyo.

36 Very few articles discuss the practical issues of forecasting. Two useful works are Ballocchi (1998) and Diebold and Lopez (1997).

37 Leicht and Tanner (1991) conclude that only a directional measure corresponds closely to trading profit from forecast models.

38 The forecast included in these league tables is usually based on fundamentals. The quantitative forecast may not feature in these league tables as its horizon is typically shorter.

39 Currency volatility is considered to be a class distinct from equity and fixed-income volatility as the former is traded with considerable liquidity and is therefore far more detached from the underlying spot. Some market participants, admittedly more of the hedge funds type, treat currency implied volatility as a separate asset class.

40 An example of such an arrangement is Vivendi's all-stock offer for Seagram. The offer was subject to a collar defined on the future Vivendi share price *expressed in US dollars*.

41 With exchange of principle at both ends. Same when referred to later.

Optimisation and Hedge Ratios

5.1 INTRODUCTION

The now ubiquitous mean–variance portfolio optimisation theory provides the foundation for the investment management industry. In the next section we briefly review the mainstream international capital asset pricing models (ICAPM) with progressively more relaxed assumptions, looking at both the theoretical and practical issues for optimisation, including currency, and emphasising the implications for currency hedging and overlay.[1] The practical relevance of these models to the topics covered in this book is probably limited, but as they provide some justification for the practice of currency hedging, this aspect will be discussed here.

The practical application of the CAPM or ICAPM is fraught with difficulties – many, but not all, of which have their roots in the assumptions made by Markowitz, Sharpe and others. On the one hand, the existence and efficiency of the market portfolio is questionable on many fronts. On the other, many empirical studies do not support the assumption of the (stable) multinormality of returns. This non-normality or instability results in constant changes of variance–covariance matrix and of the "optimal" portfolios. These problems are not unique to foreign exchange risk management, and practical solutions have been presented in volumes of studies written in the portfolio management area. In this chapter we will consider just a few topics that are specific to currencies. In many ways, it is precisely these imperfections of the world that provide the foundation of almost the whole fund management industry. The analogy applies here too: in a perfect world the currency question is quite easy to deal with, both theoretically and practically. We look at a several topics on the imperfections in the field of CAPM optimisation and discuss their relevance to currency risk management.

The currency decision in an international portfolio is often expressed as a hedge ratio, which is the percentage of the underlying exposure in a foreign currency that is hedged. Section 5.5 reviews some commonly used hedge ratios and the methods of obtaining them. Again, we focus on the practical difficulties and ways of overcoming them. The last three sections of the chapter cover practical topics related to currency optimisation. Section 5.6 briefly discusses how currency risk management is dealt with in an asset–liability optimisation (as opposed to asset allocation optimisation, which is the optimisation method used in most existing works in the field). In Section 5.7 we look at currency basket hedging, a practical currency-hedging method used by many fund managers that aims to exploit the diversification benefit of a basket of currency exposures. Section 5.8 contains a short discussion on the implications of section-based investment and currency management.

5.2 CAPM AND CURRENCIES
5.2.1 Background
The domestic version of the CAPM predicts that (1) everyone holds a combination of the domestic market portfolio and the domestic risk-free asset and (2) the domestic securities are priced according to their domestic βs. Similarly, the international version of the CAPM (ICAPM) predicts that everyone holds a combination of the world market portfolio and the risk-free asset in their own domestic currency.[2] Depending on the assumptions made in the model, this portfolio may be partially hedged against currency moves. Theoretically, the hedge ratio can be dependent on the investor's risk-aversion and his relative wealth. The hedge ratio can also be different for different assets, currencies and investors.

The extension of single-β CAPM and arbitrage pricing theory (APT) models to international pricing relationships attempts to answer several questions:

❏ are assets priced domestically or globally?
❏ does foreign exchange affect expected returns?
❏ how should currency hedging feature in a CAPM framework and how much exchange rate risk should an investor optimally hedge?

ICAPM tries to answer or explain other questions or observed abnormalities, including:

❏ why do investors hold much more of the domestic asset than predicted by the models (the so-called "home bias")?
❏ why are there such large variations in international equity flows?
❏ why is the correlation between asset returns from different countries not stable over time?

Technically, the extension from a domestic to an international setting can be complicated for the following reasons.

❏ One has to make assumptions about the behaviour of exchange rates, especially about nominal exchange rates vs real exchange rates vs local inflation. One also has to make an assumption on the validity of PPP. The nominal asset returns can be different for investors in different countries.[3]
❏ The consumption as well as investment opportunities for investors based in different countries (currencies) might be different due to different tastes and various country-specific restrictions, and the models need to address this.

Both of the above could result in heterogeneous beliefs among investors (as investors may perceive the returns on the same assets differently), whereas homogeneous beliefs is a key assumption in the original CAPM framework. One of the goals of ICAPM is to examine how these country-induced differences can affect investors' portfolio holdings and the expected returns on assets in a particular currency.

The seminal works on ICAPM are those by Solnik (1974), Sercu (1980), Stulz (1984) and Adler and Dumas (1983). These works provided the general equilibrium extension to some earlier ideas. The starting point in these studies is the modelling of portfolio holdings of representative agents in different countries and obtaining pricing relationships through aggregation and market equilibrium conditions. Another approach, the international extension of APT (IAPT), starts from the assumption that foreign exchange is simply another asset class whose returns are driven by the same set of factors that drive asset returns. Solnik (1983b) and Ikeda (1991) showed that IAPT can be applied to international investment. In our review we include only the basic ICAPM models. For comprehensive surveys in this area, refer to Stulz (1995) and Frankel (1994). This book is a practical guide to currency overlay and we do not intend to delve into detailed theoretical expositions on these topics, interesting as they may be.

5.2.2 Basic ICAPM models

5.2.2.1 Single-factor model
Stehle (1977) and Stulz (1984, 1995) developed single-factor ICAPM models where the key assumption is that PPP holds. The main assumptions are:

1. equal consumption in all countries;
2. equal investment opportunities in all countries;
3. PPP holds;
4. investors are risk-averse; and
5. investors maximise end-of-period consumption.

Additional assumptions are that:

6. in any country an asset with a risk-free return denominated in that country's currency exists and this asset has zero world market beta in real terms; and
7. the inflation in any country is uncorrelated with nominal asset returns.

It can then be shown that all investors desire a combination of the risk-free asset and a portfolio of risky assets that is common to all investors across the countries (ie, world market portfolio). Finally, no currency hedging is necessary as there is no real exchange rate risk. The pricing relationship in real terms can then be written as follows:

$$E[r_A^r] = \beta^r E[r_W^r]$$

or, with assumptions 6 and 7, in nominal terms,

$$E[r_A^n] = \beta^n E[r_W^n]$$

where E is the expectation operator, r_A^r and r_A^n are the real and nominal excess returns on an asset, r_W^r and r_W^n are the real and nominal excess returns on the world market portfolio, and β^r and β^n are the sensitivity of the real or nominal excess returns of an asset to the real or nominal excess returns of the world market portfolio. Assumption 7 above ensures that $\beta^r = \beta^n$.

Problems with the single-factor model are that:

❏ PPP does not hold;
❏ both consumption and investment opportunity sets differ across countries; and
❏ assumption 7 on inflation and returns is not supported by empirical evidence.

5.2.2.2 Solnik–Sercu currency-hedging model

A model incorporating currency hedging has been proposed by Solnik (1974) and Sercu (1980). Here the key assumptions are that PPP does not hold but that inflation is zero. The assumptions are as follows:

❏ equal investment opportunities across countries;
❏ different consumption sets across countries;
❏ perfect capital flows;
❏ zero local inflation;
❏ PPP does not necessarily hold;
❏ exchange rate is uncorrelated with stock returns in the domestic currency (relaxed in Sercu (1980));
❏ in each country a risk-free bond exists;
❏ no international trade in consumption goods.

Then,

$$E[{}^H r_A - c_A] = {}^H\beta E[{}^H r_W - c_W]$$

where E is the expectation operator, ${}^H r_A$ is excess stock return conditional on a minimum-variance foreign exchange hedge, ${}^H r_W$ is excess return on the hedged world market portfolio, and c_A and c_W

are the cost of hedging foreign exchange risk in the stock and in the world market portfolio, respectively. $^H\beta$ is the currency-hedged beta obtained by regressing currency-hedged stock returns on currency-hedged market returns. Note that the risk-free rates used on both sides of the equation may be different. Also, the pricing relationships in nominal and real terms are the same because of the zero-inflation assumption.

In a Solnik–Sercu framework, every investor in the world holds a combination of:

❏ the world market portfolio hedged against foreign exchange risk (pure market risk);
❏ a portfolio of the risk-free bonds of all countries (pure exchange risk); and
❏ the risk-free bonds of his own country (foreign exchange hedge).

The model has the following implications for investors' currency-hedging behaviour:

❏ investors will hedge currency fluctuations in equity holdings according to a minimum-variance hedge;
❏ if the expected return on the currency forward contract is not zero, investors may in addition take speculative currency positions; and
❏ stock positions are determined conditional on a minimum-variance currency hedge, ie, one should use currency-hedged stock returns and a variance–covariance matrix in the optimisation process.

5.2.2.3 Currency risk premium in the Solnik–Sercu model
One can impose equilibrium conditions on the Solnik–Sercu model in the assets and currency forward markets and derive the currency risk premium in equilibrium. To do this, the important observation must be made that in the model the riskless asset in a given country serves two fundamentally different purposes for different investors (Solnik, 1993):

❏ it is a *foreign* (risky) investment for foreign investors, who hold it for returns;
❏ it is a *domestic* (riskless) investment for domestic investors, who hold it for hedging.

It then follows that the expected currency return has two terms. The first is the traditional CAPM term associated with the correlation between currency forward returns and world market returns, and the second is the additional currency risk premium. However, the model offers very little guidance for empirical testing on the currency risk premium as the hedge portfolio is linked to investors' risk tolerance and is therefore unobservable.

5.2.2.4 Inflation model

If we introduce domestic inflation into the models, the investment in domestic bonds is no longer risk-free in real terms and investors will look to maximise their end-of-period wealth or consumption in real terms. In this setting Adler and Dumas (1983) were the first to demonstrate that the optimal portfolio for a particular type of investor will consist of two components:

❑ a universal portfolio of risky assets that is the same for all investors; and
❑ an individual portfolio that provides the closest hedging against domestic inflation (portfolio compositions will differ depending on the investor's domestic currency, the divergence of (perceived) local and foreign inflation and the local consumption basket).

The following multi-β pricing relationship can be obtained:

$$E[r_A^n] = \beta E[r_W^n] + \Sigma \beta_I E[r_I]$$

where E is the expectation operator, r_A^n and r_W^n are the nominal excess returns on an asset and the world market portfolio, respectively, r_I is the inflation premium, and β_I is the correlation between nominal excess returns on an asset and the rate of inflation in each country. β_I is summed over all countries in the world market portfolio.

The model has the following implications for investors' currency-hedging behaviour:

❑ investors will hedge a portion of their stock positions by taking short positions in deposits. The hedge ratio is a function of risk-aversion; for more risk-averse investors, the ratio is close to one.
❑ in equilibrium (net zero supply of domestic deposits), the hedge ratios for investors based in different countries are different,

depending on the (aggregate) risk-aversion of all investors and the ratio of their wealth in relation to stockmarket capitalisation.

5.2.3 Empirical evidence on ICAPM

Although a comprehensive survey of the empirical evidence would not suit our purposes here, the following relevant summary points can be made:[4]

❏ on balance, the evidence is supportive of the international capital asset pricing model, namely, that national market risk premiums are determined internationally.
❏ the ICAPM does not seem to be able to explain the variation in the returns from different securities, though this may stem from the lack of explanatory power of the CAPM. Multifactor models (such as international APT) have been shown to improve on the explanatory power.
❏ exchange rate risk is probably priced in the expected returns, and for countries other than the US it is significant. According to De Santis and Gerald (1998), almost 64% of the total excess return is attributable to currency.[5]

5.3 CAPM, FOREIGN EXCHANGE HEDGING AND OVERLAY

Except in the simplest models, where exchange rate risk is more or less assumed away (as in the single-factor model discussed in Section 5.2.2.1), investors will in general hedge the currency risk under a given ICAPM framework. But how much an investor will hedge seems to vary with different factors depending on the model. Some commentators argue that hedging reduces currency volatility without compromising expected returns, and every investor should therefore hedge the currency risk fully to take advantage of this "free lunch". The assertion can of course be challenged on empirical grounds: as we have seen in Chapter 4, there is evidence that foreign exchange returns may not be zero. On a theoretical level, one can show that if the expected return for hedging is zero for the domestic investor, it is not possible for it to be zero for the foreign investor.[6]

People sometimes claim that a currency overlay programme is not justified theoretically. For example, to determine the optimal stock allocation in the Solnik–Sercu model, one needs to know the minimum-variance currency hedge. However, to determine the minimum-variance currency hedge, one needs to know the optimal stock allocation! Therefore, only a joint optimisation will give the efficient portfolio. The overlay currency-hedging mechanism, narrowly defined (see Chapter 3, Section 3.3), means that the currency decisions are taken independently of the structure of the underlying stock selection and therefore they are theoretically sub-optimal.

So how do we reconcile the apparent disparity between the theory and the growing acceptance of currency overlay management? A few thoughts here:

❏ overlay can include a spectrum of divergent management styles and optimisation procedures;
❏ the low starting point for many funds – historically, currency risks were not even recognised by many funds;
❏ parameter uncertainty (discussed in Section 5.5.6)
❏ economies of scale – large specialist overlay funds can exploit their market power to obtain better prices and to lower administration costs;
❏ more research is needed.

Our view is that the uncertainty over parameters, which is a particularly acute problem for currency risk management, presents the main backdrop for the suitability of a separate currency optimisation process. We will develop this idea further in the next sections.

On a broader note, it is not only currency overlay that has found little love in the theoretical playground of finance. Many of the models and practices that are widely utilised by the investment profession have no place in the traditional field of finance, which, in some sense, reached a point of stagnation in the 1980s.[7] The last breakthroughs were, of course, option pricing theory and risk-neutral valuation. While awaiting new advances from the theoreticians, we think that a healthy mix of common sense and pragmatism, a keen eye for opportunities arising from market anomalies and a sound, quantitatively based risk management approach are the order of the day.

5.4 GLOBAL OPTIMISATION AND THE ROLE OF CURRENCY

Following up from the previous section, there are three possible ways of including currency in the global mean–variance

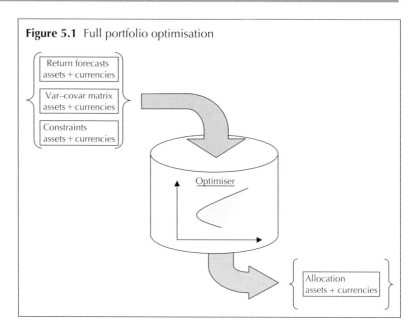

Figure 5.1 Full portfolio optimisation

Return forecasts
assets + currencies

Var–covar matrix
assets + currencies

Constraints
assets + currencies

Optimiser

Allocation
assets + currencies

optimisation (Jorion, 1994):[8]

❑ full portfolio optimisation;
❑ partial portfolio optimisation;
❑ separate currency optimisation.

In a full portfolio optimisation (Figure 5.1), currency is treated in exactly the same way as any other asset class in the portfolio and the correlation between various currencies and assets is taken into consideration during the optimisation process. The optimised portfolio can be compared with a portfolio where currency decisions are not taken separately; any difference can be attributed to the cost/benefit aspect of managing currency risk within the global portfolio. The currency positions will contain a hedge portion and a speculative portion.

In a partial portfolio optimisation approach the asset portfolio is optimised first without currency considerations (Figure 5.2). Once the allocation is determined, a separate currency optimisation is run with the underlying asset positions as given. The output of the second-stage optimisation will yield a currency allocation that is dependent on the output of the first-stage optimisation. The second-stage allocation can either be done within the investment

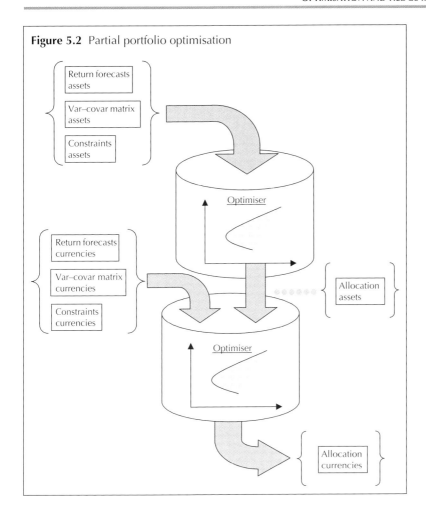

Figure 5.2 Partial portfolio optimisation

portfolio, in which case the portfolio manager retains the owner-ship of currency risks, or by an overlay manager.

In a separate currency optimisation approach, asset and cur-rency decisions are made independently of each other in two sepa-rate optimisation processes (Figure 5.3). Jorion (1994) classified this approach as currency overlay as well, but it is probably more akin to running a currency fund than an overlay.

In practice, the currency optimisation method for a given fund cannot be so easily classified and it is complicated by many factors, such as the particular optimisation model a fund chooses to use, investment constraints, risk management limits (both absolute and

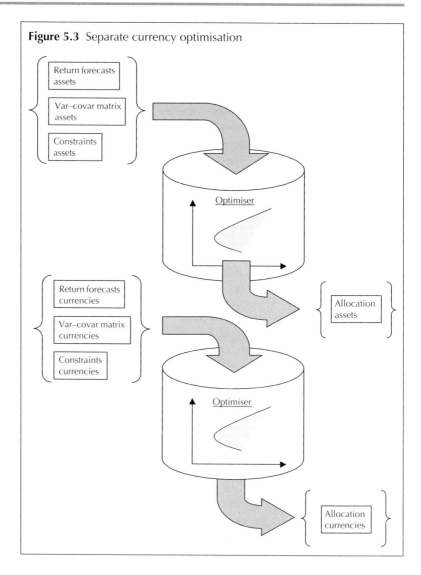

Figure 5.3 Separate currency optimisation

relative to a benchmark), and communication between different managers and between the fund and custodians, etc. For example, some mandates specify that currency be treated in a particular way that renders joint optimisation infeasible. From our experience, the overlay method used by most investment funds is closer in spirit to partial optimisation, namely, underlying positions are first optimised and then the currency decisions are taken, whether by internal or external currency managers. Some funds have better co-ordination between the different parts and the procedure is therefore more like a joint optimisation. With others there is very little timely communication between overlay and asset managers and the procedure is more like a separate optimisation.

Overall, we feel that the scope for adding value via a CAPM-type optimisation over currencies is probably limited and this is the reason why we do not devote more space to a survey of studies on this topic, many of which chart or table efficiency frontiers with and without currency optimisations. There are many known problems with CAPM optimisation in general, and additional optimisation over currencies can only be as useful as how a fund views (and remedies) the particular CAPM-type optimisation method it chooses to adopt. In fact, optimisation over currencies may well be less useful, mainly due to the problem of parameter uncertainty. As a rule of thumb in an optimisation, error in return estimates is 10 times as bad as error in variance estimates and 20 times as bad as error in covariance estimates. In practice, currency return estimates are at best arbitrary. Rather than choosing a particular set of return estimates and letting an optimiser tell him the answer he more or less expects anyway, an investor or fund manager may wish to set a passive hedge ratio in the same way he sets his strategic asset allocations. Active positions can be taken, if so desired, using one of the methods described in Chapter 2.

An alternative, minimum-variance optimisation, taken from the literature on the futures/forward relationship, alleviates the problem of return estimation. An optimal hedge ratio is chosen to minimise the variance of the combined portfolio of the underlying and the currency hedges. It is not uncommon to see tables and charts showing the risk reduction achievable through varying levels of hedge ratio. The charts often present either as a downward-sloping curve (which indicates that you should hedge fully) or as a smiley face, curling up towards both ends (which indicates that you should hedge at the lowest point).[9] Most of these results are *ex post* and some strong assumptions may have been made to obtain them: a bivariate normal distribution for foreign exchange and the underlying as well as a stable covariance between them over time. Academic studies in *ex ante* settings have cast doubt on the validity of such an approach as the optimised minimum-variance hedge ratio does not offer significant performance improvement over a simple passive hedge ratio.[10] One reason for this, we can only speculate, is the unstable covariance between currencies and the underlying. The *ex post* approach can, however, be useful on a strategic level when a passive hedge ratio is set.

5.5 HEDGE RATIOS

For many funds the currency decision is expressed in terms of a hedge ratio rather than a currency allocation weighting. The hedge ratio is defined as the percentage of the notional amount of currency hedging with respect to the underlying exposure. It can be applied to a stock, a country or a portfolio. When expressed in this way it is assumed that, at the benchmark level, the currency positions taken by a manager are restricted to those currencies where the fund has an underlying position against the base currency. Currency overlay mandates usually stipulate the benchmark hedge ratio as well as the maximum and minimum hedge ratios that active management can reach for risk control purposes.

A hedge ratio can be:

❏ *fixed* – for example, 0% or 100%, or 50% or 77%. 100% is also called the unitary hedge ratio, 50%, the minimum regret hedge ratio, and 77%, Black's universal hedge ratio; or
❏ *dynamic* (systematic) – for example, an option replication hedge ratio.

Just like the asset allocation decision, the hedge ratio can be derived from an asset–liability study or via an asset-only optimisation.[11] In practice, many fund managers simply set a hedge ratio not because it optimises anything but because it is intuitive or easy to administrate.

The optimal currency-hedge ratio, if a fixed hedge ratio is deemed appropriate, may depend on a few factors, amongst them:

❏ risk/return objectives;
❏ investment constraints;
❏ the optimisation technique used by a particular fund for its non-currency investment; and/or
❏ practicalities such as cash management (discussed in Chapter 9), parameter uncertainty, historical data, estimation methods (especially for correlation).

In this section we review some commonly used hedge ratios and proceed to discuss the practical problems a fund manager may encounter when he tries to use optimisation methods to determine a hedge ratio.

5.5.1 Unitary hedge ratio

Most work on the effectiveness of currency in portfolios has used a unitary, or 100%, hedge ratio. This makes sense if one assumes that currency only adds noise to a portfolio without adding any return or diversification benefit. Theoretical and empirical support for a unitary hedging strategy can be found in Eaker and Grant (1990) and Adler and Simon (1986). In practice, a 100% hedge ratio is common for global bond portfolios, whereas for equity portfolios or balanced portfolios there is a range of selections between 0% and 100%.

Critics of the unitary hedge ratio cite the following:

❏ it may be too large for many portfolios as it does not take potential correlation between currency and the underlying exposure into consideration.[12]

❏ it may cause large swings in the cashflow account due to the fact that hedging contracts need to be settled in cash at expiry.

❏ it may restrict the ability of currency managers to take active positions and therefore limit the scope for alpha generation. Many mandates forbid the currency manager to take on currency positions where there is no matching underlying exposure, which means that the hedging ratio cannot exceed 100%.

❏ a predefined 100% hedge ratio may not allow efficient utilisation of new information. Some academic studies show that the efficiency of currency hedging can improve significantly if hedge ratios are updated regularly, attributing this to the changing relationship between foreign exchange and the underlying. Others, however, argue that the regular update should not affect a passive hedge ratio though it should be part of active management. The latter should be policy-driven and therefore remain relatively constant.

However, a unitary hedge ratio is easy to implement and recent research has shown that, in the presence of parameter uncertainty, it may even outperform its more sophisticated relatives.

5.5.2 Dynamic hedge ratios

In contrast to other types of hedge ratio discussed in this section, a dynamic hedge ratio is not fixed. Any system trading strategy, including those reviewed in Chapter 4, can be incorporated into a benchmark to provide dynamic hedge ratios. The commonly used dynamic hedge ratio is the option replication hedge ratio, also known as delta. It is used, as its name suggests, to replicate the payoff of an option where the exposure is completely hedged when the exchange rate moves against the investor, but the exposure is left open when the exchange rate moves in a favourable direction.

An option replication hedge ratio is more complicated than a fixed hedge ratio and can potentially alleviate the cashflow problem associated with the unitary hedge ratio. Apart from marketing literature put out by currency managers who specialise in such strategies, we are not aware of any neutral research into their effectiveness. There is, however, a stream of research on whether it is cheaper to replicate an option than to purchase one, and this is reviewed, along with the topic of option replication strategies, in Chapter 8.

5.5.3 Black's universal hedge ratio

Solnik (1974) was the first to consider the existence of a universal hedge ratio, ie, a hedge ratio that is the same for all investors in all countries. Later, Black (1989, 1990) proposed a model to derive this ratio. He made the following assumptions:

❏ the risk tolerance of investors is the same across all countries/ currencies; and
❏ stockmarket capitalisation in each country is equal to net wealth in that country, and there is no domestic or foreign debt, ie, no net foreign investment.

Black solved for the optimal hedging decision assuming that investors try to minimise portfolio variance. The first assumption is needed to ensure that no investors borrow or lend aside from the basic currency-hedging motivation. The second assumption is used to link total hedging (in terms of borrowings and lendings; see Section 5.2.2.2) with the world wealth and assets in equilibrium. He arrived at the following formula for the universal hedge ratio:

$$h = \frac{r_W - \text{var}(r_W)}{r_W - \dfrac{\text{var}(e)}{2}}$$

where h is Black's universal hedge ratio, r_W is the excess return on the world market portfolio, $\text{var}(r_W)$ is the variance of the world market return and $\text{var}(e)$ is the average variance of the currencies in the world market portfolio. Using Black's suggested parameter values – world market excess return, 8%, world market volatility, 15%, and currency volatility, 10% – we obtain the often quoted value of Black's universal hedge ratio of 77%. $(0.08 - 0.15^2)/(0.08 - 0.10^2/2)$.

Black's universal hedge ratio has been criticised because of its unrealistic assumptions. First, the definitions of world market excess return, world market variance and currency variance are arbitrary (Jorion and Khoury, 1995, pp. 296–8). Second, the universality has been shown by Adler and Prasad (1990) to come directly from the assumption of no net foreign investment, which is of course violated all the time given balance of payment surpluses and deficits.[13] In the absence of net foreign investment, domestic deposits play a double role as the risk-free investment for domestic investors and as the currency hedge for foreign investors. And third, the assumption of a homogeneous risk tolerance by investors in different countries is too restrictive.

What makes Black's universal hedge ratio stand out is the idea of partial hedging. Many investment managers adopt a partial hedging approach to currency risk out of the desire to minimise regret.[14] A partial hedging approach also makes sense in theory. According to a general equilibrium ICAPM, the optimal portfolio is the world market portfolio partially hedged against exchange rate moves. That way, if everyone adopts the strategy, it will be feasible and equilibrium can be achieved.

5.5.4 Alternatives to Black's universal hedge ratio

As an alternative, Adler and Prasad (1990) propose that investors use the minimum-variance hedge ratios (regression coefficients) that result from regressing the return of an index measured in a specific currency against forward currency returns measured in that currency. A technical condition known as Jensen's inequality guarantees that the hedge ratio for a holding in a given currency will be the same for each national investor regardless of his base currency.[15] As an example, the US dollar (sterling) investor would obtain the appropriate hedge ratios for hedging the exchange rate risk of investing in the Canadian stockmarket by regressing an historical time series of Canadian stockmarket returns denominated in US dollars (sterling) against the corresponding rates of return of the forward exchange rate for the Canadian dollar quoted in terms of the US dollar (sterling). In this way, two cross-currency hedge ratios would be determined. And the two hedge ratios should be the same.

This approach offers a practical alternative to Black's method and it is sometimes used by investment managers. However, as the method is based on historical data the historical returns and variance–covariance play a key role in determining the hedge ratio. In an unconstrained regression some hedge ratios can be negative, which means that the investor actually increases his currency exposure, and they are prone to change when different sample periods are used.

5.5.5 Optimisation and hedge ratios: the empirical evidence[16]

It is easy to see that in theory the first optimisation approach discussed in Section 5.4 probably offers the most efficient outcome as all available information is exploited. Jorion (1994) used historical bond and foreign exchange return data to demonstrate the progressive efficiency loss that occurs from full to partial to separate optimisation. In fact, he computed that for an equity portfolio over the period 1978–91, joint optimisation could have added up to 173 basis points per annum. Using partial optimisation, one would have incurred a loss of 35bp, and with separate optimisation a further 66bp. The same figures for a bond portfolio are much larger due to the high correlation between bond returns and foreign exchange returns: for the same period joint optimisation would have added as much as 273bp per annum, whereas partial optimisation would have lost 171bp and separate optimisation a further 65bp. He concluded that any form of foreign exchange separation is sub-optimal and that an overlay strategy ought not to be applied to a bond portfolio.

These results are to be expected because, when the number of assets increases, the results can only improve when *ex post* parameter inputs are used. Their practical relevance is very limited since a manager would need perfect foresight when conducting his optimisations, which of course he does not have. In a real-world *ex ante* situation, the parameters required for the optimisation must be estimated from historical data. It is possible that the attempt to determine the optimal currency-hedge weights results in inferior performance compared to using a simple unitary hedge strategy, or even unhedged international investment. In an *ex ante* study, Glen and Jorion (1993) compared portfolios hedged with an optimal combination of forward contracts with a unitary hedging strategy and portfolios hedged using Black's universal hedge ratio. They found that the optimally hedged portfolios performed best, but not significantly better than the unitary hedge ratio or Black's universal hedge ratio. Moreover, they found that Black's universal hedge ratio does not outperform the unitary hedge ratio either. Their study also tested the minimum-variance hedge ratio, and this did not offer any performance improvement either. Their results are confirmed in other *ex ante* studies on the topic (see Eun and Resnick, 1994, and Larsen and Resnick, 2000). These *ex ante* studies generally show that full currency hedging is more beneficial to bond and balanced portfolios than equity portfolios. On balance, it seems reasonable to conclude that optimised hedge ratios do not necessarily improve the hedging performance over that achievable with a fixed hedge ratio and that Black's universal hedge ratio is not necessarily better than an arbitrary 100% hedge ratio.

Levich and Thomas (1993b) showed that a fully hedged bond portfolio has a higher Sharpe ratio (0.38 vs 0.29) than its unhedged counterpart. Hauser and Levy (1991) indicated that a full currency hedge is more beneficial for shorter-maturity foreign bond portfolios. Reiner (2000) contended that a fully hedged equity portfolio has a lower Sharpe ratio (0.18 vs 0.26) than its unhedged counterpart. This is somewhat at odds with an earlier study by Eaker and Grant (1990) in which they claimed that fully hedged equity portfolios outperform unhedged portfolios.

Most of these studies use Sharpe ratio as the performance measure and the result will therefore be sensitive to the sample period and base currency. Most use the US dollar as the base currency. Eun and Resnick (1994) examined hedging performance by US- and Japan-based investors. They found that a full hedge is beneficial both *ex ante* and *ex post* for US-based investors but only beneficial *ex post* for Japan-based investors. The second part of their conclusion can be attributed to the data set, in which the yen-denominated domestic bond portfolio has the highest Sharpe ratio, which is difficult to beat. It would be interesting to see whether the negative forward points from currency hedging would have compounded the problem.

Braccia (1995) looked at the impact of transaction costs on hedge ratios. He found that the optimal hedge ratio can be reduced substantially (from 80% to 30%) when transaction costs are considered.

Detzler (1997), using the return data (net of expenses) for global mutual bond funds during the period 1988–95, confirmed that returns on these funds are sensitive to exchange rate movements and that the latter contribute significantly to the volatility of passive government bond indices. She also correlated the returns of a fully currency-hedged bond benchmark to those of the mutual funds and found that the link between them is weak. This suggests that the bond portfolios may not be fully hedged against currency movements.

5.5.6 Parameter uncertainty and structural models

Larsen and Resnick (2000) performed an *ex ante* study comparing unhedged international equity investment, unitary hedging, a properly computed Black's universal hedge ratio, an arbitrary (but frequently cited) estimate of 0.77 for Black's universal hedge ratio, and the universal regression hedge ratios of Adler and Prasad (1990). They found that a unitary hedging strategy worked as well as or better than Black's or Adler and Prasad's universal hedging techniques did under parameter uncertainty.

Eun and Resnick (1988, 1994) have shown that it is important to control parameter uncertainty to capture the potential gains from international diversification and that hedging foreign exchange risk can increase the gains from international stock portfolio diversification. When neither of these risks is properly controlled, investors may not be able to realise enough of the potential benefits to justify international investment. The authors suggested that hedging exchange rate risk can be beneficial simply due to the reduction in estimation risk. Many studies in this area follow and extend Jorion's (1985) technique in which estimated returns are weighted averages of historical returns and the average return from a minimum-variance portfolio. The approach is quite technical and interested readers should consult Jorion (1985) and Eun and Resnick (1988).

Gardner and Stove (1995) investigated the effect of estimation error on hedge ratios using a bootstrap method under some fairly general assumptions. Their estimated hedge ratio in a risk/return optimisation framework with a 50% confidence level (ie, 25th and 75th percentiles) was (-4.95, 2.95), so a point estimate, as used by many practitioners, is almost useless. The key reason for the large range of hedge ratios is the large standard deviation of currency returns. When minimum-variance optimisation is chosen instead, the range of hedge ratios at the 50% confidence level is (0.72, 1.47), which is a major improvement. But a 90% confidence level range is (0.21, 2.12), which is still not very good.

Ex ante work greatly improves the relevance of academic research to the practical operation of a fund. Larsen and Resnick's (2000) work lends partial support to the commonly used unitary hedge ratio. However, one might still ask: can this be improved on? Some researchers have conducted further investigations by assuming that there are structural links between the movements in interest rates, equity prices and foreign exchange rates. Bauer (2001) looked at a structural model where foreign exchange returns and equity returns respond to common shocks. He estimated a joint signal/response model and incorporated the result into the optimisation process for currency hedging. Since the signal/response model shows that foreign exchange and equity moves are jointly predictable, he claimed that the currency hedge should be decided periodically, incorporating all new information, including equity returns and macroeconomic indicators. The author was able to separate exchange rate volatility into a fundamental part plus a noise part and, naturally, the two parts have different impacts on currency-hedging decisions. Given the difficulty in predicting exchange rates (both direction and volatility), it is hard to see how confidently a practitioner can view the output of this type of model.

5.5.7 Instability of variance–covariance matrices

A generally known problem with many CAPM-type optimisation models is that one needs to assume that the variance–covariance matrices are constant. Even with the more recent research papers, where optimisation is generally conditional on the latest information, one needs to assume that the matrices are stable over the short horizon. In reality, actual variance–covariance matrices are rarely stable, even in the short term. There is, for example, some empirical evidence to show that diversification is at its weakest (ie, correlation is highest) when global volatility is high and the benefit of diversification is needed the most.[17] In these studies currency risks are all combined with the foreign equity risks and there is no explicit conclusion on whether such phenomena would affect the hedging output of an optimisation. Solnik, Beucrelle and Le Fur (1996) looked at monthly return data denominated in local currencies over 37 years and found that the correlation between national stockmarkets and the US stockmarket was volatile and generally higher in the most recent decade than before, although in almost all cases the increase was not significant apart from the UK. They found that the correlation between the MSCI EAFE Index and US stock indices was lower, implying the benefit of international diversification and currency hedging. However, they also found that the correlations between national stockmarkets were positively correlated with the volatility levels of stockmarkets around the world, which supports the claim that diversification benefit is low when it is needed the most.

One way of dealing with such instabilities is to fit a structural model assuming that equity and foreign exchange respond to some shocks in a predetermined fashion, as was done by Bauer (2001) in the work discussed in the previous sub-section. Another way is to assume that covariances are affected by variances. Jacquier and Marcus (2000) modelled correlation across assets as due to the common dependence of returns on a market-wide, systematic factor. In such a setting, if one assumes that security (sector) β and security σ are relatively stable, then the correlation between the security and the market is driven by market volatility. Their model is better at explaining the variation of sector correlation within a country than across countries, which indicates that there is considerably more country-specific risk than industry-specific risk. Chan,

Karceski and Lakonishok (1999) fitted a three-factor model to explain the fluctuation in variance–covariance matrices. They found that the model was just as good as models with more factors, but none of the multifactor models was a dramatic improvement on the traditional CAPM model in terms of risk management. The currency decision is not explicitly modelled in their study. We have not seen any currency-hedging optimisation models that incorporate similar structures.

5.5.8 Other factors affecting choice of hedge ratio

There are a few other factors that may affect the choice of hedge ratio, but we have not seen a credible attempt to investigate them. So here we will cover these factors in the form of a short list of questions that a practitioner might ask, each followed by a brief summary discussion of the issue.

❏ *Should the hedge ratio be different for different base currencies?* Possibly. For obvious reasons, almost all of the existing research looks at the optimisation problem from a US investor's perspective. Because the US is the world's largest capital market and the US dollar is the world's most important currency, when the dollar falls or rises, in theory it usually falls or rises against every other currency. Therefore, it is plausible that conclusions on currency hedging appropriate for a US-based investor may not be so for investors based in other currencies.

Research work in this area remains sketchy. Gadkari and Spindel (1990) found that hedging is beneficial for US-based investors but not so much for Japan- and UK-based investors. They suggested that the diversification benefit for non-US dollar currencies as base is greater and, consequently, that the benefit of currency hedging is less. Both Eaker, Grant and Woodard (1991) and Eun and Resnick (1994) confirmed that hedging is far more beneficial for US-based investors than for their Japan-based counterparts. VanderLinden, Jiang and Hu (2002) also reported that forward-bias rules work differently for investors based in different currencies.

We have computed the average pairwise one-year rolling correlations for the US dollar, sterling, euro, Swiss franc and Japanese yen as base currencies for the last 10 years and the results are shown in Figure 5.4. If the diversification benefit is strong for a

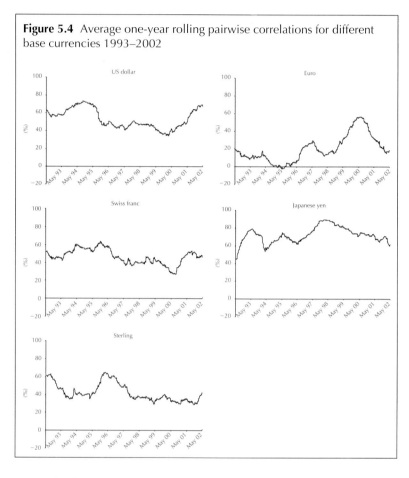

Figure 5.4 Average one-year rolling pairwise correlations for different base currencies 1993–2002

particular base currency, the average pairwise correlation should be low. But we find that the yen has higher average correlation as the base currency than, say, the dollar, which indicates that the diversification benefit for the yen-based investor is smaller than for the dollar-based investor. The 10-year average correlation coefficients are, for the US dollar, 53%; sterling, 42%; euro, 20%; Swiss franc, 46%; and Japanese yen, 72%. We suspect that the unfavourable hedging performance for yen-based *vis-à-vis* dollar-based investors as documented in academic studies may be due to the interest rate differential effect. Of course, the average correlation computed here does not take into account the fact that the weights for investment in different currencies are different or the empirical correlation between currencies and the underlyings.

❏ *What about different hedge ratios for different counter currencies?* Aside from the aforementioned fact that a currency is linked to the economic status of its country, folklore has it that currencies can be different for other reasons (where the lore is that of folk working in the currency market). For example, the yen is more jittery partly because the Bank of Japan is more likely to intervene than other central banks and partly because Japanese companies have a certain hedging pattern. Another example, the Swedish krona, is said to respond closely to the share price movement of Nokia and the technology-heavy NASDAQ Index. As another example, many commentators claim that the Australian dollar is driven by commodity prices. Given these little idiosyncrasies, whether the hedge ratio for each individual currency should be different is a natural question to ask. We feel that this "intimate knowledge" of currencies generally has more to do with return forecasting than risk control and therefore should probably be dealt with in the context of trading models.

❏ *Would the hedging decision change if one used other optimisation techniques?* This is a much larger topic than can be discussed in the present context and there is a growing body of research looking at the hedging implications of using alternative optimisation techniques – for example, the regret minimising approach mentioned in endnote 14 of this chapter. Duarte and Rajagopal (1999) investigated the application of a scenario-based approach to currency overlay using a network optimisation technique which is more flexible than the traditional optimisation techniques. In most optimisation models the objective is to maximise the Sharpe ratio, which is based on standard deviation. Other risk measures, such as value-at-risk (VAR) and conditional VAR (CVAR), are now finding their way on to the radar of currency risk managers in the investment management industry (Dowd, 1998 and 1999). It is perhaps too early to say whether new optimisation and/or risk control methods will alter the ways in which currency-hedging decisions are made, but we are hoping to see new research effort in this area.

5.6 ASSET–LIABILITY OPTIMISATION

Almost all existing works in the area of currency risk management for international investment, both theoretical and practical, focus on the asset aside of the equation. For many institutional money managers, especially pension funds and insurance funds, incorporating the liability side of the equation seems the more appropriate framework. It is not difficult to infer that, *ceteris paribus*, an optimisation done in two stages – first asset optimisation and then asset–liability optimisation – will at best be as good as a single-stage optimisation and usually worse. This is similar to the situation where joint optimisation dominates partial optimisation dominates separate optimisation.

We are aware of a few recent attempts to investigate the issue of currency hedging from an asset–liability matching perspective – for example, Prajogi, Muralidhar and van der Wouden (2000) and Muralidhar and van der Wouden (2000). The first authors gave a detailed description of such an approach using a hypothetical Canadian pension fund as an example. The basis for optimisation was mean–variance-based simulation for various market returns as well as the domestic inflation rate over a five-year period, whereas the duration of the liability was 23 years. In contrast to an asset-only optimisation, where one maximises the expected return for a given portfolio risk or minimises the portfolio risk for a given expected return, in an asset–liability optimisation one minimises the funded ratio risk for a given contribution rate or minimises the contribution rate for a given funded ratio risk (as shown in Figure 5.5).[18] The main decision variables in their example are the percentage of assets invested in foreign equities and the average currency-hedge ratio. They illustrated that these two decisions may be different under the same set of assumptions for asset-only optimisation vs asset–liability optimisation. For example, when 30% of the assets are allocated to foreign equities, 25% should be hedged in an asset-only optimisation but 0% in an asset–liability optimisation. The ratios are 40% vs 25% when 40% of the assets are allocated to foreign equities. The other sections of the study concern use of the JP Morgan currency overlay service to reduce risk and enhance return, which we do not review here.

As noted in Prajogi, Muralidhar and van der Wouden (2000), one needs to make assumptions about inflation rates as well as interest rates in order to estimate future liabilities. These two variables are also used for asset-only optimisation – the inflation rate assumption is used indirectly when one employs nominal returns.

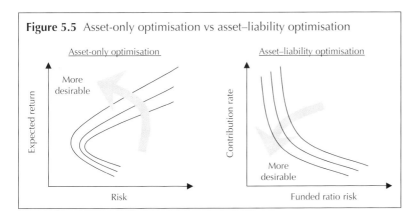

Figure 5.5 Asset-only optimisation vs asset–liability optimisation

The asset–liability framework recognises the impact of these two variables on both assets and liabilities and is therefore able to exploit the links in the optimisation – in theory. In practice, the relationship between inflation and the returns on domestic and foreign securities, including currencies, is complicated and probably time-varying. An exercise using simple correlation, either historical or forecast, to compare the performance of different asset allocation and currency-hedging decisions is, in our opinion, unlikely to be very useful, especially given the specific features of modelling currency returns which we reviewed in Chapter 4.

5.7 CURRENCY BASKET HEDGING

Optimisation techniques can be used in another context: rather than hedging every single currency in the portfolio, an investor may wish to hedge only a few. The underlying assumption is that, in many broad-based investment indices, currency risk is concentrated in a handful of major currencies and a programme consisting of three to four currencies may be sufficient to cover a large portion of the currency risk. The advantage of this so-called basket hedging approach is its simplicity, ease of administration and low trading cost. Also, by focusing on the major currency pairs, it can be easier to implement systematic active management because it is easier to open and close positions – most systematic trading strategies work better in major currency pairs. However, some recent developments have diminished the attraction of the basket approach:

❑ with the introduction of the euro, the number of currencies in investment portfolios has been reduced and the administration of a currency-hedging portfolio is significantly simplified;

❑ bid–offer spreads have, in general, been shrinking in non-G24 currencies, which brings down trading costs;

❑ the currency devaluations that occurred during the Asian crisis, the Russian debt default and the Latin American crisis reduced the effectiveness of basket hedging;

❑ online trading and portfolio management solutions have lowered the cost of administration even further.

Sorensen, Mezrich and Thadani (1993) demonstrated, using a mean–variance framework but incorporating a Garch forecasting method for variance, that a hedging portfolio of three to four currencies is able to track a portfolio with 20 odd currencies fairly closely. Their analysis was done on an equally weighted portfolio, and they showed that with only three to five currencies they could achieve a tracking error of 50–150 bp per annum. If one uses a market cap-based global portfolio where the currency risk is much more concentrated, the effectiveness of using a smaller currency universe for hedging purposes can be expected to increase significantly. In practice, one can use a shortcut: list the portfolio exposures by country and group currencies where possible (for example, the euro countries; Hong Kong dollar and Singapore dollar with US dollar, etc.), then sort weightings in descending order and hedge only the top three to four exposures.

Grouping related currencies together is often done by practitioners. Currencies are combined either on the basis of correlation or for economical reasons. The simplest approach is to use all the data (a single time window), calculate the correlations between pairs of currencies and group them qualitatively. The approach is simple, intuitive and easy to manage. However, it gives you an "average" result, and it does not tell you how far from the average you might deviate on any particular day. An improved approach is to use a time window that is shorter than the available data set and to move the time window forward. This generates a series of correlations and will tell you not only the average result but also how far you might deviate from it (ie, how sensible your grouping has proved over time). There are many alternative ways of grouping currencies and all basically involve recording variables over time and measuring the "distance" between them. Statistical packages are often required for such an exercise.

5.8 SECTOR-BASED INVESTMENT AND CURRENCY MANAGEMENT

Sector-based investment was the buzzword a few years ago in both the academic world and the fund management industry. Often quoted figures from practitioners are: in 1996, 50% of the asset allocation decision was attributable to country allocation, 30% to stock picking and 10% to sector-based allocation, whereas the estimate for 2000 shows that the split had changed to around 10%, 30% and 60%, respectively. We have not seen authoritative statistics on this and remain sceptical about the high proportion of sector-driven investment in the more recent estimate.

Some academic studies support the idea that sectors have a greater impact on expected returns than countries. Beckers, Connor and Curds (1996) found that the domestic sector is more important than the country factor in explaining returns, although they also found that the global sector factor is not as important as the country factor. Baca, Garbe and Weiss (2000) and Cavaglia, Brightman and Aked (2000) noted an increase in the importance of the sector factor over time and observed that sector influences have grown so markedly that they are more important than country factors in explaining equity returns. However, other researchers have shown that sector differences have a negligible impact (eg, Heston and Rouwenhorst (1994), Griffin and Karolyi (1998) and Rouwenhorst (1999)). A recent study by L'Her, Sy and Tnani (2002) contends that both sector and country factors are now dominated by "global risk factors" constructed from size, book-to-market ratio and momentum from national markets. We can only hypothesise that these are manifestations of two trends: the increasing level of integration between national financial markets, and the increasing globalisation of industries. None of the works mentioned above assesses the role of currency risk in these factors. Another study by Gerard, Hillion and de Roon (2002) incorporates an explicit currency-hedging portfolio, as in Section 5.2.2.2, and shows that country factors dominate sector factors but that ICAPM portfolios dominate both country and sector portfolios in terms of Sharpe ratio.

In practice, sector-based investment strategies pose new currency problems. For fund managers following a given sector-based benchmark there is an implicit amount of currency exposure. When managers take an active position, either at the sector level or at stock level, the currency exposure can easily be altered. If they do not pay close attention to the currency exposure, fund managers may find their carefully chosen strategy spoiled by unforeseen currency movements. In this case they can implement a currency overlay programme even if the passive currency-hedge ratio is zero. With the overlay, fund managers can easily align the active currency exposure against the benchmark currency exposure.

1 Arbitrage pricing theory (APT) models are not reviewed here. Similar to the difference between CAPM and APT in a closed economy, the APT approach provides a less restrictive framework to empirical testing as it does not require assumptions on investors' utility, which is difficult to implement.

2 Sometimes in the academic literature you will also see the acronym IAMP, the "capital" in CAPM being left out because a currency-hedging portfolio is introduced.

3 In general equilibrium models, exchange rates can be endogenous, ie, determined by the internal dynamics of the model.

4 For a survey see Karolyi and Stulz (2002).

5 Karolyi and Stulz (2002) observed that this result is paradoxical given that at the stock level share prices do seem to be particularly sensitive to exchange rate moves. However, recent studies show that the latter relationship is in fact significant, though non-linear. If this is the case, sensitivity can "reappear" in linear format at a portfolio level.

6 This result is also known as Siegel's paradox. Refer to note 13 and Solnik (1993).

7 For example, the term structure of interest rates, volatility smiles and term structure, the factor models used by many active fund managers, value-at-risk methodology, the equity premium puzzle, forward bias, hedge funds as an asset class and many more.

8 A dynamic option replication technique can be viewed as an add-on to one of the approaches described here.

9 Or a three-dimensional version that looks like a hammock. The extra axis shows the portion of the portfolio allocated to foreign assets.

10 See Eun and Resnick (1994) and Larsen and Resnick (2000), reviewed in Chapter 1.

11 We have seen academic papers that advocate higher foreign currency exposure from an asset/liability matching viewpoint for pension funds. The argument is that pension funds are exposed to the domestic inflation rate, which can be difficult to hedge. Foreign currencies will presumably rise in value against the domestic currency when domestic inflation is high and therefore can serve as a hedge against domestic inflation. However, as we have seen in Chapter 4, currency movements may not be a function of domestic inflation, at least in the short term (three to five years).

12 Note 11 is an example of the potential correlation between foreign currency and a fund's liability. A full hedge would completely remove such beneficial correlation (if it existed).

13 Black contributed to the universality of Siegel's paradox, which states that for a given move in the exchange rate of currency A against currency B, the impact is not necessarily equal and

opposite for investors based in those currencies. For example, if the US dollar/yen rate moves from 110 to 120, the dollar appreciates 9.09% for the dollar-based investor whereas the yen depreciates 8.33% for the yen-based investor. Black argued that the asymmetry represents a win–win opportunity for both investors and that the way to achieve this is through a partial hedge.

14 Gardner and Wuilloud (1995) proposed an optimisation framework which seeks to minimise investor's regret. They showed that when the evaluation horizon is short (less than two years) and the investor's risk tolerance is moderate or high, there is a high probability that the portfolio using an optimal hedge ratio, derived by maximising the risk-adjusted return, will substantially underperform other portfolios with simple hedging strategies (for example, full hedge or no hedge). They suggested a method for quantifying such regret, and a hedge ratio is chosen to minimise the regret. They concluded that if the cost of not using an optimal hedge ratio is small, an investor should probably choose a 50% hedge ratio.

15 See Adler and Jorion (1992) for an illustration of Jensen's inequality and how it can be applied here.

16 Refer also to Chapter 1, Section 1.4.4.

17 See Chow *et al.* (1999), Longin and Solnik (1995) and Solnik, Beucrelle and Le Fur (1996) for investigations of the time-series property of international correlations.

18 Note that the smooth lines on the chart are for illustrative purposes only. The exact shape of and relationship between such curves depends on the assumptions used and how liabilities are valued.

6

Benchmark Design and Performance Measurement

6.1 INTRODUCTION

When designing or selecting a multi-currency benchmark, the investor clearly has to make a combined decision on the underlying assets and the embedded currency exposures, and in this chapter we review some of the issues that arise in developing a benchmark. Since most foreign exchange benchmarks are tailor-made, our aim is that the topics covered here will enable readers either to have an informed discussion with professionals who specialise in designing such benchmarks, or, if needed, to construct one themselves. We emphasise that we do not endorse one kind of benchmark over another, in the same way that we do not advocate a specific hedge ratio or hedging style. We do, however, believe it important that a thorough investigation is carried out to clarify how much currency risk there is in an investment portfolio and who is responsible for such risk.[1] The benchmarking process is nothing but a formalised, and repeated, investigation process.

A benchmark is an essential tool for defining, implementing and reviewing the investment policy. It usually includes an index or a set of numerical indices. But a benchmark is also likely to incorporate a performance evaluation mechanism, whereas an index alone is not. Selecting a benchmark is therefore a vital part of the establishment of an investment policy. Academic studies have shown that the choice of benchmark can have a considerable impact on the performance of equity funds but that the performance of bond portfolios is not generally sensitive to the choice of index.[2] Unfortunately for our purposes, these studies all use single-currency indices, and we have seen no systematic investigation of how the choice of currency benchmark affects portfolio perform-ance. Adding the currency dimension complicates the picture as there is no generally accepted currency-specific index.

Since many bond portfolios hedge foreign exchange risk fully as a matter of course, for widely followed bond indices the providers usually include a currency-hedged index to accompany the unhedged ones.[3] However, how the hedge is designed and how the calculation is carried out is often not transparent and may not neces-sarily be in accordance with a manager's hedging practice. We have not seen specific studies on the effectiveness of hedging and the impact of selecting one index rather than another. Foreign exchange-hedged equity indices or broad indices have not gained much popularity, mainly due to the *ad hoc* nature of currency hedg-ing and the difficulty of designing an index that is applicable to a large number of investors.[4]

One reason for establishing a benchmark is to clarify the (*ex ante*) risk position; the other, equally important, is to facilitate (*ex post*) performance measurement. Performance measurement in currency management is fraught with difficulties, mainly because the return on currency is difficult to define, especially in relation to the treat-ment of forward points. We review two commonly used methods in Sections 6.5 and 6.6: one is the "currency surprise" method recommended by Association for Investment Management and Research (AIMR), and the other is the "excess return" method pioneered by Karnosky and Singer (1994). We will show in this chapter that the two methods, each of which has its own merits and shortcomings, are consistent.

6.2 SETTING A GOOD BENCHMARK

As there is no generally applicable approach to setting a bench-mark, here we list some practical and perhaps commonsensical guidelines. A benchmark system should aim to be:

❏ *Consistent*. It should apply the same risk/return view across dif-ferent asset classes. Many systems treat currency on an *ad hoc* basis and/or as a stand-alone asset risk category, applying currency-specific rules to deal with hedged vs unhedged returns. Such systems may lead to sub-optimal asset allocation decisions and misleading performance measures.

❏ *Transparent.* The system should be tractable in that parties involved in the process should be able to arrive at the same conclusion with the same data set, following rules defined in the performance measurement system.

❏ *Accountable.* The system should be able to distinguish different sources of return and risk, allowing meaningful comparisons between different portfolios and/or different managers. Separating the overall return into a currency part and an underlying part is difficult because the overall return is the product of the returns from both sources. The system should also be able to break down the overall risk/return profile into a currency part, an underlying part and a dead-weight part. The last item refers to the portion for which neither currency manager nor underlying manager is responsible. The dead-weight return should be made as small as practically possible.

❏ *Achievable (investable or replicable).* Computation of the indices should correspond to the transactions managers can and may take, including transaction costs and liquidity considerations.

❏ *Fair.* It should be a fair reflection of the investment universe and representative of the investment manager's habitat. Also, the system should offer neither incentive nor disincentive for managers to take currency-hedging actions – ie, all strategic hedging decisions should already be reflected in the benchmark.

❏ *Stable.* It should not produce large swings when periodical rebalancings and other adjustments are undertaken.

❏ *General.* The system should be general enough to accommodate different investment and hedging strategies.

The AIMR recommends the following set of basic rules for an effective benchmark; these are that it should be:

❏ representative of the asset class or mandate;
❏ investable (ie, a viable investment alternative);
❏ constructed in a disciplined and objective manner;
❏ formulated from publicly available information;

❏ acceptable by the manager as the neutral position;
❏ consistent with underlying investor status (eg, regarding tax, time horizon, etc.).

6.3 CUSTOMISED BENCHMARKS: RISK SEPARATION AND RISK RESPONSIBILITY

Many, if not all, currency benchmarks are customised because of the client-specific nature of currency-hedging practice and the interaction between currency and the underlying. A customised currency benchmark should incorporate the requirements of the following three important areas:

❏ the taking of a separate currency risk decision at the asset allocation stage (currency optimisation);
❏ monitoring risk transfer from underlying asset managers to currency risk managers; and
❏ performance measurement and attribution.

As we have often emphasised in this book, the key benefit of currency overlay – or for that matter any currency management approach – lies in the risk separation and risk responsibility aspects. To achieve these a fund needs a benchmark system, comprising several indices and a set of guidelines, that encompasses the overall activity of the whole fund.

A simple benchmark should include the following three (sets of) indexes, whose relationships are illustrated in Figure 6.1:

❏ *Index for the underlying manager ("a" in Figure 6.1)*. The underlying managers are measured on a fully hedged basis (hedge ratio = 100%), which means that a currency-hedged index (or a set of such indices) for the underlying needs to be chosen or established. These benchmarks reflect the underlying risk, free from currency fluctuations.
❏ *Index for the impact of currency ("c" in Figure 6.1)*. The net impact of currency on the underlying investment is measured separately by this index. The index can be divided further into the part that is hedged passively and the part that is not hedged, as shown in the lower part of Figure 6.1 (where "d" is the unhedged part). Note that part of the currency impact may not be hedgeable, and this is explored further in Section 6.4.

Figure 6.1 Illustration of risk separation

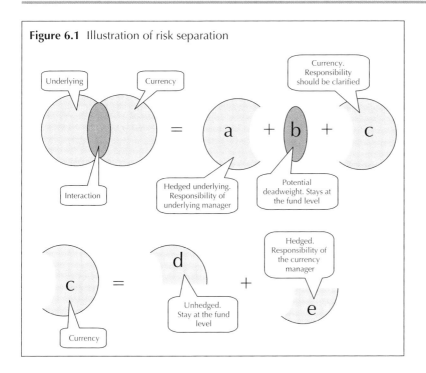

❑ *Index for the currency manager ("e" in Figure 6.1).* A currency manager's index can be established using information from the two indices above, plus other hedge-specific information such as the fund's passive hedge ratio, adjustment frequency and style (see Sections 6.8 and 6.9) and so forth. This index represents the risk that is transferred to the currency manager.

The unallocated, or "dead-weight", portion of currency risk ("b" in Figure 6.1) is the strategic currency risk a fund decides to bear. For example, a fund with a 50% currency-hedge ratio will assume half of the currency exposure, which should remain at the asset allocation level. The dead-weight portion is a result of some interrelated factors: cross-products, simplifying assumptions, intra-month strategy changes and compounding across time. Sometimes, depending on the design of the hedging policy, returns from the currency manager and underlying manager may not add up to the total portfolio return; the difference is also part of the dead-weight.

For any underlying manager who has declared a competency in currency, a separate currency benchmark is needed in addition to his fully hedged underlying index. The benchmark represents the currency risks taken on by the underlying manager given his stated competency. Thus, there are two separate measurements of his performance: one in respect of the underlying and the other in currencies.

6.4 DISSECTING CURRENCY RETURNS

An intuitive and simple way of dissecting the return from a foreign currency-denominated asset is to look at the return on the underlying asset denominated in local currency and the return on the currency against the base currency. The first part is relatively straightforward to calculate. For the second part there are, however, two commonly used methods to define the currency return – spot-on-spot and spot-on-forward – the pros and cons of which were illustrated in Chapter 2. One main difference is the treatment of the forward premium. When a hedge transaction is engaged, the investor will be contracted to pay the forward premium, which may be a benefit or a cost depending on the interest rate differentials. Some people treat the forward premium as if it were a consequence of currency hedging. They count it as part of the benefit/cost of a hedging programme if they do hedge, and they ignore it if they do not hedge. Forward premium should be part of the intrinsic benefit/cost of investing in an asset denominated in a foreign currency. The act of hedging does not create forward premium, it merely makes it explicit. Forward premium should, therefore, be explicitly incorporated when one dissects currency returns, irrespective of one's hedging decision. Also, forward premium may well be an important factor in determining one's hedging decision.

We have to stress here again that local currency returns on an asset are generally not available to investors based in other currencies. The investor can use currency-hedging instruments to eliminate the spot-on-forward return but not the forward points. Therefore, the currency-hedged return will be different from the local currency return, and only the former is available to foreign investors. Over time, the forward premium can have a significant effect on currency returns – remember from Chapter 3 that the average return from an active currency-hedging programme is around 50–200 bp per annum, whereas the forward points can easily be as much or higher.

The ramifications of the return decomposition go beyond who is responsible for the forward points in that the decomposition is linked to several issues crucial to global investment:

❑ it is clearly linked to the establishment of a currency benchmark as the forward points need to be explicitly incorporated;
❑ it is linked to the performance attribution system to evaluate sources of investment return and risk; and
❑ it should also be part of the global optimisation process as foreign exchange plays an important role in a global portfolio's overall return and risk.

In the next two sections we review the two main approaches to return decomposition or separation.

6.5 THE CURRENCY SURPRISE APPROACH

The currency surprise approach, which is endorsed by the AIMR,[5] assumes that a currency will go to where the forward rate "predicts" it will be in the future. If it does not, the extra movement is the "surprise". The approach separates the return from a foreign currency-denominated asset into the three parts shown in Table 6.1. Note that the term "forward premium" appears explicitly in both parts (a) and (b). Hedging the currency risk embedded in an asset will give an investor the local currency return plus the forward premium rather than just the local currency return itself. The local

Table 6.1 Separating currency returns in the currency surprise approach

(a) Hedged asset returns	Defined as the local currency return on the assets plus forward premium
(b) Currency surprise	Defined as the exchange rate movement (spot-on-spot) less forward premium. Currency surprise is the interest rate-adjusted movement in the spot currency
(c) Currency management return	Defined as the combined return from passive hedging plus active position-taking

Adapted from Stannard et al (1998).

Table 6.2 Parameter values for currency surprise examples

Variable	Symbol	Example 1 %	Example 2 %	Example 3 %
JPY return on Nikkei	r_{JPY}	14	14	14
USD return on S&P	r_{USD}	8	8	8
Expected change in USD/JPY spot	$e_{USD/JPY}$	−4	−4	−4
Risk-free rate, JPY	d_{JPY}	9	4	9
Risk-free rate, USD	d_{USD}	2	2	4

Table 6.3 Return decomposition using the currency surprise approach

Returns	Symbol	Example 1 %	Example 2 %	Example 3 %
(a) Hedged Nikkei returns	$r_{JPY} + (d_{USD} - d_{JPY})$	7	12	9
(b) Currency surprise	$e_{USD/JPY} + (d_{USD} + d_{JPY})$	3	−2	1
(c) Currency management return	N/A	N/A	N/A	N/A

N/A, not applicable.

currency return is not achievable for foreign investors unless the forward premium is zero. Currency hedging aims to reduce or neutralise the impact of currency surprise.

In the next tables we use numerical examples to illustrate return decomposition in this approach. For easy comparison we use the same parameters as Karnosky and Singer (1994), and values for these parameters are listed in Table 6.2. Results of the decomposition are given in Table 6.3. Given that only item (b), currency surprise, in Table 6.3 can be eliminated by currency hedging, the rational asset allocation decision would be to hedge in example 2 but to leave the currency exposure open in both examples 1 and 3.

These hypothetical examples can also serve to illustrate another important point that goes beyond the decision whether to hedge currency exposure. Given the parameters in each example – in particular, that the US dollar return on the S&P is 8% and the

Table 6.4 Optimal portfolios using the currency surprise approach

Returns	Symbol	Example 1	Example 2	Example 3
Hedged Nikkei return	$_{\$}r_{JPY}$	7%	12%	9%
Currency surprise	$_{\$}e_{USD/JPY}$	3%	−2%	1%
USD return on S&P	r_{USD}	8%	8%	8%
Asset decision	$_{\$}r_{JPY} > r_{USD}$?	S&P	Nikkei	Nikkei
Currency decision	$_{\$}e_{USD/JPY} > 0$?	FX position*	Hedge	Unhedge
Portfolio return		11%	12%	10%

*Investor will invest fully in S&P and will also take a currency position to buy Japanese yen and sell US dollars despite the fact that there is no underlying position in the yen.

Japanese yen return on the Nikkei is 14% – what should the asset allocation decision be? On paper, one may prefer the Nikkei to the S&P in all three cases as the return on the Nikkei, at 14%, is much higher. However, after taking forward points into consideration, the optimal portfolios are as given in Table 6.4.

Assuming a 50% currency-hedged benchmark and using the parameter values in example 1 from Table 6.2, we present the following example on attribution. Table 6.5(a) contains the allocation and return information needed for the exercise. Column (4) was calculated using the 50% hedge ratio from column (1). Columns (3) and (9) are the underlying and currency deviations from the respective benchmarks. Note that benchmark returns for underlying and currency in the bottom half of Table 6.5(b) are calculated using (1) and (4) in Table 6.5(a), respectively.

From the data in the tables it is easy to compute the benchmark total return as

$$10.40\% + (-2.25\%) - 0.45\% = 7.70\%$$

and the actual portfolio total return as

$$70\% \times 14\% + 20\% \times 8\% + 10\% \times 2\%$$
$$+ 70\% \times (-5\%) + 20\% \times 0\% + 10\% \times 0\%$$
$$+ ((-60\%) \times 2\% + 60\% \times 0\%) = 6.90\%$$

How do we attribute the −80bp difference between the actual portfolio return and the benchmark return? This is shown in Table 6.6.[7]

Table 6.5(a) Currency surprise attribution example: benchmark and actual portfolio allocation assumptions

| | Underlying security | | | Currency selection | | | | | |
	Benchmark % (1)	Active % (2)	Difference % (3) = (2) − (1)	Currency benchmark % (4)	Active weighting % (5) = (2)	Cash % (6)	Hedge % (7)	Currency weighting % (8) = (5) + (6) + (7)	Difference % (9) = (8) − (4)
Nikkei	45.00	70.00	25.00	22.50	70.00	0.00	−60.00	10.00	−12.5
S&P	50.00	20.00	−30.00	77.50	20.00	10.00	60.00	90.00	12.5
USD cash	5.00	10.00	5.00	N/A	N/A	N/A	N/A	N/A	N/A
Total	100.00	100.00	0.00	100.00	90.00	10.00	0.00	100.00	0.00

Table 6.5(b)[6] Currency surprise attribution example: return assumptions

	Unhedged (local currency) % (a)	Risk-free (USD) % (b)	Forward premium % (c)	Spot return % (d)	Hedged (USD) % (e) = (a) + (c)	Currency surprise % (f) = (d) − (c)
Nikkei	14.00	9.00	−7.00	−5.00	7.00	2.00
S&P	8.00	2.00	0.00	0.00	8.00	0.00
USD cash	2.00	2.00	0.00	0.00	2.00	0.00
Benchmark returns (computed)*						
Underlying	10.40					
Currency				−2.25	7.25	0.90
						0.45

*Underlying and currency benchmark returns calculated using (1) and (4) in Table 6.5(a), respectively.

Table 6.6 Return attribution in currency surprise example

	Underlying	Currency	Total
Nikkei	−0.06% = (70% − 45%) × (7% − 7.25%)	−0.14% = (10% − 22.50%) × (2% − 0.90%)	−0.20%
S&P	−0.23% = (20% − 50%) × (8% − 7.25%)	−0.11% = (90% − 77.50%) × (0% − 0.90%)	−0.34%
USD cash	−0.26% = (10% − 5%) × (2% − 7.25%)	0.00%	−0.26%
Total	−0.55%	−0.25%	−0.80%

6.6 THE EXCESS RETURN APPROACH

Karnosky and Singer (1994) proposed an alternative methodology that is consistent with the currency surprise and forward premium framework, although their framework is more general than in the currency surprise approach. The main advantage is that the new approach can easily accommodate the cross-hedging positions, whereas the currency surprise approach requires a cumbersome calculation for bilaterally hedged returns. Central to their approach, they view an investment in a given currency as a combined holding of cash and an asset. The expected return on the cash part is the local risk-free interest rate. The expected return on the asset is the local currency return above the local risk-free interest rate, ie, the excess return. Under this definition, the currency-hedging decision has a very straightforward interpretation.

Portfolio managers generally hold cash as part of strategic allocation and/or operational purposes (see Section 6.9.3). The cash may be in a mix of currencies and the return on the cash balances should be close to the risk-free interest rates in the respective currencies. It is easy to work out that if the cash holdings in non-domestic currencies are hedged, their returns will be almost exactly the same as the domestic risk-free interest rate. Namely, the cash return in a foreign currency adjusted by the forward return (premium or discount) equals the cash return in the domestic currency – a relationship that is illustrated in Appendix 2A of Chapter 2.

Table 6.7 Optimal portfolios using the excess return approach

Variable	Symbol	Example 1	Example 2	Example 3
Security excess return				
S&P	$r_{USD} - d_{USD}$	6%	6%	4%
Nikkei	$r_{JPY} - d_{JPY}$	5%	10%	5%
Cash return in USD				
USD	d_{USD}	2%	2%	4%
JPY	$d_{JPY} + e_{USD/JPY}$	5%	0%	5%
Asset decision	$(r_{USD} - d_{USD}) >$ $(r_{JPY} - d_{JPY})$?	S&P	Nikkei	Nikkei
Currency decision	$d_{USD} > (d_{JPY} + e_{USD/JPY})$?	JPY	USD	JPY
Portfolio return		11%	12%	10%

There is, however, another form of cash. When a non-cash investment position is taken – be it in equities or bonds, domestic or foreign[8] – the implicit aim is to seek a return *above* the risk-free interest rate in that currency, the latter being the return on an equivalent cash position in the currency. This provides a useful decomposition of returns on any non-cash investment into an excess return plus a cash return. In other words, the position itself can be viewed as an underlying position seeking excess return plus an equivalent cash position in that currency seeking a cash return. The net impact of a currency hedge is to substitute the cash return in the foreign currency by that in the domestic currency. It is important to note that the excess return part, defined as market return above the risk-free rate, remains the same. In Table 6.4 we rework the asset allocation examples using the excess return approach, and the results are listed in Table 6.7. Comparing Tables 6.4 and 6.7, we see that both approaches give the same asset allocations.

The attribution process is very similar to that of the currency surprise approach detailed in Table 6.6. First, however, we need to compute the relevant excess returns and cash returns, and these are given in Table 6.8. The attribution calculation is given in Table 6.9.

The results in Tables 6.6 and 6.9 are identical. We should mention here that the excess return approach can easily be applied to situations where more than two currencies are involved – one only has to deal with an array of excess returns plus a matrix of cash returns

Table 6.8 Excess returns and cash returns calculated for excess return approach from data in Table 6.5(b)

	Unhedged (local currency), % (a)	Risk-free (USD), % (b)	Excess return, % (g) = (a) − (b)	Cash return (USD), % (h) = (b) + (d)
Nikkei	14.00	9.00	5.00	4.00
S&P	8.00	2.00	6.00	2.00
USD cash	2.00	2.00	0.00	2.00
Benchmark returns Underlying			5.25	2.90

Table 6.9 Return attribution using the excess return approach

	Underlying	Currency	Total
Nikkei	−0.06% = (70% − 45%) × (5% − 5.25%)	−0.14% = (10% − 22.50%) × (4% − 2.90%)	−0.20%
S&P	−0.23% = (20% − 50%) × (6% − 5.25%)	−0.11% = (90% − 77.50%) × (2% − 2.90%)	−0.34%
USD cash	−0.26% = (10% − 5%) × (0% − 5.25%)	0.00%	−0.26%
Total	−0.55%	−0.25%	−0.80%

in different currencies. For the currency surprise approach one needs a matrix of underlying returns hedged into different currencies plus a matrix of pairwise currency surprises – a little more difficult to keep track of. Many studies of the effectiveness of currency hedging make unfortunate mistakes on precisely this point.

6.7 HOLDING-BASED BENCHMARKS

In this section we give stylised examples to show how some commonly seen benchmarks might be constructed. These benchmarks are holding-based as opposed to performance-based; the latter will be discussed later in this chapter. There are many holding-based benchmarks (which are in essence historical performances) in overlay managers' pitch books and many articles on the benefit of currency overlay. Some of the results are simply too good to be true. And they probably are. Most offer no detailed explanation on how the figures are obtained. As we have demonstrated in Chapter 2, Section 2.2, and in Section 6.4, the calculation method may have a critical bearing on the final results. To compute a benchmark is hardly rocket science, and the following examples are all constructed using easily obtainable data. In all our examples we choose three currencies: US dollar, sterling and Japanese yen, but the result can easily be modified to include more currencies. The base currency is the US dollar and the initial weightings are equally 33.33% (these are kept fixed for convenience, with no adjustment for asset drift). We assume that the equity indices have been adjusted for dividends. Tables 6.10 and 6.11 contain the raw data and calculated raw returns used in subsequent sections.

6.7.1 Passive benchmarks

The following benchmarks are passive because they all have fixed hedge ratios.

6.7.1.1 Unhedged

Most publicly available equity indices are unhedged. No adjustment is made for currency hedging in an unhedged index. Returns denominated in the base currency have two components: local currency returns and spot currency returns, the latter consisting of currency surprise (hedgeable) and forward premium (unhedgeable). Our way of computing unhedged returns may seem cumbersome as they can be obtained directly from the returns on three indices, all denominated in the US dollar, namely, $R1$, $R8$ and $R9$ in Table 6.11. However, calculating returns in this way has two distinct advantages: it lends itself directly to other passive hedge ratios, as shown in subsequent sections; and the equity return column, $P2$ in Table 6.12, which shows the underlying returns with forward points included, should be used as the index for the underlying manager, as argued in Section 6.3.

6.7.1.2 Fully hedged (unitary)

The return for each country in the fully hedged benchmark consists of the sum of the local asset market return and the currency premium. The currency surprise component of the spot currency return is eliminated, as shown in Table 6.13.

Table 6.10 Raw data used in holding-based benchmark calculation examples

	S&P ($) L1	FTSE (£) L2	Nikkei (¥) L3	USD/GBP FX1	USD/JPY FX2	$ Libor I1 %	£ Libor I2 %	¥ Libor I3 %	FTSE ($) L2/FX1	Nikkei ($) L3/FX2
31/01/00	754	6,269	19,540	0.6191	107.37	5.89	6.11	0.09	10,126	181.99
29/02/00	739	6,233	19,960	0.6336	110.14	5.92	6.16	0.13	9,837	181.21
31/03/00	815	6,540	20,337	0.6276	102.66	6.13	6.05	0.10	10,421	198.11
28/04/00	781	6,327	17,974	0.6435	108.15	6.29	6.19	0.09	9,832	166.18
31/05/00	762	6,359	16,332	0.6664	107.72	6.65	6.12	0.08	9,542	151.61
30/06/00	790	6,313	17,411	0.6588	106.02	6.64	6.07	0.15	9,583	164.22

Table 6.11 Calculated raw returns for holding-based benchmark examples.

	S&P ($) R1 %	FTSE (£) R2 %	Nikkei (¥) R3 %	USD/GBP R4 %	USD/JPY R5 %	£ − $ Libor R6 %	¥ − $ Libor R7 %	FTSE ($) R8 %	Nikkei ($) R9 %
31/01/00									
29/02/00	−2.09	−0.57	2.13	−2.32	−2.56	−0.02	0.48	−2.89	−0.43
31/03/00	9.85	4.82	1.88	0.95	7.04	−0.02	0.48	5.76	8.91
28/04/00	−4.21	−3.31	−12.35	−2.50	−5.22	0.01	0.50	−5.81	−17.57
31/05/00	−2.58	0.50	−9.58	−3.50	0.40	0.01	0.52	−2.99	−9.18
30/06/00	3.70	−0.74	6.40	1.16	1.59	0.04	0.55	0.42	7.99

£ − $ Libor and ¥ − $ Libor are differences between Libor interest rates for currencies indicated.

Table 6.12 Passive holding-based benchmarks: unhedged benchmark

	Unhedged return P1, %	Equity return P2, %	Currency surprise P3, %	Cumulative unhedged P4, %
31/01/00				
29/02/00	−1.80	−0.03	−1.78	
31/03/00	8.17	5.67	2.51	8.17
28/04/00	−9.20	−6.46	−2.74	−1.03
31/05/00	−4.92	−3.71	−1.21	−5.94
30/06/00	4.04	3.32	0.72	−1.90

$P1 = P2 + P3$; $P2 = [R1 + (R2 + R6) + (R3 + R7)]/3$ and $P3 = [0 + (R4 − R6) + (R5 − R7)]/3$. $P4$ is a simple cumulative arithmetic sum of returns to date. There are many other ways of calculating cumulative returns, but here we have chosen to use simple methods throughout the examples.

Table 6.13 Passive holding-based benchmarks: fully hedged (unitary) benchmark

	Hedged return P5, %	Equity return P6, %	Currency return P7, %	Cumulative hedged P8, %
31/01/00				
29/02/00	−0.03	−0.03	0.00	
31/03/00	5.67	5.67	0.00	5.67
28/04/00	−6.46	−6.46	0.00	−0.79
31/05/00	−3.71	−3.71	0.00	−4.50
30/06/00	3.32	3.32	0.00	−1.18

$P5 = P6 = P2$ and $P7 = 0$.

6.7.1.3 Partially hedged

A partially hedged benchmark, shown in Table 6.14, is a weighted average of unhedged and fully hedged benchmarks. If we use a 50% hedge ratio, the returns are the average of the unhedged and fully hedged benchmarks.

6.7.2 Dynamic benchmarks

When the hedge ratio is not fixed, the benchmark is referred to as dynamic. Here we consider a few such benchmarks, albeit the simpler ones, used by fund managers. In practice, many dynamic benchmarks incorporate research results similar to those discussed

Table 6.14 Passive holding-based benchmarks: partially (50%) hedged benchmark

	50% hedged return P9, %	Equity return P10, %	Currency return P11, %	Cumulative 50% hedged P12, %
31/01/00				
29/02/00	−0.92	−0.03	−0.89	
31/03/00	6.92	5.67	1.25	6.92
28/04/00	−7.83	−6.46	−1.37	−0.91
31/05/00	−4.31	−3.71	−0.60	−5.22
30/06/00	3.68	3.32	0.36	−1.54

$P9 = P10 + P11; P10 = (P2 + P6)/2; P11 = (P3 + P7)/2.$

Table 6.15 Dynamic holding-based benchmarks: momentum benchmark

Hedging decision		Portfolio return P13, %	Equity return P14, %	Currency return P15, %	Cumulative portfolio return P16, %
GBP	JPY				
31/01/00					
29/02/00	Hedge	Hedge				
31/03/00	Unhedge	Unhedge	5.67	5.67	0.00	5.67
28/04/00	Hedge	Hedge	−9.20	−6.46	−2.74	−3.53
31/05/00	Hedge	Hedge	−3.71	−3.71	0.00	−7.24
30/06/00			3.32	3.32	0.00	−3.92

$P13 = P14 + P15; P14 = P2.$ If the hedging decision is to hedge, then the currency return is zero; otherwise it takes on unhedged currency returns.

in Chapters 4 and 7. One type of dynamic benchmark not included here is the CAPM-optimised benchmark discussed in Chapter 5, Section 5.4. As argued there, we consider that this type of benchmark is too volatile in the *ex ante* setting and therefore unsuitable for practical use.

6.7.2.1 Momentum benchmark

A momentum benchmark incorporates some kind of trend-following rules. Here we assume a simple filer rule: *if last month's actual currency return is positive, then do not hedge; otherwise, hedge fully.* The benchmark can be constructed as shown in Table 6.15.

Table 6.16 Dynamic holding-based benchmarks: value benchmark

	Hedging decision		Portfolio return P17, %	Equity return P18, %	Currency return P19, %	Cumulative portfolio return P20, %
	GBP	**JPY**				
31/01/00						
29/02/00	Unhedge	Hedge				
31/03/00	Unhedge	Hedge	4.90	5.67	0.32	5.99
28/04/00	Hedge	Hedge	−6.13	−6.46	−0.84	−1.30
31/05/00	Hedge	Hedge	−3.71	−3.71	0.00	−5.01
30/06/00			3.32	3.32	0.00	−1.69

6.7.2.2 Value benchmark

Another popular benchmark explicitly incorporates forward bias. A very simple version might be: *hedge currency exposure if the foreign currency forward trades at a premium and leave it open if it trades at a discount.* In our example the yen always trades at a premium, so yen exposure will be hedged, whereas sterling initially trades at a discount and then at a premium. The hedging decisions and the benchmark are shown in Table 6.16.

6.7.2.3 Fundamental benchmark

For a fundamental benchmark the hedging decisions are made on the basis of signals from fundamental data. There are endless possible choices of which fundamental data to use and, indeed, how they are used. Here we construct a very simple example using the OECD Composite Leading Indicators (CLI).[9] We look at the monthly changes of CLI for the US, the UK and Japan. The hedging decision is taken as follows: *if the change of UK CLI for a particular month is higher than that for the US* (sterling is likely to appreciate), *the exposure is left unhedged; and vice versa.* The benchmark is detailed in Table 6.17.

6.7.2.4 Dynamic hedging benchmark

A dynamic hedging style aims to replicate the payoff of an option by hedging a portion of the exposure that is equivalent to the option delta. Delta can be loosely interpreted as the likelihood of option protection being needed. We will discuss option replication in more detail in Chapter 7, but here is an example of how a

Table 6.17 Dynamic holding-based benchmarks: fundamental benchmark

Composite Leading Indicators (CLI)			Hedging decision		Portfolio return P21, %	Equity return P22, %	Currency return P23, %	Cumulative portfolio return P24, %
USD	GBP	JPY	GBP	JPY				
31/01/00								
29/02/00 −0.19	−0.29	−0.05	Hedge	Unhedge				
31/03/00 −0.35	−0.32	−0.49	Unhedge	Hedge	7.85	5.67	2.19	7.85
28/04/00 −0.22	−0.51	0.01	Hedge	Unhedge	−7.29	−6.46	−0.84	0.56
31/05/00 0.75	−0.46	0.05	Hedge	Hedge	−3.75	−3.71	−0.04	−3.19
30/06/00 −0.53	0.08	−0.37			3.32	3.32	0.00	0.13

Source: CLI data are from OECD.

Table 6.18 Dynamic holding-based benchmarks: dynamic hedging benchmark

	Hedge ratio		Portfolio return P25, %	Equity return P26, %	Currency return P27, %	Cumulative portfolio return P29, %
	GBP, %	JPY, %				
31/01/00						
29/02/00	47	47				
31/03/00	42	19	7.00	5.67	1.33	7.00
28/04/00	59	43	−8.49	−6.46	−2.03	−1.49
31/05/00	81	43	−4.21	−3.71	−0.50	−5.70
30/06/00			3.59	3.32	0.27	−2.11

dynamic hedging benchmark can be constructed. In the example in Table 6.18 we choose two six-month put options on sterling and the Japanese yen against the US dollar, assuming implied volatilities of 9% and 12% for dollar/sterling and dollar/yen, respectively. Note that if one wants to compare the performance of the dynamic hedging benchmark with that of a purchased option benchmark, the option premium should be explicitly incorporated.

6.8 ADJUSTMENT STYLE

Once the underlying benchmark has been chosen, a hedge ratio set and various other specific issues listed above resolved, the investor needs to define how the adjustment should be carried out. This may not be as straightforward as it sounds, largely due to the interactive nature of currency exposure and the underlying investment: when a fund manager moves out of Japanese equities and into US Treasuries, a currency position is taken at the same time. The differences of adjustment style arise depending on how a currency overlay manager deals with this "extra exposure".[10]

There are three common alternatives:

❏ hedge the actual exposure;
❏ hedge the benchmark exposure; or
❏ hedge to benchmark neutral.

Below we use a simple example to illustrate these different styles. In each case, the pre-set static hedge ratio is 50% and the base currency is the US dollar.

6.8.1 Hedging actual exposure

The currency overlay manager's (moving) target is the actual exposure of the fund, which consists of the benchmark exposure and the active exposure. In the example shown in Table 6.19, the benchmark underlying position is listed in column 1 and the currency overlay manager's benchmark position is in column 5. The manager will make sure that the final position in column 9 represents the hedging positions needed for the active position in column 2. The adjustment needed in column 8 is driven by the active positions in column 2.

The pros and cons of this approach are:

❏ It requires timely communication between underlying manager and overlay manager. This is a big practical barrier for the successful implementation of an overlay programme. However, the situation is improving rapidly with the application of on-line technology as well as the new services provided by custodian banks.
❏ Because the hedging positions are a function of the actual underlying positions, the underlying manager can influence currency decisions unless the hedge ratio is 100%.
❏ The performances of the underlying manager and the overlay manager may not add up to the portfolio performance. This is due to the fact that the former can influence currency positions.

Table 6.19 Overlay adjustment: hedge actual exposure

| | Underlying security Average market weight | | | Currency selection Average currency weight | | | | | |
	Benchmark % (1)	Active % (2)	Difference % (3) = (2) − (1)	Benchmark Underlying % (4) = (1)	Hedge % (5) = −50% × (1)	Hedge Benchmark %, (6) = (1) + (5)	Actual % (7) = (6) + (3)	Adjustment % (8) = −50% × (3)	Final % (9) = (7) + (8)
Euro zone	20.0	25.0	5.0	20.0	−10.0	10.0	15.0	−2.5	12.5
Japan	20.0	20.0	0.0	20.0	−10.0	10.0	10.0	0.0	10.0
UK	10.0	10.0	0.0	10.0	−5.0	5.0	5.0	0.0	5.0
US	50.0	45.0	−5.0	50.0	25.0	75.0	70.0	2.5	72.5
	100.0	100.0		100.0		100.0			

6.8.2 Hedging benchmark weighting

This approach is straightforward: the currency overlay manager's target is simply the benchmark exposure of the fund. As shown in Table 6.20, currency positions are derived from the benchmark underlying exposures and the hedge ratio. The extra exposure portion in column 7 created by active positions is ignored. No adjustment will be made with respect to the active positions taken by the underlying manager: this is shown in column 8.

The pros and cons of the approach are:

❑ It does not require timely communication between underlying manager and overlay manager.
❑ Since underlying and overlay managers act independently, the total return on the portfolio is the sum of the returns from the underlying portfolio and the overlay portfolio.
❑ The actual currency position is influenced by the underlying manager's active positions.
❑ There is no link between actual currency exposure and the overlay programme.

6.8.3 Hedging to benchmark neutral

In this arrangement, illustrated in Table 6.21, the currency overlay manager first neutralises any deviations caused by the active underlying positions relative to the underlying benchmark, as shown in column 3. He will then take additional currency-hedging positions according to the benchmark weighting and the passive hedge ratio.

The pros and cons of the approach are:

❑ It is a commonly used method for currency overlay as it represents a complete transfer of risk from the underlying manager to the overlay manager. All additional currency positions taken by the former are neutralised.
❑ The benchmark is more complicated to compute and the approach requires timely communication between the underlying manager and the overlay manager.
❑ Again, because of the dependence between the actions of the underlying and overlay managers, total portfolio performance may not be the sum of the performances of the underlying and overlay portfolios.

Table 6.19 Overlay adjustment: hedge actual exposure

| | Underlying security Average market weight | | | Currency selection Average currency weight | | | | | |
	Benchmark % (1)	Active % (2)	Difference % (3) = (2) − (1)	Benchmark Underlying % (4) = (1)	Hedge % (5) = −50% × (1)	Hedge Benchmark %, (6) = (1) + (5)	Actual % (7) = (6) + (3)	Adjustment % (8) = −50% × (3)	Final % (9) = (7) + (8)
Euro zone	20.0	25.0	5.0	20.0	−10.0	10.0	15.0	−2.5	12.5
Japan	20.0	20.0	0.0	20.0	−10.0	10.0	10.0	0.0	10.0
UK	10.0	10.0	0.0	10.0	−5.0	5.0	5.0	0.0	5.0
US	50.0	45.0	−5.0	50.0	25.0	75.0	70.0	2.5	72.5
	100.0			100.0		100.0			

Table 6.21 Overlay adjustment: hedge back to benchmark exposure

	Underlying security Average market weight			Currency selection Average currency weight						
	Benchmark % (1)	Active % (2)	Difference % (3) = (2) − (1)	Benchmark Underlying % (4) = (1)	Hedge % (5) = −50% × (1)	Hedge Benchmark %, (6) = (1) + (5)	Actual % (7) = (6) + (3)	Adjustment % (8) = −(3)	Final % (9) = (7) + (8)
Euro zone	20.0	25.0	5.0	20.0	−10.0	10.0	15.0	−5.0	10.0
Japan	20.0	20.0	0.0	20.0	−10.0	10.0	10.0	0.0	10.0
UK	10.0	10.0	0.0	10.0	−5.0	5.0	5.0	0.0	5.0
US	50.0	45.0	−5.0	50.0	25.0	75.0	70.0	5.0	75.0
	100.0			100.0		100.0			

6.9 OTHER PRACTICAL CONSIDERATIONS

A host of other practical factors need considering prior to the actual implementation of a currency overlay, and below we list a few of them:

❑ *Hedging horizon.* How long should the maturity of a currency-hedging portfolio be, and how frequently should the positions be adjusted?

❑ *Choice of hedging instruments.* Is it better to use spot, forwards or options?

❑ *Cashflow.* How much cash should a fund set aside to settle hedging contracts?

❑ *Symmetry of constraints.* Should the overlay mandate allow positions to be taken on both sides of a passive hedge position or only on one side?

❑ *Fixing arrangements.* What foreign exchange rates should be used for benchmark calculation?

❑ *Emerging market currencies.* Should one consider only exposures in mature currencies where currency hedging is practicable at reasonable cost, or in all currencies?

❑ *Bid–offer spread.* How should bid–offer spreads be dealt with when constructing a benchmark?

In this section we take a brief look at some of these issues. The answers to the questions posed above to a large extent depend on the circumstances specific to a given fund. Consideration of emerging market currencies is deferred to Chapter 9 due to its importance, and the question of bid–offer spreads will not be discussed here as it is not a currency-specific issue.

6.9.1 Hedging horizon

In a classic CAPM framework there is no *a priori* reason to choose one particular currency-hedging horizon over another.[11] There are, however, some academic studies on the impact of investment horizon on the performance of a fund. For example, Balduzzi and Lynch (1999) show that the cost of behaving myopically and ignoring the predictability of returns can be substantial. Brennan, Schwartz and Lagnado (1997) found that longer-horizon portfolio strategies that take into account the predictability of asset returns significantly outperform short-horizon portfolio strategies that ignore it. While for other asset types one may well be able to argue that lengthening the horizon will increase predictability, in the case of currency the argument remains unconvincing, both theoretically and empirically. However, some argue that the currency-hedge ratio should be lower for funds with longer investment horizons because over a long period of time the impact of risk from currency will diminish but its effect on diversification will increase. The first point is essentially another way of stating that, in the long run, currency impact "washes out" – a point that was briefly discussed in Chapter 1. The second point is that if currency fluctuations are pure random noise, the diversification benefit of having currencies in a portfolio is as good as a lottery where the proceeds are fully distributed. If currency fluctuations are not pure noise, a stable link between them and any other economic variables remains unproven.

The choice of hedging horizon is often made on practical grounds – for example, internal hedging constraints such as rebalancing frequency, adjustment bands and allowable tracking error (related to the volatility of the underlying assets and base currency), dealing costs (which may reflect the liquidity in underlying currency pairs), administration, etc. While some of the factors are fund-specific, dealing costs can be estimated.[12] We will consider an example of a Swedish krona-based fixed-income fund with a full hedge mandate. The main exposures are in the US dollar, euro, sterling and Japanese yen.

The fund uses a mixture of rolling swaps to manage its exposure, so we can estimate the dealing cost using the relevant bid–offer spreads for currency swaps. The swap spreads are reasonably stable except in rapidly changing markets or shortly before and after central bank interest rate announcements. Figure 6.2 plots the bid–offer spread of currency swaps against the krona over different maturities. On balance, the transaction cost for the krona/yen pair is the highest, followed by sterling and euro. The US dollar/krona pair has the lowest transaction cost. The bid–offer spreads of the benchmark portfolio track those of the krona/euro closely.

The bid–offer spread for shorter horizons is smaller. However, the fund will need to roll more often in a given period. We annualise the bid–offer spread by taking the dealing frequency into

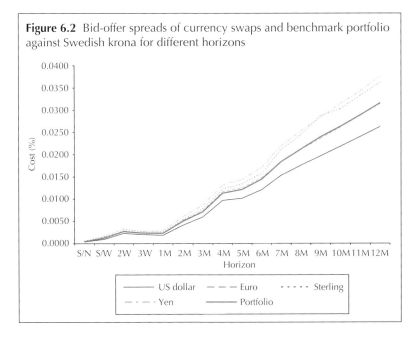

Figure 6.2 Bid-offer spreads of currency swaps and benchmark portfolio against Swedish krona for different horizons

consideration, and the results are plotted in Figure 6.3. Now we observe that the hedging cost initially declines when we lengthen the hedge horizon due to the reduced number of rolls but that it stays more or less stable beyond a one-month horizon. To judge from Figure 6.3, a hedging horizon longer than one month would be optimal. If the underlying index is rebalanced once a month (quarter), it makes practical sense to set the same hedging frequency. This way the foreign exchange impact of the monthly (quarterly) rebalancing decision can be dealt with immediately.

Some practitioners argue that the hedging horizon should be decided on the basis of the fund's views and sensitivities with respect to interest rates. When a forward position is entered into, it locks the fund into a fixed interest rate over the contract period. A longer-maturity forward will be more sensitive to interest rate changes. However, most funds' hedging horizons are shorter than six months and the difference between them is not material. We have seen a strategy where a fund will switch between a long and a short hedging horizon monthly depending on the relative interest rate differentials, but the effect on performance, which we do not know, is unlikely to be significant.

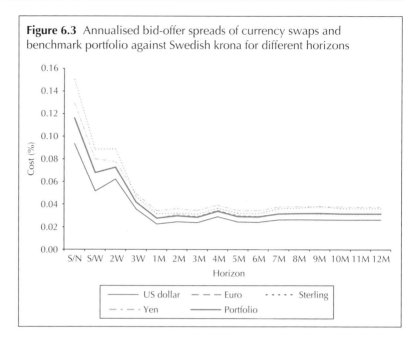

Figure 6.3 Annualised bid-offer spreads of currency swaps and benchmark portfolio against Swedish krona for different horizons

The following issues may also affect the horizon decision:

❏ *Cash management.* Foreign exchange hedging contracts need to be settled in cash (on a net basis), which may result in in- or out-flows from the cash accounts. A longer horizon will result in larger, if less frequent, swings in the cash accounts, and it may be preferable to limit the size of the flows by having a slightly shorter horizon.

❏ *Credit charges.* Dealing counterparties may levy credit charges for longer-dated trades, and these are not modelled explicitly in our view.

❏ *Administration cost.* This should be split into a fixed part and a variable part and added to the overall transaction cost. There should also be an explicit estimate of dealing errors, which can add to the cost.

6.9.2 Choice of instruments

As mentioned in Chapter 1, the foreign exchange market is highly commoditised, transaction costs are usually very small for almost all categories of foreign exchange instrument, and there is high substitutability between different instruments. Here are a few general observations; in practice, the choice is largely a function of a fund's internal objectives and constraints.

6.9.2.1 Spot vs forwards

❏ A currency manager can use either spot or forwards to hedge currency risks. If he uses spot, he can roll the spot positions forward on daily basis.
❏ The overall cost of daily rolling is usually higher than for a slightly longer horizon (see Section 6.9.1).
❏ Spot positions may be suitable for currency managers who trade actively on very short time horizons (intra-day). It is probably better to use forwards for the passive portion of the hedge.

6.9.2.2 Forwards vs futures

❏ Most foreign exchange trades are done over the counter rather than through the exchanges (see volume figure in Chapter 1, Table 1.1). There is little to distinguish them on the grounds of transaction cost. Forwards are more flexible.
❏ Some currency managers are restricted to using exchange-traded products.
❏ Credit risk is different.[13] For forwards, the currency managers take on the credit risk with the counterparty banks. For futures, credit risk is with the exchange and is largely eliminated through margining. A credit agreement must be in place before a currency manager can deal in currency forwards with a bank.

6.9.2.3 Use of options (including exotic options)

❏ Broadly speaking, there are probably some market inefficiencies in the options market (just as in the spot market, as surveyed in Chapter 4), which could be explored.
❏ There are good reasons for fund managers to use options either systematically or discreetly. However, specialist knowledge is required if a fund decides to use options.
❏ The conventional wisdom on options being too expensive for what they are is not entirely correct (but not that wrong either).

6.9.2.4 Specifically, the use of exotic options

❏ There is very little research to support or refute the use of exotic options by fund managers. This arena is still dominated by large investment banks, some corporations (in dwindling numbers) and many hedge funds.

❏ Some products are designed to solve particular problems a fund faces. However, we believe that it is even more important for a fund to acquire specialist knowledge before using exotic options.

6.9.3 Hedge cash account

One important practical question related to currency hedging is cash management: profits/losses on currency hedges need to be settled in cash,[14] whereas the currency exposure does not crystallise until the underlying investment is sold. If not properly considered, this temporal mismatch may force a fund to (partially) liquidate investment positions against its strategic asset allocation decisions. Some use this fact as an argument against currency hedging.

It is reasonably straightforward to estimate the potential passive cashflow requirement from the following factors:

❏ the size of the portfolio;
❏ benchmark weightings in different currencies;
❏ the passive hedge ratio; and
❏ the hedging horizon.

The exercise closely resembles a value-at-risk (VAR) calculation, which one can conduct using various methods: historical simulation, variance–covariance matrices or Monte Carlo simulation. If we use a variance–covariance matrix method, we can compute the foreign exchange volatility of a portfolio using the estimated matrix along with the position weightings, the latter calculated from benchmark weightings in different currencies and the passive hedge ratio. Assuming a normal distribution, one can estimate the cash requirement to settle hedging contracts as shown in Table 6.22.[15] Monthly volatilities are computed from annual volatilities using the square root of time rule.

Note that in order to estimate the cumulative cash requirements for several periods, one needs to use the square root of time rule

Table 6.22 Estimating the cash requirement for forward hedging

	FX moves (standard deviations)					
	1	2	3	1	2	3
	FX volatility = 5% per annum			FX volatility = 10% per annum		
Likelihood, %	7.93	1.14	0.07	7.93	1.14	0.07
One in how many	13	88	1,429	13	88	1,429
Hedging horizon	Cash outflow					
1-month, %	−0.72	−1.44	−2.16	−1.44	−2.88	−4.32
2-month, %	−1.02	−2.04	−3.06	−2.04	−4.08	−6.12
3-month, %	−1.25	−2.50	−3.75	−2.50	−5.00	−7.50
6-month, %	−1.77	−3.54	−5.31	−3.54	−7.08	−10.62

Lower part of table shows the potential cash outflow from settling currency hedging contracts. Outflows (indicated by minus sign) are expressed as percentage of total exposure. Potential outflow increases with foreign exchange volatility and with magnitude of foreign exchange moves. It also increases with hedging horizon, but with shorter horizons one has to hedge more frequently.

again rather than multiplying the single period number by the number of periods. Also worth bearing in mind is that investment in foreign currencies typically accounts for only a small portion of the total portfolio and the net impact is probably much smaller. Variance–covariance estimation methods have many known problems, the assumption of a normal distribution being a serious one. The normal estimate produced in the table is likely to underestimate the large moves and the associated cash requirements. There are many remedial methods that one can find in any book on VAR.

In practice, many funds will set aside some cash upfront for the currency overlay programme, and this is normally in the region of 3–5%. The cash amount can be counted towards the fund's strategic cash holdings. Alternatively, derivative contracts can be used to synthetically invest the cash in the desired asset class. This amount is periodically adjusted using a predefined band: injecting cash (funded by selling underlying positions) if the level falls towards the lower bound and allocating surplus cash to the underlying investment if the level moves towards the upper bound.

There are other ways of dealing with currency hedging:

❏ *Purchased options.* The loss on a purchase option contract is limited to the upfront premium. However, over time, cumulative option premiums, which also need to be funded in cash, can be of a similar magnitude.

❏ *Layered forward contracts.* Rather than using six-month forward contracts to hedge all the exposure, where a fund will have to deal with infrequent but potentially large cashflows, the fund can use a mix of one-, three- and six-month forward contracts that settle at different times. The result of layered forward contracts is, however, largely cosmetic.

❏ *Dynamic hedging.* Here one automatically reduces the hedge ratio when the hedging portfolio moves into the red and increases the hedge ratio when it moves into the black. For much the same reason as for the use of purchased options, the effect over time of reducing the cashflow requirement with the use of a dynamic hedging strategy is not established.[16]

❏ *An active approach.* To reduce the cash requirements associated with a passive hedging strategy, one needs to lift the hedge before the base currency depreciates and place the hedge before the base currency appreciates. There is some evidence that, *on average*, active overlay management does a better job than a random lifting/placing alternative. But that is not the same as reducing the cash requirement, the latter being achieved when hedging results move away from the average. However, a suitably controlled active currency overlay programme is unlikely to add to the cashflow requirements arising from a passive hedging strategy.

6.9.4 Symmetry of constraints

A typical currency overlay mandate will specify a passive hedge ratio that serves as the starting point for the overlay managers. Historically, the overlay managers' decision variable – the actual hedge ratio – varies from 0% to 100%. That is, he can decide to leave the exposure completely open in anticipation of an appreciation of the foreign currency; or he can hedge the exposure fully if he thinks that the foreign currency will depreciate (vs forward). He cannot take positions that may result in a negative hedge ratio (ie, going long foreign currency in addition to the exposure) or choose

Table 6.23 Symmetrical mandate vs asymmetrical mandate

Passive hedge ratio, %	Currency manager's decision	
	Overhedge, %	Underhedge, %
0	100	0
50	50	50
100	0	100

a hedge ratio that exceeds 100% (ie, going short foreign currency more than the exposure). These restrictions are in place to guard against "speculative" currency positions in the portfolio. Such constraints, though commonsensical, may affect the performance of currency overlay managers in terms of both excess return and tracking error.

The type of active positions a currency overlay manager can take will depend on the passive hedge ratio – this is illustrated in Table 6.23. It is easy to see that, with a 50% passive hedge ratio, an overlay manager can go either long or short depending on his currency views. For 0% and 100% passive hedge ratios, he is restricted to one-sided positions (albeit in twice as much). Because of this, a 50% hedged benchmark is sometimes called a symmetrical benchmark, and 0% or 100% hedged benchmarks are called asymmetrical benchmarks. It probably makes more sense to talk about symmetrical and asymmetrical *mandates* than benchmarks, as symmetry in this case really refers to the ability of a currency manager, under a specific mandate, to take positions on both sides of the passive hedge position or only one side. We believe that all mandates should be symmetrical, with the risk control consideration reflected in the maximum deviation allowed. When active decisions are taken to vary the hedge ratio, it is speculation. An investor or fund manager should decide either to speculate in currencies or not to speculate at all, in which case he sticks to a passive hedge ratio; it does not make sense to "half-speculate".

It is easy to work out that the tracking error of an asymmetric benchmark is larger than that of a symmetric one. In a very simple case, if we compare the tracking error for a 0% or 100% hedged benchmark with that for a 50% hedged benchmark, the former can be about 40% higher than the latter, assuming that short or long positions are taken with equal probability.[17] The case has been studied empirically by Acar and Pedersen (2001) using a historical simulation method, and their result confirms the above conjecture.

Some of the constraints are in place because of regulatory requirements. For example, German investment trusts are currently not allowed to carry out currency trades that are separate from the underlying investment. This situation is expected to change soon, and many overlay players are already positioning themselves to capture new business once the ban is lifted. In France, funds are generally forbidden to enter into unmatched short foreign exchange positions. Similar regulations exist in several other European countries. The regulatory reforms in respect of Swedish national pension funds, begun in January 2001 and thought to have been linked to the increased level of foreign exchange activities by Swedish funds,[18] give fund managers more freedom to pursue international diversification.

We have not seen empirical studies on the impact of mandate symmetry on the historical performance of currency overlay. This is not surprising given the scarcity of performance data in this field. Even if we assume that, on average, the performance is the same (although an overlay manager may miss half the opportunities available to him, he can take positions that are twice as large with the other half), the risk-adjusted return would be lower given the increase in tracking error.

6.9.5 Currency fixing arrangements

Fixing arrangements began to receive attention in recent years as currency hedging became more widespread and the procedures more transparent. For many types of bonds and equities, natural fixing arrangements are provided by exchanges or certain professional organisations. But with currencies the choice is not as straightforward. Generally speaking, each central bank publishes a set of daily fixing rates for its base currency against a host of other currencies. The quality[19] of these rates varies. Here are four frequently used central bank fixing sources:

❏ Bank of England hourly fixing, from London open to close;
❏ European Central Bank daily fixing, published at around 14.30 Frankfurt time;

❏ Federal Reserve Bank of New York interbank fixing, published at 10.00 and 12.00 New York time;
❏ Reuters also publishes a daily fixing at around 13.00 Frankfurt time (16 banks surveyed and the readings averaged).

Bloomberg's currency fixing rates are used less frequently for fixing purposes.

The commonly used (by fund managers as well as index compilers) rates are the WM/Reuters closing spot rates published at 16.00 GMT by the WM Company,[20] the Bank of England's closing reference rates, also at 16.00 local time, and the European Central Bank's rates at 14.15 local time. Some investment banks and custodian banks now provide a dealing service against these fixing rates. One point worth noting is that some fund managers use non-deliverable forwards (NDFs) to hedge their currency exposures in emerging market currencies, and these contracts are normally fixed against central bank fixings of the relevant currencies. There may be significant discrepancies between the different fixing sources.

Natsuko Waki of Reuters reported in November 2002 that more investors are transacting at the daily fixing points, hoping to match their peers' performance in currencies and hence eliminate a source of risk. However, the practice itself can cause greater volatility in the minutes when central banks and third parties set the fixing rates, as the counterparty banks scramble to hedge their currency positions.

6.10 PERFORMANCE-BASED BENCHMARKS

A performance-based benchmark, computed using the performance of a chosen peer group, is useful in a situation where holding-based benchmarks are not generally available or are so diffuse in their details that a fair comparison is difficult to conduct. Holding-based foreign exchange benchmarks are generally not difficult to compute, as demonstrated in Section 6.7; however, making fair comparisons between these benchmarks is not straightforward. For one thing, currency positions may not be stable and may not be disclosed. If the basis is not standardised to take into account returns and risk from different currency portfolios, the result can be erroneous if not pointless. Performance-based benchmarks offer a valuable alternative to holding-based benchmark in this case.

Currency return analysis is still in its infancy, mainly due to the fact that return data are scarce and disclosure requirements minimal. There are several areas that we feel are worth investigating:

❑ Comparing the contribution of different trading styles using a traditional style analysis.

❑ Examining currency management in a portfolio context. For example, investigating the risk reduction achievable through a currency programme.[21]

❑ Determining whether managed currency returns do display option-like characteristics.[22]

It is also important to be aware of the potential main sources of bias from aggregated returns:

❑ *Survivorship bias.*[23] With the active risk level of currency overlay funds at 2–3% per annum, survivorship bias may inflate the average historical overlay return by 20–50 bp if the bias is not explicitly handled. We have seen no published studies of the impact of this type of bias on overlay performance.

❑ *Selection bias.* Only well-performing funds are likely to report to the aggregators and/or they may report only for those accounts with the best performance.

❑ *Back-filled history bias.* Some fund managers may report back-filled (not actual) returns to the aggregator, and this is one of the reasons why the early return data for many funds are on average higher than are reported later.

---

1 The well-respected Association for Investment Management and Research (AIMR) makes the following statement on the subject: "While AIMR here does not make a recommendation in favour of the unhedged or the hedged benchmark, we do regard the determination of currency exposure in the benchmark as an important fiduciary responsibility." (Stannard *et al*, 1998.)

2 See, for example, Grinblatt and Titman (1994) and Lehman and Modest (1987) for equity indices and Blake, Elton and Gruber (1993) for bond indices. AIMR's 1997 publication *Performance Evaluation, Benchmarks, and Attribution Analysis* contains articles written by both practitioners and academics on the subject, but only a few articles deal with currency questions specifically.

3 Aside from the traditional government bond indices, Lehman Brothers, Salomon Smith Barney and Merrill Lynch have each developed new broad market indices to accommodate the much enlarged investment universe. Many of these new indices are accompanied by their currency-hedged counterparts. Salomon Brothers' (now part of Citigroup) currency-hedged indices use one-month forward contracts, rolled every month, with a hedge ratio of 100%.

4   MSCI has developed currency-hedged indices for its popular equity indices, including the EAFE series, as well as for several emerging markets on a custom basis.

5   For a fuller definition see Stannard *et al.* (1998); available on AIMR's website at www.aimr.com/standards/pps/benchmark.html. Table 6.1 is adapted from the same source.

6   Note that in this example we assume for convenience that the actual returns are the same as the passive returns. In practice, they will not be the same as the former include the returns from security selection (eg, stock picking) and active currency contribution (eg, timing). However, it is easy to incorporate these in the framework. For more details see Karnosky and Singer (1994).

7   Interested readers can re-do the example using local returns for the underlying and spot-on-spot returns for currencies and compare the result.

8   It is difficult to generalise this for derivative contracts as they have many different features.

9   More information on Composite Leading Indicators can be found on the OECD's website at www.oecd.org.

10 See Del Vecchio (1999) for a rigorous exposition. Our examples here are similar to those used by Del Vecchio.

11 This is in marked contrast to the choice of hedging horizon for corporations. Since the main concern for corporations when they hedge foreign currencies is to forecast cashflows in those currencies, the length of the hedge horizon will correspond directly to the size of the exposure. For an investor, the size of the exposure is more or less known at any given point in time.

12 Mercer Investment Consulting has teamed up with Record Treasury Management to offer a currency audit service that aims to help trustees of corporate-sponsored schemes gain a clearer picture of foreign exchange trading costs. According to their estimate, pension funds could make an annual saving of 20 bp or more by paying more careful attention to foreign currency management.

13 Interest rate exposures are slightly different too in that forward contracts are entered at fixed interest rates, whereas the margining requirement on the futures contracts renders the return on these contracts sensitive to subsequent interest rate changes as well. This is unlikely to be a major factor, however. See Lioui (1998) for a discussion and references.

14 One can, however, roll the currency-hedged forward at the original contract rate and avoid the large cash in-/outflows. This is the so-called historical rollover, which, in essence, is a loan in disguise. The practice is now prohibited by many regulators.

15 Table 6.22 is similar to the one used in a research note by Bridgewater Associates (no date (a)), but we use a one-sided tail probability rather than the two-sided probability used there. Bridgewater's estimates use actual MSCI EAFE basket weights. The results are similar to ours, which are obtained from a much simpler calculation. See also Lee and Rahman (1990) for simulated results. He investigated a single currency pair with single and multiple managers and with various assumptions on the serial correlation of exchange rate moves.

16 Record Treasury Management uses a dynamic hedging approach and, according to the company, one of the reasons for choosing such an approach is the less stringent cash requirement. The claim is at odds with the research note from another overlay manager, Bridgewater Associates (no date (a)). The note indicates that a dynamically hedged portfolio is not less risky than a comparable, 50% hedged portfolio.

17 The ratio between the volatility of a variable that moves two units half of the time and the volatility of a variable that moves one unit all the time is $\sqrt{2}$ to one.

18 See European Central Bank (2003), p. 24.

19 These are reliable fixing sources. To compare different fixing sources one needs to look at how close those rates are to where the currencies are actually traded in the market, and at how long a delay there is between the reading and publication.

20 The WM Company (www.wmcompany.com) has published daily standardised closing spot exchange rates using information provided by Reuters since 1994. Currently 103 currencies

are quoted, with bid, ask and mid rates available. Since 1997 forward rates have also been published, and nine maturities for 41 currencies are available. The closing spot rates are based on rates at 4pm UK time each trading day and are published at around 4.15pm. The published rates are based on traded rates seen on Reuters' dealing system, along with other quoted rates contributed to Reuters by market participants. Outliers are removed using the company's proprietary methodology.

21 There is currently no large-scale overlay performance database and the existing databases do not really cover the risk-reduction side of currency overlay.

22 Several recent studies have looked at the option-like return profile of hedge fund performance. See, for example, Agarwal and Naik (2001).

23 See, for example, Liang (2000) and Fung and Hsieh (2000).

Option Pricing Theory and Dynamic Hedging

7.1 INTRODUCTION

These days the finance section of any bookstore is typically filled with books on various aspects of option pricing at almost any level of sophistication: continuous-time finance, martingale representation, stochastic calculus, third (or even fourth) generation exotic derivative products in different segments of the capital market, and beyond. It is not our intention to squeeze into this already crowded space. The reason we nevertheless feel obliged to include a chapter on option pricing theory is threefold: first, we wish to illustrate the link between one of the overlay styles – dynamic hedging (also known as option replication) – and option pricing. Second, it allows us to discuss a practical question asked by many currency managers: should currency options be used in an overlay programme? To do this, we need to take another look at the concept of implied volatility, which has its roots in option prices. Third, we follow up with a brief review of option skews and smiles – the fact that the implied volatility of an option differs for different strikes. We look at why skew exists and how it may be exploited for investment. The chapter closes with some observations on the option "Greeks".

The message we would emphasise in this chapter is that option pricing theory performs one fundamental yet often neglected role: the quantification of risks, enabling insurance contracts to be priced against these risks. In this context option pricing theory is – whether options are actually used or not – very relevant to many aspects of risk management besides currency overlay.

7.2 OPTION REPLICATION AND DYNAMIC HEDGING

We start with an intuitive description of what is behind the complicated formulae one uses to price options. In the simplest scenario, a customer buys an option from a bank, either to hedge his own risk or as an investment vehicle. For many clients buying the option is the end of the story. But for a bank it is only the beginning: the bank needs to hedge its risk. No big deal – banks have been doing this over many years for many types of risk. There are, however, two special and very important features about this hedge:

❏ In all likelihood the hedge will need to be adjusted now and then, depending on how market prices change. And, in theory, it needs to be adjusted continuously – this is one of the reasons why sometimes people talk about "continuous-time finance". Not only that, the adjustment takes place in a prespecified manner according to option pricing theory.

❏ The adjustment process has nothing to do with what the underlying might be in the future. In other words, it does not matter what one thinks the price might be in the future. The option is hedged (therefore, priced) as if everyone took the risk-neutral view.

If we ignore some technical caveats, the above two features form the foundation of option pricing theory and, with it, continuous-time finance. The practical relevance of option pricing theory is mainly in the following two areas:[1]

❏ The option price is not just a price for an instrument with a funny-shaped pay-off profile. It is a price plus a DIY guidebook. If you follow the rules in the guidebook you can, with some preparation, replicate what the option is designed to achieve by trading the underlying.

❏ Using the guidebook (or, rather, the principles in the guidebook), one can derive a price for a given instrument with a given underlying distribution. In other words, option pricing theory allows the practitioner to price risks and, with the help of the guidebook, to manage these risks.

The binomial representation of option pricing theory can be found in many works on option pricing. We will apply it in the case of a hypothetical call option to illustrate the points mentioned above. Our example makes the following assumptions:

❏ The US dollar/Japanese yen spot price is 100.00;
❏ Dollar and yen interest rates are zero (to make the calculation simple);
❏ There are two possible spot movements in the next period: up to 120.00 or down to 90.00, with probabilities of 60% and 40%, respectively;
❏ A call option struck at 100.00 will pay the holder 10 yen if spot ends up at 110.00 and nothing if spot ends up at 90.00.

What should the market price of this call option be? We will denote the value of the option as V. To replicate the position, let us assume that we hold a portfolio of spot dollar/yen positions and a cash position, denoted as S and C, noting that S represents the US dollar notional amount of the spot position.[2] The spot process, option payoff and hedging process are illustrated in Figure 7.1.

We want the value of the portfolio (S,C) to be the same as the option pay-off at time 1, ie,

$$
\begin{aligned}
&\text{Up:} &&S \times 120.00 + C = 10.0 \\
&\text{Down:} &&S \times 90.00 + C = 0.0
\end{aligned}
$$

Solve the equations (without calculating the exact results) and we get:

$$
S = \frac{10.00 - 0.00}{120.00 - 90.00}
$$

$$
C = 10.00 - \frac{10.00 - 0.00}{120.00 - 90.00} \times 120.00
$$

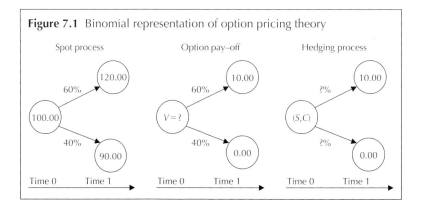

Figure 7.1 Binomial representation of option pricing theory

Therefore, if we hold such a portfolio of S and C, we will exactly replicate the pay-off of the option. And, by the argument of no arbitrage, the value of this portfolio should be the value of the option at time 0, namely,

$$V = S \times 100 + C$$
$$= \frac{10.00 - 0.00}{120.00 - 90.00} \times 100.00 + \left(10.00 - \frac{10.00 - 0.00}{120.00 - 90.00} \times 120.00\right)$$

Rearrange the last equation and we get the following:

$$V = \left(1 - \frac{100.00 - 90.00}{120.00 - 100.00}\right) \times 10.00 + \left(\frac{100.00 - 90.00}{120.00 - 100.00}\right) \times 0.00$$

This looks suspiciously like a formula for taking expectations: the terms in brackets are probabilities and the terms outside are option pay-offs. More amazingly, the "real" probability of whether the spot will go up or down does not even appear in the expression! A whole branch of science, after the seminal work of Black, Scholes and Merton, is devoted to studying the whys and hows of this equation. Luckily, the intuition is sufficient for our purpose and our excursion more or less stops here. Interested readers can turn to the many books available in this field – for example, Hull (2002) for a balanced exposition of both theory and practice, and Baxter and Rennie (1996) for some mathematics.

This simple example tells us that:

❑ Options (or, more generally, all derivatives contracts) are priced at the expected value of their future pay-offs, but the expectation is taken using a different probability set.
❑ Since the probability has only the price terms (it should also have interest rate terms but here we assume these are zero), it does not depend on people's attitude to risk. It is as if everyone were risk-neutral. Hence, some people refer to the probability as the risk-neutral probability.
❑ The method we use to price the option has one by-product. It not only tells us the value of the option in question, but it also tells us how to construct a portfolio of spot and cash to replicate the

option. This is the DIY guidebook that comes with the option pricing theory.

Of course, in the real world prices do not move up and down as in our simplistic setting, but the binomial representation can easily be extended to multiple periods and multiple branches and it can be used as a powerful tool for pricing derivative instruments. One final remark: where is the implied volatility term? In a one-period example we can link the volatility to the size of the steps. For a more volatile currency pair the up and down movement should be correspondingly bigger, and vice versa.

7.3 TRANSACTION COSTS AND OPTION REPLICATION[3]

The binomial representation of a dynamic hedge can be adapted to continuous time. However, the presence of transaction costs now becomes an important issue because even low transaction costs can become prohibitively expensive in continuous time, and it becomes impossible to construct a perfect hedge that matches the option pay-off exactly. Under such practical constraints, one needs to follow strategies that optimise a chosen objective (for example, lowest cost, closest match, easiest implementation, etc.) under a particular set of constraints. A natural solution is to abandon continuous rehedging and only to hedge when the underlying price moves by more than a predefined interval. This is the so-called "optimal band" approach.[4] Alternatively, one can follow an "optimal time interval" strategy, in which rehedging takes place only at certain time points.[5] In practice, a dynamic hedger is likely to employ a combination of the two: when the underlying moves by a certain amount and/or after a certain period since the last rebalancing. The latter is necessary because the option hedge may change over time even if the underlying price stays constant.

This topic is directly relevant for currency managers who follow a dynamic hedging approach as they will have to make these practical choices when running an actual hedging portfolio. Optimisation techniques, such as those used in the studies listed in notes 4 and 5, can be used to determine the desirable rehedging band and time interval under a set of constraints appropriate for the given circumstances.

7.4 PORTFOLIO INSURANCE[6]

An important style of overlay management is dynamic hedging, also known as portfolio insurance or option replication. Similar techniques have been used by equity investors for several decades.[7] The idea is straightforward: you hedge more when prices move against you, until you are fully hedged; and, conversely, you hedge less when prices move in your favour. The pay-off of such a strategy is increasing when the price moves in one direction, and zero when the price moves in the other direction. In its purest form a dynamic hedging programme is completely systematic, ie, it does not depend on how one anticipates the spot price movements in the future. It is easy to see the similarity between a portfolio insurance programme and the pay-off profile of a put option. In fact, if we extended the binomial exercise shown in Figure 7.1 to more than one period, we would see the near-exact correspondence between a dynamic hedging programme and what a market-maker does to replicate an option.

This brings up an important question: why should one use portfolio insurance rather than an option? One obvious answer is that it is free – compared with a purchased option strategy, portfolio insurance does not require an upfront premium. Here we make a digression on what is known as a free option, which is used by some overlay managers and investment banks. The free option gives the user an unlimited upside while flooring the downside at zero (adjusted for forward premium). How is it possible to achieve this? From our construction of the option hedging strategy in the last section, in order to replicate the profile but with no money upfront one has to be able to foretell the next spot move – ie, have perfect foresight. Then one can go long or short according to whether the spot goes up or down and accomplish the feat of replicating the option for free. So the next time someone asks whether you would like a "free option", take it only if he accepts "free money"!

People use a dynamic hedging approach instead of options for a combination of reasons:

❏ *Biased option prices.* It is a widely held belief that options are more expensive than they should be. Empirical evidence on this point suggests that they are but this is not conclusive.

❏ *Cash cost and non-cash benefit.* Options have to be purchased, and when they are not exercised they represent a sunk cost. Of course, this is balanced out by the "opportunity benefit", whereby the underlying currency exposure will be in-the-money when an option is out-of-the-money. However, in the real world the opportunity benefit may not be treated the same as the upfront cost.

❏ *Flexibility.* It is much easier to reverse a portfolio of spot/forward contracts than one of options.

❏ *Operational simplicity.* Many old systems are not designed to deal with option-type contracts where the pay-off at expiry is contingent. Options are also a lot more complicated than spot/forwards and specialist knowledge is required to deal with such contracts.

❏ *Regulatory prohibition.* Some countries have stringent regulatory requirements on what type of instruments an institutional investor, especially pension funds, can and cannot deal in and the use of option-type contracts could be excluded.

Does a portfolio insurance programme actually reduce the risk of the portfolio? The answer to this question is not as straightforward as it seems. If one purchases a put option on the currency risk of the portfolio over a certain period, the maximum currency loss is limited to the premium paid for the option. Clearly it alters the risk/return profile of the portfolio of that period (see the illustration in Chapter 3, Figure 3.1). If the original return distribution is symmetrical and bell-shaped normal, the altered distribution will have a cut-off point to the left and a hump in the left centre, indicating a greater likelihood of small losses. Over the period, an option or a portfolio insurance strategy will eliminate or reduce the likelihood of large losses at the cost of an increased likelihood of smaller losses. However, this is only true for that period. Option premiums can accumulate over time, and the effect of the changed distribution is increasingly diluted over longer horizons. If the horizon is long enough, a purchased option strategy or a dynamic hedging programme is comparable to a 50% passive hedged strategy in terms of risk reduction.

What might be the undesirable aspects of adopting a dynamic hedging approach rather than a purchased option alternative?

❏ *Slippage.* When the spot market is volatile or fast moving, a dynamic hedger may need to perform a substantial adjustment to his hedging portfolio. But when the market is volatile, the cost of dealing is high and the hedger may not be able to achieve the desired hedging levels. This can result in underperformance of a dynamic hedging portfolio relative to an option, especially during the time when the hedge is needed most.

❏ *Transaction cost.* Rather than cross the bid–offer spread in an option, a dynamic hedger will have to cross the bid–offer spread in spot (also swap or forward).[8] In theory, the bid–offer spread in an option will reflect the expected bid–offer spread in spot replication. But in practice the former is often lower as a result of competition and position netting by option market-makers.

❏ *Uncertainty.* Rather than accepting a certain upfront premium, a dynamic hedger may face the uncertain cost of providing insurance. This is partly reflected in the slippage, but also in the overall cost of hedging.[9]

❏ *Administration.* A dynamic hedger may need to do many deals and monitor spot movements constantly.

But is the portfolio insurance programme – which aims to replicate an unpaid-for option – free? It is not immediately evident what the hedging cost actually is in our one-period binomial example. In a multi-period setting, the same principle applies and the dynamic hedger adjusts his spot position. This is a costly business because, if spot has gone higher during the preceding period, he will need to buy more at a higher price; conversely, if the spot has gone down, he will need to offload some of his hedge at a lower price. So he is constantly buying high and selling low – not a smart move for making money. In fact, the cumulative loss he makes should equate to the option premium if the option is fairly priced.

A dynamic hedging programme is similar to a simple mechanical trend-following approach. Compared with a purchased option programme, a dynamic hedging programme works well when the market trends or does not move very much but not so well if the market whips around the same level. If we accept the (limited) evidence that options are more expensive than they ought to be, a dynamic hedging programme has the potential to improve portfolio performance relative to a purchased option benchmark. Also, the spot market is much more liquid than the options market and it is that much easier (and with less price distortion) to execute a dynamic hedging programme than an options alternative for large portfolios. Note, however, that because of the close link between a dynamic hedging programme and the pay-off of an option, an appropriate benchmark for evaluating the performance of the former should incorporate the option premiums.

One final comment: there has been talk, especially in the equity market, claiming that the practice of dynamic hedging will increase market volatility as hedgers will buy when the market goes high and sell when the market goes low and that it will therefore accentuate these movements. There is some evidence to support this hypothesis in the equities market, but given its depth it is unlikely to be a driving factor in the currency market.

7.5 THE REDUNDANCY OF OPTIONS

One question often asked by fund managers is whether it is necessary to use options, be they vanilla or the exotic varieties, in an overlay programme. From a theoretical viewpoint, under the classical Black–Scholes assumptions an option is a redundant asset. In Section 7.2 we demonstrated in a binomial setting that the pay-off of an option can be replicated by trading spot. It can be proven that the same principle can be applied in continuous time: one can replicate the pay-off profile of any option by continuously trading spot. If this is indeed the case, there would no reason for fund managers to use options and pay something extra for something they can construct themselves. This assertion leads to the following questions:

❏ Are options still redundant, theoretically and practically, when the classical assumptions are violated?
❏ Is the option price justified? Namely, do end-users pay over the odds for what they get in the options markets? Many end-users dismiss the use of options by saying that they are too expensive for what they are. Cynics may further add that end-users are probably net buyers of options and that market-makers – typically investment banks – raise prices accordingly to profit from this situation.
❏ Is the bid–offer spread for options, which can be some magnitudes larger than that for a spot transaction, justified by the cost of constructing them?

The second question relates to the efficiency of the currency options market, and we defer discussion of this until later in the chapter. The third question has not been systematically studied. But, given the competitiveness of the market and the fact that bid–offer spreads have gone down significantly in recent years, we think that the answer to it is probably yes. Here we will take a look at the first question.

Black and Scholes made a series of assumptions to derive the well-known option pricing formula. When these assumptions are not met in practice – which typically they are not – the pricing formula needs various adjustments. Some of these are cosmetic: for example, interest rates are deterministic but not constant, volatilities are deterministic but not constant, etc. Under these variations, the DIY rules in the guidebook are preserved, the pay-off of the option can still be replicated risklessly and so options remain redundant. But other violations of the assumptions are more serious: incomplete underlying market, stochastic volatilities, transaction costs, etc. In these cases, risk-free replication can no longer be achieved and its place is taken by somewhat risky replications (usually through some sort of fancy optimisation). When the replication is no longer risk-free, the option will not be redundant: it cannot be manufactured by trading the underlying without incurring some sort of cost and/or inaccuracy. Its price will be different for people with different risk-aversions and its market price will be set at a point where buyers' interests equate to the sellers'. Since violation of the Black–Scholes assumption is the market norm, we can conclude that options are probably not redundant.

However, this leaves one further question: to what extent are they not redundant? Are options only marginally different from what can be replicated by trading the underlying, and therefore can be ignored in practice, or are they completely different and should be viewed as an essential tool in the suite of investment tools? A direct approach to this question is difficult but there are two indirect empirical routes. One looks at whether the introduction of an option alters the price behaviour of the underlying and, if it does, then one can infer that options are not redundant. The other looks at the empirical returns and risks of options to see whether they are significantly different from those of the underlying.

Investigation along the first route has been sporadic and has concentrated mainly on stock options.[10] The findings usually support the notion that the introduction of options does significantly affect the underlying prices and therefore stock options are not redundant. The reason is often attributed to the incompleteness of the stock-market. The currency market is significantly different from the stock-market owing to its huge liquidity and standardised underlying assets. Connolly (1996) looked at the impact of options on currency futures and found no significant price effect on foreign exchange futures. He argued that the existence of other foreign exchange derivatives contracts (over-the-counter options on spot, for example) are probably close substitutes and that the new options on futures are probably redundant. In a recent study Chan and Lien (2002) examined the redundancy of options on currency futures by looking at the transmission of information between foreign exchange futures and spot markets. They found that after the introduction of options the instantaneous feedback between spot and futures markets improves drastically. They also found evidence that options play a leading role in the transmission of information in currency markets.

The second empirical approach looks at whether options provide a risk/return profile that is distinct from spot foreign exchange, or, indeed, any other asset class. To isolate the impact of spot moves on options, we need to look at volatility alone. Is volatility a separate risk class? And if it is, is volatility risk priced in a CAPM sense?

The academic methods used to answer the above questions are usually convoluted. In summary, the existing evidence from different markets seems to suggest that:

❏ Volatility is not constant.
❏ Options, both at-the-money (ATM) and out-of-the-money (OTM) types, do exhibit a distinct risk/return profile and therefore should be considered as a separate risk class.
❏ Volatility attracts a negative risk premium – ie, long volatility will, on expectation, produce a loss. In other words, options are more expensive than they should be (Jackwerth and Rubinstein, 1996).

In the equity market, Dumas, Fleming and Whaley (1998) compared the out-of-sample performance of a wide range of deterministic volatility function models and found their performance unsatisfactory. Buraschi and Jackwerth (2000) found that returns for both in- and out-of-the-money options are needed for spanning. They hypothesised that the return for the latter is probably driven by different economic factors, for example, by portfolio insurers. In the fixed-income market Collin-Dufresne and Goldstein (2001) – using data from three different countries, the US, the UK and Japan – found that changes in the term structure of swap rates have very limited explanatory power for returns on ATM straddles.[11] Their results support the notion of stochastic volatility (unspanned). Jagannathan, Kaplin and Sun (2001) and Longstaff, Santa-Clara and Schwartz (2001) have provided similar evidence. We have not seen any work on whether the spot currency market spans the option market. Practical observations on how the currency options market works lend some support to the view that currency options are a distinct type of security, not spanned by spot. For most market-makers in currency options the trading book is run independently of the spot/forward book. Both position-taking and hedging of the currency options trading book are usually done through the options market directly.

On balance, then, empirical evidence is supportive of the notion that currency options are not a redundant asset. However, it does not necessarily follow that a fund manager should use options in his portfolio. They can provide an additional source of return and/or be a powerful tool for risk management. However, they can just as easily be a turbo-charged value destroyer, as attested by a long list of stories of derivatives going horribly wrong.

Our view is that whether to use options in a currency portfolio is dependent on a particular currency manager's risk/return objectives and operational constraints. Also, it is essential that the currency manager has the necessary expertise before adding currency options to his portfolio. While we are on this point, it is also worth emphasising that expertise in currency options is a useful supplement to any fund manager's professional knowledge base, even those who do not use options.

7.6 SKEWS AND SMILES

Before we consider the efficiency of the options market and potential trading strategies using currency options, we need to make a quick detour into the subject of options skews and smiles. Both terms refer to the phenomenon that implied volatility can differ for options with different strikes but otherwise identical features. There is no provision for this in the traditional Black–Scholes set-up as volatilities are assumed to be constant across time as well as strikes.[12] In particular, skew refers to the observation that equal-delta puts and calls can be priced off different volatilities, whereas smile refers to the observation that volatility tends to increase when option strikes move away from the forward level.

There is no simple formula or model which will allow somebody to construct a volatility smile from an at-the-money volatility quote because the smile is largely driven by demand/supply in the options market. Figure 7.2 shows how implied volatility, both ATM and OTM, and vanilla option premiums are linked. Using volatility, you can apply the standard Black–Scholes model to agree on the price for an option (links 1 and 4). Banks tend to have their own proprietary models to take into account market imperfections that are not dealt with in standard Black–Scholes (links 2 and 5). However, banks generally will not quote you option prices from their own models. They instead adjust their implied volatility quote such that when the implied volatility is entered into a

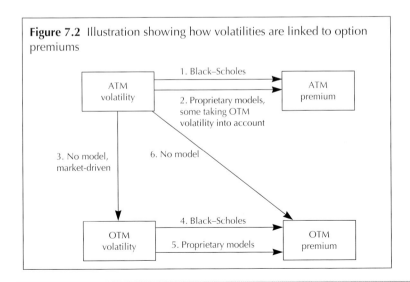

Figure 7.2 Illustration showing how volatilities are linked to option premiums

Black–Scholes calculator (links 1 and 4 again) it produces the same price as their proprietary models. The key point here is that there is no model that will give you OTM volatility from ATM volatility (links 3 and 6).

In a Black–Scholes world, all options with the same maturity date would be priced on the same volatility. This makes intuitive sense as there can only be one possible "actual" volatility for a spot process over a certain time period, and this value should not depend on the strike of the option. However, the market-makers will change their prices for OTM options to reflect, among other factors, supply and demand conditions in the market. Generally speaking, demand outstrips supply for OTM options. A main reason for this is the high leverage for an OTM option. Rather like a lottery ticket, an OTM option costs very little, but once the spot moves by a long way (admittedly this is a low-probability event), the potential gain as a percentage of the upfront premium (so-called leverage) is much larger than that of an ATM option. Therefore there are usually more buyers than sellers for OTM options – a market-makers' nightmare.

Other factors also contribute to the smile:

❏ Many corporate/institutional hedgers seek cheap insurance by purchasing OTM options;
❏ Expectation of spot movements will push up the OTM call relative to the OTM put, or vice versa (skewed smile);
❏ Empirical spot return distributions display time-varying kurtosis and skew, which often leads to adjustments in OTM volatilities (the underlying distributions may not be normal or lognormal); and
❏ Last but certainly not least, with the growing volume of exotic options in the foreign exchange market, market-makers use OTM options to statically hedge exotic risks, which means that they are unwilling to short too many OTM options. This may in turn aggravate the smile.

As one can imagine, no single model has emerged to capture all these factors, and it is very much down to demand/supply and market-makers' judgement to determine the magnitude of the smile at a particular point in time.

7.7 TRADING OPPORTUNITIES IN THE OPTIONS MARKET

Chapter 4 was, in part, a survey of trading opportunities in the foreign exchange spot market presented with the aim of helping investors to decide whether the opportunities are sufficiently attractive for them to trade currencies actively. The discussion would not be complete without a parallel review of the efficiency of the foreign exchange options market. However, here the motivation is slightly different. As discussed in Section 7.5, options can be a useful though not necessarily indispensable tool for a fund manager, and the information on market efficiency is therefore directly useful only for fund managers who choose to use options. But in view of the importance of option pricing theory in risk management in general, this section on trading opportunities in the options market will also be relevant for those fund managers who decide not to incorporate options in their portfolios.

7.7.1 Overview

The question of efficiency in the foreign exchange options market can be loosely paraphrased as whether implied volatility, being the market consensus forecast of actual volatility, is an unbiased estimate of future actual volatility. Alternatively, whether foreign exchange implied volatility incorporates information such that excess return from taking any static or dynamic position in options does not exceed the transaction cost of trading based on that information.

Two related questions are often asked by those who may not be familiar with foreign exchange options markets:

❏ Does implied volatility move a lot?
❏ Does it move in a particular way that corresponds to spot movements?

The answer to the first question is unequivocally yes. Figure 7.3 shows how six-month implied volatilities for the euro/US dollar, US dollar/Japanese yen and euro/Swiss franc have moved over a five-year period for three different horizons: daily, weekly and monthly. The same range is used on the y-axis of each plot to make

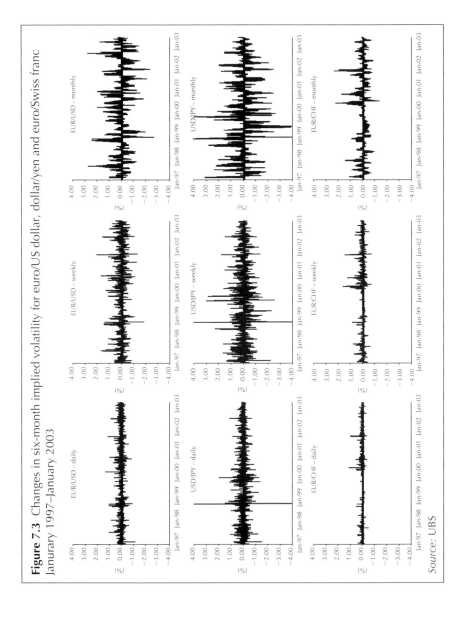

Figure 7.3 Changes in six-month implied volatility for euro/US dollar, dollar/yen and euro/Swiss franc Janurary 1997–January 2003

Source: UBS

Figure 7.4 Changes in euro/US dollar spot January 1997–January 2003

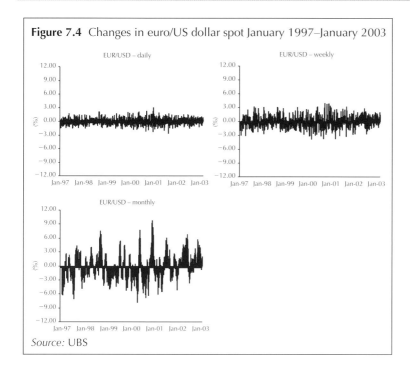

Source: UBS

it easy to see the relative magnitude of change across different currency pairs and over different horizons: US dollar/Japanese yen is the most volatile pair and euro/Swiss franc is the least volatile. Larger moves are associated with longer horizons. For a currency manager, investing in spot can work in almost exactly the same way as investing in implied volatility.[13] This point is illustrated in Figure 7.4, where we plot the equivalent changes for spot moves in euro/US dollar. This time a wider range is used for the y-axis because of the larger of movements in spot. However, this should not be interpreted as meaning that implied volatility is less important for trading purposes because it displays a narrower range of movements. Instruments or portfolios may have completely different sensitivities to spot and volatility movements.

The second question – whether the moves in spot and implied volatility are correlated in some way – is much trickier to answer. On an intuitive level, implied volatility measures the two-way movement in spot in that we would expect implied volatility to increase when spot moves away from its mean. In an ideal world a

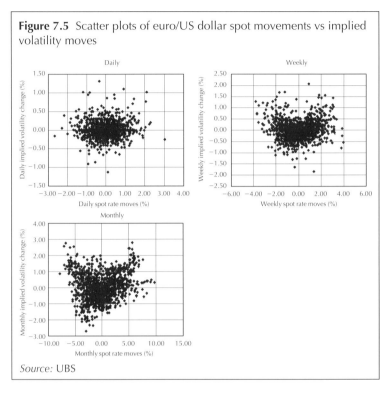

Figure 7.5 Scatter plots of euro/US dollar spot movements vs implied volatility moves

Source: UBS

scatter graph of changes in implied volatility against changes in spot should have a kidney shape – as is just about evident in the weekly and monthly charts in Figure 7.5. A correlation measure would be quite powerless in this situation as when spot went up the correlation would be positive and when it went down, negative. Models incorporating a changing volatility can be very convoluted and they do not often lead readily to an easily interpretable relationship between spot moves and implied volatility moves. Also, these models are not widely used in foreign exchange compared to, say, in equities or bonds.

7.7.2 Does implied volatility systematically overpredict actual volatility?

Many fund managers claim that implied volatility systematically overpredicts actual volatility. If this is true, it makes options less attractive than spot or forwards as hedging instruments. But any suggestion that the latter are a superior hedging instrument is easily disputed as one can just as easily sell implied volatility and make a statistical arbitrage profit if implied volatility is on average more expensive than actual.[14]

A simple test of the claim of systematic overprediction would be to compare the implied and actual volatilities for a particular period. Here we choose six currency pairs in which OTC options are actively traded (US dollar/Japanese yen, euro/US dollar, euro/Japanese yen, sterling/US dollar, euro/Swiss franc and euro/sterling), with three different time frames, one month, three months and 12 months. By definition, implied volatility is forward-looking: the one-month implied volatility today is a forecast of spot volatility for the next month. On the other hand, one-month actual volatility today is computed from last month's price data, ie, it is backward-looking. A fair comparison therefore would be to compare the one-month implied volatility from a month back with today's one-month actual volatility, which is what we do in Table 7.1.

An initial look at Table 7.1 seems to indicate that implied volatility has indeed been systematically higher than its actual counterpart. Of six currency pairs and three maturities (18 time series in total), only sterling/Deutschmark 12-month has shown higher actual volatility than implied volatility, which can be attributed mainly to the long-lasting impact on actual volatility of sterling's exit from the exchange rate mechanism (ERM). People often talk of sterling and the US dollar as a range-bound currency pair. For sterling/US dollar 12-month, the discrepancy is acutely high at 2.38%.

While the spread of implied over actual volatility may be statistically significant, it is, however, not stable over time, as represented by standard deviation.[15] In Figure 7.6 we depict all 18 series against time, and it is apparent that the spread frequently moves from positive territory to negative territory; the positive averages we get may be due to the sample period, ie, if we chose a different sample period, we might obtain negative or zero means.

Before jumping to the conclusion that the options market "overprices" the spot movement, we need to address a few questions:

❏ Is implied volatility in the data set accurate (or relevant)?
❏ Is actual volatility calculated accurately (or could it be calculated accurately)?
❏ Why should the spread be zero anyway?

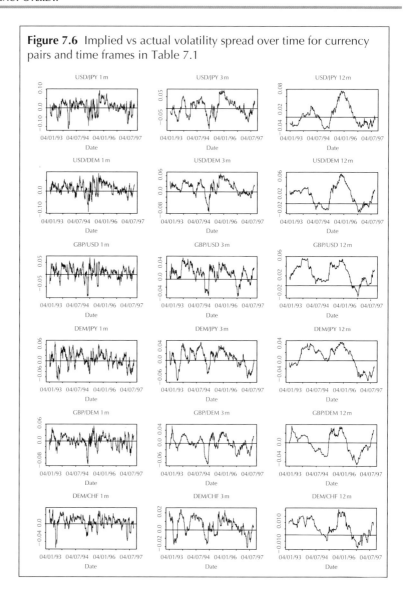

Figure 7.6 Implied vs actual volatility spread over time for currency pairs and time frames in Table 7.1

A few factors may affect the results we have presented:

❏ *Bid–offer spread*. We use mid-volatility in the test. Bid–offer spreads in these currency pairs are typically in the range 0.1–0.3%.
❏ *OTM volatilities*. Out-of-the-money volatilities are not included in the test. It seems sensible to use a weighted average of all the

Table 7.1 Comparison of implied and actual volatilities for six currency pairs January 1993–September 1998

	Expiry					
	1-month	3-month	12-month	1-month	3-month	12-month
	GBP/USD			USD/DEM		
No. obs.	1,452	1,408	1,222	1,452	1,408	1,222
Average (%)	0.99	1.51	2.38	1.30	1.54	1.75
St. dev. (%)	2.28	1.89	1.89	2.36	2.27	2.18
Max. (%)	7.06	5.48	5.69	8.24	6.83	6.76
Min. (%)	−9.02	−7.80	−9.34	−9.58	−7.55	−1.91
	DEM/JPY			USD/JPY		
No. obs.	1,452	1,408	1,222	1,452	1,408	1,222
Average (%)	0.55	0.52	0.72	0.32	0.24	0.32
St. dev. (%)	2.74	2.45	2.56	3.51	3.16	2.91
Max. (%)	8.27	5.53	4.51	9.40	7.60	7.72
Min. (%)	−9.00	−6.09	−4.94	−12.26	−8.69	−3.55
	DEM/CHF			GBP/DEM		
No. obs.	1,452	1,408	1,222	1,452	1,408	1,222
Average (%)	0.51	0.54	0.58	0.27	0.16	−0.19
St. dev. (%)	1.31	0.98	0.70	1.99	2.01	2.00
Max. (%)	3.66	2.42	2.04	5.46	5.34	3.48
Min. (%)	−5.36	−2.13	−1.05	−8.29	−6.46	−4.58

Source: Implied volatility from UBS internal data (market-maker's mid-volatility quote for at-the-money-forward (ATMF) options at Chicago close). Actual volatility is calculated from UBS internal mid-spot rates at Chicago close and centring term is the rolling mean. Sample period is January 4, 1993, to September 1, 1998.

Note: Apart from the number of observations (No. obs.), the data in the table show the difference between implied volatility and actual volatility over the same period. Implied volatility is generally higher than its actual counterpart. This is indicated by averages: 17 out of 18 are positive over the sample period.

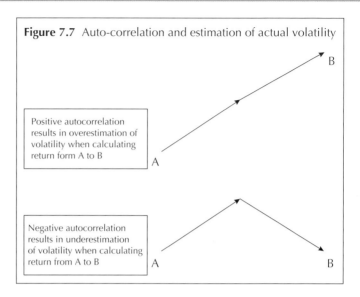

Figure 7.7 Auto-correlation and estimation of actual volatility

Positive autocorrelation results in overestimation of volatility when calculating return form A to B

Negative autocorrelation results in underestimation of volatility when calculating return from A to B

volatilities rather than only ATMF volatility. However, including OTM volatilities would probably increase the spread and they are generally higher than ATM volatilities.

❏ *Return frequency.* This is a very big topic on its own. To calculate actual volatility, should we use daily returns? Weekly returns? Hourly returns? Or multiples or fractions of them? There is no definitive answer to the question – it usually depends on what you want this number for in the first place. One thing is clear though: different return frequencies are likely to result in different estimates of the actual volatility.[16]

❏ *Autocorrelation in returns.* One of the reasons why the choice of return frequency is so important is the autocorrelation in returns. One can overestimate the actual volatility for a positively autocorrelated return series and underestimate it for negatively autocorrelated series, as illustrated in Figure 7.7.

Our results are based on a simplistic setting and do not incorporate trading constraints. More robust tests are needed to validate the claim that options are overpriced. To launch a trading programme to exploit this, one would need to consider the risk profile of such a strategy as well. If one is to sell vanilla options routinely, the gains will be small and accumulate over time. But losses, when they appear, will be large.

7.7.3 Volatility and correlation forecasting

Volatility forecasting has attracted an extensive array of research from both academics and practitioners.[17] This partly reflects the important and diverse role of volatility in investment, security valuation, risk management and monetary policy-making. For example:

❑ Volatility directly impacts the pricing mechanism of almost all options, which have become increasingly accepted as one of the main investment and risk management vehicles.

❑ Indirectly, volatility enters into the valuation of many types of assets and liabilities, either through CAPM or through analysis of option-like features in the assets and liabilities.

❑ Volatility is a key ingredient in the portfolio optimisation procedures widely used by investment managers.

❑ Additionally, volatility may influence the monetary decision-making process. The US Federal Reserve uses volatilities of stocks, bonds and currencies as one type of indicator and the Bank of England also makes frequent reference to option implied volatilities as a key financial variable.

❑ Last but certainly not least, the 1996 Basle Accord links the VAR of banks and trading houses to their capital reserves and therefore makes volatility forecasting an integral part of the risk management systems for these financial institutions.

There are two main strands of research in this area. One follows the seminal work of Engle (1982) and Bollerslev (1986) on Arch (autoregressive and conditional heteroskedastic) modelling. In a nutshell, an Arch process posits that the volatility of the next period is closely linked to the volatility of the previous period adjusted by the latest (squared) movements of the underlying prices. It is therefore capable of reproducing the often-observed phenomenon of volatility clustering: large moves are likely to be followed by large moves and vice versa. A version of the Arch model called Garch(1,1) is widely used by foreign exchange practitioners to forecast volatility.

The other strand investigates the forecasting power of implied volatility, which is a traded commodity and regarded as the market consensus forecast of future volatility.

The empirical evidence on how useful implied volatility is for forecasting purposes is at best mixed. Generally speaking, researchers find that it does contain some information about future actual volatility but that it is not necessarily a superior estimator than, say, historical volatility or an Arch forecast, and implied volatility is generally thought to be a biased estimator (see Section 7.7.2).[18] In a widely quoted paper, Jorion (1995) examined implied volatility from options on foreign exchange futures. His main finding was that implied volatility has substantially greater predictive power than time-series models (including Arch or Garch), even when the Arch models have the advantage of using *ex post* data to estimate its parameters. Jorion's results are similar to those of West and Cho (1995). Weinburg (2001) confirmed Jorion's result and also found that little discernible additional information is embedded in volatility smiles beyond the ATMF implied volatility. Neely (2002) used intra-day data and employed measures to correct a data estimation problem in Jorion's study; he concluded that, on balance, implied volatility is a biased estimator of actual volatility. However, Neely's study also contains two more interesting findings: implied volatility provides a better forecast of actual volatility computed using intra-day data; and time-series methods, including Garch, improve the forecasting power of implied volatility in an out-of-sample comparison. We should note that even with the combined help of implied volatility and statistical methods, only about a third of the variation in actual volatility is explained – in other words, these are not very good forecasts. Neely did not consider whether the apparent inefficiency can be exploited in a statistical arbitrage.

The use of implied volatility to forecast correlation is a much less investigated field. Campa and Chang (1998a) found that implied correlation from foreign exchange options outperforms time series-based correlation forecasts but that in some cases historical correlation also contains additional information. They used a criterion based on economic profit and loss, similar to that in Engle *et al* (1993), to compare the relative success of different forecasts. The method these authors employ is much closer to what a practitioner might use than those used by many academics.

7.8 SOME VOLATILITY-BASED TRADING SCHEMES

Some financial instruments, for example, the forward volatility agreement (FVA) and the volatility–variance swap, allow investors to take positions directly in volatility without committing to a particular spot level or even with no exposure to directional spot movements. Appendix 7A contains a simple explanation of how an FVA works in practice. The volatility–variance swap is not so much a swap as a forward contract. It allows investors to profit from or hedge the risk of an increase or decrease in future currency volatility. Its pay-off is computed by multiplying the notional face amount by the difference between the realised variance–volatility and the implied variance–volatility.

Volatility–variance swaps can be used as more than just a speculative vehicle on the rise or fall in volatility. Currency risk managers can use such contracts to hedge against unexpected future changes in volatility. According to a research note published in 2001 by FX Concepts, a New York-based overlay manager, some pension funds have started to look into the use of volatility products for both return enhancement and risk management purposes.[19] The report notes that currency managers, predominately systematic players, have been slow to innovate in this area mainly due to a lack of expertise in options and a good volatility database. Both situations are improving quickly. Many banks now allow their clients to analyse and download volatility data, including skews and smiles, directly from their websites.

The following sub-sections present three short examples in which investors adopt more traditional trading methods to trade volatility (or use volatility to trade spot) systematically. These represent actual trading schemes (the parameters used in some trading models can be different) as used by some market players.

7.8.1 Gamma scalping

Gamma scalping offers a means to capture the spread between implied volatility and future actual volatility as shown in Table 7.1. If the investor is of the view that the former is lower than the latter, he can buy the option and try to replicate a short option position using currency spot/forward, just as we have discussed in Section 7.2 (but bearing in mind that the example there is to replicate a long option position). If the replication is successful, at expiry the investor will have the exact same position as if he were to short the option, which will neutralise the long option position he entered upfront. He is left with two cash items: one is the cash outflow from purchasing the option in the first place, and the other is the cumulative cash inflow, reflecting the profits of carrying the replication. This time the investor will always be selling high and buying low so he will end up with a profit from his replication exercise – hence the term "scalping".[20] If his view is right, the net cashflow will be positive.

7.8.2 Selling wings volatility

If implied volatilities are generally higher than the actual volatility, could one make a profit by selling OTM strangles? A strangle consists of one OTM put option and one OTM call option, usually with similar deltas. A number of market players are consistent sellers of such options. They are usually systematic in their approach, with steady notional amounts. Some years back there were many more sellers of OTM volatilities – often on a discretionary basis and in large notional amounts – than there are now. The reason for using OTM options is that they can reduce the magnitude of the losses that one may suffer when selling volatilities. Also, due to the volatility smile, OTM volatilities are usually higher than the ATM counterpart. We are not aware of any publicly available studies on the effectiveness of this strategy, the main difficulty being to obtain a reliable data set of OTM volatilities. A UBS research note in 1999 provides some support for the existence of excess return, albeit not across different currency pairs.[21]

7.8.3 Trading spot using option skew as an indicator

When the implied volatilities for equal-delta puts and calls that are otherwise identical differ, this is referred to as option skew. As we saw in Section 7.6, there are many reasons for option skew, and one of them reflects the market's collective anticipation of a directional move on the spot market. If the spot is viewed as more likely to go up than down, call options are likely to be more expensive than the corresponding puts as some market players may wish to purchase the call in anticipation of the spot move.

One naturally asks the question: does option skew contain information about future spot movements that is not available elsewhere? Some empirical evidence is supportive of a yes answer. Campa, Chang and Reider (1998) investigated implied skewness in one- and three-month over-the-counter options on a number of different exchange rates between April 1996 and March 1997. They found that the direction of skewness was positively correlated with returns over the remaining length of the option. Malz (1997) also examined over-the-counter foreign exchange rates using one-month options from April 1992 through June 1996 and found that investors can earn excess returns (in a CAPM sense) by holding currencies whose option prices indicate positive skewness. Several banks have issued research notes that support the existence of excess return from this strategy.

7.9 SPEAKING GREEK – SOME CLOSING COMMENTS

To summarise our views, we think that foreign exchange options as financial instruments do offer a new avenue for currency management but that they may or may not be suitable for a particular fund depending on its circumstances. However, an understanding of foreign exchange option pricing theory is essential for sound risk management practice.

But how much understanding is enough? Do you have to know your delta, gamma, vega and rho and pepper your conversations accordingly? Or, if that is not enough, do you also have to know about d(vega)/d(volatility), "pin" risk, or the willow-tree implementation of the finite-difference method? Throughout the book we have tried to steer clear of such "geek" talk, which is common these days when you speak to foreign exchange sales persons from banks and their financial engineers, risk advisors and structurers (the author being one of them).[22] The concepts behind some of this jargon are essential for a basic understanding of option pricing theory, but the ability to drop technical names is, in our view, not. In many cases the fancy Greek terms have more mundane and commonsensical meanings and these are more important (and perhaps less confusing) to understand. So, next time a banker calls and tells you that gamma is bid or it is expensive to sit on a pile of rho, ask him what it means in terms of spot, forward, implied volatility and actual volatility.

APPENDIX 7A: USING A FORWARD VOLATILITY AGREEMENT TO TAKE A POSITION ON VOLATILITY

The forward volatility agreement (FVA) is a forward contract where the buyer agrees, on the trade date, to purchase an

Figure 7A.1 Sequence of events for a forward volatility agreement

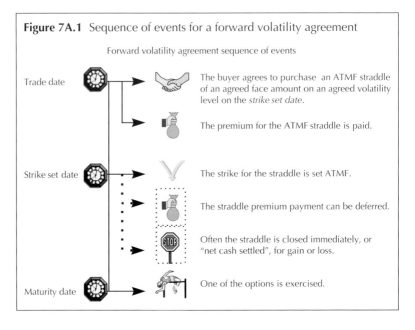

Forward volatility agreement sequence of events

Trade date		The buyer agrees to purchase an ATMF straddle of an agreed face amount on an agreed volatility level on the *strike set date*.
		The premium for the ATMF straddle is paid.
Strike set date		The strike for the straddle is set ATMF.
		The straddle premium payment can be deferred.
		Often the straddle is closed immediately, or "net cash settled", for gain or loss.
Maturity date		One of the options is exercised.

at-the-money-forward (ATMF) straddle valued on a prespecified volatility on a prespecified strike set date which falls prior to the final maturity date from the seller. The strike of the straddle is set at the prevailing rate (ATMF) on the strike set date. Figure 7A.1 outlines the sequence of events.

The buyer usually pays the premium for the contract upfront (on the trade date). On the strike set date the contract can be physically settled – namely, the buyer determines the strike of the straddle at 10.00am New York time according to the prevailing spot rate and swap points (to the maturity date) at that time, and the buyer receives the specified option.

Prior to the strike set date an FVA is not sensitive to movements in spot: its value is a function of forward–forward volatility only.[23] The sensitivity with respect to changes in the forward–forward volatility is often given as a vega amount, which reflects the sensitivity of the premium to a one percentage point change in the forward–forward volatility.

An investor can use an FVA to express directional views on the volatility curve (both level and shape) by taking a volatility position that is not affected by spot movements and time decay prior to the strike set date. For example, a buyer of an FVA may believe that implied volatilities are undervalued and will move higher. On the other hand, a seller of an FVA is able to take a short position on volatility. Buying and selling FVAs enables one to separate a view on implied volatility almost completely from a view on spot.

1   The option pricing theory, which has its origins in the Ph.D. thesis *Théorie de la Spéculation* by the French mathematician Louis Bachelier in 1900, predated Einstein's famous paper of 1905 on heat diffusion, which is based on a similar concept. However, it was 70 years before Black, Scholes and Merton came up with the ingenious argument on dynamic hedging and risk neutrality and the theory became one of the cornerstones of modern finance.

2   C should be a position in a bond or deposit, but since we assume that both interest rates are zero, we can ignore the time value of money here.

3   See Martellini (2001) for a survey on the subject.

4   See, for example, Hodges and Neuberger (1989), Constantinides (1997) and Whalley and Wilmott (1993).

5   Refer to Hoggard, Whalley and Wilmott (1993) for fixed time intervals and Henrotte (1993) or Grannan and Swindle (1996) for variable time intervals.

6   See also Bridgewater's research note "Currency observations: the dynamic hedging enigma". Available as pdf from the company's website: www.bridgewaterassociates.com/pdf/DYNAMICHEDGING.pdf.

7   See, for example, Asay and Edelsberg (1986), Garcia and Gould (1987) and Zhu and Karee (1988) for some early empirical studies and Basak and Mehra (2001) for a more recent investigation.

8   According to Bridgewater's estimate (see note 6), the expected turnover in spot for dynamic replication of a one-year option is about 200%.

9   One might ask why there could be uncertainty here: from the option replication example earlier, as long as someone follows the DIY guidebook religiously, the end result should be guaranteed irrespective of what actually happens afterwards. One main reason is that the option premium is based on the forecast of future spot volatility and the forecast can turn out to be wrong.

10 Conrad (1989), Detemple and Jorion (1990) and Sorescu (2000) used US stock data and found a significant price effect on the underlying asset as a result of the introduction of stock options. Urrutia and Vu (2001) showed that the return and volatility may increase or decrease after the introduction of stock options.

11 See also Jagannathan, Kaplin and Sun (2001), Longstaff, Santa-Clara and Schwartz (2001) and Fan, Gupta and Ritchken (2002). They find that find that swaptions and even swaption straddles can be well hedged with Libor bonds alone.

12 Of course, volatilities are generally not constant across different expiries (or maturities) either. The relationship of volatility and time is referred to as the term structure of implied volatility, analogous to the similar relationship between interest rates and time. There is a considerable literature on the forward bias present in the term structure of interest rates, where forward interest rates are said to generally overpredict the future term structure of interest rates, and investors could potentially exploit this. Campa and Chang (1998b), using daily volatility data with maturities from one month up to 12 months in four major currency pairs, showed that, unlike interest rates, the term structure of implied volatilities does predict the future shape of the implied volatility curve. Many banks provide short-term buy or sell recommendations for short-term volatilities via options or other instruments based on

whether short-term volatilities are higher or lower than the long-term counterpart. As far as we know, the effectiveness of this is unproven.

13 Well, almost. There are a few more subtle and often more technical issues, such as decay, front-end vs back-end volatility, and the spread between implied and actual volatilities.

14 Some may argue that most funds are restricted in what they can do. For example, many cannot sell options and therefore could not sell implied volatility even if they wanted to. However, there are instruments that will allow clients to sell implied volatility by buying options.

15 Standard deviation is used here only as an indicative measure of the dispersion of the implied over actual volatility spread as there is no evidence to show that such spreads are normally distributed.

16 The short-term forecasting power of Garch and implied volatility can be significantly improved if one uses intra-day returns. See Andersen and Bollerslev (1998).

17 See Mayhew (1995) and Figlewski (1997) for surveys.

18 See Canina and Figlewski (1993) and Christensen and Prabhala (1998) on equity implied volatilities and Neuhaus (1995) for fixed income.

19 Muralidhar and Neelakandan (2001).

20 Gamma refers to the fact that replication positions are sensitive to short-term spot movements.

21 UBS (1999), "Using risk reversals to predict spot movement", UBS Research note.

22 A nice remark I heard when someone tried to impress a mathematically savvy client was "Gamma so-and-so to death!".

23 The way to obtain forward–forward volatility from two straight-date volatilities is similar to calculating forward interest rates from two spot interest rates. However, one needs to remember that the *square* of volatility, rather than volatility itself, is proportional to time. Also, many people use trading days rather than calendar days in the calculation.

Emerging Market Currencies

8.1 BACKGROUND

It is generally accepted that emerging market stocks and bonds represent a distinct asset class, particularly for long-term investors.[1] They are characterised by their very high volatility as well as low correlation with the asset types available in developed economies. The growing importance of the emerging market is underpinned by its demographic trend (population increase) and superior longer-term growth prospects. Many financial advisors and consultants recommend that investors allocate up to 10% of their portfolio to emerging markets, which is roughly in line with the capitalisation of emerging stockmarkets as a proportion of that of the global equity markets.

Over the last decade or so the volatility of equity indices of the developed markets has ranged between 15% and 25%, and correlation with the MSCI World Index has been from 45% to close to 80%. In contrast, the volatility of emerging market equity indices has ranged, in general, from 25% to 50%, with a few outliers such as Brazil, Argentina and Turkey (all over 60%), and correlation with the MSCI World Index has ranged from 10% to 40%. Over the same period the volatility of the MSCI EMF (Emerging Markets Free) Index was only around 25%, which is an indication of the low correlation between the emerging markets themselves.[2]

Unsurprisingly, little research has been done on the subject of currency risk management under the umbrella of emerging market investment.[3] For one thing, market conditions – including those for emerging market currencies – are very fluid, which makes statistical analysis difficult and, when it is done, less relevant to prevalent market conditions. Even when the price data are available and stable over a period of time, the conclusions of such studies should be viewed with caution. For example, bid–offer spreads in emerging markets are often several magnitudes higher than their developed market counterparts, and failing to take this explicitly into consideration will hamper the usefulness of any statistical investigation. Also, one has distinguish between returns in local currency, US dollar-denominated returns and US dollar-hedged returns as the impact of these is even more pronounced than for mature currencies. Analysis performed using US dollar-denominated returns to show the impact of currency is almost pointless.

In this short chapter we look at the special features of emerging market currencies and their implications for the hedging decision. We review forward bias and implied–actual volatility spreads in emerging market currencies and consider whether they can be used for trading. We finish by proposing a pragmatic and dynamic approach to dealing with emerging market currencies. Appendix 9A contains a list of emerging market currencies categorised by their current convertibility, and Appendix 9B presents an example of emerging market research provided by banks for their clients.

8.2 SPECIAL CHARACTERISTICS OF EMERGING MARKET CURRENCIES

Here is a list of key features of emerging market currencies (DeRosa, 1999):

❏ periodic devaluation due to domestic economic problems or global contagion;
❏ high interest rates;
❏ on-shore controls;
❏ frequent central bank intervention; and
❏ high bid–offer spreads.

With its high risk, it would seem logical for an investor to hedge exposure to an emerging market currency completely. However, there are good practical reasons not to:

❏ the cost of hedging is too high as interest rates in these countries are usually higher than those in developed counties;
❏ the allocation is too small;
❏ the relatively high growth in these economies will eventually lead to appreciation of their currencies (a notable case being the yen);
❏ many emerging market currencies are pegged against the US dollar or a basket of mature currencies, which reduces the need to hedge;[4]
❏ very few specialist emerging market currency managers and products are available.

There are other important factors against hedging risks in emerging currencies. One is that the correlation between emerging market currencies in the same region is relatively high, especially during a crisis, but the correlation between emerging market currencies in different regions is low and often negative. Eaker, Grant and Woodard (2000) investigated this point in detail with a portfolio of nine emerging market equity investments between 1975 and 1997. They found that, for US investors, diversification virtually eliminates the impact of currencies and that there may be substantial diversification benefit if emerging market currency risks are considered in a basket. They also investigated the highest and lowest equity returns in US dollar terms every year over the same period, breaking these down into currency returns and equity returns in the local currency. They found that, out of 44 of the highest and lowest dollar-denominated equity annual returns, 29 were associated with depreciation of the local currency against the dollar by more than 10%.[5] In other words, big swings in emerging market equity returns often coincide with a large depreciation of the local currency. However, not all of the 29 cases could be described as double whammies (where the investor suffers losses in both local equities *and* currency in the same year) as the authors found that in 12 of these the dollar-denominated returns were in fact the highest of that year. In other words, when an emerging market currency devalues, the underlying investment may still produce a good return in the investor's base currency.

Acar and Middleton (2003) found that during the sample period March 1998 to October 2002 currency fluctuations in four currencies – Polish zloty, Turkish lira, Mexican peso and South African rand – accounted for around 17% of the portfolio risk in equity investment in those currencies for US-based investors; for bond investment, currency contributed around 50% of the risk. They also found that, apart from the rand, which weakened significantly during the sample period (from five to about 10 rand per US dollar), hedging generally accounted for the returns in those currencies. In some cases currency hedging improved the Sharpe ratio slightly, but this was not universal. It is not clear whether transaction costs were included in the study.

We know of no systematic study on trading performance in emerging market currencies. Many market participants believe that you are likely to lose money by passively going short emerging market spot due to forward bias (see next section) and that you are more likely to lose money by going long emerging market options. The only performance index we are aware of is provided by Parker Global.[6] In recent years emerging foreign exchange has outperformed the G10 foreign exchange counterpart, but when the large dip during the Asian crisis is taken into account, the difference is not significant. Performance indices for emerging market currencies are probably less reliable than for G10 currencies. There former are more likely to suffer from survivorship bias (some emerging market funds may cease to exist, leaving the more successful funds in the index).

It is not unusual to hear stories like the following from investors: they decided to hedge all their currency exposures in the emerging market but, because things were quiet for a time, they switched off the hedging programme due to the high rolling cost. When devaluation happened – by which time it was too expensive to reinstate the hedges – the underlying investment tumbled in value, often both in local currency and in translated terms. In effect, the investor pays twice.

Some consultants or investment advisors claim that investors should only hedge emerging market currencies before an impending currency crisis. There is very little theoretical evidence in this area to indicate that forecasting such a crisis is in any way easier than forecasting exchange rate movements in the mature currencies. There are two main explanations for the devaluation of emerging market currencies.[7] The first focuses on economic fundamentals and argues that errors in government fiscal and monetary policies lead to speculative attacks and subsequent devaluation when the means of defence are exhausted. According to this explanation, devaluation is partially predictable from stress signals manifest in, say, growing budget deficits, fast monetary growth, rising wages and prices, or overvaluation of real exchange rates. The second explanation points to self-fulfilling crises caused by speculative attacks motivated by what Keynes called "animal spirits" (Keynes, 1936; Howitt and McAffee, 1992). Empirical studies have found some evidence, albeit rather weak, that devaluation might to some degree be predictable.

Even if you did have some way of seeing a devaluation coming, you would have to be far enough ahead of the market to put a hedge in place but not so far that the cumulative cost of rolling the hedge outweighed the eventual benefit of hedging when the crisis materialised. Markets often react quickly when the whiff of crisis is in the air, and both forwards and options volatilities shoot up, which pushes up the cost of hedging.[8]

8.3 FORWARD BIAS AND EMERGING MARKET CURRENCIES

We have reviewed the large body of literature on the topic of forward bias in Chapter 4, Section 4.5.1. Most works on the topic consider the currencies of developed countries. However, a few recent studies have systematically investigated forward bias in emerging market currencies, with mixed conclusions. Francis, Hasan and Hunter (2002) have proposed, using monthly data from Chile, Colombia, Mexico, India, Korea, Pakistan, Malaysia, Thailand, and Turkey over the period 1980 to 2000, that forward bias in emerging markets is systematic in nature and more likely to be larger and more persistent than in developed markets. Flood and Rose (2002), using daily data for 23 developing and developed counties during the 1990s, found that forward bias "improved" (ie, became less pronounced) in the 1990s than in previous periods but that (1) it still exists across different countries and (2) there is no significant difference between developed and developing countries. The second conclusion stands in contrast to estimates provided by Bansal and Dahlquist (2000). Using monthly data going back to 1976, these authors found that forward bias is more frequently observed in developed economies and less frequently in emerging market currencies.

We make two further observations. First, both Francis, Hasan and Hunter (2002) and Bansal and Dahlquist (2000) noted – and this question was not investigated by Flood and Rose (2002) – that adding emerging market cash deposits to an investor's portfolio significantly improves the portfolio's performance. As discussed earlier in the book (Chapter 6, Section 6.6), an investment in a foreign currency-denominated asset can be viewed as an investment in the underlying asset seeking excess return plus an investment in the cash deposit in that currency. The implication of these two studies is that currency risk in the emerging markets, unlike in developed markets, should not be systematically hedged. Second, Flood and Rose (2002) grouped currencies according to whether they experienced a significant crisis during the sample period, and they found that forward bias is less prominent for those which did. This result indicates that the "peso problem" (Chapter 4, Section 4.5.1) is an important, but not the only, factor in explaining forward bias.

Here, as an example, we select the Hong Kong dollar, Mexican peso, Czech koruna and South African rand and look at forward bias over the last six years using UBS proprietary data on spot and forwards. Each month a long forward position against the US dollar is established in the respective emerging market currency. At the end of the month the position is closed using the spot rate at the end of that month and a new position is established. We sum the cumulative returns backwards in time so that each point on the figure represents the total return achievable from that point until the end of the sample period, June 2003.

The results are shown in Figure 8.1. As in Figures 4.6–4.9 in Chapter 4 for developed currencies, most of the data points lie above zero, indicating the extent and consistency of forward bias. The phenomenon is more pronounced for the Mexican peso and Czech koruna but is much subdued in the pegged currency, the Hong Kong dollar. Trade in the South African rand has been highly profitable recently when the currency was strengthening, but the opposite is true of the preceding period when the rand languished (more relative to the forward).

We also constructed an equal-weighted portfolio consisting of all four currencies against the US dollar. This was the best performer over the sample period, supporting the conventional wisdom that

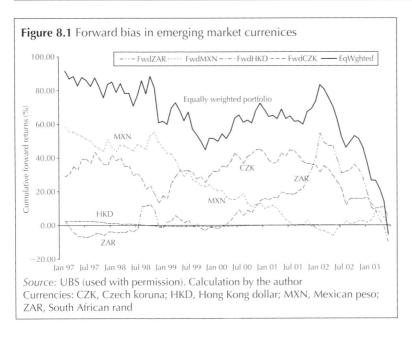

Figure 8.1 Forward bias in emerging market currenices

Source: UBS (used with permission). Calculation by the author
Currencies: CZK, Czech koruna; HKD, Hong Kong dollar; MXN, Mexican peso; ZAR, South African rand

emerging market currency exposures should be treated as a portfolio to exploit the diversification benefit.

The trading method described above is, effectively, a carry trade, one of oldest speculative trading methods around. Several commentators have investigated the profitability of carry trades in an emerging market context. Bansal and Dahlquist (2000) found that including emerging market currencies in portfolios containing investments in the developed markets improves the portfolios' Sharpe ratios. Malliaropulos (1997) concluded that the expected excess returns of foreign currency deposits are less volatile than those of equities and that the addition of US dollar deposits to an international equity portfolio can provide additional diversification benefits to non-US investors. Bridgewater Associates (no date (c)), using 15 emerging market currencies over a period longer than 20 years (1972–96), have estimated that excess returns on emerging market currencies amount to about 2–3% per annum over a long horizon. They also comment that expected volatility in any single currency will be around 10–15%. However, by combining these as a portfolio, the risk can be reduced to around 5%.

Carry trades are routinely used by many players in the currency markets. However, the mechanics of the trade mean that investors accumulate profit in small measures over time but are exposed to the risk of periodical devaluation. Also, it has been noted that carry trades with stop-loss orders may lead to episodes of sharp exchange rate movements and loss of liquidity in the trading of emerging market currencies.[9]

Finally, it is worth pointing out that, in our example, the profit is made by actively taking positions using currency forward contracts. However, if investors are investing in the equities and bonds of emerging markets, the profit potential may be realised if no currency forward positions are taken. Overall, it is reasonable to say that emerging market currency exposures should be evaluated as a portfolio and, if it is well diversified, the risk should be left unhedged as a baseline case.

8.4 IMPLIED VOLATILITY

Research on the behaviour of implied volatility in emerging market currencies is scarce, mainly due to lack of data. In practice we usually observe that implied volatility is itself more volatile and the implied–actual volatility spread is more pronounced than in developed markets. This is shown in Figures 8.2–8.4, which plot the implied and actual volatilities for three emerging market currencies over different maturities for the five-year period January 1997–January 2003. Spot rates against the US dollar are shown in the first part of each figure for comparison.

Just as with other emerging market currencies, each has its own specific characteristics. Implied volatility is generally much higher than actual volatility in the Mexican peso, particularly in the longer maturity (Figure 8.2), perhaps due to market participants' long memory of the peso crisis. Trading in the US dollar/South African rand is generally more active and consistent than in many other emerging market currencies. This is a traditional currency pair for some speculators to put on trades to exploit carry and/or implied–actual volatility spread. Hence, implied volatility bears a closer resemblance to actual volatility in this currency pair (Figure 8.3). And, finally, we look at the US dollar/Hong Kong dollar, a pegged currency pair that has seen very little spot movement over the last five years. Here, the implied volatility reflects sentiment on how likely it is that the peg will be abandoned (Figure 8.4).

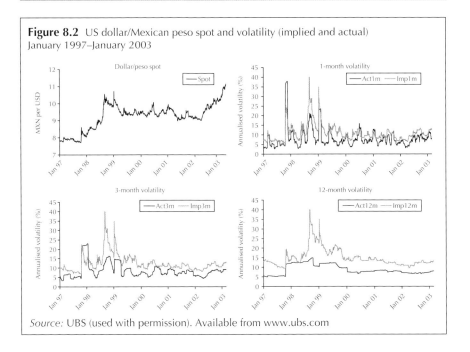

Figure 8.2 US dollar/Mexican peso spot and volatility (implied and actual) January 1997–January 2003

Source: UBS (used with permission). Available from www.ubs.com

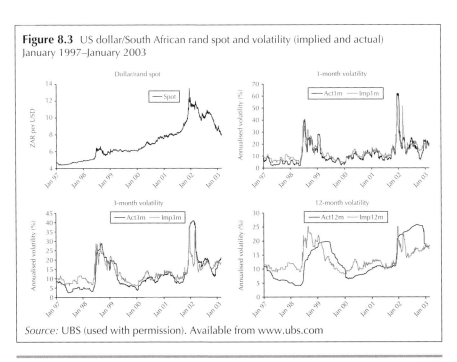

Figure 8.3 US dollar/South African rand spot and volatility (implied and actual) January 1997–January 2003

Source: UBS (used with permission). Available from www.ubs.com

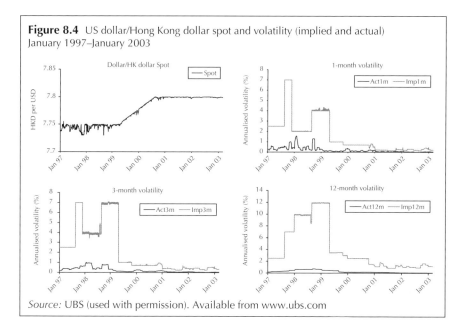

Figure 8.4 US dollar/Hong Kong dollar spot and volatility (implied and actual) January 1997–January 2003

Source: UBS (used with permission). Available from www.ubs.com

For the investor or currency manager such information is important because:

❏ implied volatility can be exploited directly as a source of additional return;

❏ implied volatility, rather than actual volatility, should be used to estimate hedging costs (so that an informed decision can be taken);

❏ implied volatility can be more informative of potential future movements than actual volatility, especially for pegged emerging market currencies, and this information can be incorporated in the risk management process.

8.4.1 Selling volatility

If implied volatility is systemtically higher than actual volatility, an investor can sell an option to exploit the discrepancy just as in mature currencies. Here is an example based on the period between 1995 and 1999 when implied volatility for the US dollar/ South African rand was, on average, higher than actual volatility.[10]

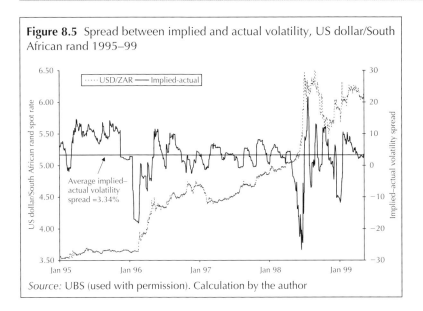

Figure 8.5 Spread between implied and actual volatility, US dollar/South African rand 1995–99

Source: UBS (used with permission). Calculation by the author

As shown in Figure 8.5, one-month implied volatility was on average 3.34% higher than its actual counterpart from the beginning of 1995. What if an investor had sold options? In parallel with the option strategies discussed in Chapter 7, we will look at the returns when an investor sells a one-month 25 delta strangle (consisting of 25 delta out-of-the-money put options and 25 delta out-of-the-money call options) on a daily basis. Transaction and carry costs are included in the exercise.

The cumulative returns are shown in Figure 8.6. Selling the one-month strangle produces a cumulative profit of 313% over the period. There are some large drops along the line, which signify big losses over the periods concerned. If we look at the profit/loss on each trade, we can see that the big losses again tend to occur in clusters. Separating the returns into puts and calls, we find that selling rand calls/dollar puts generates 275% profit and selling dollar calls/rand puts a 38% cumulative profit. This may indicate that the profit is largely due to the overall trend in the dollar/rand spot rate. To test this hypothesis, one could use a later data set where the trend reverses. Or a bootstrap method could be used to investigate the results' sensitivity to overall trends. Generally speaking, this type of strategy where investors accumulate small

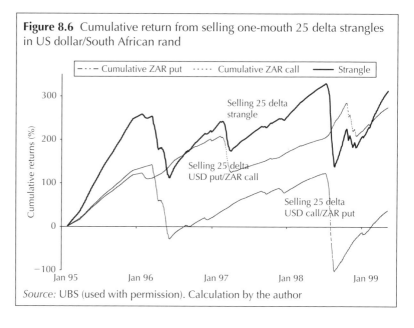

Figure 8.6 Cumulative return from selling one-mouth 25 delta strangles in US dollar/South African rand

Source: UBS (used with permission). Calculation by the author

returns and suffer large losses, albeit only occasionally, is probably not suitable for those with a low risk appetite. The "carry trades" that exploit the forward rate bias belong to the same risk category.

8.5 OTHER RELATED ISSUES

8.5.1 Using options to forecast spot

Is there potentially additional information on future spot movements embedded in option skews – ie, when a call option on a currency is more expensive than the put option of the same delta, does that signal that the currency may appreciate? It would be interesting to see whether the implied volatility of emerging market currencies can be used to forecast spot movements. The only research in this area that we are aware of is by Campa, Chang and Refalo (1999). Using currency option data from the local Brazilian exchange to test market perception of the credibility of the crawling peg regime, they found evidence that information embedded in option prices could indeed provide a better forecast of periodic realignments of the exchange rate bands than macroeconomic or interest rate-based indicators.

8.5.2 Cross-correlation

We have seen that investors or fund managers sometimes use proxies to hedge emerging market currencies. For example, they may treat exposure to the Korean won or Singapore dollar as an exposure to, respectively, the Japanese yen or US dollar and hedge accordingly. Hedging the yen or dollar obviously attracts much lower direct trading costs than trading in the won or Singapore dollar. The underlying assumption of this practice is a stable and high correlation between the Korean won or Singapore dollar and the Japanese yen or US dollar. In ordinary times such assumptions will usually hold as they are often a direct consequence of the relevant central banks' foreign exchange policies. However, during financial turbulence the policy could be abandoned and the correlation break down, resulting in a potential for big mismatches between the hedge and the underlying.

Apart from *ad hoc* research papers from investment banks and some specialist fund managers, the only systematic study of this approach we know is that by Aggarwal and Demaskey (1997). They looked at the hedging performance achieved by using the Japanese yen, sterling, the Canadian dollar, Deutschmark and Swiss franc to hedge currency risks in the Hong Kong dollar, Korean won, Singapore dollar, Taiwan dollar, Indonesian rupiah, Philippine peso and Thai baht over the period 1983–92, using Sharpe ratio as the performance measure. They found that cross-hedging generally did improve the performance for US-based investors and that the yen was the best proxy in most cases apart from the Hong Kong, Singapore and Taiwan dollars, currencies that move closely with the US dollar. However, it would be very difficult to apply their approach in practice as their minimum-variance hedge ratio varied from −900% to 3,400%.

Another related issue is the cross-correlation between emerging market currencies themselves. Low correlation between these currencies indicates a high potential for diversification, and vice versa. We are not aware of a direct attempt to quantify such cross-correlation, but the IMF's Emerging Market Bond Cross Correlation Index can be used as a close proxy.[11]

8.5.3 Basket peg

At the end of December 1996, at least 30 countries were using a basket-pegging approach according to data compiled by the IMF.

Some other currencies, notably the Singapore dollar and South African rand, may also include a pegging element. Some market participants have historically been using carry trades to explore the interest rate differentials between the basket currencies and the emerging market currency in question.[12] A recent study highlights the danger of such an approach. Christoffersen and Giorgianni (1999) developed an *ex ante* method to estimate time-varying weights and *ex ante* risk measures for a proxy hedging approach. The motivation was to analyse the potential profit/loss from carrying trades where the monetary authority of the underlying currency follows a policy of linking its currency to a basket of hard currencies but with an undeclared, and potentially time-varying, weight. They found that traditional rolling regression methods may significantly underestimate the risk involved. Taking the Thai baht as an example, when the basket peg was abandoned on July 2, 1997, the baht dropped 9.8% on that day. Using the estimated daily profit figure of 0.021% per trading day, it would take 445 trading days of average profit to make up the loss experienced on that particular day. Not to mention the trading restrictions introduced after the devaluation. For comparison, in the rolling model, which is what most people use to estimate the risk in carry trades, the crash represents a 29 standard deviation event – a near impossibility. Applying Christoffersen and Giorgianni's approach, it is only a 10 standard deviation event – still quite unlikely but not impossible.

8.5.4 Indices of risk and risk appetite

A number of financial institutions have developed indices that try to capture the risk of investing in certain markets and/or the risk appetite of investors. The indices of risk appetite are often the more subjective, some relying on investor's speculative positions, others based on survey data. One approach proposed by Kumar and Persaud (2001) in an IMF paper is based on a special type of correlation between the excess returns of currencies and the volatility of those returns. The rationale of such an approach is that a high correlation indicates that the return is commensurate with the associated risk, which in turn signifies a rising risk appetite. The authors suggest that when their risk appetite index goes up, high interest rate currencies (often emerging market currencies) will probably outperform.

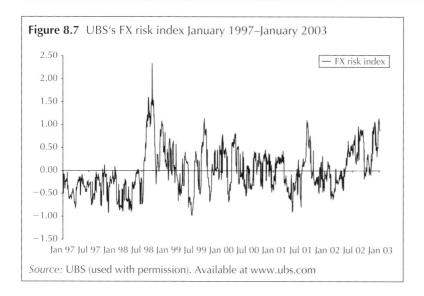

Figure 8.7 UBS's FX risk index January 1997–January 2003

Source: UBS (used with permission). Available at www.ubs.com

The risk indices are usually a statistical summary of a selection of financial market variables: for example, liquidity, actual volatility, implied volatility, option skews, credit spread, and correlations between some variables. A well-known index in this camp is the Liquidity, Credit and Volatility Index (LCVI) computed by JP Morgan Chase, the US investment bank.[13]

UBS produces a daily index called the FX Risk Index (Figure 8.7). The index is calculated as an arithmetic average of six separate factors:

❏ foreign exchange option implied volatilities;
❏ JP Morgan's EMBI+ emerging market bond spreads relative to US Treasury bonds;
❏ high-yield corporate bond spreads relative to US Treasuries;
❏ gold prices;
❏ differences in stock returns between the S&P Financials and Utilities sub-indexes; and
❏ a signal index calculated from the relationship between US bond and stock prices to capture investors' preference for liquid assets over stocks and long-dated bonds before and during a crisis.

The FX Risk Index shows high correlation with the US dollar, Swiss franc, euro and Brazilian real but not with other major emerging market currencies, including the Polish zloty, Korean won, South African rand and Mexican peso.

8.6 SUMMARY

On balance, the evidence we have reviewed in this chapter suggests that a blanket approach to emerging market currency exposures may not be appropriate, especially in view of the high hedging cost in both forwards and options markets. We would recommend a more pragmatic and dynamic programme to deal with specific problems and changing market conditions. CalPERS, the California Public Employees' Retirement System, together with consultant firm Wilshire Associates, has developed an approach to investing in emerging markets using a scoring system on a host of country- and market-related factors, including political stability, market regulation and volatility, liquidity, legal systems, transparency and so on. The same approach can be adopted for currency hedging, incorporating signals in budget deficits, monetary growth, wage and price inflation, and real exchange rate overvaluation, etc. One important factor in the decision-making process should be transaction costs. Estimates of these should be incorporated in the calculation of potential return enhancement and/or risk reduction.

APPENDIX 8A: MAJOR EMERGING MARKET CURRENCIES

Tables 8A.1–3 are compiled from the UBS database, IMF World Economic and Financial Surveys and information published on various central banks' websites. Note that we group the countries according to our criteria of convertibility. Currencies listed in Table 8A.2 may be termed either fully convertible or non-convertible by their respective central banks. The difference is really in the details.

Table 8A.1 Freely convertible currencies for offshore investors

Czech koruna	CZK	Currency forwards/options liquid up to one year. EUR/CZK is more liquid than USD/CZK.
Estonian kroon	EEK	Pegged to EUR. Low liquidity.
Hong Kong dollar	HKD	Pegged to USD. Forwards up to 10 years and options up to two years with good liquidity.

Table 8A.1 (continued)

Hungarian forint	HUF	Currency forwards/options fairly liquid up to one year. EUR/HUF is more liquid than USD/HUF.
Israeli shekel	ILS	Traded against a basket of currencies. Currency forwards/options liquid up to one year.
Kenyan shilling	KES	Very low liquidity.
Lithuanian lita	LTL	Almost fully convertible. Low liquidity.
Mexican peso	MXN	Forwards and options very liquid up to one year.
Peruvian nuevo sol	PEN	Very low liquidity.
Polish zloty	PLN	Currency forwards/options liquid up to one year. EUR/PLN is as liquid as USD/PLN.
Saudi Arabian riyal	SAR	Pegged to USD. Currency forwards/options liquid up to one year.
Singapore dollar	SGD	Forwards and options up to one year with good liquidity.
Slovak koruna	SKK	Currency forwards/options liquid up to six months.
Slovenian tolar	SIT	Very low liquidity.
Thai baht	THB	Small forwards and options market up to one year.
Turkish lira	TRL	Currency forwards/options reasonably liquid. Bid–offer spread is wide due to a tax on forward.

Table 8A.2 Partially convertible currencies for offshore investors*

Argentine peso	ARS	Convertible only onshore. NDF and options extremely illiquid.
Brazilian real	BRL	NDF and options up to one year with limited liquidity.
Chilean peso	CLP	NDF and options up to one year with limited liquidity.
Colombian peso	COP	NDF and options up to one year with limited liquidity.
Egyptian pound	EGP	Managed float. Small NDF market but extremely illiquid.
Indian rupee	INR	Small NDF and options market.
Indonesian rupiah	IDR	Both NDF and options extremely illiquid.

Table 8A.2 (continued)

Korean won	KRW	Currency NDF/options liquid up to one year.
New Taiwan dollar	NTD or TWD	Currency NDF/options reasonably liquid up to one year.
Pakistani rupee	PKR	Very illiquid.
Philippine peso	PHP	Currency NDF/options traded up to one year.
Russian rouble	RUB	Small NDF market. Very illiquid.
South African rand	ZAR	Currency forwards liquid up to one year and options liquid up to two years.

*Investors can only sell currency in line with central bank regulations. Documentation is sometimes required.

Table 8A.3 Non-convertible currencies*

Chinese renminbi/yuan	CNY	Dirty float. Currency forwards/options variable liquidity.
Malaysian ringgit	MYR	Capital control. No forward/options market.
Venezuelan bolivar	VEB	Fixed locally. No forward/options market.

*Off-shore investors can only buy currency with a payment order attached.

Currency codes vary between sources. Here we adopt the codes that are generally used by market participants; these may sometimes be different from the ISO codes, a complete list of which can be found at www.unece.org/cefact/rec/cocucod.htm. The "major emerging market currencies" we list here were chosen because they are frequently traded by banks or requested by banks' clients, largely reflecting these countries' relative economic importance.

APPENDIX 8B: EMERGING MARKET RESEARCH – AN EXAMPLE
Emerging Currencies – Foreign Exchange Guide[14]
London 24 June 2002

Singapore dollar
❏ The Monetary Authority of Singapore targets the SGD against a trade weighted basket of currencies, intervening when it feels that the SGD has become out of line with its basket.

❏ The weights used in the basket are unspecified as are the bands that the SGD is permitted to fluctuate within. Thus participants have to estimate themselves where the SGD is relative to its basket.

❏ Other key factors for the SGD are the JPY, global growth, technology stocks and regional politics.

The MAS targets the SGD against a trade weighted basket of currencies. Given the MAS currently has foreign exchange reserves of USD78bn, the central bank has the strength to closely control the SGD against this policy target. Thus the level of the SGD against its basket is a key factor for the market.

The MAS does not specify the weights of the basket or the permitted fluctuation bands of the SGD. We estimate the weights using trade data covering G10 and regional economies. For the bands we look at the long run mean level of the SGD against its basket since the end of the Asia crisis (defined as the end of 1998) and attempt to model the bands using standard deviations. Currently the SGD remains weak against its basket as Figure 8B.1 shows.

Though players track the SGD against their estimates of the basket, they also look at the JPY and IDR as guides for the SGD against the USD. For more medium term considerations, Singapore is a small open economy so global growth is important. A key data

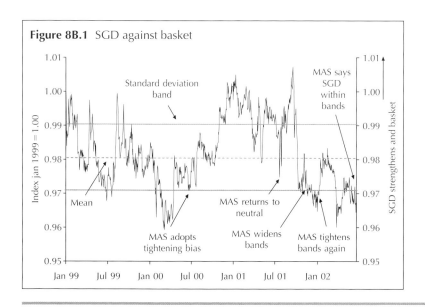

Figure 8B.1 SGD against basket

release here is monthly non-oil exports (NODX). Global stock markets are also important given Singapore's hi-tech exports. Lastly, SGD players also keep an eye on regional politics.

Thai baht

❏ The Bank of Thailand is active in the currency market tracking the THB against the USD.

❏ The central bank is keen to build up its foreign exchange reserves, depleted after the Asia crisis, while ensuring that the THB does not hurt exports or the real economy.

❏ Other key factors for the THB are foreign investors' purchases of domestic equities in Thailand, the state of the global economy, and the behaviour of regional currencies such as the SGD and JPY.

The Bank of Thailand is active in the currency market tracking the level of the THB against the USD. Like other central banks in Asia, the Bank of Thailand seeks to smooth out volatility in the market. In addition the authorities do not want to see the THB hurt exports or the real economy. As such in an environment of THB strength, the central bank is likely to check the market by buying USDs. This accords well with its medium term objective of rebuilding its

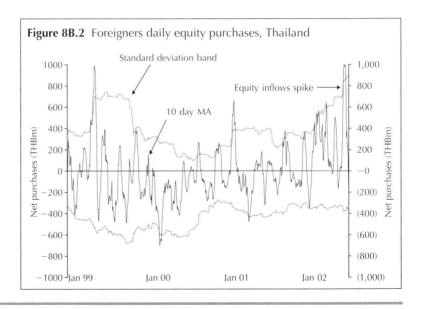

Figure 8B.2 Foreigners daily equity purchases, Thailand

foreign exchange reserves that have become depleted after the Asia crisis in 1997/1998.

Foreign investors' daily net equity buying or selling is another important factor for THB players to watch. Figure 8B.2 shows the ten day moving average of such purchases against a one standard deviation band of historic daily purchases. Recently purchases have been very high in excess of one standard deviation, supporting the THB against the USD.

For day to day price action, regional currencies are also important for THB players. In particular traders watch how the SGD and JPY are faring against the USD. For the more longer term, global growth prospects are important for the THB as Thailand is a net exporter like other East Asian economies.

Korean won

❏ The Bank of Korea on behalf of the Ministry of Finance tracks both the KRW against the USD and the KRW against the JPY.

❏ The authorities have strong foreign exchange reserves with which to control the market but are willing to tolerate substantial currency fluctuations in contrast to other central banks in Asia.

❏ Other factors for the KRW are foreigners' purchases of Korean equities, the behaviour of global stock markets such as the Nasdaq and the state of the world economy.

Exchange rate policy in Korea is set by the Ministry of Finance with the Bank of Korea acting as agent. The authorities look at both USD/KRW and JPY/KRW. For the former the authorities do not like to see sharp multi-big figure moves and may intervene to smooth the market when trading becomes volatile. For the latter, the JPY/KRW cross rate is an important target as approximately two thirds of Korean producers compete directly with Japanese producers in Japan and Korea or indirectly in third markets overseas. But as Figure 8B.3 shows policy-makers are willing to tolerate substantial moves in this cross.

Korea like other Asian economies is a net exporter so the KRW is traditionally seen as a play on global growth. Thus when global growth prospects rise the KRW usually outperforms.

KRW players also watch foreign inflows into Korean equities. These are correlated with global tech markets like the Nasdaq.

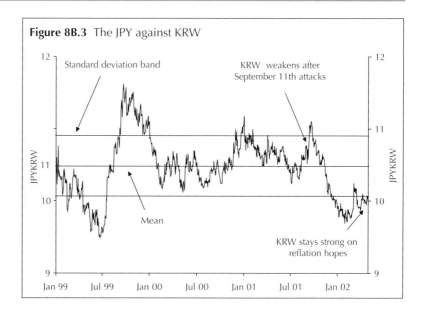

Figure 8B.3 The JPY against KRW

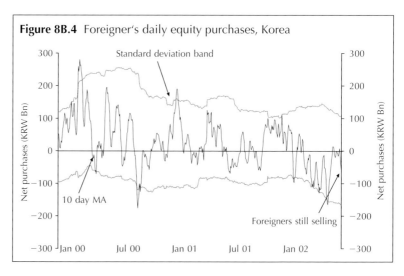

Figure 8B.4 Foreigner's daily equity purchases, Korea

Taiwanese dollar

❏ The Central Bank of China (the monetary authority of Taiwan) tracks the TWD against the USD and against the JPY.

❏ The central bank has substantial foreign exchange reserves. It uses these to control the TWD more closely than the authorities in Singapore, Thailand and Korea control their own currencies.

❏ Other factors for the TWD are foreigners' purchases of equities, the behaviour of global technology stock markets and the performance of the world economy.

The TWD like the KRW, SGD and THB is a floating currency. But in contrast the authorities in Taiwan intervene actively on a day to day basis to ensure the TWD rate against the USD does not move very much per day. Thus TWD players watch the actions of the Central Bank of China very closely. The CBC watches USD/TWD and TWD/JPY. As with Korea, Taiwan's producers compete with Japan's so the cross rate is important for Taiwan's economy.

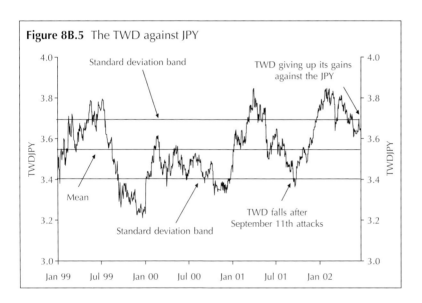

Figure 8B.5 The TWD against JPY

Also important for the TWD are foreigners' daily net purchases of Taiwanese equities. As in Korea these correlate with global sentiment on technology stocks so TWD players watch how the Nasdaq is doing.

For the medium term, Taiwan like other Asian economies is a net exporter so the long run outlook for the TWD depends on global growth prospects.

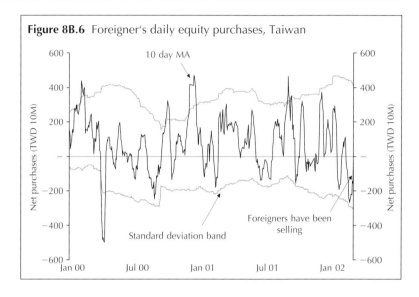

Figure 8B.6 Foreigner's daily equity purchases, Taiwan

Mexican peso
❏ Historically oil prices are have been a driver of the MXN but this correlation has been breaking down for some time now.
❏ With Mexico's economy becoming increasingly integrated with that of the United States, the fortunes of the USD globally are a key factor for the MXN.
❏ Other key factors for the MXN include global risk aversion owing to the need to fund Mexico's current account deficit, the central bank's monetary policy, regional currency contagion and domestic politics.

Historically, oil prices have been viewed as an important factor for the MXN given the Mexican economy's dependency on oil. However for some time now this correlation has been breaking down as Mexico's economy becomes more diversified. Thus as Figure 8B.7 shows the rise in oil prices in the first half of 2002 has not stopped the MXN from sliding.

The diversification of Mexico's economy has been driven by its increasing integration with the United States. This has caused the MXN to become linked with sentiment on US markets and the USD. Figure 8B.8 shows the MXN following the USD index closely. This linkage is further compounded as Mexico runs a significant

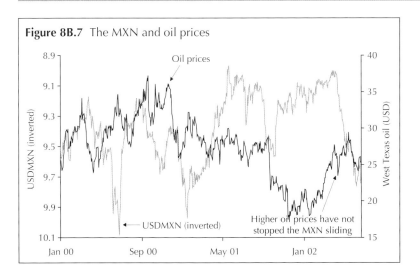

Figure 8B.7 The MXN and oil prices

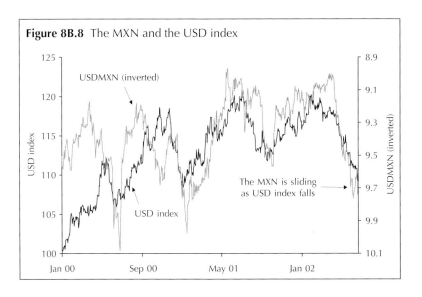

Figure 8B.8 The MXN and the USD index

current account deficit like the US. Running a current account deficit implies that the MXN also suffers during times of risk aversion like the USD.

Other factors to watch for the MXN are the central bank's interest rate policy, neighbouring currencies given the threat of contagion from regional crises and Mexico's domestic politics.

Brazilian real

❏ Commodity prices especially for soft commodities have traditionally been a key indicator for the BRL though this correlation is becoming less important.

❏ Brazil's large public debt is now the focus of the market as concerns arise over whether a future Brazilian government will default on the country's debt.

❏ Other factors for the BRL include global risk aversion as Brazil runs a large current account deficit, central bank interest rate and exchange rate policy and regional currency contagion.

As Brazil is a large producer of soft commodities, stronger global demand has historically benefited the BRL through higher commodity prices. Conversely as the world economy slowed down in 2001 and commodity prices fell the BRL lost support. This is shown in Figure 8B.9 of the BRL and the broad Journal of Commerce index that includes both soft and hard commodities.

But Figure 8B.9 also shows broadly rising commodity prices have not helped the BRL in the first half of 2002 as fears over the country's public debt have dominated sentiment instead. This is due to uncertainty over the outcome of elections in the second half of the year. Thus indicators of Brazilian debt sentiment are watched closely by BRL players. These include Brazilian C bonds and the

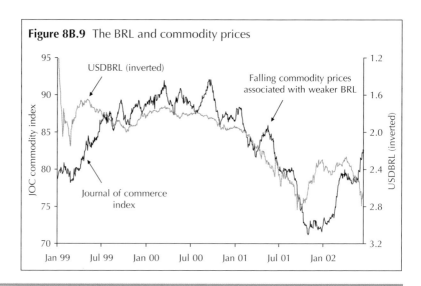

Figure 8B.9 The BRL and commodity prices

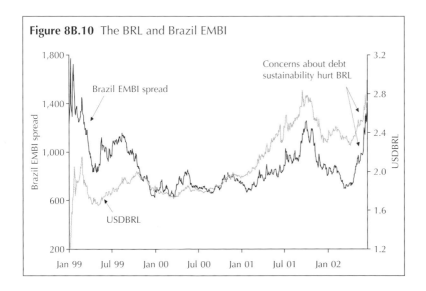

Figure 8B.10 The BRL and Brazil EMBI

JP Morgan Emerging Market Bond Index spread for Brazilian debt given in Figure 8B.10.

Other factors for the BRL are the risks of central bank intervention, interest rate, global risk aversion given Brazil's large current account deficit and regional currency contagion.

South African rand

❑ As South Africa produces precious metals, commodity prices are important for the ZAR. Similarly sentiment on commodity currencies like the AUD and CAD is also key.

❑ Unlike the dollar bloc currencies however the ZAR is also an emerging market currency so players watch global emerging market indicators and local indicators such as domestic crime and regional politics.

❑ The ZAR is also dependent on short term flows into the bond market given ongoing current account deficits. The SARB forward book however is less important now.

As South Africa is a major producer of precious metals, ZAR players watch hard commodity prices like gold. However the correlation between commodities and the ZAR waxes and wanes as Figure 8B.11 shows. For example in 1999, the ZAR did not benefit from spikes in gold because the central bank intervened to buy

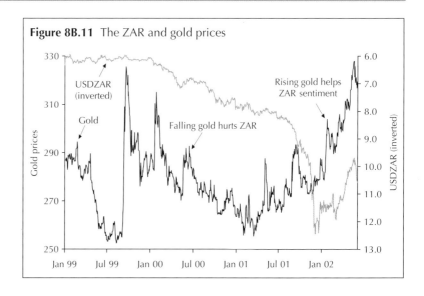

Figure 8B.11 The ZAR and gold prices

Figure 8B.12 The ZAR and EMBI spreads

USDs for its reserves. In the first half of 2002 however stronger gold prices (along with commodity currencies such as the AUD and CAD strengthening) have helped sentiment on the ZAR.

Unlike the dollar bloc, the ZAR is also an emerging market currency. Thus players watch indicators of global emerging market sentiment such as the JP Morgan EMBI given in Figure 8B.12 and more local indicators for South Africa. These include crime, the HIV situation and political risks in neighbours like Zimbabwe.

Other factors are short run inflows into the bond market. Thus players watch local yields like R153s. The central bank's forward book used to be an issue but now has become much reduced.

Polish zloty

❏ As Poland seeks to join the European Union in the next few years and the EUR later on, the PLN is a long term convergence trade. This attracts inflows into the local bond market and also foreign direct investment.

❏ The PLN is now a freely floating currency but PLN players also track the PLN against its old basket when trading the currency.

❏ Also important for PLN sentiment is Poland's current account deficit and relations between the country's politicians and the National Bank of Poland.

As Poland is a candidate to join the European Union in the next few years, the PLN is a long term convergence trade supported by inflows into local PLN denominated bonds and also by foreign direct investment. As such players watch the yields on benchmark local bonds as a guide to sentiment on the PLN. This is shown in Figure 8B.13 below.

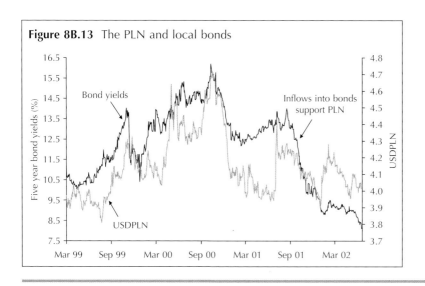

Figure 8B.13 The PLN and local bonds

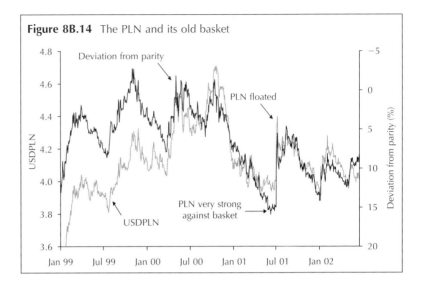

Figure 8B.14 The PLN and its old basket

The PLN was freely floated almost a year ago but PLN players still track the currency against its old basket. The weights of the basket were 55% EUR and 45% USD and the basket had a central parity rate and wide permitted fluctuation bands. Figure 8B.14 shows the PLN against its former basket.

Also important for the PLN is Poland's current account deficit and relations between the country's politicians and the National Bank of Poland. The latter is important as attempts to undermine the independence of the central bank hurt sentiment and Poland's prospective accession into the European Union.

1 Some recent research has started to question this premise, citing the increasing level of cross-correlation between emerging market asset returns and developed market asset returns as evidence. Given the disparate nature of emerging markets and the varying degree of "emergedness" of each market, we will stay with the established view here.

2 The International Monetary Fund's semiannual Global Financial Stability Report (March 2003) contains times series of such average correlations. The same publication also has useful information on market activities in emerging currencies. Available from www.imf.org/external/pubs/ft/gfsr/.

3 For general discussions of (and references for) emerging market investment, see Errunza (1997) and Aggarwal (1994). Hauser, Marcus and Yaari's (1994) early empirical study concludes that there is no benefit. Bridgewater Associates has produced two very informative research papers on emerging market currencies. Both are available from its website at www.bridgewaterassociates.com.

4 Some emerging market debt is US dollar-based – for example, Brady bonds and other dollar-denominated securities. These securities have no direct currency exposure but full credit exposure.

5 Note that in Eaker, Grant and Woodard (2000) currency returns are calculated by spot-on-spot changes and are therefore not necessarily hedgeable.

6 The Parker Emerging FX Index, available at www.parkerglobal.com/_private/emerging.htm.

7 See the comprehensive surveys by Esquivel and Larrain (2000) and Beckaert and Harvey (2003) for further references.

8 This is probably one of the reasons why the forward bias in emerging market currencies is even more pronounced and why the implied–actual volatility spread is even higher.

9 European Central Bank (2003), p. 21.

10 We did not snoop on the data set – the exercise was done in 1999.

11 The index appears in the IMF's Global Financial Stability Report – see note 2.

12 For historical studies, see Horngren and Vredin (1989), Klein (1989) and Pikkarainen (1991).

13 The LCVI also contains a risk appetite element.

14 Briefing written by Mansoor Mohi-uddin and Zoe Charny of UBS Warburg, London, UK (used with permission). The codes/currencies referred to are: AUD, Australian dollar; BRL, Brasilian real; CAD, Canadian dollar; EUR, euro; IDR, Indonesian rupiah; JPY, Japanese yen; KRW, Korean won; MXN, Mexican peso; PLN, Polish zloty; SGD, Singapore dollar; THB, Thai baht; TWD, Taiwan dollar; USD, US dollar; ZAR, South African rand.

Liquidity, Online Dealing
and E-Commerce

9.1 INTRODUCTION

In this chapter we bundle together two short and seemingly unrelated topics: foreign exchange liquidity and foreign exchange e-commerce. The first, foreign exchange liquidity, is relatively established but not necessarily well studied – not surprising given the predominantly over-the-counter nature of the foreign exchange market and, consequently, the lack of data one would need to conduct such a study. The topic of foreign exchange liquidity is often mentioned by practitioners in their jargon-peppered talk. We present a short overview on foreign exchange liquidity, including both academic findings and practical observations, with the aim of providing some background information for someone without prior practical knowledge.

The topic of foreign exchange e-commerce is, on the other hand, relatively new (even though electronic dealing has been around for over a decade), but it is fundamentally changing the operation of the foreign exchange market, including the provision of and access to foreign exchange liquidity. Hence we opt to combine these two topics in one chapter. Over the last three to five years, innovations in foreign exchange e-commerce have changed not only the way foreign exchange transactions are done but also many other aspects of the life cycle of such transactions: matching confirmation, settlement, portfolio management and so forth. The benefits of online transaction, via either a multi-bank portal or a single-bank system, and straight-through processing (STP) are easy to see, and we will use FXall and UBS, respectively, as examples to illustrate them.

We believe that the potential for efficiency improvement when online innovations are combined with the currency overlay process can be significant, and we are only seeing the beginning of it. Definitely a space worth watching in the future.

9.2 FOREIGN EXCHANGE LIQUIDITY: THEORY AND REALITY
9.2.1 Theory of foreign exchange liquidity

Foreign exchange is the largest financial market, with massive trading volumes – far larger than supported by the underlying trade flows between the countries. There are many theories on this so-called excess volume, mostly involving noisy traders. Lyons' (1997) "hot potato" theory provides a plausible explanation. It works as follows: when a client executes a large trade through a market-maker, the latter eliminates all or part of the exposure to minimise the risk of adverse price movements. He can call out on the inter-bank market and offload his exposure by hitting on other dealer's quotes.[1] The dealers hit by such positions may then wish to call out on other dealers to pass the exposure on. The original trade is thus passed around like a "hot potato", multiplying itself several times en route.

Lyons' theory fits well with two characteristics of the foreign exchange market: its dealer structure and its lack of trade reporting. If the theory is correct, new mechanisms of price dissemination could fundamentally reduce the volume, whereas the impact might not be so drastic if the noisy trader theory were true. In fact, one could argue that the volume from noise traders might actually increase if price transparency increased. The advent of electronic trading, eg, EBS and Reuters' D2000-2 systems, has fundamentally changed the price discovery process and the online multi-bank portals are pushing the boundary even further in that these B2C (business to consumer) tools, such as FXall, are pushing transparency out to customers. We have indeed seen a large reduction in foreign exchange volume between 1998 and 2001, as indicated in the triannual BIS surveys. But other factors may be at work too (see Section 9.2.2).

There are other types of foreign exchange liquidity models that attempt to explain the dissemination of information and the role of private information in foreign exchange trading. For example, Ito, Lyons and Melvin (1998) analysed data on US dollar/Japanese yen trading over a particular day when a certain trading restriction was lifted and found evidence consistent with the presence of significant private information in the foreign exchange market. Covrig and Melvin (1998) arrived at a similar conclusion. They concluded that, at intra-day level, private information is a very important factor for foreign exchange trading, even though its importance diminishes markedly for longer time periods and/or lower-frequency data. Peiers (1997) observed trading activities of Deutsche Bank in the US dollar/Deutschmark around periods of Bundesbank intervention and concluded that Deutsche Bank is a price leader over those periods. He suggested that the bank received a significant portion of the intervention-related currency trades and therefore had a temporary information advantage. His conclusion is supported by Sapp (2002). De Jong *et al* (1999) repeated Peiers' analysis but did not find evidence of price leadership.

As we mentioned in Chapter 4, Section 4.5.4, the microstructure of the foreign exchange market, where foreign exchange liquidity is also studied, is the subject of active research. Interested readers can follow up Lyons (2002) and the references therein.

9.2.2 The impact of consolidation on liquidity 1998–2003

Some recent events that are important for an understanding of changes in foreign exchange liquidity are:

❏ the impact of the euro. The introduction of the new currency has greatly reduced the number of actively traded currencies. Various fixing arrangements and target zones among Euro-in currencies used to provide abundant opportunities for speculators.
❏ the Asian crisis of 1997–98. Many investors, especially carry traders, got burnt by the large-scale devaluation of Asian currencies and, in some cases, the ensuing capital control.
❏ the poor performance of macro-funds. Many investors pulled out of fundamental-driven foreign exchange speculation after the high-profile collapse of Long Term Capital Management (LTCM).

❑ the equity market. The stellar performance of equity markets up to 2000 attracted capital away from the foreign exchange market and diminished foreign exchange liquidity. This situation reversed after the burst of the bubble.

❑ bank consolidation and the reduction in the number of niche/specialist banks. We will discuss this point in some detail below.

The foreign exchange market is still fragmented, with the top 10 banks having more than 50% of the market and increasing their share. The rest is shared among hundreds of small banks. Consolidation in this market continues, with big mergers such as those of Chase and JP Morgan. Many smaller banks have scaled back their activities since EMU. One big trend over the last two or three years has been for the small, niche banks to outsource their trading activities to large investment banks and concentrate instead on client deals. This is reflected in the growth of what is known as the "bank for bank" (or B4B) segment. The onset of continuous linked settlement (CLS) and rapid changes, as well as fierce competition, in the foreign exchange e-commerce arena have all significantly pushed up the cost of participation.

Banks have also been centralising their trading operations. For example, in 1994 UBS and the Swiss Bank Corporation between them employed about 300 spot traders in several trading centres including London, Frankfurt, Zurich, Geneva, Lugano, Basel, Zug, Lausanne, Lucerne, New York, Chicago, Toronto, Tokyo, Hong Kong, Singapore and Sydney. By 2000, the bank formed by their merger had 55 spot traders in London, Stamford, CT, Singapore and Tokyo (yen only).

With the reduced number of banks, and the reduced number of independent trading desks in those banks, liquidity has been getting tighter. According to an internal estimate by UBS in 1990, there were 27 active interbank trading banks (or desks) making the market in the US dollar/Swiss franc, with a total average nominal volume per call-out of US$255 million. By 1999, the number of active trading banks had been reduced to 14 through consolidation and centralisation and the total volume was US$105 million. And in 2000 the number was further reduced to seven and the total volume to US$50 million.

Some general observations can be made on the factors that impacted foreign exchange liquidity over the period 1998–2003:

❏ the total industry volume is static, though there are regional variations.
❏ wholesale customers have become more price-sensitive, mainly due to the improved price discovery mechanism. Therefore, a lower price can mean far greater volumes.
❏ price convergence increases the importance of differentiation between service providers through better tools or advisory services.
❏ high fixed costs are barriers to entry.
❏ huge economies of scale are to be had. Major players seek to increase volumes dramatically to support high fixed costs; second-tier players look to "get big" or "get niche" to reduce overall costs.
❏ price competition has led to shrinking margins for all players to the benefit of the end-users.
❏ many market-makers believe that only the largest players with the lowest costs will survive. Large players have a large customer base and superior information, especially from order flows. They deal in large volumes, which can sometimes affect exchange rates.

9.2.3 Studies of electronic dealing and its impact on liquidity

Figure 9.1 shows the proportion of foreign exchange spot transactions via direct interbank trades, voice brokers and electronic brokers according to the BIS's triannual survey of foreign

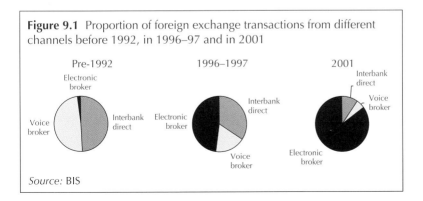

Figure 9.1 Proportion of foreign exchange transactions from different channels before 1992, in 1996–97 and in 2001

Source: BIS

exchange and derivatives market activities published in 2002. In the 1992 survey, transactions were divided almost equally between direct interbank and voice broker trades, with electronic brokers channelling only about 2% of total trades. In the 1998 survey direct interbank trades accounted for roughly a third of all transactions, but close to half of the trades were done via electronic brokers. It is interesting to note that the source of these trades has remained relatively stable over the period – roughly a third of all trades originated from clients.

Huang and Masulis' (1999) study, using data for 1992–93, indicates that bid–offer spreads increase with foreign exchange volatility and decrease with competition. However, the bid–offer spread in the spot foreign exchange market has been relatively stable over the most recent five-year period for all mature currency pairs, barring the one-off adjustment during the introduction of the euro. Goodhart, Ito and Payne (1996), in a study of trading activities via the Reuters D2000-2 electronic brokering system, observed that bid–offer spreads in the foreign exchange market are determined by market convention rather than potential cost. Spot market-makers generally make their money by active position-taking rather than by capturing the spread.[2] This transition was almost completed by 1997.

The vanilla options business has not been the subject of a systematic study in the style of Goodhart, Ito and Payne (1996). However, the bid–offer spread was falling steadily until 2000–01 and has since stabilised. In the mid-1990s option market-makers were able to capture up to 40% of the implied volatility bid–offer spread by matching client flows, clever risk management and spot replication. Now some indicate that most of the money is no longer made in this way but, rather, by active position-taking.

9.3 E-COMMERCE

9.3.1 General observations

Currency trading is by far the most "electrified" capital market activity in both depth and width. Section 9.2 gave an overview of the extent of automation in the execution process, but in recent years the process of automation has spread to other aspects of currency trading, from pre-trade to at-trade to post-trade – in other words, to the whole process. At the pre-trade stage the delivery of research materials has gone electronic: there is now a whole range of internet-based tools that allow the user to conduct *ad hoc* studies with an increasing degree of flexibility and sophistication. At the at-trade stage, automatic liquidity and execution are now taken for granted, and the new standard is on whether the trades are electronically captured by the different systems used by clients. The post-trade stage is being revolutionised by automation and connectivity: straight-through-processing (STP), prime brokerage and continuous linked settlement (CLS) are technologies and methods that are bringing significant efficiency gains to end-users and are increasingly being adopted by different clients.

9.3.2 Straight-through processing

Traditionally, foreign exchange deals between a bank and its customers have been executed over the phone. Once the details are agreed, they are entered manually by both institutions into their respective systems. This process is error-prone, given that dealers are usually under time pressure. And errors can be costly in the fast-moving foreign exchange markets. Once the deals are captured in the systems, they are processed further by middle- or back-office staff to add confirmation and settlement details. The process is largely automated now, but manual intervention is frequently required, which again can result in errors. Settlement errors can be expensive too because of the related interest charges and penalties.

The emergence and increasing acceptance of online dealing platforms over the last five years is rapidly changing the way in which foreign exchange transactions are executed. Many asset managers have signed on to proprietary systems provided by banks or multi-bank portals or both. Many of these systems enable them to automate the dealing process, reduce errors and achieve best execution. Clients can choose to integrate their own trading and back-office systems with these systems and achieve straight-through processing. The integration process is becoming standardised and the cost has been falling rapidly over recent years. All these factors have contributed to an increasing acceptance of online trading systems and straight-through processing. In the next two sub-sections we will look at examples of multi- and single-bank systems.

9.3.3 Multi-bank platforms

Currently there are three main multi-bank platforms: FX Connect (100% owned by State Street), Currenex and FXall (both owned by shareholders), all launched between 2000 and 2001. The main advantage of a multi-bank platform lies in competitive pricing and it is ideal for clients with a fiduciary responsibility to obtain the best execution. However, all platforms have expanded (and continue to expand) their services to include pre-trade and post-trade activities. Here we use FXall as an example to explain what a multi-bank platform offers. The offerings of different platforms are usually only marginally different. The panel in Section 9.3.5 contains an example of how a multi-bank platform is used by overlay managers in practice.

Like other online multi-bank portals, FXall's value proposition as a financial intermediary can be categorised as follows:

❏ *trading*. Trading is the core competency. FXall requests prices from participating banks according to the client's specifications. The prices are displayed and best prices highlighted. The client only needs "click and deal" within a specified time. The price-making process is highly automated and more than half of all price requests are answered within one second.
❏ *operation*. Modules allow pre- and post-trade allocation and amendment.
❏ *settlement*. The deal matching, confirmation and settlement process is also automated between the liquidity-providing banks and FXall through STP. The client can opt to integrate its own systems fully with FXall to realise the full potential of online dealing with STP. The integration service is provided by a host of system providers partnered with FXall.
❏ *information*. Aside from identifying the best-quoting banks in real time, FXall can also measure the performance of chosen banks. The client can also access participating banks' proprietary research materials.

The trading platform's execution methods are designed to improve efficiency. For example, it offers a "batch" function that allows customers to send entire portfolios to their chosen bank for pricing. A greater degree of efficiency than the traditional dealing channels can be achieved by reducing the time to price small trades

Figure 9.2 Screenshots of the FXall trading platform

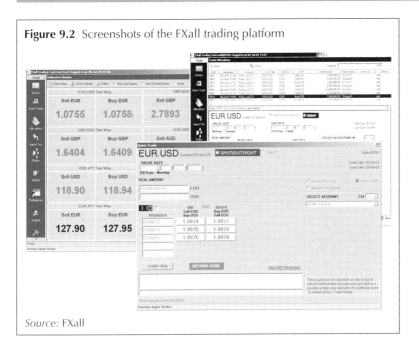

Source: FXall

through automation; by standardisation of confirmation and settlement; and by centralisation of training and support. In contrast to
the online dealing tools provided by banks, FXall's services and
products are provided by a neutral, independent entity, which
avoids potential conflicts of interest. Figure 9.2 shows screenshots
provided by FXall.

Other benefits, no less important, lie in the automation of other
steps of a deal's life cycle. FXall's settlement centre has the following capabilities:

❑ automated confirmation matching;
❑ clients can "enrich" settlement instructions by adding specific
   instruction;
❑ seamless notification of custodians using SWIFT;[3]
❑ support for multiple custodians; and
❑ automated calculation of netting instructions.

According to the latest figures released by FXall, more than half
of its trading volume originates from European clients and around
one-third from the Americas. Corporations account for more than

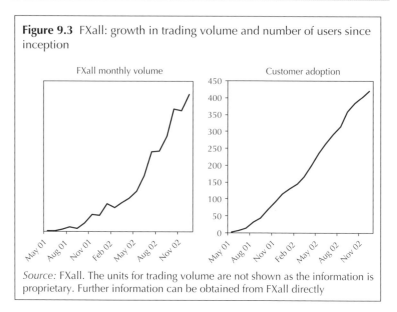

Figure 9.3 FXall: growth in trading volume and number of users since inception

FXall monthly volume

Customer adoption

Source: FXall. The units for trading volume are not shown as the information is proprietary. Further information can be obtained from FXall directly

half of the trading volume, institutional investment managers and banks accounting for the rest. Figure 9.3 shows the growth in volume and participating client numbers since inception. FXall won a succession of awards in 2002, including Best Multibank Portal from the influential *Euromoney* FX Poll 2002, Number 1 Multibank Portal from *Global Investor*'s FX Survey 2002, and Best Multibank FX Trading Portal from *FX Week*'s Best Bank Awards 2002.

9.3.4 Single-bank platforms

Nearly all large foreign exchange banks offer eFX solutions of one form or another. Apart from the fact that just one bank provides the dealing prices in these systems, their functionality is fairly similar to that of multi-bank portals. Because the number of such systems is much larger than the number of multi-bank portals, they do vary in the range and depth of services provided. Here we offer a general overview of such facilities using UBS's online system as an example. The choice may seem biased as the author is an employee of UBS. However, it has been chosen for illustration mainly because of its ease of access. Moreover, UBS's e-tool suite was voted number one in several surveys in 2002, including the *Euromoney* FX Poll 2002, in which it was voted the Best Overall Bank in E-Commerce,

Best Online Execution, Best Online Research and Best STP. So, we trust that the choice is justified.

UBS's e-tool suite is designed to address the whole trading process from pre-trade to post-trade. It includes:

❑ pre-trade (decision support)
  ❑ *FX Web* (which includes online foreign exchange research and analytics)
  ❑ *Interchange Chat* (instant messaging system)
❑ at-trade (liquidity)
  ❑ *FX Orders* (limit-order module)
  ❑ *FX Trader* (spot, forward, swap, money market module)
  ❑ *FX Option Trader* (option pricing and execution module)
❑ post-trade
  ❑ *FX KeyLink* (confirmation, settlement and payment module)
  ❑ *FX2B* (system-to-system integration for banks, corporations and intermediaries where UBS provides liquidity to clients' front-end systems. Also referred to as "white label" foreign exchange liquidity)

The website is designed to reduce information overload. A variety of short cuts, tags and filters (which online technology is most suited to delivering) are used to assist users to locate relevant information with speed and accuracy. The commentaries can be distributed to clients via email, Bloomberg, chat, web, or third-party channels (such as FXall). Its Analytics section allows users to access a range of data-mining tools for analysing historical and real-time data – in particular, UBS's proprietary implied volatility data. The website also offers a black box-driven technical trading model complete with data on positions and historical performance.

The execution modules provide firm, dealable prices for a range of products on a click-and-deal basis. "Firm" means that prices cannot be changed or revoked over a specific time window when they are sent to the client for acceptance or rejection. According to UBS, most deals going through its dealing modules do not require dealer intervention. Figure 9.4 has screenshots of some different modules.[4]

The post-trade module, KeyLink, can handle a variety of functions, including trading, confirmation, cash management and security management across different asset classes. Because it is

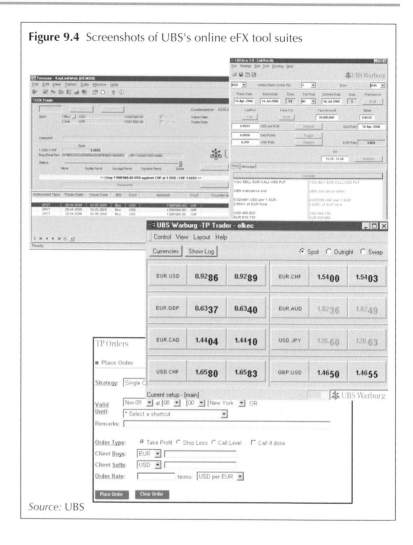

Figure 9.4 Screenshots of UBS's online eFX tool suites

Source: UBS

SWIFT-based, clients can use it to access confirmation and payment information from any SWIFT-based bank. Standardised message formats facilitate STP.

9.3.5 eFX and currency management in practice

For a fund manager the main and most direct benefit of eFX is the reduction of error and other types of operation risk. Other direct benefits of eFX include better price discovery, lower overheads and better management of credit relationships. Because the whole dealing process is done electronically, audit and reporting capabilities are also greatly increased.

According to a survey conducted by *Euromoney* and SunGard at the end of 2002, end-users (not exclusively currency managers) consider the following factors to be important when they choose an online platform:

❏ ease of use;
❏ built-in access to existing trading and settlement systems;
❏ security;
❏ better prices;
❏ multi-bank prices;
❏ overall efficiency gains from STP;
❏ multi-instrument trading.

In the same survey respondents also thought that, with the spread of multi-bank platforms, liquidity is likely to be concentrated in the hands of a few large players. Curiously, they considered that competitiveness and transparency would probably not be adversely affected. Currently, around two-thirds of foreign exchange trades are done via traditional means, but the proportion is expected to decline to around one-half within the next two years, particularly for smaller tickets.

This represents a remarkable shift from the sceptical position that was generally held until almost 2002. Before then, many currency managers on the buy-side expressed reservations on the likely impact of eFX on their business. While most acknowledged the potential for error reduction through STP, there was concern about the cost of integration. They were even less enthusiastic about other benefits the online foreign exchange paradigm might bring. However, the situation has changed significantly, with sell-side institutions – including banks and multi-bank portals – making rapid progress on the services they provide. Technological advances, coupled with alliances between liquidity providers and system providers, are driving down the cost of integration while increasing its scope.

The current discussion on eFX (including the example shown in the Panel) focuses on the online foreign exchange transaction and the steps immediately before and after the point of transaction.

We can expect eFX to penetrate many other aspects of currency management, for instance:

❏ exposure identification and aggregation;
❏ passive hedge execution;
❏ allocation of trades to clients' accounts;
❏ portfolio construction according to individual constraints;
❏ risk control;
❏ cash management; and
❏ performance measurement and real-time reporting.

We have seen some fund managers' internal systems that are streamlined to varying extents and offer a good glimpse of what is to come in the world of currency managers. Admittedly, these funds are all comparatively large and have the clout and economy of scale to develop such systems internally. A good foreign exchange system can usually:

❏ collect exposure data from underlying portfolios within a short period;
❏ compute passive currency-hedging requirements using in-built hedge ratios relevant for each account;
❏ implement active currency decisions across different accounts under their individual risk limits;
❏ aggregate net currency positions and generate the new trades required;
❏ check counterparty credit limits;
❏ route the new trades through single- or multi-bank platforms on the dealer's instruction;
❏ report back prices and, if accepted by dealers, capture the trades in internal risk control systems;
❏ confirm and settle all trades and/or, if required, send details to custodians;
❏ generate reports for different purposes.

We must, however, quickly add that good systems which perform all the above tricks seamlessly are still exceptions rather than the norm. Most fund managers carry different IT baggage due to corporate restructuring and/or a lack of investment/initiatives. A complaint we frequently hear from currency managers is that it is extremely difficult to know the underlying currency exposure

PANEL 1 eFX TRADING SOLUTIONS IN THE CURRENCY OVERLAY BUSINESS
Paul Duncombe and James Smith, State Street Global Advisors

(Reprinted with permission from *e-Forex*, October 2002, pp. 56–7.)

State Street Global Advisors has been using electronic trading platforms for over two years, and was probably one of the first fund management firms to start using the technology. Two factors always made it likely that we would be one of the initial asset managers to go down this route. First, we are one of the leading currency overlay managers of institutional assets and have a dedicated team of currency managers and traders executing large volumes of foreign exchange. Second, as a division of State Street Corporation, we were given an early opportunity to use the electronic trading platform, FX Connect, developed by the treasury division of our parent company.

It is worth stating at the outset that our experience with e-trading platforms has been very positive, and the impact on our business significant. Prior to installing an electronic dealing system, we were processing a considerable volume of foreign exchange tickets. In addition to handling third party currency overlay accounts, the team runs currency overlay mandates for in-house managed bond and equity portfolios, and also executes all foreign exchange trades generated within SSgA London.

Before e-trading, the execution process followed a time consuming pattern familiar to many readers – phoning counterparties, agreeing prices, sorting out split bookings and entering all the details into the trading software. Tickets were forwarded to settlements for reconciliation, and inevitably there would be a small percentage of tickets which did not match – through manual errors on both sides.

The e-trading environment has both increased the efficiency of our dealing desk and reduced the error rate to virtually zero. Additionally, one of the major advantages of e-trading was the progression to paperless dealing.

The FX Connect team integrated the platform into our trading and accounting systems, allowing all communications, signatures, and settlements to be performed electronically. A further important development is that since all of our counterparty banks are now connected to the platform, we can exploit the benefits of the system fully.

The day-to-day management of accounts in a currency overlay team typically involves trading a combination of a small number of high value active foreign exchange deals and a high volume of relatively small foreign exchange deals. The smaller flows can emanate from the need to fund the purchase and sale of securities, the sale of coupons and dividends or the re-balancing of positions in line with benchmarks. The larger transactions are still best dealt by a telephone conversation with a salesperson. However, where smaller deals are involved, there is a clear case for automating execution to the highest degree possible. Our business has expanded rapidly in recent years resulting in a large increase in the number of foreign exchange trades. Without the efficiencies that have resulted from the use of this new technology, we would have struggled to cope with these increased volumes.

We have found that the main advantages of electronic platforms are the ability to manage batch trades, and the straight through processing achieved. FX Connect is particularly useful for streamlining the execution of our numerous daily batches of multiple trades. The system is especially good at aggregating these trades and executing the orders in one hit. The batches tend to have the same base currency, and the final order usually consists of only a few different currency pairs.

The system calculates the net position of these trades – both for ourselves and the counterparty bank – at the press of a button. The procedure might initially seem lengthy – pulling the trades from our portfolio management system into the FX Connect platform, transmitting the trades to the counterparty, waiting for the rates to be entered, checking the rates, and then pulling the completed trade details back into our system. However, in fact, the whole process usually takes no more than 2 minutes and moreover the possibility of manual error is virtually eliminated, since our currency dealers do not enter either the trade or the rate at any point.

Additionally, we regularly have batches of trades which need to be executed at certain times to match benchmark fixings, usually the 4pm WM rate.[5] FX Connect allows us to send these trades to a counterparty at any time of the day, and the trades stay on the system until the counterparty sends them back with the fixing rate. At no point is there a "time-out" period when the system is logged off. The chat box facility enables us to highlight the fact that the trades must be executed to coincide with the benchmark fixing. The counterparty bank sends the completed trades back once the benchmark rate has been calculated and these deals remain on our system until we go onto the platform and manually accept them. At busy times, electronic dealing is much more effective than executing these trades over the telephone, as we may send several batches of benchmark fixes to several different counterparties. Not only is it faster, and with less margin for error, as mentioned above, but it is also easier to keep the batches separate and well organised.

This means there is no need for the traders to write down the rates and check them when they are sent back from the counterparty. The traders just go into each batch, check the "fills" and accept them when they have the time.

A further advantage of e-trading is the time-savings from the ability to obtain simultaneous competitive quotes. The recently updated version of FX Connect allows trading with up to 4 counterparties in competition on either one-way or 2-way prices. The prices from each counterparty are displayed in real-time on the screen and the best bid and offer prices are automatically highlighted. The dealer simply clicks on the best price to execute the trade. The counterparties do not know who they are competing with, and if unsuccessful, they are not told whether we have executed the trade, or have decided to wait. Pricing trades competitively in this way can be done by just one trader, thereby avoiding the difficulties of co-ordination when more than one person is telephoning for prices and the counterparties respond at different times.

Some concern has been voiced about the "impersonality" of trading on electronic platforms, but we have not found this to be the case. Our traders are immediately advised who has picked up the transmission at the counterparty end, and the chat box is very fast, allowing conversation in real-time. There is no doubt that e-trading has had a positive impact on our business, allowing us to handle larger trading volumes more efficiently, and without the need to increase trading or operations resources to the same extent.

with the accuracy and timeliness required as the information is lost in a labyrinth of incompatible IT systems (sometimes in addition to a fund's internal politics). We believe, with a reasonable degree of confidence, that this aspect of currency overlay management will see the most significant changes in the next few years. Some further candidates for change are discussed in the next section.

9.4 CUSTODIAN BANKS AND eFX

We have not mentioned the role of custodian banks so far. Traditionally, custodians monitor transaction flows, provide periodic position reports to investors and execute foreign exchange transactions arising from underlying security transactions on the investor's behalf. These foreign exchange transactions were considered to be auxiliary and best execution was never an issue: a custodian's main objective is to minimise the risks associated with the settlement of securities. Consequently, the reduced bid–offer spreads in foreign exchange trading and the adoption of time-saving systems bypassed this kind of transaction to a certain extent. Sometimes one still meets fund managers who are forced to deal with custodian banks at spreads that – to borrow a phrase often used by dealers – are wide enough to drive a truck through.

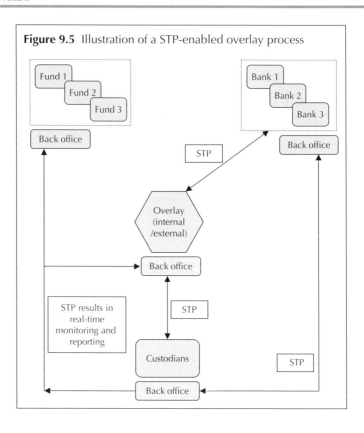

Figure 9.5 Illustration of a STP-enabled overlay process

Custodians play another very important role in currency overlay. An overlay programme is unlikely to be effective if the underlying portfolio is not marked-to-market and consolidated with a given accuracy and timeliness. Custodians traditionally help to provide such information to investment managers, though not necessarily with the desirable level of accuracy and timeliness. The market for custodians has been consolidating at some pace in recent years, with many banks exiting the business and those remaining able to exploit economies of scale. These custodians have begun to offer online services to investment managers that cover both execution and risk management solutions. The change is partly driven by the demand from investment managers, who increasingly view foreign exchange as an asset class for returns and want to consolidate foreign exchange trading and reduce transaction costs.

Some custodians are offering what is known as 360° STP. This automates several tasks in the overlay process, including exposure identification and consolidation, price discovery (execution), confirmation and settlement, and position reporting and risk analysis. With all these STP links, we can redraw the typical overlay process depicted in Chapter 3, Figure 3.3, in Figure 9.5. Compared with the process shown in Figure 3.3, the STP-enabled overlay process is significantly simplified. The custodian bank acts as a hub for most of the STP links, automatically collating information at pre-, at- and post-trading stages. The information can be processed promptly and accurately and provided to both fund managers and overlay managers to act on.

APPENDIX 9A: SOME SERVICE PROVIDERS

This appendix lists some of the treasury system providers, foreign exchange banks, dealing platforms and information sources related to eFX. The list of foreign exchange banks is compiled from various foreign exchange surveys, and we have marked the entries for the most recent *Euromoney* FX Poll. Information on the service providers is taken mainly from the companies' websites. The inclusion of a particular service provider does not constitute a recommendation.

Table 9A.1 Systems providers

Provider	Website	Comments
360T Treasury Systems	www.360t.com	Development, marketing and implementation of integrated systems for deal execution, intra-group trading, risk and portfolio management of financial instruments in the OTC market segment.
AVT Technologies	www.avt.co.uk	Specialises in providing technology to financial institutions and their customers to conduct foreign exchange and money market transactions

Table 9A.1 (continued)

Provider	Website	Comments
		in a real-time environment over the internet. Bought by Reuters in 2002.
Brokerage Services Group	bsg.adp.com	Multi-product/entity/ currency STP solutions, delivering fully automated front- to back-office functions throughout the life cycle of a trade, starting with deal capture, portfolio and risk management functions all the way to trade confirmation and settlement.
Cognotec	www.cognotec.com	Supplier of e-commerce foreign exchange and money market trading solutions. Core product AutoDeal CONNECT is a web-based trading solution.
FairEx	www.fairex.com	Web-based financial systems solutions for trading and risk management in foreign exchange dealing.
Financial Software Systems	www.fssnet.com	Provides treasury management and back-office systems using both web-based technology and Sybase and Microsoft SQL Server technology.
One-Ten	www.one-ten.com	STP solutions.
SunGard	www.risk.sungard.com	Provides enterprise-wide solutions for trading, risk management and operations. Web-enabled solutions for achieving straight-through processing and for managing risk.

Table 9A.2 Banks[6]

Bank	Website
ABN Amro*	www.abnamro.com
AIG International	www.aigi.com
ANZ International	www.anz.com
Bank of America	www.bankofamerica.com
Bank of New York	www.bankofny.com
Bank One	www.bankone.com
Barclays Capital*†	www.barcap.com
BNP Paribas	www.bnpparibas.com
Brown Brothers Harriman	www.bbh.com
CIBC	www.cibc.com
Citigroup*†	www.citigroup.com
Commerzbank	www.commerzbank.com
Commerzbank	www.commerzbank.com
Credit Agricole Indosuez	www.indosuez.com
Credit Suisse First Boston*†	www.csfb.com
Den Danske Bank	www.danskebank.com
Den Norske Bank	www.dnb.no
Deutsche Bank*†	www.deutsche-bank.com
Dresdner Kleinwort Wasserstein†	www.drkw.com
Fleet Bank	www.fleet.com
Goldman Sachs*†	www.gs.com
Halifax	www.halifax.co.uk
HSBC*†	www.hsbcib.com
ING Barings	www.ingbarings.com
Investec	www.investec.com
JP Morgan Chase & Co.*†	www.jpmorganchase.com
Lehman Brothers	www.lehman.com
Lloyds TSB	www.lloydstsb.co.uk
Merrill Lynch	www.ml.com
Morgan Stanley*	www.morganstanley.com
Rabobank International	www.rabobank.com
Royal Bank of Canada	www.royalbank.com
Royal Bank of Scotland	www.rbs.co.uk
SEB	www.seb.se
Société Générale	www.socgen.com
Standard Chartered Bank	www.stanchart.com
State Street Bank and Trust†	www.statestreet.com
Sumitomo Bank	www.sbcm.com
UBS*†	www.ubs.com
Wells Fargo	www.wellsfargo.com
WestLB	www.westlb.com

*Voted one of top 20 banks in *Euromoney* FX Poll 2003.
†Voted one of top 10 banks for single bank execution in *Euromoney* FX Poll 2003.

Table 9A.3 Other dealing systems

System/company	Website	Comments
FXall	www.fxall.com	Electronic trading platform offering customers foreign currency trade execution, access to research, and straight-through processing.
FX Connect	www.globallink.com	Multi-bank online trading platform, backed by State Street.
Currenex	www.currenex.com	Online global currency exchange that links institutional buyers and sellers worldwide in foreign exchange and money markets.
Fenics	www.fenics.com	Interface for price discovery, trade entry and decision support in foreign exchange options.
Superderivatives. com	www.superderivatives. com	Online brokerage for foreign exchange options and structured products.
ICor Brokerage Ltd	www.icorbrokerage. com	Online FX options brokerage. Joint venture between ICor Brokerage and Reuters.
GCI	www.gcitrading.com	Margined currency trading on the internet for corporations and institutions.
FXDirectDealer	www.fxdd.com	Retail-oriented online currency trading system.

Table 9A.4 Online information sources

Company/journal	Website	Comments
MCM	www.mcmwatch.com	Analysis of events influencing world currency markets. Fundamental and technical analysis on majors, emerging currencies and exotic and foreign exchange options markets.

Table 9A.4 (continued)

Company/journal	Website	Comments
Trademade International	www.trademade.com	Real-time technical analysis solutions.
FX Week	www.fxweek.com	Weekly magazine published by Risk Waters Group.
FX Street	www.fxstreet.com	Online information aggregator.
Profit & Loss	www.profit-loss.com	Monthly trade magazine with emphasis on trading and information system vendors.
e-Forex Magazine	www.aspmedialtd.com	Quarterly trade magazine on online technology for foreign exchange.

1   A market-maker "calls out" when he tries to obtain prices, usually simultaneously, from other market-makers. He then chooses to deal one or several of the obtained prices; in other words, he "hits" on these quotes. A call-out offers one of the most entertaining glimpses of the life on a foreign exchange trading floor, where several traders punch furiously at their dealing terminals and shout prices or instructions at one another. Its occurrence is now increasingly less common.

2   Larger banks do have the advantage of a larger client base and a high potential for matching clients' trades. This has been one of the rationales behind the fierce race between the top foreign exchange banks to expand their market share in recent years.

3   SWIFT, the Society for Worldwide Interbank Financial Telecommunication, is an industry-owned cooperative that provides a standardised and secure messaging service used by banks, broker/dealers and investment managers for payments, securities and trades.

4   The similarity between Figures 9.2 and 9.4 is due to the fact that UBS and FXall used the same IT development company to develop their trading platforms. Systems provided by other banks may have different layouts but the essential functionality is similar.

5   WM Company – for details of WM/Reuters' online spot exchange rates (intra-day, closing and forward) see Chapter 6, note 20.

6   As bank's websites are usually password protected we are unable to provide summaries or reviews in this table. Polls and surveys on their online product and services are periodically conducted by *Euromoney*, *Global Investor*, *FX Week*, *The Banker* and *Profit & Loss*. Details of the *Euromoney* FX Poll can be obtained through *Euromoney* via subscription.

Conclusions and an Overlay Checklist

10.1 SUMMARY OF THE MAIN ARGUMENTS

We set out to survey and explain the concepts and practices of currency overlay in a neutral, practical and comprehensive manner, but we ended up with a book that is probably much broader in its scope. The expansion was, in our opinion, necessary to achieve the original objective.

The variability in investment returns caused by currency movements is an avoidable and direct consequence of investing globally. Additional variability in returns can also be introduced indirectly as a consequence of the globalisation of both the goods and services markets and the financial markets around the world. Some investors treat such variability as a risk factor while others do not. Those who do not view currency as a risk factor often liken currency returns to a random walk whose long-term impact on investment returns will wash out. Among those who do treat currency variability as a risk factor, some also subscribe to the random walk hypothesis. For them, predicting currency returns is all but futile and they usually opt for some form of passive hedging to remove part or all of the return variability caused by currencies. Some, on the other hand, believe that currency markets are inherently inefficient and that currency movements can be predicted to a certain extent. They therefore view currency variability as a profit opportunity in that positive impact can be retained while negative impact is eliminated.

This divergence in investors' views on the existence of currency risk provides a rich and complex background against which the question of currency overlay is discussed. For many investors, or for those involved in currency risk management, these views have typically formed over a long period of time and have, so to speak, ossified.

Discussion of currency overlay is often sidelined by the much broader question of how to deal with currency risk in an investment portfolio. We therefore started our exploration from the standpoint of this second question. We argued that no matter what view an investor might have on whether currency movements represent a random walk (or any of the questions covered in Chapter 1, Section 1.3), the currency component of a portfolio should be separated from other risk factors – for example, risks in bonds and risks in equities. Our view on risk separation provided us with a framework for surveying the theoretical as well as the practical aspects of currency overlay, which, according to our definition, represents nothing more than a process of separating the variability of returns caused by currency moves.

The reason for our belief in currency separation – and our favourable disposition to currency overlay – lies not so much in our view on the predictability of currency movements, a topic on which we spent some time (in Chapter 4 and parts of Chapters 7 and 8) reviewing the existing evidence; nor in the body of empirical work which generally favours currency management (Chapter 1, Section 1.4.4); nor in the track record of the specialist currency overlay managers or their well-organised market presence (Chapter 3). Our belief in currency separation stems from a simple premise: any investment should be managed by a manager with a declared core competency in managing that particular type of risk factor or factors (Chapter 2, Section 2.5). If currency fluctuation, be it a risk factor or not, does not fall under a fixed-income or equity manager's core competency, then currency impact should be excluded from that manager's remit, ie, the manager's performance should be measured on a fully currency-hedged basis. Even in cases where the underlying managers do declare additional core competency in currencies, they should still be measured on a fully currency-hedged basis for the underlying and their currency decisions should be evaluated separately.

Although we promote fully currency-hedged asset allocation and a performance measurement framework (Chapter 6), we do not, however, encourage or discourage an investment manager to actually carry out the full currency-hedging transaction. In fact, we have no fixed view on particular hedge ratios, active or passive hedging styles, or specific trading models. These are not necessarily contradictory statements. The fully currency-hedged framework will ensure that investment decisions are separated, at least conceptually.

What does an investor do with the separated and centralised currency part? We think the decision should be made in more or less the same manner in which he makes other choices: bonds vs equity, domestic vs overseas, growth vs value, index vs active, etc., typically via an optimisation process to achieve a desirable risk/return objective. We have presented factual information on the risks and returns of currencies, as well as on methods for quantifying these risks and returns (mainly in Chapter 2 but also in Chapters 4, 6, 7 and 8), which we hope can be used as input variables in the investor's decision-making process. We also discussed, at considerable length, some specific issues related to currency and optimisation techniques, including the hedge ratio (Chapter 5). If the investor's currency decisions entail more than just passive hedging, he can entrust the currency decisions to managers who have a core competency in currency management.

Of course, the above picture – where an investor performs optimisation, takes currency decisions and selects managers according to their core competency – is a gross oversimplification of the real-life situation where the relationship between investor and investment managers is much more complex, as are the decision-making processes. This is particularly the case in large institutions. We feel that it is precisely in this type of complex situation that the currency overlay process can bring substantial, if less quantifiable, benefits. In order to run an overlay efficiently, an investor or investment manager will likely need to know, with a certain degree of accuracy and timeliness, his investment positions in nearly all asset classes so that he can figure out the currency exposures on which an overlay programme will run. The process of collecting, distilling and sharing these data, together with clarified risk responsibility, will undoubtedly help to improve the overall efficiency of investment institutions.

We are of the opinion that the (external) specialist overlay industry will continue to grow. However, the main growth area will be organic, in that institutional managers will set up their own, internal overlay processes in some shape or form, not only to seek returns and/or reduce risks but also exploit the informational benefit of currency overlay. The cost of setting up a currency overlay programme will continue to fall, largely thanks to the proliferation of online dealing and risk management tools (see Chapter 9). How to realise the full potential of e-commerce in a currency overlay process is one of the big challenges that lies ahead of institutional fund managers. And how to deal with emerging market currencies exposures is another (see Chapter 8).

10.2 A CURRENCY OVERLAY CHECKLIST

As this book is a practical guide, we conclude with a checklist for the investment manager who is looking to start a currency overlay process.

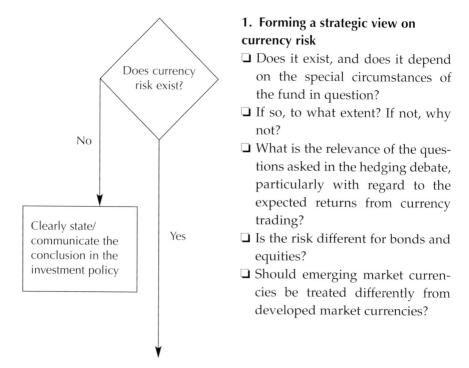

1. Forming a strategic view on currency risk

❏ Does it exist, and does it depend on the special circumstances of the fund in question?

❏ If so, to what extent? If not, why not?

❏ What is the relevance of the questions asked in the hedging debate, particularly with regard to the expected returns from currency trading?

❏ Is the risk different for bonds and equities?

❏ Should emerging market currencies be treated differently from developed market currencies?

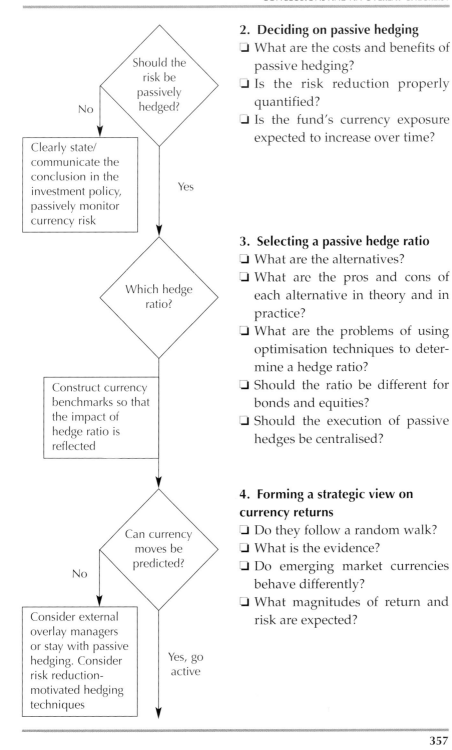

2. Deciding on passive hedging

❏ What are the costs and benefits of passive hedging?

❏ Is the risk reduction properly quantified?

❏ Is the fund's currency exposure expected to increase over time?

3. Selecting a passive hedge ratio

❏ What are the alternatives?

❏ What are the pros and cons of each alternative in theory and in practice?

❏ What are the problems of using optimisation techniques to determine a hedge ratio?

❏ Should the ratio be different for bonds and equities?

❏ Should the execution of passive hedges be centralised?

4. Forming a strategic view on currency returns

❏ Do they follow a random walk?

❏ What is the evidence?

❏ Do emerging market currencies behave differently?

❏ What magnitudes of return and risk are expected?

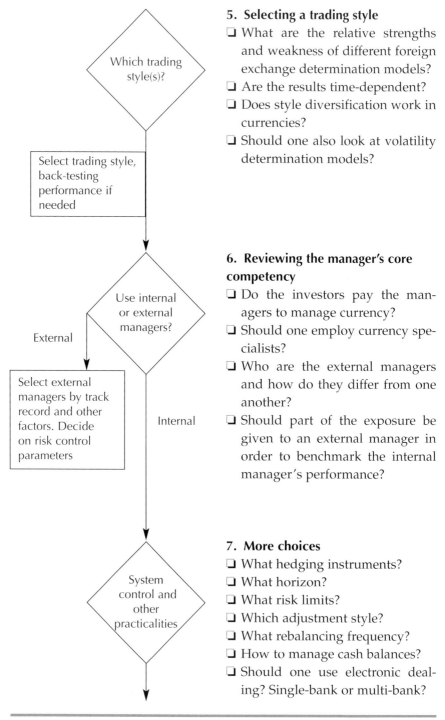

5. Selecting a trading style

❏ What are the relative strengths and weakness of different foreign exchange determination models?

❏ Are the results time-dependent?

❏ Does style diversification work in currencies?

❏ Should one also look at volatility determination models?

6. Reviewing the manager's core competency

❏ Do the investors pay the managers to manage currency?

❏ Should one employ currency specialists?

❏ Who are the external managers and how do they differ from one another?

❏ Should part of the exposure be given to an external manager in order to benchmark the internal manager's performance?

7. More choices

❏ What hedging instruments?

❏ What horizon?

❏ What risk limits?

❏ Which adjustment style?

❏ What rebalancing frequency?

❏ How to manage cash balances?

❏ Should one use electronic dealing? Single-bank or multi-bank?

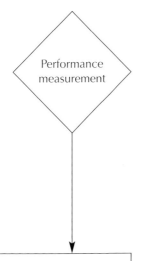

Performance measurement

Clearer and cleaner investment policy;
Competency-based approach to investment and risk management decisions;
Better understanding of the portfolio risk as a whole and in its constituents;
Centralisation of currency trading and other administration functions, with improved efficiency;
Potential benefit of risk reduction so that the risk budget can be spent more productively;
Potential source of alpha, uncorrelated with underlying returns

8. Evaluation before and after

❏ What are the main issues in evaluating currency performance?

❏ What are the strengths and weaknesses of the different approaches?

❏ How to construct/use a holding-based vs a performance-based benchmark?

❏ What are the contributions, in both return and risk terms, of passive hedging and active hedging?

Appendix A: Euro fixings

These are the irrevocably fixed conversion rates between the euro and the currencies of those EU member states which adopted the euro as of December 31, 1998, apart from Greece, whose irrevocable conversion rate was fixed as of January 1, 2001. More details can be found on the European Central Bank's website at www.ecb.int.

Table A1 Euro fixed conversion rates

EUR 1	=	BEF	40.3399	(Belgian franc)
	=	DEM	1.95583	(Deutschmark)
	=	ESP	166.386	(Spanish peseta)
	=	FRF	6.55957	(French franc)
	=	IEP	0.787564	(Irish punt)
	=	ITL	1936.27	(Italian lira)
	=	LUF	40.3399	(Luxembourg franc)
	=	NLG	2.20371	(Dutch guilder)
	=	ATS	13.7603	(Austrian Schilling)
	=	PTE	200.482	(Portuguese escudo)
	=	FIM	5.94573	(Finnish markka)
	=	GRD	340.750	(Greek drachma)

Appendix B: Currency abbreviations

Currency names and codes vary between sources. Here we use names and codes that are commonly used by foreign exchange market participants. A full list of ISO currency names and codes can be found at www.unece.org/cefact/rec/cocucod.htm.

Table B1 Currencies for which cash/derivatives products are commonly traded

Currency	Code
Australian dollar	AUD
Argentinean peso	ARS
Austrian Schilling*	ATS
Belgian franc*	BEF
British pound sterling	GBP
Brazilian real	BRL
Canada dollar	CAD
Czech koruna	CZK
Chilean peso	CLP
Chinese yuan (renminbi = RMB)	CNY
Cyprus pound	CYP
Dutch guilder*	NLG
Danish krone	DKK
German mark*	DEM
Estonian kroon	EEK
European currency unit	XEU
Euro	EUR

Table B1 (continued)

Currency	Code
French franc*	FRF
Finnish markka*	FIM
Greek drachma[†]	GRD
Hungarian florint	HUF
Hong Kong dollar	HKD
Italian lira*	ITL
Indian rupee	INR
Irish punt*	IEP
Indonesian ruppiah	IDR
Israeli shekel	ILS
Japanese yen	JPY
Korean won	KRW
Latvian lat	LVL
Lithuanian litas	LTL
Mexican peso	MXN
Malaysian ringgit	MYR
Maltese lira	MTL
Norwegian krone	NOK
New Zealand dollar	NZD
Portuguese escudo*	PTE
Philippine peso	PHP
Polish zloty	PLN
Romanian leu	ROL
Russian rouble	RUB
Singaporean dollar	SGD
Slovakian koruna	SKK
Slovenian tolar	SIT
Spanish peseta*	ESP
Swiss franc	CHF
Swedish krona	SEK
Saudi riyal	SAR
New Taiwan dollar	TWD
Thai baht	THB
Turkish lira	TRL
US dollar	USD
Venezuelan bolivar	VEB
South African rand	ZAR

*Replaced by the euro on January 1, 1999.
[†]Replaced by the euro on January 1, 2001.

Table B2 Full list of currencies, including precious metals but excluding currencies of euro member states

Code	Country	Currency
AED	United Arab Emirates	Dirham
AFA	Afghanistan	Afghani
ALL	Albania	Lek
AMD	Armenia	Dram
ANG	Netherlands Antilles	Guilder
AOA	Angola	Kwanza
ARS	Argentina	Peso
AUD	Australia	Dollar
AWG	Aruba	Guilder
AZM	Azerbaijan	Manat
BAM	Bosnia and Herzegovina	Convertible mark
BBD	Barbados	Dollar
BDT	Bangladesh	Taka
BGL	Bulgaria	Lev
BHD	Bahrain	Dinar
BIF	Burundi	Franc
BMD	Bermuda	Dollar
BND	Brunei Darussalam	Dollar
BOB	Bolivia	Boliviano
BRL	Brazil	Brazil real
BSD	Bahamas	Dollar
BTN	Bhutan	Ngultrum
BWP	Botswana	Pula
BYR	Belarus	Ruble
BZD	Belize	Dollar
CAD	Canada	Dollar
CDF	Congo/Kinshasa	Congolese franc
CHF	Switzerland	Franc
CLP	Chile	Peso
CNY	China	Yuan/Renminbi*
COP	Colombia	Peso
CRC	Costa Rica	Colon
CUP	Cuba	Peso
CVE	Cape Verde	Escudo
CYP	Cyprus	Pound
CZK	Czech Republic	Koruna
DJF	Djibouti	Franc
DKK	Denmark	Krone
DOP	Dominican Republic	Peso
DZD	Algeria	Algeria dinar
EEK	Estonia	Kroon
EGP	Egypt	Pound
ERN	Eritrea	Nakfa
ETB	Ethiopia	Birr
EUR	Euro member countries	Euro
FJD	Fiji	Dollar
FKP	Falkland Islands (Malvinas)	Pound

Currencies of euro member states are listed in Table A1.
*Renminbi (literally means "people's money") is the name of the currency of China. It is sometimes shortened to RMB, which is used instead of the proper code, CNY. Yuan is the currency unit.

Table B2 (continued)

Code	Country	Currency
GBP	United Kingdom	Pound sterling
GEL	Georgia	Lari
GGP	Guernsey	Pound
GHC	Ghana	Cedi
GIP	Gibraltar	Pound
GMD	Gambia	Dalasi
GNF	Guinea	Franc
GTQ	Guatemala	Quetzal
GYD	Guyana	Dollar
HKD	Hong Kong	Dollar
HNL	Honduras	Lempira
HRK	Croatia	Kuna
HTG	Haiti	Gourde
HUF	Hungary	Forint
IDR	Indonesia	Rupiah
ILS	Israel	New shekel
IMP	Isle of Man	Pound
INR	India	Rupee
IQD	Iraq	Dinar
IRR	Iran	Rial
ISK	Iceland	Krona
JEP	Jersey	Pound
JMD	Jamaica	Dollar
JOD	Jordan	Dinar
JPY	Japan	Yen
KES	Kenya	Shilling
KGS	Kyrgyzstan	Som
KHR	Cambodia	Riel
KMF	Comoros	Franc
KPW	Korea (North)	Won
KRW	Korea (South)	Won
KWD	Kuwait	Dinar
KYD	Cayman Islands	Dollar
KZT	Kazakhstan	Tenge
LAK	Laos	Kip
LBP	Lebanon	Pound
LKR	Sri Lanka	Rupee
LRD	Liberia	Dollar
LSL	Lesotho	Loti
LTL	Lithuania	Litas
LVL	Latvia	Lat
LYD	Libya	Dinar
MAD	Morocco	Dirham
MDL	Moldova	Leu
MGF	Madagascar	Malagasy franc
MKD	Macedonia	Denar
MMK	Myanmar (Burma)	Kyat
MNT	Mongolia	Tugrik
MOP	Macau	Pataca
MRO	Mauritania	Ouguiya
MTL	Malta	Lira
MUR	Mauritius	Rupee

Table B2 (continued)

Code	Country	Currency
MVR	Maldives (Maldive Islands)	Rufiyaa
MWK	Malawi	Kwacha
MXN	Mexico	Peso
MYR	Malaysia	Ringgit
MZM	Mozambique	Metical
NAD	Namibia	Dollar
NGN	Nigeria	Naira
NIO	Nicaragua	Gold cordoba
NOK	Norway	Krone
NPR	Nepal	Nepal rupee
NZD	New Zealand	Dollar
OMR	Oman	Rial
PAB	Panama	Balboa
PEN	Peru	Nuevos sol
PGK	Papua New Guinea	Kina
PHP	Philippines	Peso
PKR	Pakistan	Rupee
PLN	Poland	Zloty
PYG	Paraguay	Guarani
QAR	Qatar	Rial
ROL	Romania	Leu
RUR	Russia	Rouble
RWF	Rwanda	Rwanda franc
SAR	Saudi Arabia	Riyal
SBD	Solomon Islands	Dollar
SCR	Seychelles	Rupee
SDD	Sudan	Dinar
SEK	Sweden	Krona
SGD	Singapore	Dollar
SHP	Saint Helena	Pound
SIT	Slovenia	Tolar
SKK	Slovakia	Koruna
SLL	Sierra Leone	Leone
SOS	Somalia	Shilling
SPL	Seborga	Luigino
SRG	Suriname	Guilder
STD	São Tome and Principe	Dobra
SVC	El Salvador	Colon
SYP	Syria	Pound
SZL	Swaziland	Liangeni
THB	Thailand	Baht
TJR	Tajikistan	Ruble
TMM	Turkmenistan	Manat
TND	Tunisia	Dinar
TOP	Tonga	Pa'anga
TRL	Turkey	Lira
TTD	Trinidad and Tobago	Dollar
TVD	Tuvalu	Tuvalu dollar
TWD	Taiwan	New dollar
TZS	Tanzania	Shilling
UAH	Ukraine	Hryvnia
UGX	Uganda	Shilling

Table B2 (continued)

Code	Country	Currency
USD	United States of America	Dollar
UYU	Uruguay	Peso
UZS	Uzbekistan	Sum
VEB	Venezuela	Bolivar
VND	Viet Nam	Dong
VUV	Vanuatu	Vatu
WST	Samoa	Tala
XAF	Communauté Financière Africaine BEAC	Franc
XAG	Silver	Ounce
XAU	Gold	Ounce
XCD	East Caribbean States[†]	Dollar
XDR	International Monetary Fund (IMF)	Special drawing right
XOF	Communauté Financière Africaine BCEAO	Franc
XPD	Palladium	Ounce
XPF	Comptoirs Français du Pacifique	Franc
XPT	Platinum	Ounce
YER	Yemen	Rial
YUM	Yugoslavia	New dinar
ZAR	South Africa	Rand
ZMK	Zambia	Kwacha
ZWD	Zimbabwe	Zimbabwe dollar

[†]Comprising Antigua and Barbuda, Dominica, Grenada, St Kitts and Nevis, St Lucia, St Vincent and the Grenadines, Anguilla and Montserrat.

Bibliography

Acar, E., and A. Middleton, 2003, "Currency returns in emerging markets", *Profit & Loss*, February, pp. 38–9.

Acar, E., and H. Pedersen, 2001, "Which currency benchmarks for an active international investor?" *Profit & Loss*, February.

Acar, E., and S. Satchell, 1997, *Advance Trading Rules* (Butterworth Heinemann).

Acar, E., and R. Toffel, 2000, "Stop-loss and investment returns", Working paper, Faculty and Institute of Actuaries, Hatfield Heath.

Adler, M., and B. Dumas, 1983, "International portfolio choice and corporation finance: a synthesis", *Journal of Finance,* 38, pp. 925–84.

Adler, M., and P. Jorion, 1992, "Universal currency hedges for global portfolios", *Journal of Portfolio Management*, Summer, pp. 28–35.

Adler, M., and B. Prasad, 1990, "On universal currency hedges", *Journal of Financial and Quantitative Analysis,* 27, pp. 19–38.

Adler, M., and D. Simon, 1986, "Exchange risk surprises in international portfolios. *Journal of Portfolio Management*, Winter, pp. 44–53.

Agarwal, V., and N. Y. Naik, 2001, "Characterising hedge fund risks with buy-and-hold and option based strategies", Working paper, London Business School.

Aggarwal, R., 1994, "Investing in emerging markets: challenges and opportunities", in R. Aggarwal and D. Schirm (eds), *Global Portfolio Diversification*, pp. 261–88 (San Diego, CA: Academic Press).

Aggarwal, R., and A. L. Demaskey, 1997, "Using derivatives in major currencies for cross-hedging currency risks in Asian emerging markets", *Journal of Futures Markets,* 17(8), pp. 781–96.

AIMR, 1997, *Performance Evaluation, Benchmarks, and Attribution Analysis*, Charlottesville, VA: Association for Investment Management and Research.

AIMR, 1997, *Managing Currency Risk*, Charlottesville, VA: Association for Investment Management and Research.

AIMR, 1998, "Benchmarks and performance attribution", Subcommittee report, AIMR (August). Available at www.aimr.com/standards/pps/benchmark.html.

AIMR, 1999, *Currency Risk in Investment Portfolios,* Charlottesville, VA: Association for Investment Management and Research.

Amihud, Y., 1994, "Exchange rates and the valuation of equity shares", in Y. Amihud and R. Levich (eds), *Exchange Rates and Corporate Performance,* pp. 49–55 (Illinois: Irwin).

Andersen, T., and T. Bollerslev, 1998, "Answering the skeptics: yes, standard volatility models do provide accurate forecasts", *International Economic Review,* 39(4), pp. 885–905.

Andersen, T. G., T. Bollerslev, F. X. Diebold, and P. Labys, 2001, "The distribution of exchange rate volatility", *Journal of the American Statistical Association,* pp. 42–55.

Annaert, J., 1995, "Estimation risk and international bond portfolio selection", *Journal of Multinational Financial Management,* 5(2/3), pp. 47–71.

Artzner, P., F. Delbaen, J. M. Eber, and D. Heath, 1999, "Coherent measures of risk", *Mathematical Finance,* 9, pp. 203–28.

Asay, M., and C. Edelsberg, 1986, "Can a dynamic strategy replicate the return of an option?" *Journal of Futures Markets,* 6(1), pp. 63–70.

Azoff, E. M., 1994, *Neural Network Time Series Forecasting of Financial Markets* (New York: John Wiley & Sons).

Baca, S. P., B. L. Garbe, and R. A. Weiss, 2000, "The rise of sector effects in major equity markets", *Financial Analysts Journal,* September/October, pp. 34–40.

Bachelier, L., 1900, "Théorie de la spéculation", *Annales Scientifiques de l'Ecole Normale Superieure,* III-17, pp. 21–86 (English translation in S. Haberman and T.A. Sibbett (eds) 1995, *History of Actuarial Science,* Vol. VII, pp. 15–78 (London: Ashgate Publishing Company).)

Baillie, R. T., 1996, "Long memory processes and fractional integration in econometrics", *Journal of Econometrics,* 73, pp. 5–59.

Baldridge, J., B. Meath, and H. Myers, 2000, "Capturing alpha through active currency overlay", Frank Russell Research Commentary (May).

Balduzzi, P., and A. Lynch, 1999, "Transaction costs and predictability: some utility cost calculations", *Journal of Financial Economics,* 52, pp. 47–78.

Ballocchi, G., 1998, "The statistical evaluation of financial market forecasts", Unpublished manuscript, Olsen & Associates. Available at forecasting.olsen.ch/html/forecastpaper/paper.html.

Banerjee, A. V., 1992, "A simple model of herd behaviour" *Quarterly Journal of Economics,* 107, pp. 797–817.

Bank for International Settlements (BIS), 2002, *BIS Triennial Central Bank Survey of Foreign Exchange and Derivatives Market Activities 2001,* Available at www.bis.org.

Bansal, R., and M. Dahlquist, 2000, "The forward premium puzzle: different tales from developed and emerging economies", *Journal of International Economics,* 51, pp. 115–44.

Barberis, N., A. Shleifer, and R. Vishny, 1998, "A model of investor sentiment", Working paper, University of Chicago.

Bartov, E., and G. M. Bodnar, 1994, "Firm valuation, earnings expectations and the exchange-rate exposure effect", *Journal of Finance,* 49, pp. 1755–85.

Basak, S., and R. Mehra, 2001, "A comparative study of portfolio insurance", *Journal of Economic Dynamics and Control,* 26, pp. 1217–41.

Basak, S., and A. Shapiro, 1998, "Value-at-risk based risk management: optimal policies and asset prices", Working paper, Wharton School, University of Pennsylvania.

Bauer, G. H. 2001, "Conditional currency hedging and asset market shocks", Working paper, William E. Simon Graduate School of Business Administration, University of Rochester, Rochester.

Baxter, M., and A. Rennie, 1996, *Financial Calculus: An Introduction to Derivative Pricing* (Cambridge University Press).

Baz, J., F. Breedon, V. Naik, and J. Peress, 2001, "Optimal portfolios of foreign currencies – trading on the forward bias", *Journal of Portfolio Management*, 28, pp. 102–11.

Beckers, C., G. Connor, and R. Curds, 1996, "National versus global influences on equity returns", *Financial Analysts Journal*, March/April, pp. 31–9.

Bekaert, G., and C. R. Harvey, 2003, "Emerging market finance", *Journal of Empirical Finance*, 10, pp. 3–55.

Bekaert, G., and R. J. Hodrick, 1993, "On biases in the measurement of foreign exchange risk premium", *Journal of International Money and Finance*, 12, pp. 115–38.

Bennett, D., 1997, *Managing Foreign Exchange Risk: How to Identify and Manage Foreign Currency Exposure*, (Financial Times/Prentice Hall).

Berben, R. B., and D. J. van Dijk, 1998, "Does the absence of cointegration explain the typical findings in long horizon regression?" Report 9814, Econometrics Institute, Erasmus University Rotterdam.

Berben, R. P., and D. J. van Dijk, 1999, "Unit root tests and asymmetric adjustment: a reassessment", Research report 9902/A, Econometrics Institute, Erasmus University Rotterdam.

Berkowitz, J., and L. Giorgianni, 2001, "Long-horizon exchange rate predictability?" *Review of Economics and Statistics*, 83, pp. 81–91.

Bessembinder, H., and K. Chan, 1998, "Do the profits from technical trading rules reflect inefficiencies?" Working paper, University of Utah and Hong Kong University of Science & Technology.

Billingsley, R., and D. Chance, 1996, "Benefits and limitations of diversification among commodity trading advisors", *Journal of Portfolio Management*, 23, pp. 65–80.

Bilson, J. F. O., 1981, "The 'speculative efficiency' hypothesis", *Journal of Business*, 54(3), pp. 435–51.

Bjerve, S., and K. A. Doksum, 1993, "Correlation curves: measures of association as functions of covariates", *Annals of Statistics*, 21, pp. 890–902.

Black, F., 1989, "Universal hedging: optimizing currency risk and reward in international portfolios", *Financial Analysts Journal*, July/August, pp. 16–22.

Black, F., 1990, "Equilibrium exchange rate hedging", *Journal of Finance*, 45, pp. 899–908.

Blake, C. R., E. J. Elton, and M. J. Gruber, 1993, "The performance of bond mutual funds", *Journal of Business*, 66(3), pp. 371–403.

Blyth, S., 1996, "Out of line: non-linear models of correlation", *Risk*, 9(10), pp. 82–4.

Bollerslev, T., 1986, "Generalized autoregressive conditional heteroscedasticity", *Journal of Economics*, 31, pp. 307–27.

Bollerslev, T., and M. Melvin, 1994, "Bid–ask spreads and volatility in the foreign exchange market", *Journal of International Economics*, 36, pp. 355–72.

Braccia, J. A., 1995, "An analysis of currency overlays for US pension plans", *Journal of Portfolio Management*, Fall, pp. 88–93.

Brennan, M., E. Schwartz, and R. Lagnado, 1997, "Strategic asset allocation", *Journal of Economic Dynamics and Control*, 21, pp. 1377–403.

Brenner, M., and Y. H. Eom, 1997, "No-arbitrage option pricing: new evidence on the validity of the martingale property", Working paper, New York University.

Bridgewater Associates (no date (a)). Currency observations. Developing an effective currency overlay program: the nuts and bolts. Available at www.bridgewaterassociates.com/pdf/NUTSBOLTS.pdf.

Bridgewater Associates (no date (b)). Currency observations. The dynamic hedging enigma. Available at www.bridgewaterassociates.com/pdf/DYNAMICHEDGING.pdf.

Bridgewater Associates (no date (c)). Currency observations. Emerging market currencies: what to expect. Available at www.bridgewaterassociates.com/pdf/EMC.pdf.

Brock, W., J. Lakonishok, and B. LeBaron, 1992, "Simple technical trading rules and the stochastic properties of stock returns", *Journal of Finance*, 47(5), pp. 1731–64.

Buraschi, A., and J. C. Jackwerth, 2001, "The price of a smile: hedging and spanning in option markets", *Review of Financial Studies*, 14(2), pp. 495–527.

Bureau of Economic Analysis (BEA) 2002, Survey of current business (July 2002). Available at http://www.bea.doc.gov/.

Burik, P., and R. M. Ennis, 1990, "Foreign bonds in diversified portfolios: a limited advantage", *Financial Analysts Journal*, 46(2), pp. 31–40.

Campa, J. M., and P. H. K. Chang, 1998a, "The forecasting ability of correlations implied in foreign exchange options", *Journal of International Money and Finance*, 17, pp. 855–80.

Campa, J. M., and P. H. K. Chang, 1998b, "Learning from the term structure of implied volatility in foreign exchange options", in Z. Chen (ed), *Currency Options and Exchange Rate Economics*, pp. 98–115 (Singapore: World Scientific Publishing Co. Pvt. Ltd).

Campa, J. M., P. H. K. Chang, and J. F. Refalo, 1999, "An option-based analysis of emerging market exchange rate expectations: Brazil's real plan, 1994–1997", Working paper 6929, National Bureau of Economic Research, Chicago.

Campa, J. M., P. H. K. Chang, and R. Reider, 1998, "Implied exchange rate distributions: evidence from OTC option markets", *Journal of International Money and Finance*, 17(1), pp. 117–60.

Canina, L., and S. Figlewski, 1993, "The informational content of implied volatility" *Review of Financial Studies*, 6, pp. 659–81.

Canova, F., and J. Marrinan, 1993, "Predicting excess returns in financial markets", Working paper 93-17, European Institute – Economics Department.

Caporale, G. M., and N. Spagnolo, 2001, "Modelling East Asian exchange rates: a Markov-switching approach", Working paper, South Bank University, London.

Cassel, G., 1916, "The present situation on the foreign exchanges", *Economic Journal*, 26, pp. 62–5.

Cavaglia, S., C. Brightman, and M. Aked, 2000, "The increasing importance of industry factors", *Financial Analysts Journal*, 56(5), pp. 41–54.

Chan, L., and D. Lien, 2002, "Are options redundant? Further evidence from currency futures markets", Working paper, Mount Union College/University of Texas.

Chan, L. K. C., J. Karceski, and J. Lakonishok, 1999, "On portfolio optimization: forecasting covariances and choosing the risk model", *Review of Financial Studies,* 12(5), pp. 937–74.

Chase/Risk Publications, 1996, *The Chase Guide to Risk Management* (London: Risk Publications).

Chow, E. H., W. Y. Lee, and M. E. Solt, 1997, "The economic exposure of U.S. multinational firms", *Journal of Financial Research,* 20, pp. 191–210.

Chow, G., Jacquier, E. M. Kritzman, and K. Lowry, 1999, "Optimal portfolios in good times and bad", *Financial Analysts Journal,* 55(3), pp. 65–73.

Christensen, B., and N. R. Prabhala, 1998, "The relation between implied and realized volatility", *Journal of Financial Economics,* 50, pp. 125–50.

Christoffersen, P., and L. Giorgianni, 1999, "Interest rate arbitrage in currency basket: forecasting weights and measuring risk", Working paper WP/99/16, International Monetary Fund, Washington, D.C.

Clarida, R. H., and M. P. Taylor, 1997, "The term structure of forward exchange premiums and the forecastability of spot exchange rates: correcting the errors", *Review of Economics and Statistics,* 79, pp. 353–61.

Clarida, R. H., L. Sarno, M. P. Taylor, and G. Valente, 2001, "The out-of-sample success of term structure models as exchange rate predictors: a step beyond", Working paper, Columbia University.

Clarke, R. G., and M. P. Kritzman, 1996, *Currency Management: Concepts and Practices,* Charlottesville, VA: Association for Investment Management and Research.

Coakley, J., and A. M. Fuertes, 2001, "A nonlinear analysis of excess foreign exchange returns", Working paper, The Manchester School.

Collin-Dufresne, P., and R. S. Goldstein, 2001, "Do bonds span the fixed income markets? Theory and evidence for unspanned stochastic volatility", Working paper, Carnegie Mellon University, Department of Finance/Washington University, St. Louis, and John M. Olin School of Business.

Connolly, R., 1996, "Price and trading volume effects of introducing foreign exchange futures options trading", *Advances in Econometrics,* 11, pp. 249–66.

Conrad, J., 1989, "The price effect of option introduction", *Journal of Finance,* 44(2), pp. 487–98.

Constantinides, G. M., 1997, "Transactions costs and the pricing of financial assets", *Multinational Finance Journal,* June, pp. 93–9.

Comett, M. M., T. V. Schwarz, and A. C. Szakmary, 1995, "Seasonalities and intraday return patterns in the foreign currency futures market", *Journal of Banking and Finance,* 19, pp. 843–69.

Covrig, V., and M. Melvin, 1998, "Asymmetric information and price discovery in the FX market: does Tokyo know more about the yen?" Working paper, Arizona State University.

Cremers, M., 2000, "Stock return predictability: a Bayesian model selection perspective", Working paper, Stern School of Business, New York University.

Dacorogna, M. M., U. A. Müller, C. Jost, O. V. Pictet, R. B. Olsen, and J. R. Ward, 1995, "Heterogeneous real-time trading strategies in the foreign exchange market", *European Journal of Finance,* 1, pp. 383–404.

Dacorogna, M. M., U. A. Müller, R. J. Nagler, R. B. Olsen, and O. V. Pictet, 1993, "A geographical model for the daily and weekly seasonal volatility in the foreign exchange market", *Journal of International Money and Finance,* 12, pp. 413–38.

de Jong, F. R., R. Mahieu, P. Schotman, and I. Van Leeuwen 1999, "Price discovery on foreign exchange markets with differentially informed traders", Discussion paper 99-32/2, Tinbergen Institute.

Del Vecchio, F., 1999, "Currency overlay, strategies and implementation issues", in AIMR conference proceedings: *Currency Risk in Investment Portfolios*, Charlottesville, VA: Association for Investment Management and Research, pp. 70–6.

de Roon, F. A., T. E. Nijman, and B. J. M. Werker, 2003, "Currency hedging for international stock portfolios: the usefulness of mean–variance analysis", *Journal of Banking and Finance*, 27, pp. 327–49.

DeRosa, D., 1999, "Emerging markets and currency crises", in AIMR conference proceedings: *Currency Risk in Investment Portfolios*, Charlottesville, VA: Association for Investment Management and Research, pp. 92–9.

De Santis, G., and G. Gerard, 1998, "How big is the premium for currency risk?" *Journal of Financial Economics*, 48, pp. 375–412.

Detemple, J., and P. Jorion, 1990, "Option listing and stock returns: an empirical investigation", *Journal of Banking and Finance*, September, pp. 781–801.

Detzler, M. L., 1997, "The performance of global bond mutual funds", Working paper, University of Massachusetts.

Diebold, F. X., and J. A. Lopez, 1997, *Forecast evaluation and combination, vol. 14, Handbook of Statistics,* (Elsevier Science B.V.).

Doníelsson, J., and R. Payne, 2002, "Real trading patterns and prices in spot foreign exchange markets" *Journal of International Money and Finance,* 21, pp. 203–22.

Donnelly, R., and E. Sheehy, 1996, The share price reaction of U.K. exporters to exchange rate movements: an empirical study, *Journal of International Business Studies,* 27, pp. 157–65.

Dooley, M. P., and J. R. Shafer, 1982, "Analysis of short-run exchange rate behavior: March 1973 to November 1981", in D. Bigman and T. Taya (eds), *Exchange Rate and Trade Instability: Causes and Consequences*, Ballinger, pp. 43–69.

Dornbusch, R., 1976, "Expectations and exchange rate dynamics", *Journal of Political Economy*, 84, pp. 1161–76.

Dowd, K., 1998, *Beyond value at risk* (John Wiley & Sons).

Dowd, K., 1999, "A value at risk approach to risk–return analysis", *Journal of Portfolio Management*, 25, pp. 60–7.

Driessen, J., B. Melenberg, and T. Nijman, 2000, "Common factors in international bond returns", Working paper 2000-91, Department of Economics, Tilburg University.

Duarte, A. M., and R. Rajagopal, 1999, "A scenario-based approach to optimal currency overlay", *Journal of Portfolio Management*, 25(4), pp. 55–9.

Dumas, B., J. Fleming, and R. E. Whaley, 1998, "Implied volatility functions: empirical tests", *Journal of Finance*, 53(6), pp. 2059–106.

Duncombe, P., and J. Smith, 2002, "eFX trading solutions in the currency overlay business", *e-Forex*, October, pp. 56–7.

Dunis, C., and B. Zhou, (eds), 1998, *Non-linear Modelling of High Frequency Financial Time Series* (John Wiley & Sons).

Eaker, M., and D. Grant, 1990, "Currency hedging strategies for internationally diversified equity portfolios", *Journal of Portfolio Management*, 17, pp. 30–2.

Eaker, M., D. Grant, and N. Woodard, 1991, "International diversification and hedging: Japanese and US perspectives", *Journal of Economics and Business*, 43(4), pp. 363–74.

Eaker, M., D. Grant, and N. Woodard, 2000, "Realized rates of return in emerging equity markets", *Journal of Portfolio Management,* 26(3), pp. 41–9.

Ederington, L. H., and J. H. Lee, 1993, "How markets process information: news releases and volatility", *Journal of Finance,* 49, pp. 1161–91.

eFinancial News, March 14, 2000, *UK pension funds warm to currency overlay mandates.*

eFinancial News, July 9, 2001, *Currency overlay on the agenda.*

Elliott, G., and T. Ito, 1998, "Heterogeneous expectations and tests of efficiency in the yen/dollar forward exchange rate market", Working paper, University of California, San Diego.

Elton, E. J., M. J. Gruber, and C. R. Blake, 2001, "Incentive fees and mutual funds", Working paper, New York University.

Embrechts, P., C. Klüppelberg, and T. Mikosh, 1997, *External Events in Finance and Insurance* (Springer).

Enders, W., and C. W. J. Granger, 1998, "Unit root tests and asymmetric adjustment", *Journal of Business and Economic Statistics,* 16, pp. 304–11.

Engel, C., 1994, "Can the Markov switching model forecast exchange rates?", *Journal of International Economics,* 36, pp. 151–65.

Engel, C., 1996, "The forward discount anomaly and the risk premium: a survey of recent evidence", *Journal of Empirical Finance,* 3, pp. 123–92.

Engel, C., and C. S. Hakkio, 1997, "The distribution of exchange rates in the EMS", *International Journal of Finance and Economics,* 33, pp. 15–32.

Engel, C., and J. D. Hamilton, 1990, "Long swings in the dollar: are they in the data and do markets know it?", *American Economic Review,* 80, pp. 689–713.

Engle, R. F., 1982, "Autoregressive conditional heteroscedasticity with estimates of the variance of U.K. inflation", *Econometrica,* 50, pp. 987–1008.

Engle, R., C. Hong, A. Kane, and J. Noh, 1993, "Arbitrage valuation of variance forecasts using simulated options", *Advances in Futures and Options Research,* 6, pp. 393–415.

Errunza, V., 1997, "Research on emerging markets: past, present and future", *Emerging Markets Quarterly,* Fall, pp. 5–18.

Esquivel, G., and F. Larrain, 2000, "Determinants of currency crises", *Trimestre Economico,* 67, pp. 197–237.

Eun, C. S., and B. G. Resnick, 1988, "Exchange rate uncertainty, forward contracts and international portfolio selection", *Journal of Finance,* 43, pp. 197–215.

Eun, C. S., and B. G. Resnick, 1994, "International diversification of investment portfolios: US and Japanese perspectives", *Management Science,* 40, pp. 140–61.

Eun, C. S., and B. G. Resnick, 1997, "International equity investment with selective hedging strategies", *Journal of International Financial Markets, Institutions & Money,* 7, pp. 21–42.

Eun, C. S., and B. G. Resnick, 2001, *International Financial Management,* 2nd edn (New York: Irwin McGraw-Hill).

Euromoney, 2003. FX Poll 2003. Euromoney (May).

European Central Bank (ECB), 2003, Review of the foreign exchange market structure. Frankfurt am Main: ECB (March), Available as pdf from http://www.ecb.int/pub/pdf/fxmarketstructure200303.pdf.

Evans, M. D., and R. K. Lyons, 1999, "Order flow and exchange rate dynamics", Working paper, University of California Berkeley.

Fama, E. F., 1965, "The behaviour of stock market prices", *Journal of Business*, 38, pp. 34–105.

Fama, E. F., 1984, "Forward and spot exchange rates", *Journal of Monetary Economics*, 14 (November), pp. 319–38.

Fama, E. F., 1998, "Market efficiency, long-term returns, and behavioural finance", Center for Research in Security Prices (CRSP), Working paper 448, University of Chicago.

Fan, R., A. Gupta, and P. Ritchken, 2002, "Hedging in the possible presence of unspanned stochastic volatility: evidence from swaption markets", Weatherhead School of Management Finance Department, Working paper, Case Western Reserve University.

Faust, J., J. Rogers, and J. H. Wright, 2001, "Exchange rate forecasting: the errors we've really made", Working paper, International Finance Division, Federal Reserve Board, Washington, D.C.

Fernández-Rodríguez, F., S. Sosvilla-Rivero, and J. Andrada-Félix, 1999, "Exchange rate forecasts with simultaneous nearest-neighbour methods: evidence from the EMS", *International Journal of Forecasting*, 15, pp. 383–92.

Fernández-Rodríguez, F., S. Sosvilla-Rivero, and J. Andrada-Félix, 2000, "Technical analysis in foreign exchange markets: linear versus nonlinear trading rules", Working paper, Fundación de Estudios de Economia Aplicada.

Figlewski, S., 1997, "Forecasting volatility", *Financial Markets, Institutions and Investments*, 6, pp. 2–87.

Fleming, J. M., 1962, "Domestic financial policies under fixed and under floating exchange rates", IMF Staff discussion papers, 9 (November), pp. 369–79.

Flood, R. P., and A. K. Rose, 2002, "Uncovered interest parity in crisis", *IMF Staff Papers*, 49(2).

Francis, B., I. Hasan, and D. Hunter, 2002, "Emerging market liberalization and the impact on uncovered interest rate parity", Working paper 2002-16, Federal Reserve Bank of Atlanta.

Frankel, J. A., 1994, "Introduction", in J. A. Frankel (ed), *The Internationalization of Equity Markets*, Chicago: National Bureau of Economic Research (NBER).

Frankel, J. A., and A. K. Rose, 1995, "Empirical research on nominal exchange rates", in G. Grossman and K. Rogoff (eds), *Handbook of International Economics*, Vol. III, pp. 1689–729 (Amsterdam: North-Holland).

Froot, K. A., 1993, "Currency hedging over long horizons", Working paper 4355, National Bureau of Economic Research, Chicago.

Froot, K. A., and J. A. Frankel, 1989, "Forward discount bias: is it an exchange risk premium?", *Quarterly Journal of Economics*, February, pp. 139–61.

Froot, K. A., and K. Rogoff, 1995, "Perspectives on PPP and long-run real exchange rates", in G. Grossman and K. Rogoff (eds), *Handbook of International Economics*, Vol. III, pp. 1647–88 (Amsterdam: Elsevier Science Publishers BV).

Froot, K. A., and R. H. Thaler, 1990, "Anomalies: foreign exchange", *Journal of Economic Perspectives*, Summer, pp. 179–92.

Fung, W., and D. A. Hsieh, 2000, "Performance characteristics of hedge funds and commodity funds: natural vs. spurious biases", *Journal of Financial and Quantitative Analysis*, 35, pp. 291–307.

Fung, W., and D. A. Hsieh, 2001, "The risk in hedge fund strategies: theory and evidence from trend followers", *Review of Financial Studies*, 14(2), pp. 313–41.

Gabbi, G., R. Colombo, R. Branmante, M. Viola, P. Vito, and A. Tumietto, 1999, "Predicting the exchange rate: an application of econometric models, neural network and trading systems", Working paper, Euro Working Group in Financial Modelling, Vienna.

Gadkari, V., and M. Spindel, 1990, "Currency hedging and international diversification – implication of a world reserve currency effect", *Journal of International Securities Markets,* 4, pp. 35–42.

Garcia, C., and F. Gould, 1987, "An empirical study of portfolio insurance", *Financial Analysts Journal,* 43(4), pp. 44–54.

Gardner, G. W., and D. Stone, 1995, "Estimating currency hedge ratios for international portfolios", *Financial Analysts Journal,* 51(6), pp. 58–64.

Gardner, G. W., and T. Wuilloud, 1995, "Currency risk in international portfolios: how satisfying is optimal hedging?", *Journal of Portfolio Management,* Spring, pp. 59–67.

Gerard, B., P. Hillion, and F. A. de Roon, 2002, "International portfolio diversification: industry, country, and currency effects revisited", EFA 2002 Berlin Meetings Presented paper (March).

Glen, J., and P. Jorion, 1993, "Currency hedging for international portfolios", *Journal of Finance,* 48, pp. 1865–86.

Goetzmann, W. N., L. Li, and K. G. Rouwenhorst, 2001, "Long-term global market correlations", Working paper, Yale School of Management, Yale University.

Goldberg, P., and M. Knetter, 1997, "Goods prices and exchange rates: what have we learned?", *Journal of Economic Literature,* 35 (September), pp. 1243–72.

Goodhart, C., T. Ito, and R. Payne, 1996, "One day in June 1993: a study of the working of the Reuters 2000–2 electronic foreign exchange trading system", in J.A. Frankel, G. Galli and A. Giovannini (eds), *The Microstructure of Foreign Exchange Markets,* pp. 107–79 (Chicago: University of Chicago Press).

Granger, C. W. J., and Z. Ding, 1996, "Varieties of long memory models", *Journal of Econometrics,* 73, pp. 61–77.

Grannan, E. R., and G. H. Swindle, 1996, "Minimizing transaction costs of option hedging strategies", *Mathematical Finance,* 6, pp. 341–64.

Griffin, J. M., and G. A. Karolyi, 1998, "Another look at the role of the industrial structure of markets for international diversification strategies", *Journal of Financial Economics,* 50, pp. 351–73.

Grinblatt, M., and S. Titman, 1994, "A study of monthly mutual fund returns and performance evaluation techniques", *Journal of Financial and Quantitative Analysis,* 29(3), pp. 419–44.

Halpern, P., 1993, "Investing abroad: a review of capital market integration and manager performance", *Journal of Portfolio Management,* 19(2), pp. 47–57.

Hann, T. H., and E. Steurer, 1996, "Much ado about nothings? Exchange rate forecasting: neural networks vs. linear models using monthly and weekly data", *Neurocomputing,* 10, pp. 323–39.

Harvey, C. R., and R. D. Huang, 1991, "Volatility in the foreign currency futures market", *Review of Financial Studies,* 4, pp. 543–69.

Hauser, S., and A. Levy, 1991, "Optimal forward coverage of international fixed income portfolios", *Journal of Portfolio Management,* 17(4), pp. 54–9.

Hauser, S., M. Marcus, and U. Yaari, 1994, "Investing in emerging stock markets: is it worthwhile hedging foreign exchange risk?", *Journal of Portfolio Management,* 20 (Spring), pp. 76–81.

Hazuka, T. B., and L. C. Huberts, 1994, "A valuation approach to currency hedging", *Financial Analysts Journal,* March/April, pp. 55–9.

Henrotte, P., 1993, "Transactions costs and duplication strategies", Working paper, Stanford University.

Hersey, B., and J. Minnick, 2000, "Active managers generating positive excess returns over benchmarks", *Global Pensions*, February.

Hersey, B., and K. Ogunc, 2000, "Designing portable alpha engines", *Investments and Pensions Europe*, October.

Heston, S. L., and K. G. Rouwenhorst, 1994, "Does industrial structure explain the benefits of international diversification?", *Journal of Financial Economics*, 36, pp. 3–27.

Hodges, S. D., and A. Neuberger, 1989, "Optimal replication of contingent claims under transaction costs", *Review of Futures Markets*, 8, pp. 222–39.

Hodrick, R. J., 1987, "The empirical evidence on the efficiency of forward and futures foreign exchange markets", Vol. 24 in J. Lesourne and H. Sonnenschein (eds), *Fundamentals of Pure and Applied Economics* (Harwood Academic Publishers).

Hodrick, R. J., and M. Vassalou, 2002, "Do we need multi-country models to explain exchange rate and interest rate and bond return dynamics", *Journal of Economic Dynamics and Control*, 26, pp. 1275–99.

Hoggard, T., A. E. Whalley, and P. Wilmott, 1994, "Hedging option portfolios in the presence of transaction costs", *Advances in Futures and Options Research*, 7, pp. 21–35.

Hong, H., and J. C. Stein, 1997, "A unified theory of underreaction, momentum trading and overreaction in asset markets", Working paper W6324, National Bureau of Economic Research, Chicago.

Horngren, L., and A. Vredin, 1989, "Exchange risk premia in a currency basket system", *Weltwirtschaftliches Archiv*, 125, pp. 311–25.

Howitt, P., and R. P. McAffee, 1992, "Animal spirits", *American Economic Review*, 82, pp. 493–507.

Hu, M. Y., G. Zhang, C. X. Jiang, and B. E. Patuwo, 1999, "A cross-validation analysis of neural network out-of-sample performance in exchange rate forecasting", *Decision Science*, 30(1), pp. 197–216.

Huang, R. D., and R. W. Masulis, 1999, "FX spreads and dealer competition across the 24-hour trading day", *Review of Financial Studies*, 12, pp. 61–93.

Hull, J., 2002, *Options, Futures and other Derivatives*, 5th edn (Prentice-Hall).

Ikeda, S., 1991, "Arbitrage asset pricing under exchange risk", *Journal of Finance*, 46, pp. 447–55.

InterSec Research Corp, 2001, "Global investment management industry study", Research paper.

Isard, P. 1995, *Exchange Rate Economics* (Cambridge University Press).

Ito, T., R. K. Lyons, and M. Melvin, 1998, "Is there private information in the FX market? The Tokyo experiment", *Journal of Finance*, 53, pp. 1111–30.

Jackwerth, J. C., and M. Rubinstein, 1996, "Recovering probability distributions from option prices", *Journal of Finance*, 51(5), pp. 1611–31.

Jacquier, E., and A. J. Marcus, 2000, "Asset allocation models and market volatility", *Financial Analysts Journal*, 57(2), pp. 16–30.

Jagannathan, R., A. Kaplin, and S. Sun, 2001, "An evaluation of multi-factor CIR models using LIBOR, swap rates, and cap and swaption prices", *Journal of Econometrics*, 105(1), pp. 59–83.

Jorion, P., 1985," International portfolio diversification with estimation risk", *Journal of Business*, 58, pp. 259–78.

Jorion, P., 1990, "The exchange rate exposure of U.S. multinationals", *Journal of Business*, 63(3), pp. 331–45.

Jorion, P., 1994, "A mean–variance analysis of currency overlays", *Financial Analysts Journal,* (May), pp. 48–56.

Jorion, P., 1995, "Predicting volatility in the foreign exchange market", *Journal of Finance,* 50, pp. 507–28.

Jorion, P., and S. Khouri, 1995, *Financial Risk Management* (Blackwell).

JP Morgan Fleming Asset Management, 2003, Alternative investment strategies survey – 2002 results.

Juzczenko, E., and B. Maillet, 2001, "The three-moment CAPM: Theoretical foundations and an asset pricing models comparison in an unified framework", Working paper, University of Paris.

Karnosky, D. S., 1993, "Global investment in a CAPM framework", in *The CAPM Controversy: Policy and Strategy Implications for Investment Management*, Charlottesville, VA: Association for Investment Management and Research, pp. 56–61.

Karnosky, D. S., and B. D. Singer, 1994, *Global Asset Management and Performance Attribution,* Charlottesville, VA: The Research Foundation of the Institute of Chartered Financial Analysts.

Karolyi A., and R. M. Stulz, 2002, "Are financial assets priced locally or globally?", Working paper, Ohio State University.

Kedia, S., and A. Mozumdar, 1999, "Foreign currency denominated debt: an empirical examination", Working paper, Harvard University.

Keynes, J. M., 1936, *The General Theory of Employment, Interest and Money* (Cambridge University Press).

Kho, B. C., 1996, "Time-varying risk premia, volatility and technical trading rule profits: evidence from foreign currency futures markets", *Journal of Financial Economics*, 41, pp. 249–90.

Kilian, L., 1999, "Exchange rate and monetary fundamentals: what do we learn from long-horizon regression?", *Journal of Applied Econometrics*, 14, pp. 491–510.

Kilian, L., and M. P. Taylor, 2001, "Why is it so difficult to beat the random walk forecast of exchange rates?", Working paper, Centre for Economic Policy Research, London.

Klein, M., 1989, "Arbitrage and interest rates on currency baskets", *Weltwirtschaftliches Archiv,* 125, pp. 296–310.

Knez, P J., R. Litterman, and J. Scheinkman, 1994, "Explorations into factors explaining money market returns", *Journal of Finance,* 49, pp. 1861–82.

Kritzman, M., 1993, "The optimal currency hedging policy with biased forward rates", *Journal of Portfolio Management*, Summer, pp. 94–100.

Kroll, Y., and G. Kaplanski, 2000a, "Efficient VaR portfolios", Working paper, Hebrew University.

Kroll, Y., and G. Kaplanski, 2000b, "Value-at-risk equilibrium pricing model", Working paper, Hebrew University.

Kuan, C. M., and T. Liu, 1995, "Forecasting exchange rate using feedforward and recurrent neural networks", *Journal of Applied Econometrics,* 10, pp. 347–64.

Kumar, M. S., and A. Persaud, 2001, "Pure contagion and investors' shifting risk appetite: analytical issues and empirical evidence", Working paper 01/134, International Monetary Fund, Washington D.C.

Larsen Jr, G. A., and B. G. Resnick, 2000, "The optimal construction of international diversified equity portfolios hedged against exchange rate uncertainty", *European Financial Management,* 6(4), pp. 479–514.

LeBaron, B., 1992, "Do moving average trading rule results imply nonlinearities in foreign exchange markets?", Working paper, Social Systems Research Institute, University of Wisconsin–Madison.

LeBaron, B., 1998, A dynamic trading strategy approach to deviations from uncovered interest parity, Working paper, Brandeis University.

LeBaron, B., 1999, "Technical trading rule profitability and foreign exchange intervention", *Journal of International Economics,* 49(1), pp. 125–43.

Lee, C. I., and I. Mathur, 1996, "Trading rule profit in European currency spot cross-rates", *Journal of Banking and Finance,* 20, pp. 949–62.

Lee, C., and S. Rahman, 1990, "Market timing, selectivity, and mutual fund performance: an empirical investigation", *Journal of Business,* 63(2), pp. 261–78.

Lehmann, B., and D. Modest, 1987, "Mutual fund performance evaluation: a comparison of benchmarks and benchmark comparisons", *Journal of Finance,* 42(2), pp. 233–65.

Leibowitz, M. L., L. N. Bader, and S. Kogelman, 1993, "Global fixed income investing: The impact of the currency hedge", *Journal of Fixed Income,* 3(1), pp. 7–18.

Leicht, G., and J. E. Tanner, 1991, "Economic forecast evaluation: Profits versus the conventional error measures", *American Economic Review,* 81(3), pp. 580–90.

Levich, R. M., and L. R. Thomas, 1993a, "The significance of technical trading-rule profit in the foreign exchange market: a bootstrap approach", *Journal of International Money and Finance,* 12, pp. 451–74.

Levich, R. M., and L. R. Thomas, 1993b, "The merits of active currency risk management: evidence from international bond portfolios", *Financial Analysts Journal,* September/October, pp. 63–70.

Lewis, K., 1995, "Puzzles in international financial markets", in G.M. Grossman and K. Rogoff (eds), *Handbook of International Economics,* Vol. 3, pp. 1913–71 (Amsterdam: North-Holland).

L'Her, F., O. Sy, and M.Y. Tnani, 2002, "Country, industry, and risk factor loadings in portfolio management", *Journal of Portfolio Management,* 28(4), pp. 70–9.

Liang, B., 2000, "Hedge funds: the living and the dead", *Journal of Financial and Quantitative Analysis,* 35, pp. 309–26.

Lioui, A., 1998, "Currency risk hedging: future vs. forward", *Journal of Banking and Finance,* 22, pp. 61–81.

Lisi, F., and A. Medio, 1997, "Is a random walk the best exchange rate predictor?", *International Journal of Forecasting,* 13, pp. 252–67.

Litterman, R., and J. Scheinkman, 1991, "Common factors affecting bond returns", *Journal of Fixed Income,* 1, pp. 62–74.

Lo, A. W., H. Mamaysky, and J. Wang, 2001, "Foundations of technical analysis: computational algorithms, statistical inference, and empirical implementation", *Journal of Finance,* 55, pp. 1705–65.

Longin, F., and B. Solnik, 1995, "Is the correlation in international equity returns constant: 1960–1990?", *Journal of International Money and Finance,* 14, pp. 3–26.

Longstaff, F., 1995, "Option pricing and the martingale restriction", *Review of Financial Studies,* 8, pp. 1091–124.

Longstaff, F., P. Santa-Clara, and E. Schwartz, 2001, "The relative valuation of caps and swaptions: theory and empirical evidence", *Journal of Finance*, 56, pp. 2067–109.

Longworth, D., 1981, "Testing the efficiency of the Canadian–U.S. exchange market under the assumption of no risk premium", *Journal of Finance*, 36(1), pp. 43–9.

Luca, C., 2000, *Technical Analysis Applications in the Global Currency Markets*, 2nd edn (Prentice Hall).

Lyons, R. K., 1995, "Tests of microstructural hypotheses in the foreign exchange market", *Journal of Financial Economics*, 39, pp. 321–51.

Lyons, R. K., 1997, "A simultaneous trade model of the foreign exchange hot potato", *Journal of International Economics*, 42, pp. 278–98.

Lyons, R. K., 2002, *The Microstructure Approach to Exchange Rates* (MIT Press).

Malliaropulos, D., 1997, "A multivariate GARCH model of risk premia in foreign exchange markets", *Economic Modelling*, 14(1), pp. 61–79.

Malz, A., 1997, "Estimating the probability distribution of the future exchange rate from option prices", *Journal of Derivatives*, Winter, pp. 20–36.

Martellini, L., 2001, "Efficient option replication in the presence of transaction costs", Working paper, Marshall School of Business, University of South California.

Mayhew, S., 1995, "Implied volatility", *Financial Analysts Journal*, 51, pp. 8–20.

Meese, R., and K. Rogoff, 1983a, "Empirical exchange rate models of the seventies: do they fit out of sample?", *Journal of International Economics*, 14 (February), pp. 3–24.

Meese, R., and K. Rogoff, 1983b, "The out-of-sample failure of empirical exchange rate models: sampling error or misspecification?", in J. Frenkel (ed), *Exchange Rates and International Macroeconomics*, pp. 67–105 (National Bureau of Economic Research and University of Chicago Press).

Mercer Investment Consulting, 2003, *Defined Contribution Universe Summary Q2, 2002.*

Miller, K. D., and J. J. Reuer, 1998, "Firm strategy and economic exposure to foreign exchange rate movements, *Journal of International Business Studies*, 29, pp. 493–514.

Mundell, R. A., 1960, "The monetary dynamics of international adjustment under fixed and flexible exchange rates", *Quarterly Journal of Economics*, 74 (May), pp. 227–57.

Muralidhar, A., and H. Neelakandan, 2001, "Options to enhance currency overlay programs", FX Concepts working paper, Alternative Investment Management Association (AIMA), London (November).

Muralidhar, A., and R. J. P. van der Wouden, 2000, "Optimal ALM strategies for defined benefit pension funds", *Journal of Risk*, 2(2), ——.

Murphy, J. J., 1991, *Intermarket Technical Analysis: Trading Strategies for the Global Stock, Bond, Commodity and Currency Markets* (John Wiley & Sons).

Murphy, J. J., 1999, *Technical Analysis of the Financial Markets: A Comprehensive Guide to Trading Methods and Applications* (Prentice Hall).

Neely, C. J., 2002, "Forecasting foreign exchange volatility: is implied volatility the best we can do?", Working paper 2002-017, Federal Reserve Bank of St. Louis.

Neely, C. J., and P. Weller, 2001a, "Technical analysis and central bank intervention", *Journal of International Money and Finance*, 20(7), pp. 949–70.

Neely, C. J., and P. Weller, 2001b, "Intraday technical trading in the foreign exchange market", Working paper, Federal Reserve Bank of St. Louis.

Neely, C. J., P. Weller, and R. Dittmar, 1997, "Is technical analysis profitable in foreign exchange markets? A genetic programming approach", *Journal of Financial and Quantitative Analysis*, 32, pp. 405–26.

Nesbitt, S. L., 1991, "Currency hedging rules for plan sponsors", *Financial Analysts Journal*, March/April, pp. 73–81.

Neuhaus, H., 1995, "The information content of derivatives for monetary policy", Discussion paper 3/95, Economic Research Group, Deutsche Bundesbank.

Obstfeld, M., and K. Rogoff, 1996, *Foundations of International Macroeconomics* (Cambridge, MA: MIT Press).

Okunev, J., and D. White, 2001, "Do momentum based strategies still work in foreign currency markets?", Working paper, University of New South Wales.

Osler, C. L., 2000, "Support for resistance: technical analysis and intraday exchange rates", *Federal Reserve Bank of New York Policy Review*, 6(2), pp. 53–68.

Osler, C. L., and P. H. K. Chang, 1995, "Head and shoulder: not just a flaky pattern", Staff report 4, Federal Reserve Bank of New York.

Pardo, R., 1992, *Design, Testing, and Optimisation of Trading Systems* (John Wiley & Sons).

Peiers, B., 1997, "Informed traders, intervention and price leadership: a deeper view of the microstructure of the foreign exchange market", *Journal of Finance*, 52, pp. 1589–614.

Perold, A., and E. Shulman, 1988, "The free lunch in currency hedging: implications for investment policy and performance standards", *Financial Analysts Journal*, 44(3), pp. 45–52.

Phillips, P. C. B., and A. S. Maynard, 2001, "Rethinking an old empirical puzzle: econometric evidence on the forward discount anomaly", *Journal of Applied Econometrics*, 16(6), pp. 671–708.

Pictet, O. V., M. M. Dacorogna, U. A. Müller, R. B. Olsen, and J. R. Ward, 1992, "Real-time trading models for foreign exchange rates", *Neural Network World*, 6, pp. 713–44.

Pikkarainen, P., 1991, "International portfolio diversification: the basket-peg regime", *Journal of International Money and Finance*, 10, pp. 432–42.

Prajogi, R., A. Muralidhar, and R. J. P. van der Wouden, 2000, "An asset–liability analysis of the currency decision for pension portfolios", *Institutional Investor (Derivatives Quarterly)*, Winter, pp. 47–56.

Ramaswami, M., 1993, *Active Currency Management*, Charlottesville, VA: Association for Investment Management and Research (AIMR).

Reid, D., 2000, "Overlay worth the effort", *Investment & Pensions Europe*, September.

Reiner, T. F., 2000, "Practical active currency management for global equity portfolios", *Journal of Portfolio Management*, 26(4), pp. 41–8.

Reuters, September 12, 2001, "New science tries to unlock secrets of the markets", by Hament Bulsara.

Reuters, October 26, 2001, Currency weary funds look to outsource FX headache.

Reuters, November 1, 2002, FX fixing proves popular among nervous investors, by Natsuko Waki.

Roberts, J., 1999, "Using double moving average rule as spot trading system", Research paper, UBS.

Rogoff, K., 1996, "The purchasing power parity puzzle", *Journal of Economic Literature*, 34(2), pp. 647–68.

Rouwenhorst, K. G., 1999, "European equity markets and the EMU", *Financial Analysts Journal,* 55(3), pp. 57–64.

Saake, P., 2002, "Technical analysis and the effectiveness of central bank intervention", *Journal of International Money and Finance,* 21, pp. 459–79.

Sapp, S. G., 2002, "Price leadership in the spot foreign exchange markets", *Journal of Financial and Quantitative Analysis,* 37(3), pp. 425–48.

Sarantis, N., 1999, "Modeling non-linearities in real effective exchange rates", *Journal of International Money and Finance,* 18, pp. 27–45.

Schulmeister, S., 1988, "Currency speculation and dollar fluctuations", *Quarterly Review of Banca Nazionale del Lavoro,* no. 167 (December), pp. 343–65.

Sercu, P., 1980, "A generalization of the international asset pricing model", *Revue de l'Association Française de Finance,* 1(1), pp. 91–135.

Shleifer, A., and L. H. Summers, 1990, "The noise trader approach to finance", *Journal of Economic Perspectives,* 4, pp. 19–33.

Simotas, P., 2002, "Bring prime brokerage to currency overlay", *FX Week,* December 23, 2002.

Smithson, C. W., and C. W. Smith, 1998, *Managing Financial Risk: A Guide to Derivative Products, Financial Engineering, and Value Maximization,* 3rd edn (McGraw-Hill).

So, J. C., 1987, "The distribution of foreign exchange price changes: trading day effects and risk measurement – a comment", *Journal of Finance,* 42, pp. 181–8.

Solnik, B., 1974, "An equilibrium model of the international capital market", *Journal of Economic Theory,* 8, pp. 500–24.

Solnik, B., 1983a, "The relation between stock prices and inflationary expectations: the international evidence", *Journal of Finance,* 38(1), pp. 35–47.

Solnik, B., 1983b, "International arbitrage pricing theory", *Journal of Finance,* 38(2), pp. 449–57.

Solnik, B., 1993, "The performance of international asset allocation strategies using conditioning information", *Journal of Empirical Finance,* 1, pp. 33–55.

Solnik, B., C. Beucrelle, and Y. Le Fur, 1996, "International market correlation and volatility", *Financial Analysts Journal,* September/October, pp. 17–34.

Sorensen, E. H., J. J. Mezrich, and D. N. Thadani, 1993, "Currency hedging through portfolio optimisation", *Journal of Portfolio Management,* Spring, pp. 78–85.

Sorescu, S., 2000, "The effect of options on stock prices: 1973–1995", *Journal of Finance,* 55, pp. 487–514.

Stannard, J. C., M. C. Cottrill, J. P. Davis, J. E. Hollis III, J. L. Kermes, R. E. Pruyne, N. E. Riddles, B. D. Singer, and P. T. Willett, 1998, *Benchmarks and Performance Attribution Subcommittee Report,* Charlottesville, VA: Association for Investment Management and Research, August, Available on AIMR's website at www.aimr.com/standards/pps/benchmark.html.

Stehle, R., 1977, "An empirical test of the alternative hypotheses of national and international pricing of risky assets", *Journal of Finance,* 32, pp. 493–502.

Stulz, R. M., 1984, "Pricing capital assets in an international setting: an introduction", *Journal of International Business Studies,* Winter, pp. 55–72.

Stulz, R. M., 1995, "International portfolio choice and asset pricing: an integrative survey", in V. Maksimovic and W. Ziemba (eds), *The Handbook of Modern Finance,* pp. 201–23 (Amsterdam: North-Holland).

Sullivan, R., A. Timmermann, and H. White, 1998, "Data-snooping, technical trading rule performance, and the bootstrap", Working paper, University of California at San Diego.

Surajaras, P., and R. J. Sweeney, 1992, *Profit-making Speculation in Foreign Exchange Markets* (Boulder, CO: Westview Press).

Sweeney, J., 1986, "Beating the foreign exchange market", *Journal of Finance*, 41, pp. 163–82.

Szakmary, A. C., and I. Mathur, 1997, "Central bank intervention and trading rule profits in foreign exchange markets", *Journal of International Money and Finance*, 16, pp. 513–35.

Taylor, A. M., 2001, "Potential pitfalls for the purchasing-power-parity puzzle? Sampling and specification biases in mean-reversion tests of the law of one price", *Econometrica*, 69, pp. 473–98.

Taylor, M. P., 1995, "The economics of exchange rates", *Journal of Economic Literature*, 83, pp. 13–47.

Taylor, M. P., and H. Allen, 1992, "The use of technical analysis in the foreign exchange market", *Journal of International Money and Finance*, 11, pp. 304–14.

Taylor, M. P., and D. A. Peel, 2000, "Nonlinear adjustment, long-run equilibrium and exchange rate fundamentals", *Journal of International Money and Finance*, 19, pp. 33–53.

Taylor, S. J., 1986, *Modelling Financial Time Series* (Chichester, England: John Wiley & Sons).

Taylor, S. J., 1992, "Efficiency in the yen futures market at the Chicago Mercantile Exchange", in *Rational Expectations and Efficiency in Futures Markets*, Routledge, pp. 109–28.

Taylor, S. J., 1994, "Trading futures using a channel rule: a study of the predictive power of technical analysis with currency examples", *Journal of Futures Markets*, 14, pp. 215–35.

Thatcher, J. T., and L. P. Blenman, 2001, "Synthetic trades and calendar day pattern: the case of the dollar/sterling markets", *Financial Review*, 37, pp. 177–99.

The Economist, March 16, 2000, Test-driving a new model – do currency-forecasting techniques need to be redesigned?

The Economist, May 31, 2001, Predicting the unpredictable.

Thomas III, L. R., 1989, "The performance of currency-hedged foreign bonds", in L.R. Thomas III (ed), *The Currency Hedging Debate* (London: IFR Publishing). (First published in *Financial Analysts Journal*, May/June, pp. 25–31.)

Thomas III, L. R. (ed), 1990, *The Currency Hedging Debate* (London: IFR Publishing).

UBS Global Asset Management, 2002, "The case for global investing", Research note.

Urrutia, J., and J. Vu, 2001, "The impact of primes and scores on the price, volatility and trading volume of the underlying stocks", *Journal of Financial Practice and Education*, Fall.

VanderLinden, D., C. X. Jiang, and M. Hu, 2002, "Conditional hedging and portfolio performance", *Financial Analysts Journal*, 58(4), pp. 72–82.

Wasserfallen, W., 1989, "Flexible exchange rates: a closer look", *Journal of Monetary Economics*, 23 (May), pp. 511–21.

Weigend, A. S., D. E. Rumelhart, and B. A. Huberman, 1991, "Generalisation by weight-elimination with application to forecasting", *Advances in Neural Information Processing Systems*, 3, pp. 875–82.

Weinberg, S. A., 2001, "Interpreting the volatility smile: an examination of the information content of option prices", International finance discussion paper 706, Federal Reserve Board of Governors.

West, K. D., and D. Cho, 1995, "The predictive ability of several models of exchange rate volatility", *Journal of Econometrics,* 69(2), 367–91.

Whalley, A. E., and P. Wilmott, 1993, "An asymptotic analysis of the Davis, Panas & Zariphopoulou model for option pricing with transaction costs", OCIAM Working paper, Mathematical Institute, Oxford.

Zhang, G., and M. Y. Hu, 1998, "Neural network forecasting of the British pound/US dollar exchange rate", *International Journal of Management Science,* 26(4), 495–506.

Zhu, Y., and R. Karee, 1988, "Performance of portfolio insurance strategies", *Journal of Portfolio Management,* Spring, pp. 48–54.

Zitzewitz, E. W., 2001, "Measuring exaggeration by analysts", Working paper, Stanford University.

Index